Cuba: A Cruising Guide

www. nws. fsu. gov /
http: il weather. noaa. gov /fax /marine. shtmT

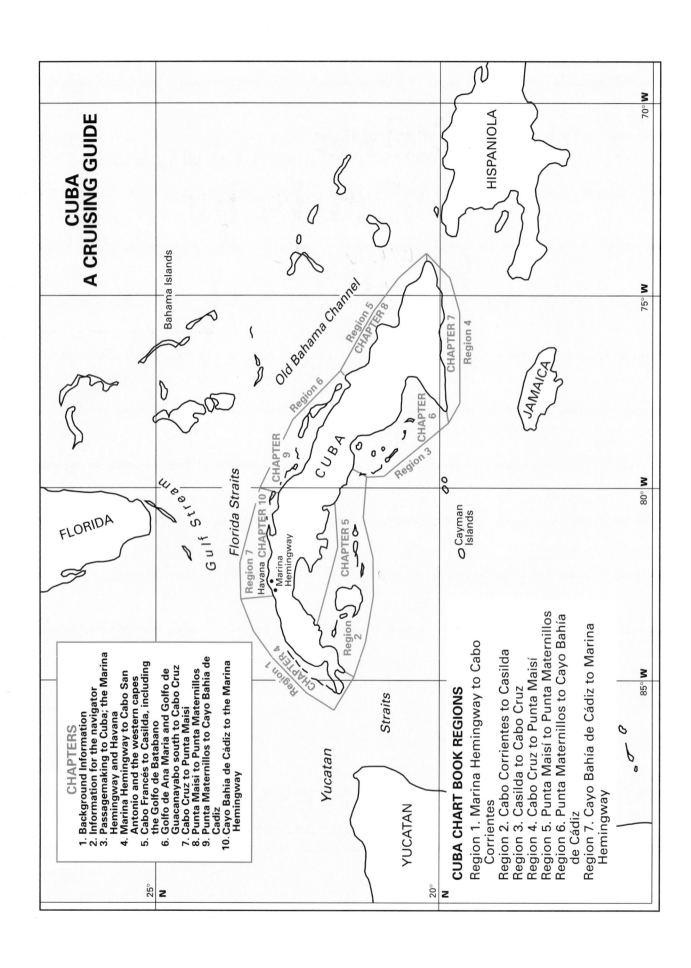

CUBA
A CRUISING GUIDE

FLORIDA

Gulf Stream

Florida Straits

Bahama Islands

Old Bahama Channel

YUCATAN

Yucatan Straits

Cayman Islands

CUBA

JAMAICA

HISPANIOLA

CHAPTER 10
CHAPTER 9
Region 7
Havana
Marina Hemingway
Region 2
CHAPTER 5
Region 1
CHAPTER 4
Region 6
Region 9
Region 5
CHAPTER 8
CHAPTER 6
Region 3
CHAPTER 7
Region 4

25° N
20° N
85° W
80° W
75° W
70° W

CHAPTERS

1. Background Information
2. Information for the navigator
3. Passagemaking to Cuba; the Marina Hemingway and Havana
4. Marina Hemingway to Cabo San Antonio and the western capes
5. Cabo Francés to Casilda, including the Golfo de Batabano
6. Golfo de Ana Maria and Golfo de Guacanayabo south to Cabo Cruz
7. Cabo Cruz to Punta Maisi
8. Punta Maisí to Punta Maternillos
9. Punta Maternillos to Cayo Bahía de Cadiz
10. Cayo Bahía de Cádiz to the Marina Hemingway

CUBA CHART BOOK REGIONS

Region 1. Marina Hemingway to Cabo Corrientes
Region 2. Cabo Corrientes to Casilda
Region 3. Casilda to Cabo Cruz
Region 4. Cabo Cruz to Punta Maisí
Region 5. Punta Maisí to Punta Maternillos
Region 6. Punta Maternillos to Cayo Bahía de Cádiz
Region 7. Cayo Bahía de Cádiz to Marina Hemingway

Cuba:
A Cruising
Guide

NIGEL CALDER

Imray Laurie Norie & Wilson Ltd
St Ives Cambridgeshire England

Published in Great Britain by
Imray Laurie Norie & Wilson Ltd
Wych House, St Ives, Huntingdon
Cambridgeshire PE17 4BT, England
☎ +44 (0)1480 462114 *Fax* +44 (0)1480 496109
E-mail ilnw@imray.com
Web http://www.imray.com

1st edition 1997
Revised edition 1999
© Nigel Calder 1999

ISBN 0 85288 413 3

Library of Congress Catalog Card Number:
96-72359
British Library Cataloguing in Publication Data.
A catalogue record for this book is available from the British Library.

CAUTION
Every effort has been made to ensure the accuracy of this book. It contains selected information, and thus is not definitive and does not include all known information on the subject in hand; this is particularly relevant to the plans, which should not be used for navigation. The author and publishers believe that it is a useful aid to prudent navigation, but the safety of a vessel depends ultimately on the judgment of the navigator, who should assess all information, published or unpublished, available to him.

BEARINGS
All bearings given in the text, and shown on the plans, are related to true north.

CORRECTIONS
The author would be glad to receive any corrections, information or suggestions which readers may consider would improve the book. Letters should be addressed to the publishers. The more precise the information the better, but even partial or doubtful information is helpful, if it is made clear what the doubts are.

The last input of technical information was April 1999.

Printed in Great Britain at Bath Press Colourbooks Ltd, Blantyre, Scotland

Contents

Royal Navy ships attacking the castle and battery of Choera on June 11th 1762

Havana castle being taken by troops under the command of the Earl of Albemarle on 30th July 1762

A perspective of Havana harbour on 16th August 1762 by Keppel in *Valiant*

Preface

PREFACE TO THE SECOND PRINTING

For this printing, we have made minor corrections, added a certain amount of information collected since the first printing, and inserted a section of color photographs. The bulk of the text, however, is unchanged.

It should be noted that hurricane *Georges* hit the north coast of Cuba hard in 1998. We have not resurveyed since the hurricane so extra care should be exercised when navigating in this areas.

Nigel Calder
January 1999

Dedication

This book is dedicated to:

John (Jake) Crump, who endured months of hard work in the cramped environment of our family boat with unfailing good humor.

José Miguel Escrich, the Executive Director of the International Yacht Club at the Marina Hemingway, Havana, who bailed us out when the security forces detained us, and who provided indispensable backup in Cuba.

Rolando Feitó Sarduy and his colleagues at the Cuban Hydrographic Office, who made available their incomparable charts of Cuba.

The folks at KVH Industries; without their magical Quadro chart-plotter and six-channel GPS this guide would not have been possible.

And, of course, to Terrie and the children, who didn't get a decent break in six months but only occasionally threatened to mutiny.

Acknowledgements

This book is the product of several years of intermittent planning, followed by six weeks in the Marina Hemingway, Havana (spent negotiating with Cuban officials, collecting information, getting to know some of the people, and studying Cuban politics and the Cuban economy). There was then a frenetic five-month circumnavigation of the island, during which we worked 12, 16 and sometimes 24 hours a day (sailing at night, doing surveys in the daytime, and then sailing again at night, grabbing catnaps on the off-watches). Subsequently, we added numerous bits of information gleaned from a variety of sources.

It would be absurdly arrogant to claim that we could get to know such a large and complex island in such a short period of time. Nevertheless, I think you will be amazed at the mass of data we managed to collect; reading through the finished manuscript, I certainly am! I am confident that there is in this book more than enough solid information to enable any sailor to circumnavigate the island of Cuba. In future editions we will, perhaps, pencil in some missing entries and flesh out the details.

Given the tremendous speed and enormous pressure with which we conducted our circumnavigation, there is no way we could have succeeded in producing useful results without a great deal of help from a large number of individuals and institutions. In particular, we owe a substantial debt of gratitude to the following (in no particular order):

John (Jake) Crump, who was persuaded to join us from England for a 'short, exploratory trip to Cuba', and who was then put to two months' hard work rerigging and painting the boat, followed by six gruelling months in Cuba. He never complained once, although he has told me before he comes over again he will require a duly signed and notarized statement that the boat is in the water, fully rigged and ready to sail.

The people at KVH, who donated a Quadro chart plotter, GPS, 'brain box', and associated display units for the project; and who went out of their way to develop a program to log data on a laptop computer. In particular, I wish to thank Jim Dodez, Per Hojfeldt and Ian Palmer. Without the Quadro system and KVH's backup, this guide would simply not have been possible.

Mercury Marine, and in particular Charlie Flores, who donated a Quicksilver inflatable and 9·9hp outboard motor as our primary survey platform.

The British Admiralty, and in particular Mr G.D. Taylor, who donated a complete set of the British Admiralty's Cuba charts to get us going.

The United States Defense Mapping Agency, and in particular Mark Ford, who donated an English translation of a Cuban two-volume *Sailing Directions for the Coast of Cuba*.

The Instituto Cubano de Hidrografía (Cuban hydrography institute – now called GeoCuba), and Rolando Feitó Sarduy in particular, for making available their wonderful charts of Cuba, and giving us permission to reproduce sections of those charts in this guide. Without the Cuban charts this guide would have taken many times longer to produce, and still would not have been nearly as good as I hope it is.

José Miguel Escrich and the International Yacht Club at the Marina Hemingway in Havana, together with Yvonne, Marie and Leandro, for enthusiastically supporting our project from day one and being absolutely indispensable in securing the official sponsorship which made this guide possible, ensuring our release when we were detained, and generally maintaining communications with various Cuban governmental agencies.

The Guarda Frontera (the Cuban coastal defense forces) for always maintaining a sense of humor, even when they detained us and our boat, and in spite of our sometimes provocative behavior.

Numerous Cuban skippers, fishermen, dive instructors and others who supplied us with detailed information on passages and anchorages which we would otherwise never have thought of exploring.

Ned and Kate Phillips, Geoffrey and Susanna Nockolds, Syd Stapleton, Jim Brown and family, Philip and Marilyn Lange and Mike Stanfield, all of whom sent us detailed notes on their cruises in Cuban waters.

Numerous other sailors who have sent in updated information since first publication.

The crews of *Uthorn*, *Fair Hippolyta*, *Neige D'Ete*, *El Magnifico*, *Wenonah*, *Flying Cloud*, and especially Michael Baxendale and Freddy Fajardo Ponce on *Cavu* (who helped to secure our speedy release after we were detained by the Guarda Frontera).

Willie Wilson, Nell Stuart, Jill Eaton and Debbie Lee at Imray, Laurie, Norie and Wilson for doing such an outstanding job in the production of this guide. M E Malone helped with proof reading and Elizabeth Cook compiled the index.

Finally, of course, there are Terrie and the children (Pippin and Paul). For them this trip was frequently no fun at all – nothing but work, work, work, all day, and sometimes all night, seven days a week, for month after month. They hardly ever complained, and remained in good spirits to the end. Next time we go to Cuba, the cruise will have to be for them.

To all of them, and many more, my heartfelt thanks!

Nigel Calder
Alna, Maine
December 1996

Introduction

Cuba is almost the last major destination in the Caribbean unexplored by the cruising community. For thirty-five years this island on the doorstep of America has been off-limits – a tantalizing Shangri-La hidden behind an iron curtain of gunboats and coastal defenses. Today, although the communists are still in power, the iron curtain has been partially lifted; tourists, including cruising sailors, are welcome, albeit with certain qualifications which we discuss later. The principal remaining bar to travel remains the intransigent hostility of the US government to the Castro regime, a hostility which only affects US travelers and even then is more rhetoric than substance. For several years a steady trickle of adventurous sailors have been making it to Havana, Santiago de Cuba, and other destinations, and starting to explore the island. Within a few years, as the last barriers to travel are eliminated, this trickle will likely turn to a flood.

What these early explorers are finding is that Cuba is BIG – much bigger than most people realize. It is by far the largest island in the Greater Antilles, with a land mass of more than 44,000 square miles, a length of almost 650 nautical miles, a coastline of 2,000 to 3,000 miles, and anywhere from 1,300 to 4,000 offshore islands (depending on the size limit used to define an island). It is in fact, not much smaller than England, but with a longer coastline. A cruise of months, rather than weeks, is required to do the island justice.

The coastal waters include a great deal of variegated cruising, including hundreds of miles of mangroves, hundreds of miles of beaches (many of them among the finest in the Caribbean), and dramatic mountains that march down almost to the edge of the sea. A good deal of this coastline is essentially still wild and largely untouched by human hand; only a handful of the islands are inhabited. The kind of manicured sand-and-coconut beaches found in the eastern Caribbean and beloved by advertisers are few and far between – if this is what you are looking for, then you will be disappointed.

The reefs that line much of the coast are once again some of the finest in the Caribbean, with spectacular snorkeling and diving. Numerous species of fish are abundant. We have never seen so many lobster, nor lobster of such a size.

Ashore, although there are few cities accessible to the cruiser, those that are accessible should not be missed. In spite of the fact that there is little in the way of supplies, the Cuban people should be enjoyed at every opportunity. They have to be some of the most spontaneously generous and friendly people to be found anywhere in the world, with a rich culture and traditions dating back hundreds of years. The cities themselves, though frequently crumbling, contain much fine architecture from colonial times – Cuba was, after all, one of the first islands in the Caribbean to be settled by Europeans, and for centuries played a key role in the Spanish empire.

And of course it is a fascinating experience to see first-hand the present-day experiment in Soviet-style communism. Given the mass of propaganda, both pro and con, that the Cuban revolution has generated, it is impossible to come to the island without at least some pre-conceived ideas. We defy anyone who arrives with an open mind to leave with those ideas intact; simply being in Cuba is a rich educational experience (albeit, an exceedingly frustrating one at times, particularly when it comes to dealing with the surfeit of officialdom).

In short, cruising in Cuba is far removed from the stereotype of Caribbean cruising. It is for the self-sufficient cruiser who wants to blaze a trail, experience nature in its pristine (and often unkempt) state, and live off the bounty of the sea. It is for the amateur historian and sociologist who wants to see first-hand one of the great social experiments of this century. And it is for all those who want to immerse themselves in an incredibly friendly and culturally rich Caribbean society.

To some it will be frustrating and disappointing; since this guide was first printed I have received letters from several disappointed, exasperated and even angry cruisers. But to many who are looking for a little more adventure, a cruise in Cuba will be remembered and savored long after leaving the island. For every negative letter sent to me I have received twice as many from cruisers for whom Cuba was the high point of a Caribbean cruise. Speaking for ourselves, we have mixed feelings. When we were there, we were working too hard to fully appreciate the island. But now that we have a cruising guide in hand, we intend to go back and enjoy it at our leisure; perhaps we'll see you there!

1. Background information

This chapter deals with a whole hodgepodge of information necessary or useful for getting around in Cuba. Much of it is not particularly interesting, but it is nevertheless worth plowing through. First, let's start with the legal situation as it affects US citizens and permanent residents (green card holders). Other nationals should also read this section as some of it impacts them.

Trading with the enemy

Under the terms of the Cuban Assets Control Regulations, issued by the US government in 1963 as part of the Trading With The Enemy Act, it is illegal for any US citizen, or US resident, to engage in unlicensed economic transactions with Cuba. The Regulations have a pretty broad scope which effectively prohibits the spending of any money in Cuba (and not just dollars; the prohibition includes all currencies). However, it should be noted that the Regulations do not prohibit visiting Cuba; there is simply a prohibition on spending money (of course, it is pretty difficult to visit without spending money, particularly since one of the first encounters most sailors have is with the immigration officials, who demand $25 for an entry visa). The penalties for non-compliance with the Regulations are Draconian – up to twelve years in jail and a fine of up to $250,000.

There are certain exceptions under the Regulations, the most notable being those that allow travel to Cuba for journalistic purposes or research, or for cultural and sporting activities. Other exceptions include American citizens with family in Cuba, people who are 'fully hosted' by the Cubans (which is to say all entry fees are waived and the Cubans pick up any other costs; they do this for certain races), and people who are 'sponsored' by someone not subject to US jurisdiction (for example, if cruising in company with Canadians, the Canadians could pick up the bill). In the case of sponsorship, it must be possible to prove that the sponsoring person or organization really did pay all expenses, and it is not legal to subsequently pay back the money. Even when covered by an exception, travelers are limited as to how much they can spend, and on what they can spend it (primarily accommodations, and food and research materials, but not souvenirs).

Until 1998, if someone went to Cuba, the onus was on the government to prove that money was spent. However, in May 1998 the law was changed to create 'a rebuttable presumption that travelers subject to US jurisdiction who traveled to Cuba without a general or specific license have engaged in prohibited transactions. Travelers may rebut the presumption by presenting a signed explanatory statement, with supporting documents, showing they were able to travel without spending money in Cuba. Appropriate enforcement action will be taken in those cases where the traveler is unable to provide sufficient evidence that all expenses were paid for while in Cuba.' Although enforcement action has been rare, there have been isolated cases resulting in fines of hundreds of dollars.

The original embargo was also tightened by Presidential Proclamation in March 1996, following the shooting down by Cuba of two US civilian aircraft. Bill Clinton declared a 'State of Emergency' under which most of coastal Florida, including the Florida Keys, was listed as a 'Maritime Security Zone'. In May 1998 this zone was expanded to include all of Florida with the exception of the Panhandle west of Panama City. All non-commercial vessels (including foreign-flag vessels) which depart from any port in the security zone and which intend to sail inside the Cuban 12-mile limit, must now have a US Coast Guard 'Acknowledgement of Security Zone and Permit to Depart During a National Emergency'! This permit can be obtained (free) from the Coast Guard at:

USCG Marine Safety Office
Claude Pepper Federal Bldg, 5th Floor
51 SW First Avenue
Miami, FL 33130-1608
☎ (305) 536-5691/5693/5607
Fax (305) 536-7005

In Fort Lauderdale, ☎ (954) 927 1611; Marathon, ☎ (305) 743 1945; Key West, ☎ (305) 292 8862; Tampa, ☎ (813) 228 2195/2189; Fort Myers, ☎ (941) 463 5754; Jacksonville, ☎ (904) 232 2640.

The permits are issued quite rapidly. Penalties for non-compliance are once again Draconian, including vessel forfeiture, fines of up to $10,000, and up to 10 years in jail. The Coast Guard passes on a copy of the permit to the US Treasury Department's Office of Foreign Assets Control ('OFAC'). OFAC sends the boat owner a letter that 'places you on notice that your authorization from the US Coast Guard does not authorize you to engage in any travel-related or other transactions that are prohibited by the Cuban Assets Control Regulations', such as 'the payment of fees required for vessels entering and departing Cuban waters and ports, including fees for your tourist visa, inward clearance, cruising permits, marina dockage and exit permits. These restrictions also apply to crew members and passengers on your vessel who are subject to the jurisdiction of the US, including all US citizens and residents.' In other words, OFAC is letting you know that it has you on its list, so you had better take care to establish that you did not spend money.

The net result of the Trading With The Enemy Act and these other measures is to effectively ban the general American public from going to Cuba. This has not, however, stopped a steady trickle of people from going, some of them many times over. As mentioned above, in isolated cases, notably when people have admitted to spending money, or when there has been clear evidence that money has been spent (such as receipts), fines have been levied, but in general few people have been harassed by the US Customs and other officials on their return to the USA.

For whatever reason, current US policy seems to be to more or less turn a blind eye to boats visiting Cuba, so long as those boats leaving from Florida have the Coast Guard permit. The Cubans aid and abet this process by not stamping the passports of visiting US citizens. If a boat clears in and out of Cuba from the Bahamas or Mexico, there is really no evidence that it has been to Cuba. On returning to the USA, if Coast Guard and customs officials know a boat has been to Cuba they are likely to ask if any money was spent, and if the answer is 'No' they seem content to leave well enough alone. Which is not to say that things might not change, but that's where they stand right now . . .

So where does this leave US sailors? If you want to go, the judgment call has to be yours. Given the interest in Cuba at all levels of American society, you could strengthen your hand vis-a-vis US authorities by promising to write stories for a local newspaper, or perhaps some company or other newsletter, and in return obtaining a letter identifying you as an official 'press representative'. This will not cover other members of the crew, but will at least cover the bearer and necessary expenses incurred by the bearer (marina and entry fees?). To remain legal, the crew will have to avoid spending money (just one of the reasons for fully stocking a boat before departing US waters – a subject I deal with in more detail later.)

Another approach would be to 'buddy-boat' with good friends not subject to the embargo (such as

Canadians or Europeans), and have your friends pick up the bill for you while in Cuba. The various entry and exit permits for a typical cruising boat in 1998 were running around $200 – not an unreasonable expense for someone to pay to have the benefit of another boat's company. Over and above these costs are whatever marina fees you opt to pay, and shoreside expenditures.

Maybe, by the time this is published the Regulations will have been rescinded. Let's hope so.

Copies of the Regulations can be obtained from the Office of Foreign Assets Control, US Department of the Treasury, Washington, DC 20220.

Note After a trip abroad, US boats with just US nationals on board can clear into any port in south Florida by calling the customs service at one of the following toll-free numbers:

1-800 432 1216
1-800 458 4239
1-800 451 0393

Normally, the boat and crew will be cleared in over the phone and that's that! However, owners of boats over 30 feet long must purchase a yearly 'Customs User Fee Decal'. This is best bought in the USA before setting sail, because if you don't have it when you clear back in, the customs are going to require you to buy it, and may come to your boat to sell it to you.

A note on the embargo

This is a cruising guide, not a political treatise. As such, we have left politics out of it. However, I feel morally bound to make a statement of my position concerning the embargo.

The current US policy is immoral, hypocritical, counter-productive, and bad for business.

It is immoral in so far as it is designed to punish the Cuban people for the perceived sins of the Cuban government. It is the people, especially the poor people, and not the government, that have to suffer the worst effects of the embargo.

It is hypocritical in so far as its chief rationale today is the lack of democracy and human rights in Cuba, whereas the USA has actively supported many a regime with a far worse record on democracy and human rights than the Castro regime (Pinochet in Chile, a succession of brutal generals in Guatemala and El Salvador, the present regime in China, and so on; the list is a long one), and continues to trade with many a country with a worse record than Cuba.

It is counter-productive in so far as it provides Castro with a fig leaf with which to cover the economic inefficiencies of his regime. In Cuba, all ills are currently, with some plausibility, blamed on the US embargo and US hostility. Without the embargo the Cuban people would have to come to terms with many of the manifest absurdities of the current system.

It is bad for business in so far as it prevents US companies from competing in the opening Cuban economy; currently the Canadians and the Europeans are being given a free hand. The US response to this is to seek ways to penalize non-US corporations for trading with Cuba (Jesse Helms' *La Libertad* Act); it seems the USA would rather fall out with its allies than admit that its policy is fundamentally flawed.

I believe the presence of people such as ourselves in Cuba, with the interaction and dissemination of ideas that takes place (which is a two-way process – there are things we can learn from Cuba) will do more to bring about change in Cuba, and do it peacefully, than will any amount of stick-waving by the USA. You'd think that after 35 years of failure, the US government would realize that a change of emphasis was needed.

That's it for politics – now let's get into the guide. First, a short history, just to get us oriented.

History

The following abbreviated history has elicited an angry response from those who believe Cuba is a brutal police state with no redeeming features, and also from those who see it as a benevolent socialist state based on a workers democracy. I have done what I can with my limited knowledge of Cuban history to be as objective as I know how. To those who are still offended, I apologize in advance!

Since the original Indian population of Cuba was almost entirely wiped out by the Spanish conquistadors, written Cuban history does not go back beyond Columbus' first voyage to the Americas in 1492. After landing somewhere in the Bahamas, Columbus continued broadly westward to make a landfall on the north coast of Cuba. He sailed somewhat further west before turning around to return in triumph to Spain believing that he had reached the Indies. Subsequent voyages penciled in considerable additional sections of both the north and south coasts of Cuba, but it was not until 1508, when Sebastian de Ocampo circumnavigated, that the Spanish discovered that Cuba was in fact an island.

Spanish colonization continued throughout the succeeding decades. The Indians put up what little fight they could against European arms, but were soon defeated and enslaved. The most notable resistance was led by a chief named Hatuey, whom the Spaniards captured and burned at the stake. Reputedly, his captors offered conversion to Christianity before he died so he could go to heaven. He asked, 'Will I meet more people like you in this heaven?' 'Oh yes,' they replied, 'we are all going

there'. 'In that case I'll stay as I am,' he said! Fairly soon after the conquest, the indigenous population was destroyed through a combination of disease and incredible abuse.

Cuba rapidly became a most important link in the Spanish chain of possessions in the Americas for reasons which are abundantly clear to sailors – the island sits squarely in the path of the Gulf Stream, which sweeps up through the Yucatan Straits and then parallels the Cuban coastline through the Straits of Florida. In other words, Cuba dominates the major trade route from south and central America to Europe.

Much of the plunder of the Americas, whether brought overland from South America to Porto Bello on the isthmus of Panama, or hauled through the jungles of Guatemala to the Río Dulce, was shipped to Havana and then on to Spain in the annual treasure fleet. Havana itself was in many ways a perfect port in which to assemble this fleet since it has a wonderfully protected harbor with a narrow entrance easily defended by massive fortifications (El Morro) built on high ground at the mouth of the harbor. It was from here that the largest treasure fleet of all set sail in 1622, only to be overtaken by a hurricane when just a day out. The principal galleon, the *Atosha*, was driven ashore in the Marquesas Keys with the loss of all aboard. 350 years later Mel Fisher and his fellow treasure hunters uncovered the 'mother lode', much of which is on display today in Fisher's museum in Key West (well worth a visit).

Havana became a flourishing trading post, and as plunder gave way to colonization valuable crops were grown to be shipped back to Europe. Tobacco, sugar and coffee predominated with native slave labor replaced by imported blacks as the Indians died off. On the heels of the French Revolution (1789) came a slave revolt in neighboring Haiti, which was then the richest colony in the Caribbean and the region's major sugar producer. Years of warfare resulted in the almost total elimination of Europeans from Haiti, and the collapse of the great sugar plantations. Cuba moved in to fill the gap, and sugar became king, with an ever-increasing proportion of the crop being shipped to the rapidly growing United States.

As the wealth and power of the Spanish colonies in the Americas grew, so too did frustration at the hand of bureaucratic control from Spain, sparking a long and bloody struggle for independence. A ten-year rebellion from 1868 to 1878, which forever established Antonio Maceo as one of the great heroes of Cuba, went down to defeat. This was followed by years of sporadic revolt. In 1895 José Martí, the pre-eminent figure in the Pantheon of Cuban nationalists, once again raised the standard of revolt, only to be killed in the first weeks of the rebellion. After three years of bloody fighting, the

US government, spurred on by an hysterical press campaign orchestrated by Randolph Hearst and others, entered the war not so much on the side of the rebels as against Spain.

The 'Spanish-American War' of 1898 resulted in the rapid destruction of a good part of the antiquated Spanish navy, and a quick surrender by the Spaniards. As a result of this war, Spain pulled out of Cuba, which was granted nominal independence, but the United States reserved the right, in the Platt Amendment, to intervene at will to 'preserve the island's independence'! In order to facilitate such interventions, the USA took out indefinite leases on 12 natural harbors around the coast of Cuba, but subsequently (1912) relinquished all claims bar that to Guantánamo Bay, which it has occupied to this day. With such inauspicious beginnings, 'democracy' was brought to Cuba. Over the years the USA has intervened repeatedly in Cuba's internal affairs, sending in the marines to enforce its will on a number of occasions, and threatening to do so on many another occasion. In addition, through its control of the Cuban sugar market the US has exercised a stranglehold on the Cuban economy.

In 1933 the economic depression in the USA brought devastation to the Cuban economy. A period of turmoil resulted in the primacy of the army, under the control of the late Sergeant Fulgencio Batista. Symptomatically, one of his first acts was to add $0.15 to the cost of all army uniforms, to be paid directly to him (by the time he was overthrown in 1959 he had salted away several hundred million dollars in overseas accounts). Throughout the 1930s, Batista, with at least the tacit support of the USA, continued to pull the strings behind a series of nominally independent governments. During this period (the New Deal era in the US) he consolidated a political base in the peasantry and working classes by promoting a fair amount of socially progressive legislation. Finally, in 1940, he promulgated a new constitution and, with the active support of the Cuban Communist Party, was elected President (this was the period of the Popular Front in which Communist parties throughout the world, under direct orders from Moscow, made many a strange political alliance). In 1944, in a surprise outcome, his appointed successor lost the presidential election to Ramon Grau, head of the Authentic Revolutionary Movement (nominally committed to progressive social policies). Batista temporarily retired to Florida.

In the words of the notable historian, Hugh Thomas, 'Grau turned his presidency into an orgy of theft, ill-disguised by emotional nationalistic speeches. He did more than any other single man to kill the hope of democratic practice in Cuba'. The corruption was accompanied by widespread gangsterism, with frequent murders and assassinations across the entire political spectrum. Grau's successor in 1948, Carlos Prio, was little better. The government continued to shamelessly pillage the country, protecting at the same time the interests of the Cuban and American rich, including the American mafia. Havana became an international playground while the majority of Cubans lived in illiterate poverty. Finally, in 1952 Batista, using the widespread corruption and disorder during that year's presidential election campaign as an excuse, seized power, overthrowing his own constitution of 1940 and initiating a period of open, brutal, dictatorship in which the police and armed forces ran amok, with torture and murder common. The USA hastened to recognize the new government.

Batista's coup found the old opposition parties in a state of internecine warfare. Into the breach stepped a charismatic young radical politician, Fidel Castro. On July 26, 1953, he captured center stage with a desperate assault on the Moncada police barracks in Santiago de Cuba, in which his poorly armed forces were outnumbered 10 to 1 (in today's Cuba, references to July 26th are to be found everywhere). The attack (denounced, incidentally, by the communists) was repulsed with few losses, but in the ensuing days dozens of Castro's supporters were captured, brutally tortured and murdered. A number of the survivors, including Castro and his brother Raúl, were jailed for a while on the Isla de la Juventud (the jail is now an interesting museum – see the relevant chapter), but released in 1955 under an amnesty.

Castro regrouped in Mexico and then sailed with 82 armed comrades to the southern coast of Cuba in December 1956 (the large cabin cruiser, the *Granma*, that was used to convey them is now on display in Havana). A day or two after landing the party of guerrillas was ambushed; only 15 escaped to the hills to continue the struggle. These then organized the rebellion that was eventually successful, with Castro and his comrades entering Havana in triumph on January 8, 1959. Foremost amongst the revolutionists were Castro, his younger brother Raúl (currently head of the armed forces in Cuba), Ché Guevara (killed in Bolivia in 1967), Camilo Cienfuegos (lost when his plane disappeared in late 1959), and Frank País (leader of the movement's supporters in Santiago de Cuba, killed during the struggle) – their names and images pop up everywhere in contemporary Cuba.

The revolutionists inherited an economy in ruins, and moreover one which had been seriously distorted to serve the interests of foreign investors, tourists and gamblers rather than the indigenous population. Castro and his comrades initiated radical steps to change the direction of the economy. Over the course of the next year, an almost continuous diplomatic duel took place between Castro and the US, during which the Castro regime expropriated many of the larger land holdings, and then took over three American-owned oil refineries (for their refusal to refine a shipment of Soviet oil – the Soviets were beginning to cautiously move into the breach between Cuba and the US). The US responded to these moves by imposing an economic embargo, which has not been lifted to this day. By 1960 the CIA had also already laid the framework for a program of destabilization, including numerous armed incursions into Cuba (the most dramatic being the ill-fated Bay of Pigs expedition) and attempts on the life of Castro.

With the loss of its principal overseas trading partner, Cuba was thrown into the arms of the Soviets, who were more than happy to subsidize the new regime in return for an outpost on the very doorstep of the United States. Castro had, in any event, been moving closer to the communists. The Soviet connection resulted in the primacy of the Cuban Communist Party, with Castro at its head. However, although Cuba soon took on many of the trappings of the former East European communist police states, there are, nevertheless, fundamental differences between Cuba and these states in as much as the Cuban revolution was a genuinely popular revolution which still retains a fair measure of loyalty amongst the population. For example, Hugh Thomas notes: '... the break from corrupt officials, corrupt judiciary, corrupt politicians, corrupt unionists and corrupt men of business was, in the minds of the majority, a stark, extraordinary, maybe baffling, but wonderful contrast', and 'for the majority, for nearly all the country-dwellers and for most of those who lived in towns ... for the first time they knew that authority was on their side, that justice could not be bought by their landlord or employer...'.

Following severe shortages in the years immediately after the revolution, and in spite of the inherent inefficiencies of a centralized, state-run economy, the combination of the undoubted idealism of the revolution and the Soviet subsidy finally produced the most egalitarian, best educated society in the Caribbean and Central America, with an enviable public health system, little unemployment, and, until recently, a relatively high standard of living. In the space of a single generation Cuba changed from a primarily manual-labor based agrarian society into a highly mechanized primarily urban society. The successes of the revolution, and the ability of Castro to thumb his nose at successive American presidents, have contributed to a sense of pride and self respect among Cubans which is sadly lacking in many of the region's other nations.

But with the collapse of the Soviet Union in 1990 Cuba lost both its subsidy and all its major trading partners; the economic glue of modern Cuba

dissolved. The economy was once again reduced to a shambles, with severe shortages of everything from oil to basic foodstuffs; the American embargo, which was largely ineffective so long as the Soviets and its allies filled the economic gap, finally had a severe impact by preventing Cuba from developing trade links with its natural trading partner.

Not only were most of the factories idled, but Cuban agriculture, already suffering from the inefficiencies of Soviet-style State farming, was also thrown into a deep crisis. Castro has always believed in large-scale, mechanized farming, and in addition has actually reinforced the dependence of the Cuban economy on sugar cane (following some unsuccessful attempts to diversify in the early years of the revolution). The earnings from sugar, and, to a lesser extent, coffee, tobacco and other produce, have been used to finance overseas purchases of oil, fertilizers and other feedstuffs (for factory-farming type production of cattle, pigs and chickens), and also foodstuffs for human consumption (such as grains for bread). Overnight, Cuba lost its market for sugarcane, and its supply of oil, fertilizer, animal feeds and grains. The sugar cane harvest plummeted from eight million tons a year to three million tons in 1997, while the production and importation of milk and dairy products, meat, and grains dropped catastrophically.

To feed the population, and maintain minimal sugar cane production, the government has been forced to adopt pre-revolutionary agricultural methods, including widespread use of ox- and horse-drawn ploughs and carts. These methods are suited to small-scale peasant agriculture, rather than large-scale state-controlled agriculture. In order to stimulate small-scale production of foodstuffs, for the first time in decades in 1995 private sale of foodstuffs was allowed through the state-licensed 'farmers' markets'. Many state-owned farms have been broken up into smaller cooperatives, which are also allowed to sell a percentage of their output in the farmers' markets (currently 20%), distributing the profits among the members of the cooperative. The result has been a marked improvement in the food situation in the past year or two.

The long-term goal of the government, however, is still to find a means to earn the foreign exchange necessary to buy the oil which will both restore large-scale mechanized production in the countryside, and also re-start the idle factories in the cities. The expansion of the tourist industry, which is currently the single largest foreign exchange earner, is the number one economic priority for the country; at the same time the Cubans are actively seeking foreign investment to jump-start their factories. As part of these moves to increase tourist revenues, foreign sailors are being allowed into Cuba, and given permits to cruise the island's waters, although the freedoms accorded visiting yachts are tempered by a substantial degree of bureaucratic oversight in the form of much paperwork, and close supervision by the Guarda Frontera (the Cuban coastal defense forces).

The one thing certain about the present situation in Cuba is that it will change before this is published. The government is under pressure from all sides, including at one extreme those in Cuba fearful of any change, and at the other extreme radical right-wingers in Florida more than prepared to initiate another civil war and to drown the revolution in blood. We hope that the Cuban people will be able to find a path which restores life to their economy and gives them greater political freedom, while at the same time preserving the social gains of the revolution, and that in the process foreign cruisers will be allowed to cruise unhampered in Cuban waters.

Security

I mentioned above the close supervision of foreign boats. This should not be taken lightly. A couple of examples will serve to illustrate this. A boat arrived off the Marina Acua in the night and hove to until dawn in order to enter. Shortly thereafter a gunboat showed up and ordered it into port. We ourselves have been boarded by the Guarda (often not in uniform, and on one occasion in his underpants with an automatic hidden in the crotch!) in the most obscure and remote locations.

On the other hand, there is no need to be overly paranoid. The scenic lighthouse on Cayo Piedras del Norte also serves as a lookout post for the military. It is actively manned 24-hours a day, with a soldier constantly patrolling and scanning the horizon. When we started to take pictures, a man in a boat offshore started shouting at us. We assumed he was ordering us not to take photographs, since the lighthouse is a military installation, so pretended we did not understand him and hastily carried on (we hadn't yet got the shots we wanted). He came rowing into the beach. We had visions of our films being ripped out of our cameras. However, he just wanted to tell us that we would get a much better picture from the lookout post.

Wherever we went, we got the same kind of helpful, open and enthusiastic reception. The sailors on the gunboats at the naval base next to the Marina Gaviota simply waved as we passed by in our dinghy, complete with electronic survey equipment and electronic plotter which were in full view, and taking photos as we went (this was before our detention, and subsequent endorsement by the highest levels of the Guarda). The high level of security is, in other words, almost always maintained with the utmost courtesy, not to mention very often downright friendliness. Cuba is one of the few countries where most officials do not openly bear arms, and is the only country we have visited in which the officials have frequently asked us if they should remove their shoes before coming aboard, or have simply removed them before we could say there was no need.

This friendliness and courtesy should not, however, lead the visitor to conclude that Cuba is an open society in the western sense. Cuban internal security is tight; the supervision of its people close, particularly since the shooting down of the two planes in 1996. Comments critical of the government are seen as subversive, rather than as an application of the principle of freedom of speech. When dealing with Cuban people it is important to remember this, and to be careful about what you say, and to whom you say it, not only to protect yourself, but also to protect the people with whom you talk. The best advice is to simply refuse to be drawn into political discussions. Note also that Cubans, with the exception of officials, are not allowed on visiting boats (even in marinas), and should not be invited on board.

Language

Spanish is the national language. Aside from Spanish, a fair number of people speak Russian, Hungarian, and (East!) German, but few speak English. However, this is changing rapidly as everyone in Cuba recognizes that English (or more particularly, American) will be the prime foreign language in the future. In the meantime your stay in Cuba will be made a whole lot easier if you can acquire at least a minimal acquaintance with Spanish before going there.

Health

The Cubans have an excellent public health system (we have never seen fitter and healthier people anywhere, but this, of course, has something to do with the current non-fat diet, and the fact that almost everyone has to ride a bicycle or else walk in order to get around). We were told that there is a doctor for every 60 people on the island. Be that as it may, there is always one within easy reach, and of course they are free.

Medicines, on the other hand, are not so easy to come by. At least in part as a result of the US embargo, even aspirin are in very short supply, and in fact sick people die every day because of the inability of the drug stores to fill the most basic prescriptions. *If you need any special medicines you must be sure to take an adequate supply with you.* Having said that, it *is* possible to get many specialized medicines, but it may take quite a bit of running around, and the medicine will have to be paid for in dollars, probably at a higher price than back home.

Should you or any of your crew need to be hospitalized you will be sent to a special tourist hospital in which the level of health care is excellent, but at prices that rival those in the USA. So if you don't already have health insurance, you would be well advised to take out a traveler's policy before setting sail.

Money and shopping

The currency and shopping situation in Cuba is unusual. The national currency is the peso, subdivided into one hundred centavos, but overshadowing everything is the almighty American dollar. The government has established an entirely arbitrary official exchange rate of one peso to the dollar, whereas the black market has established a radically different rate (which has been hovering around 20 pesos to the dollar for the past four years, but has been as high as 200 pesos to the dollar). Outside of Cuba the peso is not convertible on world currency markets, and is therefore not worth anything.

The Cuban people are paid in pesos at rates which seem absurdly low by western standards (typically 120 to 400 pesos a month). But the government guarantees everyone a basic monthly ration at equally low prices. This ration includes rice, dried peas, beans, and so on (and at one time included a bottle of rum per family!), and would be, if met in full, just about enough to feed someone. However, in recent years, because of the economic dislocations, the ration has almost never been met in full (meat, dairy products, soap, detergents, cooking oil, propane for cooking, and many other basic commodities have been, and continue to be, extremely scarce; this list includes toilet paper, which is missing from even some first-class hotels, so be sure to always carry some when leaving the boat).

In the past, all agricultural production (both from state-owned and private farms) had to go to the government for distribution. If there was any surplus beyond that needed to fill the basic rations, it was sold at somewhat higher prices in what were called 'parallel markets' – here many Cubans bought the luxuries of life (additional meat and dairy products, ice cream, and so on). With the economic crisis, the parallel markets essentially ceased to exist. Now their place has been taken by the farmers' markets. Eighty percent of agricultural production, both from the small-scale, privately owned farms and the state cooperatives, still has to go to the state to meet the monthly rations, but the remaining 20% is sold in the farmers' markets (at prices many times higher than those formerly found in the parallel markets). In time, Castro has said, as agricultural production increases, it may be possible to release 30% to 40% of production for sale in the farmers'

markets. These markets are accessible to foreigners, but pesos are normally required, although as time passes more and more goods are priced in dollars only. Depending on the exchange rate, although the prices may seem high to Cubans, they are still very low by western standards. In these markets it is possible to find a supply of fresh vegetables and fruits, and even some meat (mostly pork and chicken).

To meet the needs of the burgeoning tourist industry, the government also opened dollar stores. These initially were for tourists only, and made available to tourists all kinds of goods that ordinary Cubans could not buy. Cubans themselves were not allowed to own dollars. However, many acquired dollars either through tips, or through remittances from relatives in the USA, so a substantial dollar-based black market developed. In 1994 the government made a major change of direction, legalizing the holding of dollars by Cubans, and opening the dollar stores to its own people (although if there is a queue, priority is given to tourists, which is extremely frustrating to many Cubans who, in the pursuit of foreign currency, have been made second-class citizens in their own country).

As the dollar-based economy grew, there were simply not enough dollars in circulation to lubricate the wheels of commerce. The government responded by issuing what are known as 'convertible' pesos. These are quite distinct from normal pesos. Convertible pesos have official parity with the dollar (i.e. one convertible peso is officially worth one dollar) but in this case there really is parity since the government, and any tourist-based facility, will redeem convertible pesos on a one-for-one basis. There is also small change in convertible pesos which is freely interchangeable for US small change (inside Cuba). In addition to convertible pesos, various tourist resorts issue their own currency (beads, etc.) but this is NOT redeemable outside the resort in question.

The longer-term goal of the government is to make the peso stable enough to be convertible on foreign exchange markets; but it remains to be seen if this can be done, and if so at what rate of exchange.

So where does this leave the cruiser? Although not good, the selection of goods in the dollar shops is considerably better than that in the peso stores, but with prices that are higher than in the States. In other words, a certain amount of re-provisioning can be done, but nevertheless it is best to stock the boat as fully as possible before departure, and to rely as little as possible on local supplies. Milk and dairy products, in particular, are very hard to obtain anywhere, so if the boat has refrigeration it is worthwhile freezing and refrigerating as much as possible, supplementing whatever milk can be carried with dried milk. (Note that the Cubans have strict rules on the importation of foodstuffs – designed to protect them from foreign bugs – and in the past have been known to confiscate fresh produce, especially fruit. But lately these rules have been applied with discretion although every once in a while I get a report of some over-zealous official sticking to the letter of the law. So long as there is no obvious insect life around your fruit, and no weevils burrowing around in your flour and dried goods, and so long as meats are properly refrigerated, most times there should be no problem with importing as much as you can carry.)

The peso stores are frequently almost bare with long queues for what meager supplies are available. The farmers' markets are a much better proposition, particularly for fresh produce. As the food situation in Cuba improves they will become an even better source of supplies. However, to shop in these markets, pesos are generally required (although this is changing – see above), and if exchanged at the official rate all produce becomes prohibitively expensive. But if dollars are exchanged on the black market, the supplies in the farmers' markets are very cheap (depending, of course, on the rate of exchange). Having de-criminalized the possession of dollars by Cubans, the government has, for the time being, criminalized the possession of pesos, other than those exchanged at the official rate, by foreigners. This is simply one of those anomalies that arise when a currency is not fully convertible, and which will disappear as the government moves towards a convertible peso. If you decide to change dollars on the black market, in general it is best to do this through someone you have gotten to know, since there are many stories of sharks on the streets setting up innocent tourists and making off with their money. However, in some places there are now (1999) semi-official money-changers operating from booths with posted exchange rates. These are safe to use. It remains to be seen whether they will survive the political vicissitudes in Cuba. Black-market money changers are more common in the tourist areas than elsewhere, so it is best to get a stock of pesos in hand from one of these areas before taking off for a cruise in the boonies.

This difference between the official exchange rate and the black-market rate produces some odd situations. For example, if postage stamps or medicines are bought in a tourist area, they will be priced in dollars based on the official exchange rate, but if bought in a 'downtown' area will be priced in pesos. So if bought in pesos which have been obtained at the black-market rate, the price will be many times lower (currently twenty times lower) than the dollar price. In general, if products are available in both dollar stores and peso stores, they will be many times cheaper in the peso stores so long as the pesos have been obtained on the black market.

Finally, as a practical matter, although the dollar is now almost universally accepted in Cuba, change is in short supply. You should take a large number of dollar bills of small denomination ($1 and $5) to Cuba. Large bills (such as $100) will be hard to change outside recognized tourist areas. European credit cards, and travelers checks drawn on European banks, can be used in Cuba, but American credit cards, and travelers checks drawn on American banks (even if issued in Europe), cannot always be used (some places will now change American travelers checks but sometimes at a heavy premium, presumably to cover the cost of laundering the money in violation of the US embargo).

Note 1 One of the side effects of the differing official and black market rates for the peso is that in black market terms the typical monthly wage of most Cubans, which varies from 100 to 400 pesos, is only worth a few dollars. As a result, a $1 tip, for example, may be worth as much as a week's wages. Today, Cubans will work on sailboats in the Marina Hemingway for $15 a day, since when converted on the black market, this represents much more than a month's pay. (In 1996 the Cuban government put a stop to this activity but this is only intermittently enforced.) Cubans of all professions are competing to work in any environment that brings them into contact with tourists and tourist dollars. There are university professors who have resigned their posts to become receptionists or bellboys in hotels; even sadder are the highly qualified women who turn to prostitution (which is rampant in the tourist areas; periodically the police engage in a mass round up of prostitutes, many of whom are filling the gaols, but they soon reappear on the streets). Presumably, much of this economic distortion will disappear if the peso becomes fully convertible.

Note 2 Some of the larger coastal towns have an office of Mambisa (SUMARPO), a national ship's chandler. SUMARPO can provide extensive reprovisioning at reasonable dollar prices.

Using credit cards in Cuba

US credit cards are often not usable in Cuba, although this will end if the embargo is lifted, and the Cubans are, in any case, finding ways to circumvent the embargo. All major European cards work, although in general cards are only accepted in the tourist hotels, major restaurants, and dollar stores; in some places the processing of the card is quite rapid, but in others, where they are less used to 'plastic', it can take quite a while. One or two of the marinas also accept payment by credit card (Marina Hemingway at Havana, Marina Acua at Varadero, Marina PuertoSol at Cayo Largo), and others are considering it (for example, Marina Jagua at Cienfuegos).

It is currently difficult to obtain cash with a credit card outside of Havana and Varadero. In Havana, an office in the Hotel Havana Libre (formerly the Hilton), and also the Banco Financiero Internacional (BFI), will advance you as much cash as your card can stand; in Varadero go to the BFI.

Note Reportedly, BFI branches in Cienfuegos, Manzanillo and several other cities have started advancing cash against both European and American credit cards. Nevertheless, it is a good idea to bring plenty of cash!

Supplies and essential services

As mentioned above, it is currently possible to buy most basic foodstuffs in Cuba, including fresh fruits and vegetables, but the availability is highly localized and sporadic. In Havana, for example, there are several supermarkets which between them have a reasonable supply of commodities such as eggs, cheese, meat and cooking oil that are otherwise exceedingly scarce in Cuba. But west of Havana the pickings get increasingly slim the nearer you get to Cabo San Antonio, and in fact if sailing in this direction you will find the next reasonable source of supplies is Nueva Gerona, on the Isla de la Juventud, which is weeks of cruising time away. What this means is that if you see something you like you should stock up while the going is good.

Some things you will just about not see at all. For example, breakfast cereal, oatmeal, decent tea or instant coffee, pre-packaged frozen goods (Paul loves 'chicken nuggets'; we had to load the freezer with them before leaving the USA), fresh milk (the supermarkets have powdered milk, but it is the full-fat variety which has a distinct flavor; it is worth stocking up on low-fat dried milk in the USA since this tastes more or less like regular milk), butter (canned and packaged margarine is available), and numerous other specialized foods (any kind of sauces, such as spaghetti or taco sauce, barbecue sauce, and so on; parmesan cheese; taco shells; salad dressings; pancake or biscuit mix; etc.). These you will have to carry yourself.

Then there are other things that are either scarce or far more expensive in Cuba than elsewhere. Of the basic commodities, flour, and flour-based products such as spaghetti noodles, are the most significant (you may be baking a fair bit since bread is often almost impossible to buy outside the big cities – see below; you also need to carry yeast). Sugar, believe it or not is rarely seen (it all goes for export). Looking at our list of food to have on board (which, obviously, is quite personal) there are cookies (biscuits) and other snack foods, raisins, honey, macaroni, cocoa and chocolate mix, canned fruits and vegetables (particularly the latter, which are needed to tide you over those periods when no fresh vegetables are available), brown rice, baked beans, canned sardines and tuna, and canned or dried soups.

Bread is supplied to the Cuban people as part of the basic State food ration. All towns of any size have a bakery, with all the bakeries apparently using the same recipe. Each bakery has a list of all the households in town, together with the number of people in each house. Bread is sold to Cubans at a highly subsidized price, on the basis of 400 grams per person per day. There is no mechanism to sell it to foreigners. We tried to buy it many times without success. What normally happened was that we would be told we couldn't have any, and then as we left someone would sidle up to us and either tell us to come back later or to go around the back, when we would be given some. We tried to pay, since we certainly do not need to be subsidized by people who have so much less than we do, but never succeeded. However, we generally found we could press a bar or two of soap on the donors, although even this was difficult (the Cubans are incredibly generous, but reluctant to take anything in return; soap, incidentally, is a much appreciated gift as it is in very short supply).

Where does this leave us? There is clearly no source of supplies that even comes close to a well stocked American supermarket. You should load the boat to the gunwales before setting sail for Cuba. If you start to run low on your favorite foodstuffs or snacks, and you are getting tired of rice, beans and dried peas, Key West is less than a day's sail from a good part of the north shore of Cuba, Isla Mujeres and Cancun are about the same distance from Cabo San Antonio, and the Cayman Islands and Jamaica are readily accessible from the south coast.

Drinking water

Water is available at all the marinas, and at many of the Guarda docks. It is not a problem.

Fuel

Diesel and gasoline are available at all the marinas. In addition, every town of any size has a dollar-based gas (petrol) station with diesel and gasoline. There are two grades of gasoline, regular and special, with the price fixed by the government (1998) at $0.65 a liter for regular, and $0.90 for special (you should use special). In 1998 diesel varied in price from $0.45 a liter to $1.00 a liter with the difference being a function of where it was bought, rather than changes in State pricing policies (the cheap diesel was from a commercial dock; the expensive from the marina on Cayo Largo).

LPG (propane and butane)

Propane for cooking (LPG, called *gas liquado* in Cuba) is hard to obtain. Like bread, this is something that is supplied as part of the basic State-provided ration; there is no mechanism to sell it outside of this framework. However, one or two of the marinas (Marina Hemingway; Marina Jagua in Cienfuegos) can arrange refills. Otherwise you will simply have to find the nearest office that deals with the paperwork for the Cuban people, talk them into giving you the necessary piece of paper to get a refill, and then take your cylinder to the re-filling station (which is normally outside of town for safety reasons). You should allow all day for this process. Better yet, come with a large enough supply to see you through your cruise.

Note Cuba uses propane, not butane, with American-style cylinder fittings. European boats will need to obtain an American-style propane cylinder with the appropriate fittings before setting sail (in the UK, Calor Gas can supply the cylinders and fittings).

Electricity

Cuba uses the American electrical system, which is to say the primary household voltage is 110-volts, with larger appliances (such as electric stoves and air conditioners) using 220-volts. The frequency is 60 Hz (as opposed to 50 Hz in the UK).

All the marinas have shoreside hookups, but typically there are neither proper outlet boxes, nor proper outlets. Every time a new boat pulls in, the marina's electrician jury-rigs a connection. These connections leave much to be desired, commonly with reverse polarity and/or no grounding connection. Most times the boat's electrical system works fine, although we did see the electrician put a dead short across one boat's AC system, burning up the shore power cord and some of the onboard wiring. But even when the boat's AC system appears to be working OK, in reality there is frequently a potentially lethal situation both on board, and also should anyone swim in the surrounding water.

We strongly advise all skippers to carry a multimeter or tester, and to learn how to use it to check both the polarity of the incoming shore power, and also to test for a proper ground connection. The electrician will be more than happy to work with you in correcting any deficiencies. *If you cannot check the polarity and ground, you should not plug in.* Finally, children must be warned to stay away from the electrical boxes (most of which are open; this goes also for many street lights and other electrified systems in public places), and also kept out of the water in the area of the marina.

Note Even where there are decent dockside receptacles, they may be miswired internally. In the Marina Jagua at Cienfuegos we came across the first proper-looking outlets that we had seen in Cuba, only to find the 110-volt receptacle had 220-volts on it, while under the waterproof cover for the 220-volt receptacle there were three live prongs sticking out of the panel! After the marina electrician had 'rewired' the 110-volt outlet, it still had 220-volts on it, so we respectfully declined to plug in.

Telephones/fax/mail/e-mail

Once outside of the big cities, the internal Cuban telephone system is simply appalling. It took six hours of continuous dialing one day to get two connections. However, inside the big cities the system more or less works, although a lack of lines means that much of the time you get a busy signal. When it comes to international calls, so long as you are in a tourist area the system works fine since most of the hotels now have satellite connections. The cost, however, is horrendous – $2.50 a minute to the USA; close to $6.00 a minute to Europe and the rest of the world.

International faxes also are reasonably common in the tourist areas and work well. These are often a more efficient (and certainly cheaper) means of communicating with the rest of the world. E-mail is also becoming available through an agency called INFOTUR. In 1998 it cost $1.00 to send or receive a message.

The international telephone code for Cuba is +53. This is then frequently followed by a 7 (denoting the Havana area).

The mail system is not so hot. Its not so much that letters don't get through, its just that they may take forever to get to their destination. It is not unusual for a letter posted in Havana to take three months to get to Miami. Most of the marinas will be happy to act as a mail drop, but you might not want to wait for the mail to arrive!

For more reliable delivery (but at a high price) you should use DHL, the only courier service that operates in Cuba. They have an office in most major cities. But even with a courier it may take up to ten days to get packages in or out, and even longer if the contents get snarled up in customs (whatever you do, don't try importing or exporting any electronics; the Cubans are quite paranoid about this stuff).

Photography

Film and camera batteries are widely available in the tourist zones at prices similar to those in the States. Photo processing is less common and less reliable – it would be better to have this done after leaving Cuba.

Guns

Guns must be declared every time the boat is cleared into a new port. The local officials then remove the guns and all ammunition, returning them when you clear out for the next port, or to leave the country.

Pets

Pets must be properly vaccinated, with a certificate to prove this has been done.

Fishing

For one reason or another fish and lobster are abundant in Cuban waters. Just about any kind of a lure trailed behind the boat will sooner or later (sooner rather than later) land a barracuda. With a little luck it might instead be a mackerel or tuna. For the big-game fishing types, there are plenty of marlin. There is no problem getting enough fish to eat, but it should be noted that the barracuda on the north shore are reported to contain *ciguatera* (those on the south shore are reported as OK). We played it safe by putting all barracuda back (that was a lot of barracuda).

The lobster have to be seen to be believed! On one occasion we saw a single trap with twenty-five in it, all but one of which were large enough to eat. In some places they have been so little fished that they are relatively unafraid. That's the good news. The bad news is that it is completely illegal to take any. Not only that, but the fishermen are not allowed to sell any (since the catch belongs to the government). However, in practice most cruisers do harvest the odd one for personal consumption, added to which, if asked, the fishermen will almost always be happy to trade a ½ dozen or so for a few bars of soap or a six-pack of beer (actually, they mostly gave them away – we had to press some small gifts on them in return). There is no reason not to eat your fill. Just remember to observe the closed season in June and July (this is when the females lay their eggs) and don't be greedy – if you are caught with a freezer full you will be in serious trouble.

Traveling inland, lodging and eating out in Cuba

No cruise to Cuba would be complete without at least a trip or two into the interior. However, as a result of the present shortage of oil and hard currency the first problem likely to be encountered is transportation. All along the roadsides are groups of people seeking a ride. Buses are few and far between, and likely to be extremely crowded, while taxis tend to be prohibitively expensive. Cars can be rented, but once again the cost is high, and since very few of the (surprisingly good) roads in the countryside are sign-posted, unless you have at least some command of Spanish, once off the beaten track you may soon get lost.

The various hotels and government-run tourist agencies will provide day-long tours to a number of beautiful destinations (at a cost of up to $40 per person per day), or else rent an air-conditioned vehicle and driver for the day ($160 for a maximum of five people), but by far the best bet is to strike a deal with a private car owner, renting the car and driver for the day. Rates vary according to the distance to be covered and the owner of the car. We have paid as little as $15 for a jaunt to Havana from the Marina Hemingway (see the relevant section of this guide) up to $80 for a 250-mile all-day exploration of the province of Pinar del Río (with five people in the car, this worked out at $16 a head and was made all the more worthwhile since our driver gave us a running commentary on the countryside through which we passed, took us to some of his favorite places, and found us an excellent black-market restaurant in which to eat).

Renting a private car is illegal; the driver, in particular, can get into expensive trouble. Nevertheless, it is commonly done. The best way to find a driver is to talk to other cruisers when first arriving in a marina, or else to hang around outside the marina, or in the tourist area of a town, looking like you need a ride. Most times sooner or later (normally sooner) someone will sidle up to you asking if you need a car. Be sure to agree on the price before taking off.

In common with most visitors, before going to Cuba we had read a good deal of propaganda about the multitude of armed police and the frequent road blocks in the countryside. We traveled the length and breadth of the island and never saw anything other than the occasional traffic cop, and never came across a roadblock. We found no more restriction on the freedom of movement than in any western country, and felt a darn sight safer wandering around Cuban towns and cities, particularly after dark, than in most American cities. (There is a certain amount of street crime in the larger cities – mostly purse snatchings – but very little violent crime. This probably has something to do with the fact that Cuba, for all intents and purposes, has no drug problem: in six months we were never offered drugs, nor asked for any, and never saw anyone using them).

Should you decide to spend some nights ashore, once away from the glitzy hotels in the designated tourist areas, official lodgings tend to be few and far between, and uninspiring, yet not particularly cheap. However, if you ask around in town for somewhere to stay, sooner or later someone will discretely offer you accommodations in their house, which is likely to be far more interesting and will certainly be cheaper (but once again, may be illegal).

Eating out in Cuba is another challenge. In many government-run restaurants, particularly those outside the main tourist areas, the service is poor, the choices limited, and the food somewhere between uninspiring and downright awful. As a result, in the early 1990s, a flourishing black market developed in the restaurant business, operating out of private homes, and providing delicious meals at reasonable prices. In 1995 the government legalized these restaurants in order to tax them, but then raised the taxes so high that many went out of business or underground again. If they are underground at the time of your visit, the best way to find one is to simply ask around for somewhere good to eat (without specifying a black-market restaurant). If directed to a public restaurant, simply ask passers-by if there is another restaurant near by, or one they would recommend more highly. Sooner or later someone will take the bait and lead you to a private restaurant.

So much for the mechanisms of travel. The purpose, of course, is to experience the countryside which presents a series of startling contrasts between often spectacularly beautiful, essentially prerevolutionary landscapes, and what to western eyes are incredibly ugly decaying post-revolutionary industrial and urban developments. The latter, which are based on the Eastern European communist model, have not a shred of beauty or sensitivity to the environment.

At the present time the dramatic impact of these two types of landscape is heightened by the lack of fuel, which has forced much of the countryside to return to ox and horse-drawn ploughs and carts, producing a rural landscape that pre-dates the industrial revolution. Quite fascinating to the tourist and highly photogenic, but you should not expect the Cubans to share either an enthusiasm for these landscapes, or a revulsion at the ugly modern developments. The current lack of mechanization has imposed a tremendous burden on the countryside and the entire country, while the monstrous apartment blocks, schools and hospitals represent a dry roof with water and electricity, a TV, and a fridge, backed by an education and an excellent health-care system: a welcome contrast to the dirt-floored shacks of the Batista days in which an illiterate population, deprived of many basic necessities, frequently went to an early grave.

Pinar del Río

One of our favorite trips was along the north road (Carretaria del Norte) from the Marina Hemingway to the province of Pinar del Río. We mention it here because it is otherwise likely to get overlooked. The road follows the coastline for many miles, with ugly suburban developments gradually giving way to extensive sugar cane fields, and trucks and buses giving way to ox-drawn carts and ploughs. In the distance a range of mountains provides an increasingly dramatic backdrop. As the mountains draw nearer, the sugarcane in turn gives way to tobacco, with rice paddies in the low-lying ground.

The road turns south through a wide fertile valley with sheer limestone cliffs. Inside this valley lies the pretty colonial town of Vinales, with interesting caves to the north. El Cuevo del Indio (the cave of the Indian) in particular is worth a tour, which includes a short boat ride down an underground river.

Immediately to the south of Vinales is the Hotel Jazmines. Once the home of a fabulously wealthy planter, the house has now been converted to an expensive tourist hotel which is worth visiting simply to enjoy the gorgeous panoramic view from its parking lot and balcony (surely one of the finest views in Cuba, and one which is featured on tourist posters).

Further south still is the provincial capital, Pinar del Río. This town too has some attractive colonial architecture. The cigar factory is well worth touring; in addition, there are a couple of other rather dry and dusty museums covering local history (all in Spanish) and the natural sciences (interesting collections of bugs, butterflies, shells, birds and stuffed animals). From Pinar del Río an interstate provides a fast road back to Havana and the Marina Hemingway.

Some notes for the skipper

Insurance

Most American boats are currently uninsurable in Cuban waters. American policies generally have an exclusion written in, while European companies do not want to insure American boats because of the excessive litigation in the USA.

However, Americans who belong to the Seven Seas Cruising Association can get coverage for Cuba through Blue Water Insurance:

725 North A1A, Suite E–201
Jupiter, FL 33477
☎ (800) 866-8906 and (407) 743-3442
Fax (407) 743-8751

There is currently no problem insuring boats registered in Europe.

Paperwork

The Cubans are lovers of their paperwork. Most visitors ascribe this to the inherent bureaucracy of a Soviet-style communist regime, but those who have cruised in other parts of Central and South America will recognize a more illustrious pedigree. This is one of the legacies bequeathed to all its former colonies by Spain. Guatemala, Honduras and Venezuela are the same. As far back as the 16th century every ingot, jewel, coin and artifact looted from the New World and loaded onto the Spanish galleons to be shipped back to Europe was recorded in triplicate and signed and stamped for by numerous officials.

To this bureaucratic heritage the Cubans have added their own special gloss as a result of the perceived threat from the USA just to the north, and also to keep tabs on their own people. The result is a complex system of paperwork which can be intensely frustrating to the cruising sailor. However, the officials are friendly, with (in most instances) no corruption, and come to your boat (as opposed to having to chase all over town to find them as in some other countries). The process goes something like this:

Clearing in

On arrival in Cuba you should be flying the Cuban flag and beneath it a yellow quarantine flag. (An excellent source for all flags is Christine Davis Flags, 923 SE 20th Street, Fort Lauderdale, FL 33316, USA. ☎ (305) 527-1605).

Note The Cuban flag consists of a series of blue and white stripes, with a white star set on a red triangle. The flag looks as if it can be flown either way up, but this is not so. The star has five points. The flag must be flown with the point of the star facing up. To fly it the other way up is considered to be a declaration of a state of war, as was pointed out to us at the time of our detention!

The boat must first be cleared in by the Guarda Frontera, who will need to see a clearance from the last port of call (currently not necessary if this was in the USA) and who will carry out a search (normally pretty perfunctory, but we have seen a boat completely unloaded, with all the floorboards taken up to provide access for drug- and arms-sniffing dogs; the entire search took six hours, after which the owner still had to reload all his stores and supplies). The Guarda will take down details of the boat (length, width, draft, color, gross and net weight, registration number, home port, national flag, inboard engine make and horsepower, dinghy details, and outboard motor make and horsepower), together with a crew list which includes the full name, nationality, date of birth, and passport number of every person on board. Some sort of certificate of registration will be needed for the boat, and, if possible, a bill of sale.

Following the Guarda, the boat will be boarded (in no particular order) by immigration officers, customs officials, a doctor, and representatives of both the ministry of agriculture and the ministry of transport. All will probably write down the same information as the Guarda! The immigration officers will need to see a passport for all on board, and will then issue 30-day tourist visas ($25 each in 1999, renewable in most provincial cities for 30 days at a time at a cost of $25); the customs officials will issue an 'inward clearance' ($20); the doctor will give a health clearance (at which point the yellow flag comes down), the ministry of agriculture will check the food supplies (fresh, refrigerated and dry), and the ministry of transport will check the boat's safety systems (life jackets, fire extinguishers, flares, navigation lights, the VHF) and the bilge (to see that it is clean). The ministry of transport will issue a cruising permit for the boat which is valid for six months (including multiple exits and entries to and from Cuban waters during this six months). After six months the inspection must be repeated for a renewal. In 1999 the cruising permit cost $25 for boats up to 10m (33ft) in length, $50 for those from 10–20m (33–66ft), and $75 if longer than 20m (66ft).

The check-in procedures will be greatly speeded up if you have sheets of carbon paper and pre-prepared crew lists to hand out to each boarding officer (six copies would be a good idea, plus dozens more to spread around at other times if you are planning to cruise in Cuban waters). The crew list (*Lista de Tripulantes*) should include the following information:

- Full name (as it appears in each passport)
- Passport number
- Date of birth
- Date of issuance of passport
- Position on board (I suggest *capitan*, *piloto*, and *marinero* – captain, pilot and crew member).

Other information concerning the boat is also well advised, selected as appropriate from the following list:

Nombre Name
Bandera Flag
Matriculo Port of Registry
Folio Registration number
Tipo (*Motor yate* motor yacht; *yate de vela* sailboat)
Eslora Length
Ancha Width
Puntal (Calado) Draft
Tonnelado Weight
Color Hull color (*blanco* white; *azul* blue; *negro* black; *rojo* red; *verde* green; *amarillo* yellow)
Hecho de: fibra Made of: fiberglass
    madera wood
    acero steel
    aluminio aluminum
Tipo de motor Make of motor (e.g. Volvo)
Caballos Horsepower
Combustible: petroleo Fuel: diesel
    gasolina gasoline
Lanchita hecho de . . . Dinghy made of . . . (see above, plus *Balsa de goma* for inflatable)

The following is issued by the Cuban Ministry of Agriculture. In practice there has not been a problem in importing for personal consumption limited quantities of frozen meats, milk and other dairy products, and eggs, although all are technically illegal.

INFORMATION TO TRAVELERS

The Ministry of Agriculture is pleased to inform you of the animal and plant health regulations which rule the animal and plant origin importations into the Republic of Cuba.

These regulations are aimed at preventing the introduction of pests and hazardous diseases in our agricultural economy, flora and wildlife.

1. Absolute Prohibitions
Importation of:
- Live animals of any species;
- Un-canned meat and milk products, fresh eggs, and natural honey;
- Non-identified trade mark canned products of animal origin;
- Leathers and craftsmanship products of animal or plant origin that have not undergone industrial processing;
- Earth or organic matter in any form;
- Organisms and micro-organisms hazardous to plants and animals, products for laboratory use, and biologicals (vaccines, sera, antisera, microbial strains);
- Plants, or plant parts, fresh fruit and vegetables, seeds, and agricultural and forestry products.

2. Facilities
Passengers are informed they may import dogs and cats vaccinated against rabies, accompanied by veterinary certificates issued in the country of origin. The introduction of small volumes of registered mark vaccines for use in these species is allowed. Also, exotic fish may be imported.

Any approved imported animal shall be subjected to quarantine for a variable period of no less than two (2) weeks.

Travelers may import small quantities of canned meat products, milk, and vegetables of recognized trade marks, as well as ornamental goods duly treated.

3. Instructions
Visitors arriving at the country and carrying animals, plants or any of the above mentioned products must declare and show them for their inspection to the authorities of the Veterinary Border Services or Plant Health Services, who will gladly inform passengers regarding applicable regulations in each case. Importations or exportations of animals, products of animal or plant origin with donation, commercial or research purposes will be carried out only with the approval of the Direction of Animal Health or the Direction of Plant Health.

We thank you for your collaboration in protecting our natural resources, and wish you a pleasant stay in our country.

Tipo de motor de lanchita Make of outboard motor (Mariner, Yamaha, etc.)
Caballos de motor de lanchita Horsepower of outboard
Combustible de motor de lanchita Fuel of outboard (*gasolina*)

Moving from port to port inside Cuba

Cuba is one of those countries in which visiting boats are required to clear from port to port. It is not necessary to clear in and out with all the officials, but it is always necessary to clear with the Guarda, and frequently necessary to check with immigration and customs, particularly if moving from one province to another (Cuba has 13 different provinces). The key document is known as a *despacho* (the same as a *zarpe* in other Hispanic countries). It is issued by the Guarda and lists boat details, crew details, the port of departure, and the next port of entry. It is handed in to the Guarda on arrival at the new port, and then an application must be made for another *despacho* to continue on to the next port of call.

To lessen the paperwork, the best policy is to draw up a comprehensive list of all the places you wish to visit, beginning and ending with a major port or marina (e.g. the Marina Hemingway or the Marina Acua) and to present this to the Guarda (in the marinas, simply hand your list of intended destinations to the marina officials and let them take care of it). The Guarda will check the list for any places that are currently off-limits to visiting boats and will scrub these from the list. With any luck they will then issue a *despacho* including the rest of the places you have listed. This process can take from an hour or so up to 72 hours, so it is best to present the list well before a planned departure time. Once the *despacho* is in hand, you (or the marina) should also inform the customs and immigration, if available, of your intended departure time, so that they too can clear you out.

When arriving at any of the points (*puntos intermedios*) in between the starting and ending ports, the Guarda, if in evidence, should always be contacted (if not in evidence, depending on how far off the beaten track you are, they may well come and find you). With a little luck it will be possible to get the Guarda to simply stamp the existing *despacho*, rather than go through the process of issuing a new one. Note, however, that if you arrive at some location not covered by the *despacho* you may get into some extremely protracted 'discussions', so be sure to get a comprehensive list of *puntos intermedios* on the *despacho*.

Clearing out

To clear out from Cuban waters, and frequently from one province to the next, another *despacho* will be needed from the Guarda, and also outward clearance from the immigration and customs officials. The process is the same as for clearing from port to port inside Cuba. In 1996 the Cubans began levying a $10–15 exit charge.

Note 1 In general the officials on the south coast are more relaxed than those on the north coast – on the south coast it is possible to sail for weeks with just a single *despacho* periodically rubber-stamped by the officials, whereas on the north coast the whole rigmarole will have to be gone through repeatedly.

Note 2 In many of the more remote towns the Guarda are reluctant to allow visiting sailors ashore (*a la tierra*). If problems arise, show them the yellow entry card (visa) which will have been issued by the immigration officials on your arrival in Cuba. *This card is your passport to go ashore and is valid throughout Cuba*; you should insist on your right to use it. The more of us that do this, the easier it will get for those that follow.

Crew changes and laying-up a boat

There are plenty of international flights in and out of Cuba from all but the United States (for the US normally you have to go via Canada, the Bahamas, Mexico, or some other intermediate country although there are flights from Miami, primarily for Cuban Americans). Within Cuba there is regular air service between the major cities. So one way or another there are a number of places where it is relatively easy to bring in new crew or fly out old crew members (we make some specific suggestions in the relevant chapters). However, new crew members flying in may have trouble at the airport if they have no hotel reservations. It might be best to book a flight with a package tour, and simply not use the hotel reservation, or else reserve a hotel room for a couple of nights on arrival and use this to do some sightseeing.

Laying up a boat is also not difficult. The marinas are quite happy to have the long-term slip rental, and will help to arrange any necessary paperwork. There are a number of foreign boats in Cuban marinas that stay there year-round, with the owners flying in periodically for a vacation. On occasion, cruisers have even left their boats anchored out in secluded bays for weeks or even months while they flew home to take care of unexpected problems, but we would not recommend this – it is better to have some official body (such as a marina) keeping an eye on the boat.

National holidays

Law 1240, dated 14th December 1972, promugated by the Council of Ministers of the Republic of Cuba, declared the following days to be holidays:

1st January National Liberation Day
1st May International Workers Day

26th July Day of National Rebellion – celebration of the assault on the Moncada Barracks in 1953
10th October We are not sure what this celebrates
2nd December Celebration of the *Granma* landing

In addition, three weekends in July used to be given over to celebrating Carnival, but in recent years, with Cuba's straitened circumstances, little celebrating has taken place.

In spite of these holidays, since Cuban officials mostly work on a 24-hours on, 48-hours off, basis, there is always someone on duty (this includes Sundays) in the Guarda, customs and immigration offices. We checked into (and out of) all kinds of places at all hours of the day or night. At no time were any overtime charges levied, although there was some talk of these being introduced.

The people

We have left the best for last. The people of Cuba are wonderful. They are quite the most spontaneously friendly and generous people that we have met anywhere in our travels. You should go to Cuba just to meet them.

Books

Cuba: the Pursuit of Freedom, by Hugh Thomas, Harper and Row, 1971. A detailed, but nevertheless readable, history of Cuba from 1762 to 1962 which will give you a tremendous feel for the historical roots of the present situation.

Ché Guevara: A Revolutionary Life by Jon Lee Anderson, Grove 1997. A fascinating and compelling biography of this most famous of all Cuban revolutionaries. It provides considerable insight into the driving forces underlying the current regime.

Cuba, by Simon Calder (no relative) and Emily Hatchwell, published by Vacation Work, 1994 (9, Park End Street, Oxford, England). An excellent shoreside guide to Cuba.

2. Information for the navigator

This chapter contains a mixed bag of background information for navigators, much of which is essential for safe sailing in Cuban waters, so it should be read with care.

Time

Cuba is in the same time zone as the eastern United States, which is to say Eastern Standard Time. In the wintertime this is Universal Time (UT) minus 5 hours; when on summertime, UT minus 4 hours. Or, put the other way, in the wintertime add 5 hours to local time to find UT; in the summertime, add 4 hours.

Weather

Temperatures, humidity and rainfall

Cuba is in the sub-tropical zone, which means by and large the climate is warm (the yearly temperature average is 25°C, 77°F) and humid (average 75% relative humidity). Of course, averages frequently don't mean much, since the highs and lows may be quite extreme, but in the case of Cuba there are no great temperature differences. The nights and winters are a little cooler, with January and February being the coolest months (typically averaging about 22°C, 72°F, with daytime temperatures around 25°C, 77°F); the days and summers a little warmer, with July and August being the hottest months (typically averaging about 27°C, 81°F, with daytime temperatures around 30°C, 87°F). Humidity, however, is more variable.

In broad terms, Cuba has two seasons – the dry season, from November to April, and the wet season, from May to October (which also more or less correlates with hurricane season). The combination of lower relative humidity and slightly cooler temperatures makes the dry season exceedingly pleasant, whereas the higher humidity levels and higher temperatures can make the wet season quite steamy, particularly inland. (The wet season also brings the mosquitoes out in unbelievable numbers, and these mosquitoes don't observe regular hours – instead of just attacking in the evenings, they engage in kamikaze assaults all day long.) So it is fortunate that the dry season is also the predominant cruising season.

Winds

Cuba is in the Trade Wind belt, with prevailing winds from the ENE. In the winter months the winds tend to back more to the NE, in the summer they tend to veer into the SE. The average wind speeds are higher in the winter (10–15 knots) than in the summer (5–10 knots), when there can be a fair number of calms.

In many areas, particularly those where the mountains approach the coastline, there is a distinct daily wind pattern, with the winds decreasing at night and coming off the coast, then increasing during the course of the day and blowing onshore (what is known as the *katabatic* effect – we will have more to say about this in the relevant chapters).

The prevailing wind patterns are upset by two major kinds of disturbances – *cold fronts* in the winter months, and *tropical depressions, storms* or *hurricanes* in the summer. We need to look at these in more detail.

Cold fronts

Cold fronts (*frente frio*), more colloquially known as northers (*nortes*), are common from November to April, with the highest incidence in January and February (sometimes one after the other in February, 3 to 7 days apart). Cold fronts follow a predictable pattern, sweeping across the southern United States and the Gulf of Mexico from west to east and then disappearing into the north Atlantic.

During the passage of a typical cold front the prevailing easterly winds gradually veer into the south and then the SW, frequently decreasing in strength, but sometimes with fierce gusts from the south. With the slower moving fronts a period of steady drizzle may set in, but with the faster moving fronts this often does not occur. In any case, the arrival of the front is generally announced with a line of squalls containing winds of anywhere from 25 to 60 knots, blowing from the SW and then veering suddenly into the NW. The squall line normally passes over in an hour or two, after which the winds settle down at a steady 25 to 45 knots from the NW, slowly decreasing and veering into the north and then the NE over the next day or two, until finally the prevailing easterlies reassert themselves.

Northers can hit the north coast of Cuba with particular ferocity, made all the more dangerous by the fact that as the wind veers to the NW and north, the entire coast becomes a lee shore. If sailing the north coast in the winter months it is essential to monitor the weather forecasts on a regular basis, and to head for a protected anchorage well ahead of any front (finding such anchorages was one of our priorities when researching this guide). *You should on no account attempt most of the marina and reef entries during a norther* – if you can't find shelter before one strikes, you will probably have to weather it at sea. Fortunately, all such northers are predictable at least two days in advance of their arrival, so there is no need to get caught out.

On the south coast of Cuba the effects of a norther are muted owing to the fact that the winds tend to lose some of their steam as they pass across the island, in addition to which the stronger winds generally come off the land so the waves do not build up to the same extent as on the north shore. Nevertheless, conditions can get exceedingly uncomfortable at times, so it is just as well to play safe and seek a well protected anchorage in advance of the arrival of any front.

Tropical depressions, storms and hurricanes

Tropical depressions occur with some frequency in the summer months, with the occasional one building in intensity until it reaches storm, or even hurricane, force. In the early part of the summer these depressions tend to form in the south Atlantic and eastern Caribbean, and so can be tracked for a number of days before getting anywhere near Cuba, giving time to take evasive action, but in the late summer and fall months (September, October, November) hurricanes sometimes develop in the western Caribbean with far less warning of their arrival.

In terms of their incidence, for Cuba the most dangerous months are September and October, with the west end of Cuba being the region most frequently hit, while the east end is almost never hit. From a cruiser's perspective, statistically speaking it is relatively safe to sail anywhere in Cuba in early hurricane season (June and July) so long as regular weather broadcasts are monitored, and reasonably safe to sail in the eastern half of Cuba for the rest of the hurricane season (once again, paying close attention to weather broadcasts).

Weather forecasts

On the north coast of Cuba, from Havana to Mariel, it is possible to pick up the 24-hour-a-day weather bulletins broadcast on the VHF by the NOAA radio stations (National Oceanographic and Aeronautical Administration – a US government agency); simply press the 'weather' button on the radio.

For a more thorough treatment of the weather, and when out of range of NOAA, it is hard to beat the US Coast Guard short wave weather broadcasts from Portsmouth, Virginia. To receive these a

Table 1. Short wave weather broadcasts (NMN Portsmouth, Virginia)

UT	Local time Winter	Summer	Frequency
0400	2300	2200	4426, 6501, 8764
1000	0500	0600	4426, 6501, 8764
1600	1100	1200	6501, 8764, 13089
2200	1700	1800	6501, 8764, 13089

Notes
1. All broadcasts are on Upper Side Band.
2. The broadcasts do not always start on time.
3. If reception is poor on one frequency, try another; the higher frequencies seem to be better during the day, the lower at night.
4. There are other US stations transmitting short wave weather forecasts, notably WOM Miami, and WLO Mobile – consult a radio users guide for times and frequencies.

Single Side Band (SSB) radio is required. The times and frequencies of broadcast are given in Table 1. All broadcasts follow the same format, beginning with the forecast for New England and the northern North Atlantic, followed by that for the mid-Atlantic states and the mid-North Atlantic, then the Caribbean Sea and the SW North Atlantic, and finally the Gulf of Mexico. The various regions are in turn sub-divided (e.g. the Caribbean is divided into the NW Caribbean, the SW Caribbean, and the E Caribbean, while the Gulf of Mexico is divided into the NW Gulf, the SW Gulf, the mid-Gulf and the E Gulf).

Each section of the broadcast follows a common format including a general synopsis, the specific forecast of wind and weather patterns and wave heights for the next 36 hours, and a longer-range forecast for the following 48 hours. At the end of each section of the broadcast the announcer says: 'Break; more to follow'. There is then a brief silence (maybe 5–10 seconds) before the next section begins. For a novice listener it can be a little hard to follow so it would be wise to listen to a few broadcasts to get the feel for them well before the weather ever gets to be of critical importance. We suggest you also copy the sketch map of weather forecast zones, and make a number of copies. You can then write the pertinent information from each broadcast in the relevant zone on the sketch map.

So far as Cuba is concerned, it is at the convergence of three broadcast zones (see sketch map) – the SW North Atlantic (the northern coast of Cuba from around Varadero eastward), the NW Caribbean (the south coast) and the eastern Gulf of Mexico (the north coast from Cabo San Antonio to Varadero). Regardless of where you are in Cuba, in the winter months, in addition to the forecast for your specific region, you should always listen to the entire Gulf of Mexico forecast; this will give advance warning of impending northers. In the summer

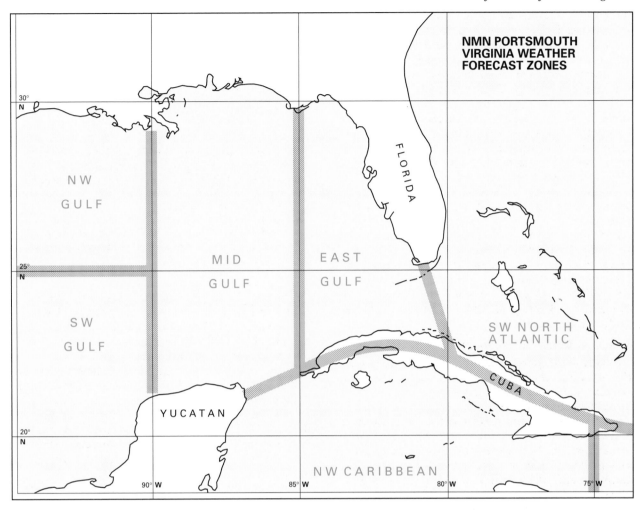

months, you should always listen to the general synopsis at the beginning of the Caribbean forecast; this will give advance warning of impending tropical depressions or more serious disturbances.

These Coast Guard forecasts are for waters 'beyond 50 miles from shore' and so will not take account of local anomalies and variations in the weather. Nevertheless, they do give an excellent picture of the overall weather situation, and a general idea of what to expect. For detailed local information you will have to consult local sources (in which case, you will need some Spanish).

Currents

Currents are a significant navigational consideration both when sailing to and from Cuba, and when sailing around its coastline.

The dominant feature is the Antilles Current, which itself is a branch of the North Equatorial Current. The Antilles Current sweeps up through the Caribbean in a generally northwesterly direction, with the greater part of its flow running to the south of Cuba (the Caribbean Current) and a lesser branch flowing to the north. The southern

portion of the current is eventually compressed into the narrow space between Cabo San Antonio and the Yucatan peninsula, from where it hooks around the north coast of Cuba to the Florida Straits to rejoin the northern portion of the Antilles Current off the Bahamas.

Where the Antilles Current is spread out in the Caribbean it does not attain great velocities (generally a knot or so toward the NW). Between the Yucatan Straits and the Florida Straits it speeds up considerably, with an average speed along the axis of the stream of 2–3 knots, and maximum speeds of up to 7 knots – a formidable force with which to have to contend, especially when the wind is blowing against the current (a norther).

The northern portion of the Antilles Current, which flows through the Old Bahama Channel, is nowhere near as powerful. Typically, it flows at a knot or so, but in certain wind conditions it may stall out or even reverse its flow.

These currents at times create eddies and counter-currents closer inshore. In general, these counter-currents are not as predictable as the main flow. Nevertheless, there is enough consistency to some of

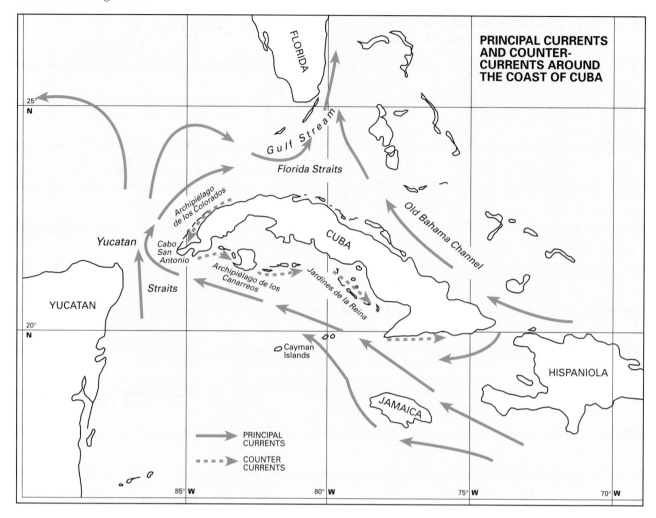

PRINCIPAL CURRENTS AND COUNTER-CURRENTS AROUND THE COAST OF CUBA

them to be able to say that much of the time there will be a ½ to 1 knot current flowing close inshore in a counterclockwise direction along the Archipiélago de los Colorados (the NW coast of Cuba), around Cabo San Antonio, and along a good part of the south coast. This generally counterclockwise inshore rotation is sometimes sustained on the NE coast by the Antilles Current in the Old Bahamas Channel.

Naturally, in all this there are some significant localized variations. Some of these are dealt with in more detail in the relevant chapters. For the general circulation, an *Atlas of Pilot Charts for Central American Waters* (DMA publication *NVPUB 106*) is an invaluable and highly recommended resource (see the Bibliography at the end of this chapter).

Tides

Tides around the coast of Cuba are quite modest, typically varying from about 0·3m (a foot or so) to 0·6m (a couple of feet), with an average of 0·5m (1½ft). The greatest tidal range is found in the region bordering on the SW North Atlantic (the NE coast) where tides of up to 1·2m (4ft) have been recorded. The tidal range diminishes the further west you go along both the north and south coasts (see Table 2).

Although these tidal ranges are not that big, because of the vast amount of relatively shoal water around the reefs and cays off the coast of Cuba, they are of considerable significance to cruising sailors. Cruisers should buy a set of tide tables for Cuba, the best being that produced by the Cuban hydrographic institute (ICH, now called GeoCuba – see below for more on this great organization).

The general tide pattern is semi-diurnal (approximately 6 hours flood followed by 6 hours ebb, as in much of the rest of the world), but in substantial areas this pattern is somewhat irregular, with the wind having a considerable influence. That section of the coastline bordering on the Gulf of Mexico (the Archipiélago de los Colorados) has a single daily tide, in common with the rest of the Gulf of Mexico. The interior region of the Golfo de Batabano (on the south coast) has very little tide at all, and what there is is largely determined by meteorological factors

Tidal currents

In open waters, because of the relatively small rise and fall of the tides, there are no strong tidal currents. In general, what current there is tends to set in a westerly direction on the flood tide, and an easterly direction on the ebb. However, in those areas where large bodies of water are more or less enclosed (the pocket bays, and the vast bays behind some of the barrier reefs and islands) tidal currents of up to 6 knots are sometimes found in the channels. When these currents are opposed by the winds, exceedingly rough local conditions can occur; in these circumstances it is important to time passages for slack water. We have more to say on this in the relevant chapters.

Magnetic variation

Magnetic variation changes markedly from one end of Cuba to the other. At the western tip (Cabo San Antonio) it is close to 1°W (January 2000); at the eastern tip (Punta Maisí) it is 8°00'W. Throughout Cuba it is increasing annually at a rate of 8'W to 9'W.

All bearings given in this guide are related to true north. To convert these to a magnetic bearing you must *add* the appropriate variation figure. (This can be obtained from the relevant chart; if using an old chart be sure to adjust the given variation adding 8' or 9' for each year from the date of issue. Remember, there are 60 minutes in a degree, not 100!)

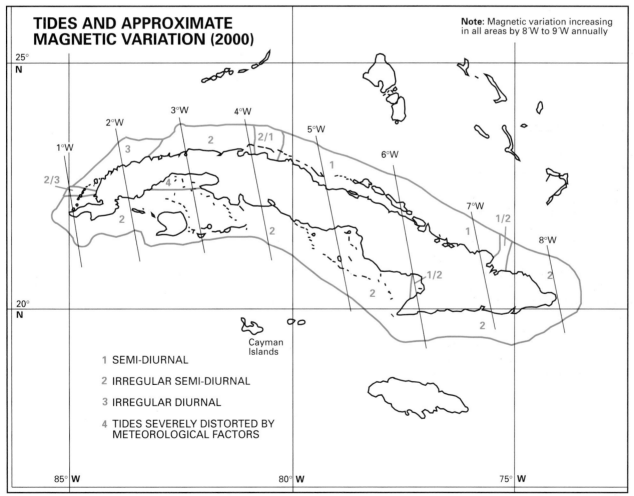

TIDES AND APPROXIMATE MAGNETIC VARIATION (2000)

Note: Magnetic variation increasing in all areas by 8'W to 9'W annually

Cayman Islands

1 SEMI-DIURNAL

2 IRREGULAR SEMI-DIURNAL

3 IRREGULAR DIURNAL

4 TIDES SEVERELY DISTORTED BY METEOROLOGICAL FACTORS

Courtesy GeoCuba

Table 2. Average tides for ports around the coast of Cuba

Location	Position	Average tide	
		cm	in
Cabo San Antonio	21°54·4'N 84°54·4'W	15	5·9
Bahía Honda	22°56·3'N 83°11·2'W	22	8·7
Cabañas	22°59·4'N 82°58·6'W	24	9·5
Mariel	23°00·6'N 82°46·1'W	25	9·8
Siboney	23°05·5'N 82°28·3'W	24	9·5
Havana	23°08·6'N 82°20·3'W	29	11·4
Santa Cruz del Norte	23°09·6'N 81°56·2'W	32	12·6
Matanzas	23°03·7'N 81°33·1'W	36	14·2
Punta Hicacos	23°11·6'N 81°07·6'W	40	15·8
La Isabela	22°56·8'N 80°06·6'W	46	18·1
Cayo Francés	22°38·5'N 79°13·7'W	51	20·1
Nuevitas	21°32·1'N 77°15·8'W	40	15·8
Punta Prácticos	21°36·0'N 77°06·2'W	36	14·2
Manatí	21°21·4'N 76°49·5'W	57	22·4
Puerto Padre	21°12·1'N 76°36·0'W	60	23·6
Gibara	21°06·7'N 76°07·5'W	55	21·7
Banes	20°54·2'N 75°43·5'W	62	24·4
B. de Nipe (Preston)	20°46·2'N 75°39·3'W	62	24·4
B. de Nipe (entrada)	20°46·6'N 75°34·8'W	59	23·2
Levisa	20°43·1'N 75°33·1'W	57	22·4
Tánamo	20°40·7'N 75°20·1'W	51	20·1
Moa	20°39·4'N 74°54·6'W	50	19·7
Baracoa	20°21·3'N 74°30·0'W	52	20·5
Maisí	20°14·0'N 74°09·0'W	43	16·9
Guantánamo	19°54·0'N 75°09·0'W	–	–
Santiago de Cuba	20°00·7'N 75°50·2'W	28	11·0
Pilón	19°54·6'N 77°19·1'W	25	9·8
Cabo Cruz	19°50·3'N 77°43·7'W	21	8·3
Manzanillo	20°19·9'N 77°09·2'W	48	18·9
Casilda	21°45·3'N 79°59·3'W	22	8·7
Bahía de Cienfuegos (entrada)	22°02·2'N 80°26·4'W	19	7·5
Bahía de Cienfuegos (interior)	22°10·8'N 80°29·2'W	28	11·0
Playa Girón	22°03·8'N 81°02·1'W	22	8·7
Carapachibey	21°27·0'N 82°55·0'W	20	7·9
La Coloma	22°14·5'N 83°34·5'W	17	6·7

Aids to navigation

In recent years Cuba has converted all its aids to navigation to the IALA Region B system. This is more easily remembered as the 'red, right, returning' system, which is to say that when entering (returning to) a harbor you proceed with the red channel markers on your right (starboard) side, and the green markers on your left (port) side. To make this system work, it has to be assumed that all channels are leading into a harbor, anchorage, river or whatever. Most are, so there is no problem in determining which is the *returning* direction, but occasionally there is the odd channel which is running between two navigable areas with no clear sense of direction. In this case the *returning* direction is determined quite arbitrarily. Fortunately, there are few instances in which this occurs in Cuba, and when it does a glance at the chart will tell you on which side to leave the various markers.

The IALA Region B system is further refined by making starboard-hand markers pointed (cone, or nun, buoys; triangle topmarks; etc.) and the port-hand markers square-topped (can buoys; square topmarks; etc.). Mid-channel markers (can be passed on either side) have red-and-white or black-and-white vertical stripes; topmarks are round. All-in-all this is an exceptionally easy system to use, even for those not accustomed to it.

Lighthouses and reefs

The entire Cuban coastline is ringed with lighthouses, many of which are more than 100 years old and yet are still in excellent working condition. Contrary to reports in the American Sailing Directions to the Caribbean (Pub. 147) these lights are kept in an excellent state of repair by the Cuban Institute of Hydrography. Every single one that we observed at night (which is most of them) was working fine, which is just as well because

IALA SYSTEM B BUOYAGE
(APPLICABLE TO CUBA)

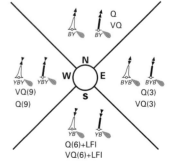

substantial sections of the Cuban coastline are fronted by dangerous reefs.

These reefs extend for hundreds of miles on both the north and south coasts. Being partially submerged, or at best identified by low-lying islands, they are frequently hard enough to spot in the daytime. At night the potential danger is compounded by the fact that the bottom comes up with incredible rapidity as the reefs are approached (a depth sounder will often not sound an alarm until it is too late to take evasive action), in addition to which *there are sometimes strong onshore currents*. The lighthouses are frequently the only visual warning of danger.

But these lighthouses must be treated with caution. *Many of them are set well inside the reefs, and so must be given a wide berth* (a couple of miles in some cases). A number of the more powerful ones are specifically designed to be used by ships standing off the coast in the shipping lanes, and are not intended to be used for close inshore navigation. So be warned, and before approaching a light too closely check the relevant chart for hazards; otherwise, like a moth attracted to a candle, you may be struck with disaster.

Charts

In the 1960s and '70s the Soviets sent a team to Cuba to train up a hydrographic office, and to do a thorough survey of the entire island and the adjacent waters. The result is that today the Cubans have a world-class hydrographic department (the Instituto Cubano de Hidrografía, or ICH for short, which is pronounced *ee see achay*), and a set of up-to-date charts *which are GPS accurate*. Whatever your views on the revolution and the subsequent Soviet penetration, this is an incredibly valuable side effect for cruising sailors.

The primary series of charts for the island are at a scale of 1:150,000. This is the ICH *1100* series, with 26 charts covering the entire island (Nos *1122* to *1147* inclusive). There are then more detailed charts for various areas and harbors, but not for the whole island, ranging in scale from 1:100,000 all the way down to 1:5,000.

Given the existence of these charts, *we would strongly recommend that all cruisers sailing in Cuban waters use the Cuban charts* rather than the available British Admiralty and Defense Mapping Agency charts (DMA – the US government agency that produces charts for non-US waters). The Cuban charts are more up-to-date and often more accurate for GPS use than their British and American counterparts. We have based this guide on them, and all chart references are to them. If you should use BA or DMA charts, check the notation on each one carefully to see what chart *datum* has been used in making the chart, and what corrections are

needed to make the latitudes and longitudes GPS accurate (in some cases, the lines of latitude may have to be shifted by up to ½M to correlate with GPS readings based on WGS 84, the default datum on most GPSs – for more on datums, see below).

The key Cuban charts are the 1:150,000 series. However, while they are fine for coastal cruising, they are not adequate for gunkholing. Although it is possible to use these charts to pick your way through numerous reef entries and into all kinds of bays and anchorages, in reality the detail is not there to do it with confidence. Which is, of course, where a guide such as ours comes in. We cannot reproduce a complete set of coastal charts for Cuba (apart from anything else, it would make this book prohibitively large and expensive), but what we can do, and hope we have done, is give you the information and confidence to go from these charts into any navigable destination of your choice.

The one snag is that this still leaves the cruiser having to buy up to 26 charts at $16.00 a piece. We had some extensive discussions with the ICH with a view to consolidating the necessary charts into a series of cheaper chart books, or else a dozen regular-sized charts. ICH decided to follow the chart book route. There is now a chart book that correlates with each regional chapter in this book, as follows:

REGION 1: Marina Hemingway to Cabo Corrientes (Chapter 4)
REGION 2: Cabo Corrientes to Casilda (Chapter 5)
REGION 3: Casilda to Cabo Cruz (Chapter 6)
REGION 4: Cabo Cruz to Punta Maisí (Chapter 7)
REGION 5: Punta Maisí to Punta Maternillos (Chapter 8)
REGION 6: Punta Maternillos to Bahía de Cádiz (Chapter 9)
REGION 7: Bahía de Cádiz to Marina Hemingway (Chapter 10)

The charts or chart books are still a significant expense, but it has to be born in mind that Cuba has almost 4,000 miles of coastline; you simply cannot expect to get coverage of an area this large at little or no cost. Whatever you do, we would advise you not to skimp on the charts; *it is not worth putting your boat at risk to save a few dollars* (we say this in all sincerity; we have no commercial interest in the sale of the Cuban charts).

At the moment the Cuban charts are most easily obtained from the Tienda de Navigantes in Havana (see the relevant section in Chapter 3), but the ICH has depots around the coast, so as more cruisers visit Cuba the sales network should be expanded to cover most of the major marinas and ports. The main address for the ICH is:

GeoCuba,
Carretera de Berroa Km 2½,
Habana del Este
Cuba
☎ (53) 765-0324; fax (53) 733-2869

Notes on Cuban survey methods

1. The placement of landmasses, reefs, soundings and other details is exceedingly accurate. The datum used is not always indicated on the charts but was North American 1927 (NAD 27), not WGS 84 (which is the default datum on most GPSs). However, since there is almost no difference between NAD 27 and WGS 84 in Cuban waters, if a GPS does not contain the NAD 27 datum, it can be used in WGS 84 mode in conjunction with the 1:150,000 Cuban charts with a great deal of precision. In any case, as the charts are re-issued, and during the adaptation to the chart books, they are being converted to WGS 84.

2. In as much as most of the surveys were done up to 25 years ago, in places (particularly some of the cays on the south coast) the mangroves have grown by up to a mile.

3. In terms of charting depths, the surveying practice seems to have been to run more or less straight survey lines, generally ½M apart (but much closer for harbor charts), logging the soundings every ½M, and simply running along the coast ½M from one survey line to the next. As a result, in relatively shoal waters with an irregular bottom the surveyors may have missed isolated shoals or coral heads, and in fact we have occasionally found this to be the case. Of more significance is the fact that the 2m line has often been interpolated (a fancy word for guessed!), rather than actually sounded out. Given the relatively wide spacing of many of the survey lines, this has inevitably lead to some errors (we have found spits of shoal water, up to a mile long in rare cases, which have projected out from the land between survey lines). As always, the charts should not be relied upon as the sole means of navigation, particularly in coastal waters.

4. The Cubans have adopted the convention of coloring many areas of rock and coral in the same color as is used to denote shoal water, irrespective of the depth over the rocks and coral. Particularly on the south coast, this gives some of the charts a fearsomely coral-strewn appearance, whereas in fact many of these areas are navigable. However, since the 2m and 5m isobaths are often omitted, and soundings may be up to ½M apart, it is exceedingly difficult to interpret the underwater topography of these areas, so it is best to simply avoid them unless the light is adequate to see any shoals, or explicit instructions are given to the contrary in this guide.

Methods used to make the plans in this guide

Two methods were used to make the plans in this guide. If there was a Cuban chart available at a suitably detailed scale, we simply checked the information and amended it as necessary. Since the Cuban charts show soundings in meters, and since this seems to be the way the whole world is going, we have also used meters throughout (abbreviated as 'm').

Where there was no sufficiently detailed Cuban chart, we made our own chart. We did this using a KVH six-channel GPS hooked to a Quadro electronic chart plotter and a depth sounder.

The Quadro system (*Yeoman* in Europe) consists of an electronic grid embedded in a plotting table, together with a hockey-puck position-indicating device that is connected to the GPS. With this system we were able to place a blank piece of paper on the table (we used universal plotting sheets), draw in a latitude and longitude grid at the scale we wished to use for plotting (generally 1:12,000, but sometimes 1:24,000), and then initialize this piece of paper to the plotting table. From this point on, the Quadro system indicated exactly where we were on that piece of paper, enabling us to plot depths, and the location of other significant features. The whole rig was portable, so we could use it in the dinghy as well as on our 'big' boat.

We chose as our controlling depth 2m (6½ft) at low tide, which is to say we only plotted depths of less than this in exceptional circumstances. In general, we would first plot any landmasses. We then ran along the 2m lines, plotting these on our chart. By running the 2m lines we achieved a high degree of accuracy in plotting the boundaries of shoal water (as opposed to interpolating the 2m line from survey lines run at fixed intervals). Lastly, we ran survey lines across the deeper water to fill in the depths.

The problem with this methodology is that the US Defense Department constantly programs random errors into the GPS signal (known as Selective Availability – SA for short). These errors are less than 100m 95% of the time, but can be more than 100m the rest of the time. At a scale of 1:12,000, 100m is approximately 0·8 centimeter (⅓ inch) – a significant shift, and more than enough to create havoc with our chart-making. So we also used a series of cross-bearings from fixed points to weed out the worst errors introduced by SA. In addition, so far as we could we ran straight survey lines so that we could see when the signal was jumping from side to side, and at constant speeds so we could see when it was jumping backward and forward.

One way or another we felt we were able to 'fudge' the data to get acceptable results, but it must still be born in mind that these are 'sketch plans' and as such must be treated with due caution. Nevertheless, what we have is more accurate than anything else that is available, and in some cases is more accurate than the official government charts. Coupled with prudent navigation and conservative seamanship, our plans should be adequate to get you safely in and out of all the places we cover.

For all our surveys we used the WGS 84 datum, since this is the way the rest of the world is going. At the kind of scales we were using this did produce some minor differences with the Cuban charts (NAD 27), but these were not big enough to cause significant problems (the *maximum* difference between NAD 27 and WGS 84 in Cuban waters is less than 2 *seconds* of latitude, which translates to 60m on the ground, which in turn is around ½cm, less than ¼in, on a chart made to a scale of 1:12,000; it is less than some of the SA errors programmed into the GPS signal).

All bearings are given in relation to *true north*.

Both in the text and on the plans, we dropped the initial zero from all longitudes (i.e. 083°W is written as 83°W).

Finally we should point out that on our plans, and in this guide, frequent reference is made to sticks, posts, stakes, etc. We eventually adopted the following convention, based upon the size and likely permanence of the mark (but not until some way into the survey, so the convention is rather loosely applied, particularly on the north coast from Varadero to Cabo San Antonio):

Stick – literally a stick; small, fragile, and easily obliterated but nevertheless often surprisingly permanent and in any case frequently replaced by the local fishermen if damaged or destroyed.

Stake – more substantial than a stick; should last for a few years.

Post – more substantial than a stake; often an official aid to navigation and sometimes lit; liable to be reasonably permanent.

Beacon – a solid, official, aid to navigation with more than one supporting leg, normally a concrete structure, often lit, which can be considered more or less permanent.

Tools of the trade

It is not our place to tell you how to navigate. Nevertheless, a few comments might prove useful. First and foremost, given the accuracy of the Cuban charts, every boat sailing in Cuban waters should have a GPS on board. And given the low price of the cheaper units, a second unit as a back-up would not be such a bad idea.

We hooked our primary GPS (the KVH six-channel receiver – a great unit) to the Quadro electronic plotter, and with this and the Cuban charts were able to navigate through many a tight corner with pinpoint accuracy. In fact, so far as we are concerned this combination of electronics and traditional paper charts is superior to fully computerized navigation systems – we cannot recommend the Quadro system (known as the *Yeoman* in Europe) highly enough.

For those who like fully computerized on-screen systems, many of the DMA and BA charts are already available on disc, but the Cuban charts have not yet been scanned and digitized. However, this work is being done right now so it should not be long before electronic versions are available. If using BA or DMA charts, *make sure that the GPS datum is the same as that on the chart* (see the comments above).

As always on this kind of a trip we used a hand-bearing compass constantly as a supplement to the electronics, fixing our position with a couple of cross-bearings, determining entry and exit headings, delineating navigable and dangerous zones, and so on. We have an excellent hockey-puck type, which is great for general use, and a KVH *Datascope,* which is unbeatable for pinpoint accuracy.

Aside from these toys, even in this electronic age there is still the need for basic navigation and plotting skills, and a certain amount of dexterity with parallel rules and dividers. Personally, I think one-handed dividers are worth their weight in gold, and when it comes to laying off course lines and bearings there is no substitute for a high-quality set of parallel rules, marked off in degrees around the circumference.

Scope of this guide

Most cruising guides are written without official sponsorship. Cuba is a different case. It was clear to us from the first that if we were to do the kind of thorough surveys necessary to provide anchorage and reef passage charts, we would rapidly arouse the suspicions of the Guarda Frontera and end up in trouble. So from the outset of this project we sought some sort of official sanction, notably through the Instituto Cubano de Hidrografía (ICH) which we were eventually successful in obtaining.

However, this was not enough. We found ourselves repeatedly experiencing friction with the local Guarda forces (who were naturally suspicious of the electronic charting equipment we used in the dinghy from dawn to dusk). This culminated in our detention for nine days when several weeks into the project, which in turn resulted in a high-level conference between ourselves, the International Yacht Club at the Marina Hemingway (who have been incredibly supportive from the outset), the Guarda, and the Immigration authorities. As a result of this we were (sort of) taken under the umbrella of the Guarda, but in return they vetted our progress, asked us to emphasize certain locations which are of particular interest to the Cuban tourist industry, and told us to by-pass other locations which for one reason or another they would like (or they require) foreign boats to by-pass.

We found this to be an acceptable compromise. Cuba is unique in many ways, and has unique political problems. It is not an open society in the western sense. Given the current situation, and the history of hostility from the USA, we found the Cuban authorities to be far more open and friendly than we had expected, and in fact they imposed few frustrating limits on the territory that we could cover, with the exception of a stretch of the northern coastline which contains five of Cuba's magnificent pocket bays, four of which were put off limits, and our access to the fifth severely restricted.

The net result is a guide that has some significant omissions, but which will enable cruising sailors to circumnavigate the entire island and enjoy the country to the full. In the future, as the Cubans become more accustomed to the ways of visiting sailors, we are sure it will be possible to pencil in the missing details, but in the meantime, if you wish to sail in areas not covered by this guide, we suggest you first get explicit clearance from the local Guarda.

How to use this guide

When writing a guide of this nature, the entries have to be ordered in some fashion. In this guide they are organized for a counterclockwise circumnavigation, beginning at the Marina Hemingway. Since this may not accord with your plans, we have tried to make the individual entries as multi-directional as possible. To get the most out of the book, regardless of the direction in which you are sailing, first read the general notes at the beginning of each chapter, and then read the general notes at the beginning of your next destination. After this, read the notes under your next destination which are specific to your direction of travel.

At the beginning of each regional chapter (Chapters 4–10) we have a 'locator chart' which shows the entire region covered by that chapter, and also all the places covered in the chapter. We hope this will provide some overall orientation for the detailed plans in the body of the chapter, although we know at times it is a little hard to gain this perspective. A Cuban chart kit, or 1:150,000 chart, is really needed to complete the picture.

Finally, please note that harbor and channel entry positions, when given, are generally for a point immediately offshore, and not for the center of the channel. This is a conservative approach that provides a small measure of insurance against navigational errors.

Books

Sailing Directions for the Coast of Cuba, Two volumes (North and South), published (in Spanish) by the Instituto Cubano de Hidrografía in Havana (1989). This is a long-winded and hard-to-follow description of Cuba's entire littoral. Even if you read Spanish, we would not recommend you buy a copy.

The Cruising Guide to Cuba 2nd Edition (1997) by Simon Charles, published by Cruising Guide Publications. This updated guide has significantly more shoreside information than we do, but nowhere near the navigational detail. It is in many respects complementary to our guide. We suggest buying both!

Sailing Directions for the Caribbean Sea (DMA *NVPUB 147*). General piloting information aimed at big ships rather than cruising sailors. Somewhat dated.

West Indies Pilot, Vol. 1 British Admiralty (*NP 70*), same comments as above.

Tide Tables for Cuba, issued by the Instituto Cubano de Hidrografía. A most worthwhile investment if you intend to spend any length of time in Cuban waters.

Reed's Nautical Almanac for the Caribbean. A useful compendium of much government information, particularly the light lists.

List of Lights, Vol. J British Admiralty (*NP 82*).

Atlas of Pilot Charts (DMA *NVPUB 106*).

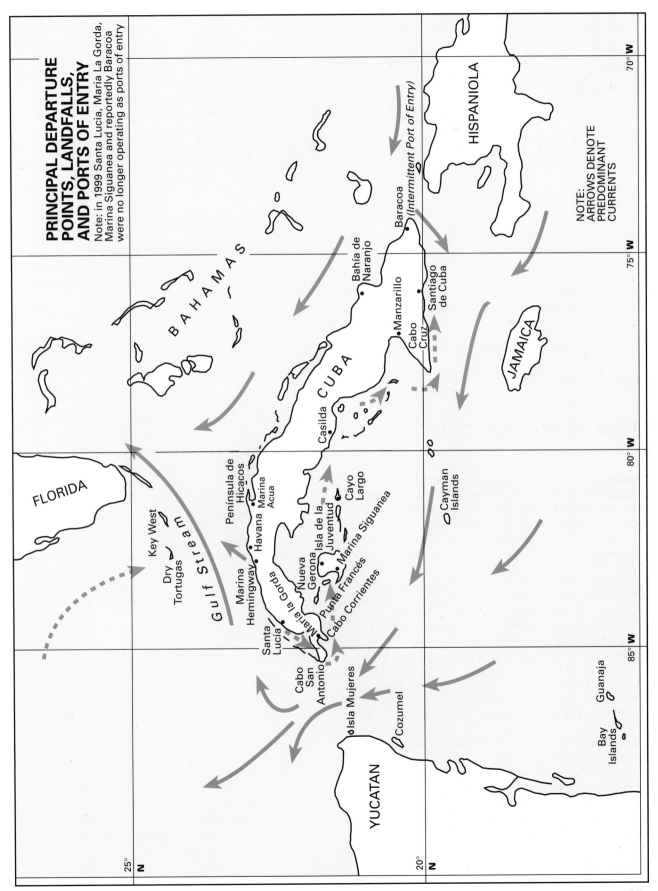

PRINCIPAL DEPARTURE POINTS, LANDFALLS, AND PORTS OF ENTRY

Note: in 1999 Santa Lucia, Maria La Gorda, Marina Siguanea and reportedly Baracoa were no longer operating as ports of entry

NOTE:
ARROWS DENOTE PREDOMINANT CURRENTS

HISPANIOLA

Baracoa
(Intermittent Port of Entry)

Bahía de Naranjo

Manzanillo

Cabo Cruz

Santiago de Cuba

JAMAICA

BAHAMAS

CUBA

Casilda

Cayman Islands

FLORIDA

Key West

Dry Tortugas

Gulf Stream

Península de Hicacos

Marina Acua

Marina Hemingway

Havana

Nueva Gerona

Isla de la Juventud

Cayo Largo

Marina Siguanea

Santa Lucia

Maria la Gorda

Punta Francés

Cabo Corrientes

Cabo San Antonio

Isla Mujeres

Cozumel

YUCATAN

Bay Islands

Guanaja

25°

20°

N

N

70° W

75° W

80° W

85° W

3. Passagemaking to Cuba; the Marina Hemingway and Havana

Passagemaking

Typically, Cuba is approached from one of three directions: the USA (Florida); the eastern Caribbean; or Central America. We will take a brief look at all three.

Passages between the USA (Florida) and Cuba

The usual jumping-off/return point in the USA is Key West in Florida; the most common port of entry/point of departure in Cuba is the Marina Hemingway (9M SW of Havana). Neither is necessarily the optimum choice. Depending on the weather conditions, and your cruising plans, it might be better to sail between the Dry Tortugas, and any one of a dozen locations on the north coast of Cuba. However, since it would be too complicated to cover all permutations, in what follows we focus on Key West, the Dry Tortugas, the Marina Hemingway and a couple of other marinas which are accustomed to dealing with foreign yachts – the Marinas Acua and Chapelín, both of which are located in the Península de Hicacos.

The Dry Tortugas are approximately 65M west of Key West. In common with Key West, the islands enclose an excellently protected anchorage which can be entered from both the north and the south in any weather conditions.

The Península de Hicacos is approximately 75M east of the Marina Hemingway. Its eastern end can be rounded in any weather conditions. Both the Marina Acua and the Marina Chapelín can be entered from the protected water in its lee. This makes these marinas accessible even in a norther, whereas the Marina Hemingway channel may be too dangerous to use (see later in this chapter). What is more, although the Marina Hemingway is a great location from which to visit Havana and take one or two other tours into the interior, there is no interesting cruising in its vicinity (and no place to anchor out to avoid marina charges). The Península de Hicacos, on the other hand, has a number of well protected anchorages in the immediate vicinity of the marinas, and some interesting cruising in the nearby waters and cays.

With these points in mind, below we summarize some of the principal factors to be considered when deciding which locations to use as a departure point and landfall.

Note Magnetic variation (January 2000) is 3°25'W at Key West; 2°50'W in the Dry Tortugas; 2°50'W at the Marina Hemingway; and 3°45'W in the Península de Hicacos. It is increasing annually at a rate of about 8'W.

US East coast to Cuba

Regardless of whether the inside route (Intracoastal Waterway) or the outside route is taken down the east coast of the USA, the last port of call is likely to be Key West (which is well worth a visit in its own right).

From Key West the rhumb line course to the Marina Hemingway is 203°, the distance approximately 100M. Passage time is likely to be between 12 and 20 hours, so a mid-afternoon departure will bring you to the Marina Hemingway some time after dawn the following day. The rhumb line course to the Península de Hicacos is 155°, the distance approximately 90M, after which another 10M may have to be traversed to get into a marina (see the relevant section in Chapter 10). Passage time will be similar to that to the Marina Hemingway, so once again a mid-afternoon departure is recommended.

Whatever the destination in Cuba, the Gulf Stream must be crossed. This surges through the Straits of Florida at 3 knots or more toward the ENE. A heading of 10° to 20° west of the rhumb line course must be maintained to compensate for the current. Such a heading from Key West to the Marina Hemingway, however, puts the boat more or less head-on into much of the current, and in addition runs into a lesser coastal current, running at a knot or so, which is deflected off the curve of the Cuban coastline in the vicinity of the Marina Hemingway. The course to the Península de Hicacos, on the other hand, cuts directly across the

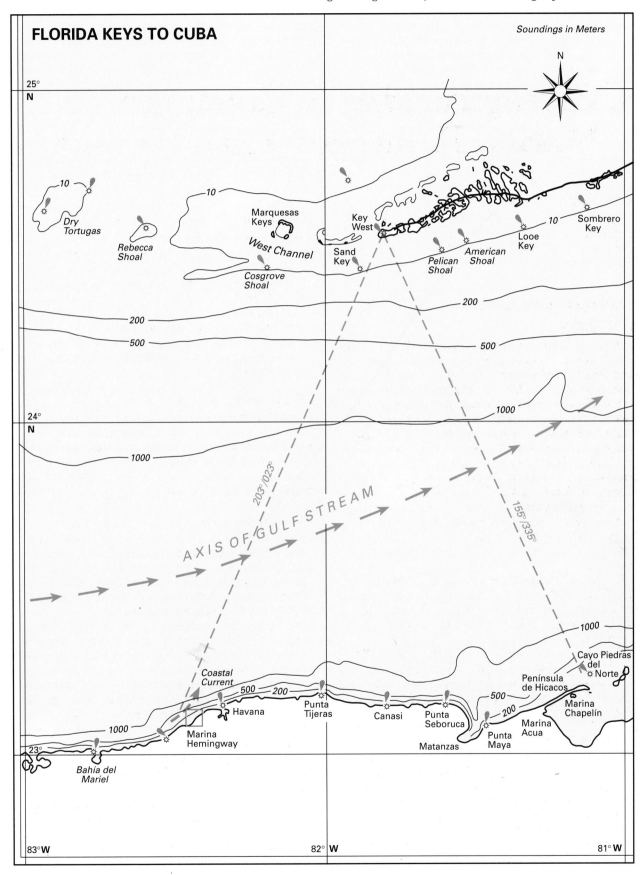

FLORIDA KEYS TO CUBA

Soundings in Meters

N

25° N

10

10

Marquesas Keys

Key West

10

Sombrero Key

Dry Tortugas

Rebecca Shoal

West Channel

Sand Key

Pelican Shoal

American Shoal

Looe Key

Cosgrove Shoal

200

200

200

500

500

1000

24° N

1000

203°/023°

155°/335°

AXIS OF GULF STREAM

1000

1000

Cayo Piedras del Norte

Coastal Current

Península de Hicacos

500

200

Punta Tijeras

Canasi

Punta Seboruca

500

200

Marina Chapelín

Havana

Marina Acua

1000

Marina Hemingway

Matanzas

Punta Maya

23°

Bahía del Mariel

83° W

82° W

81° W

axis of the stream, resulting in a favorable push to the east. In other words, the Península de Hicacos is normally much easier to lay and should be carefully considered as the initial landfall in Cuba.

If in spite of these considerations you decide to go to the Marina Hemingway, to avoid fighting both the Gulf Stream and the coastal current, the best strategy is to make well to the west on the Florida side of the Straits, and then when the full Gulf Stream flood is encountered to cut directly across the current on a southerly heading, or even slightly east of south if you have sufficient westing in hand.

To gain as much westing as possible before crossing the Gulf Stream, at the least the SW Channel should be taken when leaving Key West. Better yet, the West Channel can be followed as far as the Marquesas Keys, and even the Dry Tortugas, before heading out into the open sea (the Dry Tortugas are, in any case, well worth visiting).

There are limits to this strategy. If the wind is veering into the SE (quite common, especially in the summer months), the resulting southerly heading needed to cross the Gulf Stream may result in the boat being uncomfortably close-hauled. Clearly there has to be a balance struck here between the amount of westing made on the Florida side and the wind direction – the more the wind is in the east or north of east, the more the westing that can be made while still maintaining a comfortable angle to the wind at all points of the passage.

Northers The most favorable wind angle for any crossing from Florida to Cuba will be found during, or just after, the passage of a cold front. As the front passes over, the wind will clock around to the NW, typically at 25–35 knots, and then slowly shift in a clockwise direction through the north and NE over the next couple of days, providing following winds for the entire passage. The downside is that the passage of a cold front over the Gulf Stream can produce large steep waves with substantial breaking crests, added to which the downwind passage is likely to be quite rolly and uncomfortable. Finally, if a cold front is used to make the crossing to Cuba, and you are headed to the Marina Hemingway, you should time your departure to make sure that you do not arrive while the wind is still in its early (NW) phase (see the section on the Marina Hemingway later in this chapter).

Gulf coast states and Florida west coast to Cuba

If the wind is at all south of east, as it frequently is, any point of departure from around the US Gulf Coast can result in a stiff beat toward Havana, and an even stiffer beat to the Península de Hicacos. In this case, the Marina Hemingway is without question the preferred destination.

Navigation is also once again complicated by the Gulf Stream, which surges up through the Straits of Yucatan into the mid-Gulf region at speeds of up to 4 knots. The stream tends to divide somewhere south of New Orleans with westerly and easterly branches looping broadly around the 100-fathom line, but there is considerable variation in this pattern. Before departing, you would be well advised to obtain the latest 'Gulf Stream Loop Current' chart which should delineate the major eddies, and hopefully the direction of rotation. The US Navy provides information on the Internet at the following Web site:

http://www.nlmoc.navy.mil/

Try also Florida State University at:

http://www.nws.fsu.edu

For a thorough analysis, contact Jenifer Clark at:

http://www.erols.com/gulfstrm ☎ 301 952 0930. *Fax* 301 574 0289. Jenifer's charts and analysis are far superior to anything else around. A one time black and white chart and text cost $25; in color, $30. There are discounts for 2 or more.

The most favorable wind conditions for passaging across the Gulf of Mexico will be found during the course of a norther, but conditions are likely to be uncomfortable. The alternative is to stay inshore, following the Intracoastal Waterway around to Tampa before heading out to sea for the last stretch. Either way, since the Dry Tortugas are en route, it would be well worth stopping a day or two here before making the final (approximately 100M) crossing to the Marina Hemingway (for this crossing, see above).

Cuba to the USA

The passage from either the Marina Hemingway or the Península de Hicacos to Florida is straightforward. In prevailing easterly winds you can lay any destination from the Dry Tortugas to Miami. However, if a norther is passing through the Straits of Florida, you should wait until it has blown itself out before making a move. From the Marina Hemingway the Gulf Stream provides a substantial boost to all destinations east of the Dry Tortugas; from the Península de Hicacos, on the other hand, to lay any point west of Key West a substantial course correction will be needed to counteract the current.

Passages between the eastern Caribbean and Cuba

It is generally a glorious downwind run from any point in the eastern Caribbean to Cuba. Those boats coming to the south of Hispaniola (the Dominican Republic and Haiti) should aim to make a landfall at Santiago de Cuba, from where the best course of action is to work westward along the southern coast; those passing to the north of Hispaniola should aim to make a landfall at Baracoa (although it may be difficult to enter here: Baracoa only operates intermittently as a port of entry), and then work westward along the northern coast. In either case, you will have the wind and seas at your back for most of the time, resulting in some easy and relaxing cruising.

Passages between Central America and Cuba

If we were coming from any point in Central America to Cuba, we would not want to miss the wonderful cruising in the Bay Islands of Honduras, the Río Dulce, and Belize (see the *Cruising Guide to the NW Caribbean* by Nigel Calder, International Marine Publishing, PO Box 220, Camden, Maine 04843, USA). If the NW Caribbean is cruised, it is almost inevitable that the boat will end up at Isla Mujeres in the Yucatan, which is then the jumping-off point for Cuba.

From Isla Mujeres to Cabo San Antonio (at the western tip of Cuba) the rhumb line course is 070°, the distance 105M. This does not sound too bad, but in the course of getting to Cabo San Antonio, the Gulf Stream, setting northward at 3 knots, must be crossed. To compensate for the current a course of more or less east must be set, which is pretty much dead into the prevailing wind. In the winter-time the early stages of a norther provide a favorable wind, but also make the Gulf Stream exceedingly rough and potentially dangerous. As a result of these generally unfavorable conditions, most people wait for a relatively calm patch, and then scurry across the Yucatan Straits under power, or motorsailing.

In terms of a landfall, a choice has to be made as to whether to proceed along the south or north coast of Cuba (see below), either of which is likely to be something of an arduous beat to windward. If the north coast is chosen, a landfall is made at Cabo San Antonio, hooking around to the north of the cape and trying to clear in at Santa Lucia when you get there (Chapter 4; Santa Lucia only operates intermittently as a port of entry). From the cape there is relatively protected water for the next 100M to the east (Chapter 4). If the south coast is chosen, from Isla Mujeres it is better to head for Cabo Corrientes, on a rhumb line course of 078°, and approximately 130M away clearing in at Maria la Gorda (Chapter 4, once again; Maria la Gorda only operates intermittently as a port of entry). From here there is still another 30M to cover before gaining the relative protection of Cabo Francés, or the Cayos de San Felipe, but you should be out of the Gulf Stream and quite likely will have a favorable current (Chapter 5).

From Cuba to Isla Mujeres the wind is at your back but the rhumb line course from Cabo San Antonio to Isla Mujeres (250°) runs more or less head-on into the Gulf Stream. The best approach is to work south for maybe as much as 60M before proceeding a little south of west more or less directly across the axis of the Stream, allowing it to set you north to Isla Mujeres. However, if the plan is to visit the NW Caribbean and then return to the USA, an even better strategy is to depart Cuba from the Isla de la Juventud or Cayo Largo (see Chapter 5), sailing to the Cayman Islands, and then to Guanaja, the easternmost of the Bay Islands (both passages should be a comfortable reach), after which the wind and current will be in your favor all the way back to Isla Mujeres.

Strategies for circumnavigating Cuba

The primary factors to be considered are the generally easterly winds, but with a northerly set in the winter months and a southerly set in the summer months, the inshore currents, which tend to flow in a counterclockwise direction, and the prevalence of northers in the wintertime.

Because of the northers, so far as it is possible we would recommend cruising the south coast in the winter months, particularly January and February, and the north coast in Spring (March and April) or Fall (November and December). (We learned this the hard way, after spending a good bit of January and February searching for secure anchorages on the north coast in which to ride out northers.)

Sailing along either the north or south coast from east to west at any time of year is likely to be a comfortable reach or run, but this leaves the other coast to be sailed upwind. So the decision on which way to go around is best made on the basis of how to make the windward leg as least troublesome as possible, and to do this on the assumption that the boat will be on the south coast in the middle of winter, at which time the winds tend to be out of the NE.

In these circumstances we recommend a counter-clockwise circumnavigation. With a NE wind it is possible to lay most courses on the south coast from Cabo Francés to Cabo Cruz and beyond, in addition to which there will be a favorable current for much of the way. If the wind moves into the east, a good bit of the distance can at least be covered in reasonably protected waters behind the various barrier reefs and island groups, in addition to which it will still be possible to lay courses from Casilda to Cabo Cruz. If the wind moves into the SE (as it did with us, since we didn't arrive on the south coast until April), it is going to be a hard slog all the way, and you may wish you had gone the other way around. But a little reflection will show that this would be even worse since on the north shore not only would you be fighting the wind, but also the current.

Recommended cruises other than a circumnavigation

The majority of sailors will be coming to Cuba from the US east coast, or from the eastern Caribbean. In either case, if there is not sufficient time for a circumnavigation we would recommend a somewhat different strategy from any discussed so far, which is to make a landfall toward the eastern tip of Cuba, either by working down through the Bahamas (from the US east coast), or by sailing west from Puerto Rico or Hispaniola. Depending on the time available, there are then three attractive choices, all basically with favorable winds:

1. The longest cruise (a couple of months or more): clear in at Santiago de Cuba (Chapter 7), and then cruise the south coast as far as the Isla de la Juventud. After this, sail to the western tip of Cuba, pick up the Gulf Stream, and ride it back to the Florida Keys.
2. An intermediate cruise (a month or so): try to clear in at Baracoa (Chapter 8) and sail the north coast from here to either Varadero or the Marina Hemingway before heading up to the Florida Keys.
3. A short cruise (a couple of weeks): clear in at Bahía Naranjo (Chapter 8) and cruise the northern cays as far as Varadero before heading up to the Florida Keys.

Our reasons for picking these cruising regions should become clear in the following chapters.

Dry Tortugas

The Dry Tortugas are included in this guide since they make such a useful and delightful stopping point on many passages between the USA and Cuba.

The Dry Tortugas are the end of the line in the Florida Keys. A substantial reef area, intersected by several deep-water passages, contains a half dozen small islands, the most notable of which is Garden Key on which the US government built an enormous fort in the mid-1800s. In the lee of the fort is a well protected anchorage – surely one of the most dramatic in north America. The surrounding keys and waters have some lovely beaches and excellent snorkeling (though the water will seem cold to those used to the Caribbean – a wet suit of some sort is advised). The Dry Tortugas is a 'must-see' destination. It is also an excellent jumping off point for Cuba, or a convenient stop on the return passage to the USA, especially for boats headed to the west coast of Florida or to other Gulf Coast states.

Chart

DMA 11438, which is a highly accurate and very detailed chart produced by the Americans.

Approaches

There are three substantial channels through the surrounding reef to Garden Key – the NW, SW and SE channels. All three are straightforward and clearly shown on the chart, but note the substantial mid-channel shoals in the SW channel. All three channels can be attempted in any weather conditions, and with accurate navigation (a GPS) can be safely transited at night. Once inside the general reef area, even in rough conditions a fair measure of protection will be found. Final approach to the anchorage should only be made in daylight since entry is via narrow, curving channels with shoals on both sides.

Anchorage

The most protected anchorage is immediately SE of the fort. It is entered from the north via channels on both the east and west sides of Garden Key. The east channel is the most direct. Both channels are clearly marked with a plethora of stakes (so many, in fact, that it can be a little confusing if using the west channel!). Anchorage is made immediately off the dock, or else, if no space is available, in an area with 5m depths to the SE. Note, however, that this latter area is surrounded by shoals with the bottom coming up quite suddenly – it is necessary to proceed with caution, especially if the light does not allow a view of the bottom, and to check your swinging room before dropping the hook. Holding is generally good in a sand bottom, but there are some areas with thin sand over rock so the set of the anchor should be double-checked. We have ridden out everything from 25-knot southeasterlies to a 45-knot norther with nothing more than mild rolling.

If this anchorage is crowded, there is another substantial anchorage area to the SW of Garden Key, off Bird Key, but this is not as well protected nor as convenient for access to the fort.

Dinghy docking

Dinghies are beached on the sand immediately to the west of the dock which is in front of the fort.

Things to do

Fort Jefferson The fort was built by the USA to defend the sea lanes from New Orleans through the Straits of Florida to the eastern seaboard. It was started in 1846 at the tail end of the era of wooden ships, sail, and smoothbore cannon. With 50ft high, 8ft thick outer walls, and a planned complement of more than 400 cannons, the largest of which had 15in barrels and could throw a 60lb cannon ball as

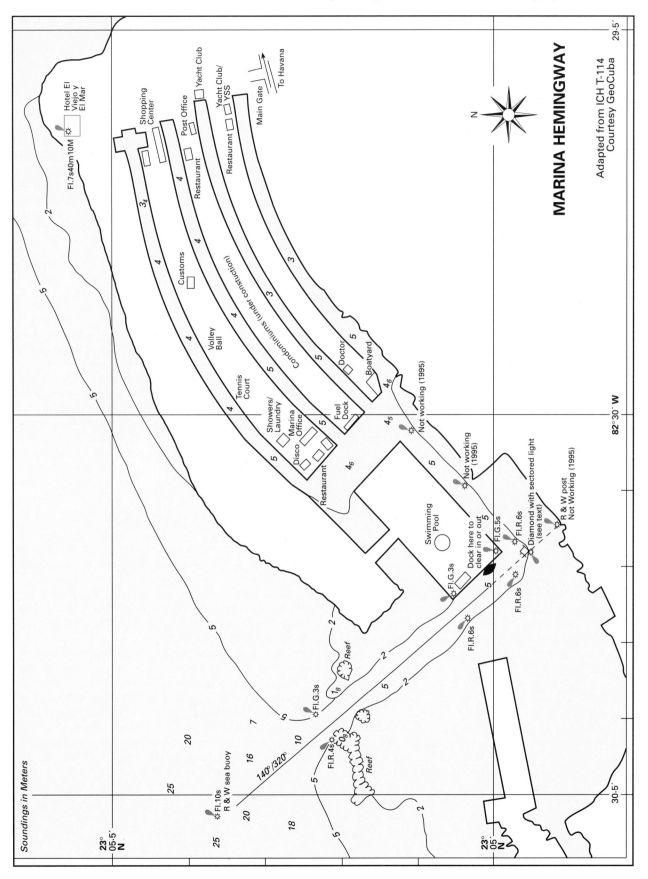

MARINA HEMINGWAY

Adapted from ICH T-114
Courtesy GeoCuba

Soundings in Meters

Hotel El
Viejo y
El Mar

Fl.7s40m10M

Shopping
Center

Post Office

Yacht Club

Restaurant

Yacht Club/
YSS

Main Gate

To Havana

Customs

Volley
Ball

Condominiums (under construction)

Tennis
Court

Showers/
Laundry

Marina
Office

Disco

Restaurant

Fuel
Dock

Doctor

Boatyard

Swimming
Pool

Reef

Dock here to
clear in or out

Fl.G.3s

Fl.G.5s

Fl.R.6s

Diamond with sectored light
(see text)

R & W post
Not Working (1995)

Not working (1995)

Not working (1995)

Fl.R.6s

Fl.R.6s

Fl.G.3s

Fl.R.4s

Reef

Reef

140°/320°

Fl.10s
R & W sea buoy

23°
05.5′
N

23°
05′
N

82° 30′ W

30.5′

29.5′

N

33

far as 3 miles, it was intended to be one of the most powerful maritime defenses in the world, barring the Straits of Florida to any enemy nation. But before the fort was ever completed the civil war broke out, and with the war came rifled cannon capable of demolishing walls of even this magnitude in a matter of hours. After twenty years of construction, and the laying of more than 16 million bricks, Fort Jefferson was obsolete before it was ever completed. It was intermittently used as a federal prison, and then as a coaling station for the emerging steam-powered navy, before being abandoned to the elements and passing cruisers.

Today the fort is the centerpiece of a National Park. Inside is a small bookstore and theater with a video program, while historical information is displayed at various key locations. A half day or more can easily be spent roaming this massive structure.

Snorkeling There is some moderately interesting snorkeling on the outside of the moat surrounding the fort, particularly around the pilings to the north and south which once supported coaling docks, but far better snorkeling will be found on the west side of Loggerhead Key, which also has a couple of interesting wrecks. In normal conditions you can anchor on the east side of Loggerhead Key and walk across the island to snorkel the other side.

Bird life Bush Key is home to a substantial colony of frigate birds, pelicans and sooty terns. It is off-limits during the nesting season (March to September) but the rookery can be observed from the anchorage or, at closer quarters, from a dinghy. During mating season the male frigate birds put on a particularly splendid display, blowing up a large red 'balloon' beneath their beaks.

Marina Hemingway

The Marina Hemingway is the principal port of entry for cruising boats going to Cuba. The marina stands by on VHF Ch 72, and should be contacted (English is spoken) soon after you cross the Cuban 12-mile limit. With any luck, by the time you reach the marina the various authorities will be on hand to expedite the clearance procedures (which in any case will take some time – see Chapter 1).

The marina is totally protected in all conditions, with a minimum of 5m of water in the entry channel, and 4m in most slips. The staff is large, friendly, and experienced in dealing with visiting boats. The services are continually being improved, but already include water (intermittent) and power in every slip, spotlessly clean showers and toilets, laundry facilities, a number of small shops (including a grocery store), a post office, a small boatyard, support services for larger yachts, a burgeoning yacht club, and a medical center. The marina is also an excellent base from which to explore Old Havana, or in which to leave a boat unattended for extended periods (while flying home, etc.).

Charts and magnetic variation

The coastline in the vicinity of the marina and westward is covered by ICH *1124*. ICH *1125* covers the coastline from just east of the marina to the Bahía de Cárdenas. There is a very detailed chart (1:5,000 – ICH *T114*) of the marina itself, but this is not necessary. Magnetic variation (January 2000) is 2°50'W, increasing annually by 8'W.

Approaches

The coastal shelf is close to the shore along this section of the Cuban coastline, so deep water is found until almost on the beach. The initial objective is the red and white marina sea buoy (Fl.10s), located at approximately 23°05·4'N 82°30·6'W. This buoy is about ¼M offshore, but less than this from the reef, and not readily visible during the daytime until close inshore (especially if any seas are running), nor at night due to the background lights. In other words, since you will be maneuvering close to the reef and the beach, a fairly accurate landfall is needed, and a nighttime entry is not recommended, particularly if this is your first visit (as I write this, the wreck of a 43ft sailboat is grinding to pieces on the reef after attempting a night entry and missing the channel by just a few meters).

From the east, the skyscrapers of Havana will be visible from many miles out.

From the west, the coastline is relatively featureless. Immediately to the west of the marina entrance are the low houses of the town of Santa Fé. Further west (2½M west of the marina) are a series of conspicuous apartment buildings (the Cuban naval academy on the Santa Ana river) together with a conspicuous water tower.

As you get closer to the sea buoy, from any direction you will see a largish hotel (with the Dársena de Barlovento light on its roof – Fl.7s40m10M). This is The Old Man and the Sea (El Viejo y el Mar) hotel. A distinctive water tower will appear to the right of the hotel, and then a little further west, at the present time, an undistinctive band of scrubby vegetation against which will be seen the masts of the sailboats in the marina (this vegetation will give way to condominiums over the next few years). The marina entry comes next, approximately ¾M to the west of the hotel. In addition to the sea buoy, the entry channel is marked by a couple of stakes. The green is left to port, the red to starboard, on entering – see sketch.

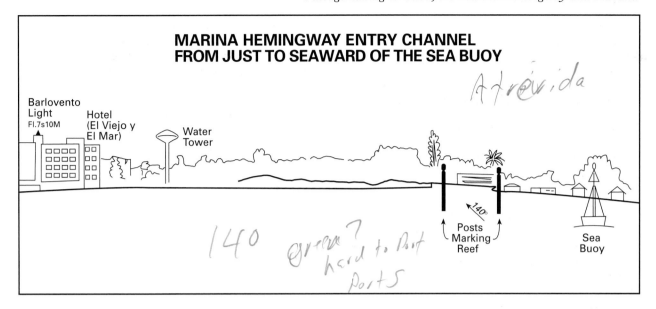

**MARINA HEMINGWAY ENTRY CHANNEL
FROM JUST TO SEAWARD OF THE SEA BUOY**

Both stakes are lit – the green flashes every 3 seconds; the red every 4 seconds.

Entry

The sea buoy is more or less on the edge of the coastal shelf, in over 25m – it can be taken on either side. From the buoy the channel is 140° straight into the marina. The depths shoal rapidly. Within less than ¼M of the buoy the channel is down to 10m as you pass between the two stakes (which are on the reef – it is essential to stay in mid-channel from this point until inside the marina). Ahead is a large diamond, behind which is a red and white post, forming a range, but these (particularly the latter) may not be easy to pick out. In any event, keep to 140° to come in directly parallel to the dock, which houses the Guarda Frontera. At night the diamond has a white flashing range light with a very narrow sector – if you stray to either side of the channel, the light changes color (red if you are on the port side of the channel; green if on the starboard side).

The seaward corner of the Guarda dock has a light (Fl.G.3s), opposite which is a lighted pylon (Fl.R.6s); beyond the Guarda post is another light (Fl.G.5s), opposite which is another lighted pylon (Fl.R.6s).

Entering the Marina Hemingway in a norther

Since the marina channel faces to the NW, during the early stages of a norther (the NW phase associated with the passage of the front itself) large breaking seas run straight up the channel – entry can be quite hazardous. In other words, if using the favorable winds of a norther to sail to the marina, the passage should be timed so as to arrive after the wind has shifted toward the NE and moderated, at which time the breakers tend to sweep across the entry channel with less force, rather than directly into it, making entry less hazardous. Even so, to avoid the risk of broaching and being thrown onto the reef, you will need to keep to the windward side of the channel, and to come in with sufficient speed to maintain steerageway (underpowered sailboats should be wary of entering in these conditions). When the wind is from the prevailing east the entry channel is calm.

Clearance procedures

Clearing in The first dock contains the office of the Guarda. All entering boats should by now be flying their Cuban and yellow (quarantine) flags, and must stop at this dock. The dock, as with all docks in the marina, is relatively high with an overhanging lip which in some places is a little beat up; in places there is a submerged ledge. *You will need at least two, and preferably three or four, good-sized fenders to prevent damage to your topsides and to hold you out from the ledge*, especially if any residual swells are making their way up the channel (only likely in the early stages of a norther; in these conditions the Guarda sometimes allow boats to follow the channel around the first turn to port, and then tie up). These fenders will also be needed in the marina itself.

The clearance procedures are protracted (see Chapter 1). However, all concerned are friendly – it is simply a matter of being patient.

Clearing out At least two days before departing for any cruise in Cuban waters you should take a copy of your planned itinerary (listing all potential stops) to the marina office, which will pass the itinerary on to the Guarda. The Guarda will in turn advise you if any of your planned stops are off-limits to visiting sailors, and then issue a detailed *despacho* (see Chapter 1). (Note that since two days is adequate for a brief exploration of Old Havana, to expedite matters those planning on cruising should leave their itinerary with the marina officials as soon as possible after arrival.)

Well ahead of leaving, you must give your intended departure time to the customs officers, who occupy a small building in the center of the marina, and the marina office (who will notify the immigration officers and Guarda). When talking to the customs officers, arrange to have them board at least half an hour before your appointment with the Guarda, and make this, in turn, at least half an hour before you actually want to leave!

Marina facilities

There are four substantial canals in the marina, with the boats docking alongside the walls. Depths alongside are generally 3–4m, but in a few places there are underwater protrusions, some of them quite close to the surface (notably on the outermost wall of the outer canal, which has horizontal pieces of re-bar, up to a meter in length, sticking out at right angles to the wall just below the surface – no place to be caught with an inflatable dinghy). The marina disco is situated close to the entrance to the outermost canal, so you should ask to dock well away from this area (it is noisy until late at night). Marina charges as of 1998 were $0.45 per foot per day, dropping to $0.35 per foot per day for stays of more than three months.

Electricity The marina was built in the 1950s with large yachts in mind. To service these yachts a high-quality, high-powered electrical system was installed, with distribution boxes spaced regularly along the docks. Forty years later these boxes were still in place, but without the proper outlets for most shore power cords. Every time a new boat pulled in, the marina's electrician jury-rigged a connection. These connections left much to be desired and in fact could be both damaging to a boat and potentially lethal (refer back to Chapter 1). Reportedly, new distribution boxes have been installed. Nevertheless, *you should not get hooked up unless you can check the installation for correct polarity and grounding.* Electricity is billed at $0.30/kWh. The marina will also provide a phone connection if so desired.

Water All the electrical distribution boxes also have spigots for hose connections with water metered at $0.05 a gallon. However, drinking water is only intermittently available. It is advisable to top off tanks whenever possible. The showers, toilets and laundry, on the other hand, always have water (this is not potable water). Soap (pretty awful) and towels are provided, but not toilet paper (it is a good idea to carry soap and a roll of toilet paper when traveling away from the boat since both are rare commodities as a result of the embargo; at the time of writing, soap makes a much appreciated gift).

Other facilities The fuel dock is between the second and third canals with plenty of water alongside. In 1998 diesel cost $0.65 a liter while gasoline was $0.90 a liter. Propane can be obtained via the marina office (they telephone the propane people who come and pick up your cylinders, returning them the same day – the cost is just a little higher than in the USA).

There are various bars, restaurants and stores scattered around the marina complex, but neither the food nor the shopping are particularly exciting, and the prices are at least as high as Stateside. (Given the general scarcity of supplies in Cuba, this is hardly surprising; the supplies nevertheless include many items that most Cubans hardly ever, or never, see.) There is a post office, but it should be noted that stamps are charged for in dollars at the official exchange rate, which makes them expensive. The marina complex includes a couple of hard court tennis courts, a volleyball court and a swimming pool. On the perimeter of the complex is the Old Man and the Sea hotel, with an open invitation to its swimming pool and bar, and in the center of the marina, the new El Jardin d'Eden hotel with a tour desk and 24-hour-a-day doctor's office ($20/visit).

Prescriptions have to be filled at a pharmacy downtown, most commonly at the International Farmacia in the Hospital Cira Garcia, which is known to all the taxi drivers. This pharmacy is a 'dollar only' pharmacy: the same prescription can be filled at a peso pharmacy for a fraction of the price, but to do this you will need to know a Cuban to take the prescription in for you. Sick people are likely to find the doctor making one or two boat calls a day (on foot or on bicycle) to see how they are doing. More serious cases of illness, requiring hospitalization, are dealt with at one or two tourist medical institutions – the service is excellent, with prices similar to those in the States.

Dockside help Various Cubans eager for work come to the docks whenever the security guards allow it (some weeks, almost no one is allowed into the marina without a special card; other weeks just about anybody can come through the gates). The most prominent are prostitutes who openly solicit clients, but there are also many young people prepared to do a hard day's work for relatively low wages, or to go shopping in the local farmers' market for fresh produce, charging a minimal amount for the service (a dollar or two). During those periods when the guards clamp down, it is often possible to find people looking for work hanging around by the shopping center.

Mail drops Mail addressed to the marina or the yacht club (see below) sometimes arrives, but normally only after weeks.

Marina office 'Despachos' are applied for, and bills are paid (on leaving) at the marina office which is located in the long, low building close to the disco and 'Papa's' bar and restaurant.

Address Marina Hemingway, 5ta Avenida y Calle 248, Santa Fé, Havana, Cuba. ☎ (53) 733-1150 and (53) 733-1831; fax (53) 733-1831.

Boatyard

There is a small boatyard at the seaward end of the innermost canal. The yard uses a crane, rented from elsewhere, to haul boats. It is professionally done (using spreader bars and substantial slings – the boatyard operator, Julio Dager, is an English-speaking naval engineer who knows what he is doing). Boats up to 12m (40ft) in length and 30 tons can be handled. Cost, depending on boat size, is likely to be from $300 to $500. The workforce includes a carpenter, a mechanic, a welder and an electronics man. Fiberglass repairs can also be handled. The standard labor rate is $12 an hour. The biggest problem is in obtaining parts and supplies – if you need work done on your boat, it is best to bring your own materials. When the US embargo on trade with Cuba is lifted, supply problems should end.

International Yacht Club

The International Yacht Club (Club Náutico) is a non-governmental, non-profit organization more or less independent of the marina but with its facilities within the marina grounds. As with many US and European yacht clubs, there is a substantial initial membership fee ($300 to $450) with the membership theoretically controlling the organization and electing the officers at an annual meeting (all except the executive director, who is appointed by the marina; this is what I mean by more or less independent!). An additional fee of $30 a month is charged during the period that a member's boat is moored in the marina. Members

get to use the club's almost new facilities – including a bar and comfortable lounge with cable TV and videos. In addition, members receive substantial discounts (35%) on the marina's mooring fees, and in bars and restaurants (20%) on the marina campus, together with free use of the tennis courts and swimming pool and a discount (15%) on car rentals made through Cubanacan. The club has a functioning phone and fax with direct-dial connections to the USA and the rest of the world.

Visiting North American sailors can obtain temporary yacht club membership at a cost of $25 a week. In simple economic terms alone it is an excellent investment (the reduction in marina fees will probably more than pay the $25), while the yacht club itself is well worth supporting in any way possible in as much as its executive director, José Escrich, has campaigned tirelessly to ease restrictions on cruising yachts, with significant progress being made.

Address International Yacht Club, 5ta Avenida y Calle 248, Santa Fé, Havana, Cuba. ☎ and fax (53) 733-1689.

Supermarkets

Aside from the small supermarket in the marina shopping center, there are two substantial dollar-only supermarkets on the way into Havana. The Diplotienda, a supermarket for diplomats in the Miramar district of Havana, on Avenida 3 and Calle 70, close to the Russian Embassy (which can't be missed either from seaward or the land – it looks like it has been built from Lego blocks); the other one, whose name we have lost, is close by (any taxi driver will know).

There is a dollars-only bakery at the corner of Avenida 7 and Calle 40.

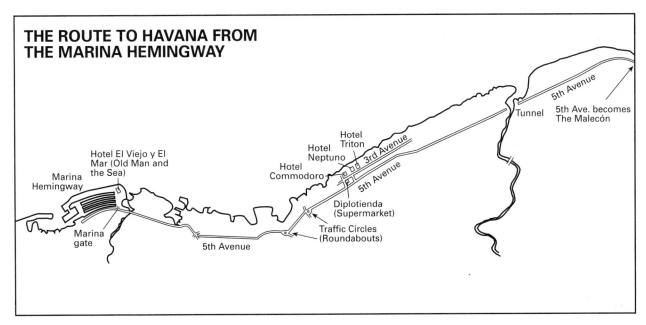

THE ROUTE TO HAVANA FROM THE MARINA HEMINGWAY

Local markets

The town of Santa Fe, to the west of the marina (turn right out of the gate) has a farmers' market with a fair supply of vegetables.

Exploring old Havana

From the earliest days of the Spanish colonization of central and south America, Havana was a most important defensive installation. This resulted in the construction of several magnificent fortresses, the two most spectacular being on either side of the entrance to Havana Harbor. These remain substantially intact, in the midst of a number of grand old buildings. Some of these date back to those early years, but most are a product of the enormous wealth subsequently generated by the sugar and tobacco plantations, which has left a legacy of much fine colonial architecture concentrated in an area known as the 'Old City'.

When these buildings were in a state of good repair Havana must have been one of the finest cities in this hemisphere. But in recent years it has fallen on extremely hard times. Much of the Old City has seen little or no maintenance in several decades. Many of the oldest buildings are in a state of imminent collapse, shored up with numerous balks of timber. Even those standing unaided are mostly crumbling into the surrounding streets. The old town, in short, has the air of just having come through a war.

On a first visit, the sense of shock engendered by this air of decay is often the first, and overwhelming, impression left with visitors. On subsequent visits there is a tendency to see more of what is still left standing (and there is much of this) and to concentrate on those buildings and areas of the city that have been salvaged and restored – the four principal forts, including El Morro and the Castillo de la Fuerza, and one or two other complete streets. Overall it is clear that many fine buildings have slipped beyond the point of no return, but in spite of this, perhaps even in a sense because of it, the Old City is a fascinating place that should not be missed. A half day at least should be spent simply wandering the streets; a full day will be needed to take in a tour of some of the buildings and museums open to the public.

Transport to and from the city

Taxis are available from the marina, with fares varying from $12 to $20 for a one-way trip (the metered taxis are the cheaper ones). But for most cruisers the best option is to arrange a ride by private transport. The driver will take you into Havana, drive you around the city, wait while you go sightseeing, shopping, or eat a meal, and then take you back to the marina. The cost varies from $15 to $30 for a day. On arrival, check with other cruisers to find out who is available – depending on demand, you may need to book a car and driver a day or two ahead of your trip to the city. Alternatively, ask around for a ride among the cars parked outside the marina shopping center.

Tienda el Navigantes

The Tienda el Navigantes, located in the Old City, is the retail outlet for the Cuban Hydrographic Department. Here, at a price of from $14.50 to $16 a sheet, you can purchase quite the best charts available for Cuban waters. The chart kits cost around $40 each (1999).

4. Marina Hemingway to Cabo San Antonio and the western capes

It is 165M from the Marina Hemingway to Cabo San Antonio, the western tip of Cuba. The first 50M or so the coastline is mostly rocky and relatively inhospitable, although it is broken by a number of small estuaries, and three of Cuba's 'pocket bays' – large bodies of navigable water with narrow, deep-water entrances creating superbly well protected anchorages.

To the west of the third of these bays (the Bahía Honda) a reef starts which runs in a more or less constant line from here all the way to Cabo San Antonio. Initially the reef is close inshore, but within a few miles it diverges far enough to create a navigable channel between it and the mainland, enabling passage to be made in relatively protected waters. Ashore, the rounded hills that have formed a backdrop ever since leaving the Marina Hemingway give way to increasingly dramatic, sheer-sided mountains.

At its western end the reef diverges up to 25M from the mainland, enclosing a large body of water known as the Golfo de Guanahacabibes. The cays fade out, and the depths increase. The mountains give way to miles of untended, wooded hills. The towns are few, far between and dirt poor. This is the most remote corner of Cuba.

In general, this region, although interesting, has neither the variety nor the attractions found on the NE coast, or much of the southern coast – there are an awful lot of mangroves and few centers of civilization for light relief! If pressed for time, we would prioritize these other regions. Nevertheless, many cruisers happily spend a week or two puttering through the cays. The area is also well worth taking in as part of a passage to or from the NW Caribbean.

Winds

The prevailing winds are from the ENE, with an average strength of 8–10 knots. Within this average, there is a marked daily wind pattern, beginning with light breezes from the east to SE early in the morning, gradually building in intensity (frequently to 15–20 knots) and shifting to the NE during the course of the day, and then dying overnight.

This pattern is broken by numerous northers in the wintertime, and calms or the effects of tropical depressions in the summertime (Chapter 2). The northers hit this section of the coastline with greater force than elsewhere in Cuba, commonly making conditions offshore decidedly rough (especially out in the Gulf Stream), and making many of the reef and harbor entries dangerous. It is best to find a secure anchorage before the advent of a norther, and not to venture out until it has passed by.

Currents and tides

Offshore, the Gulf Stream dominates everything, flowing ENE with great constancy. Closer inshore there is very often a westward setting counter-current, running at anything from 0·5 to 2·0 knots. The effects of this current can almost always be felt from the Bahía Honda westward; sometimes it begins as far east as the Bahía del Mariel and even the Marina Hemingway (though this is rare).

Tides are small, with an average amplitude of 0·2 to 0·3m (about 1ft), and maximums of 0·5m (1·5ft). The tide is diurnal, which is to say there is only one low tide and one high tide each day. Tidal currents are insignificant except in some reef passages and narrow channels between cays, and the entry channels into the pocket bays. Here, tidal currents can attain a velocity of up to 2·5 knots.

Sailing strategies

Going west, an early morning start from the Marina Hemingway benefits from the generally lighter winds and easier conditions, and makes it possible to gain the shelter of the Bahía Honda well before dark. Beyond the Bahía Honda, once inside the reef and cays of the Archipiélago de los Colorados there is adequate protection, and enough secure anchorages, to provide generally pleasant sailing conditions all the way to Cabo San Antonio. To round the cape, see the specific section at the end of this chapter.

Going east, an early morning start will at all times benefit from the lighter winds and the generally more favorable wind direction than that found later

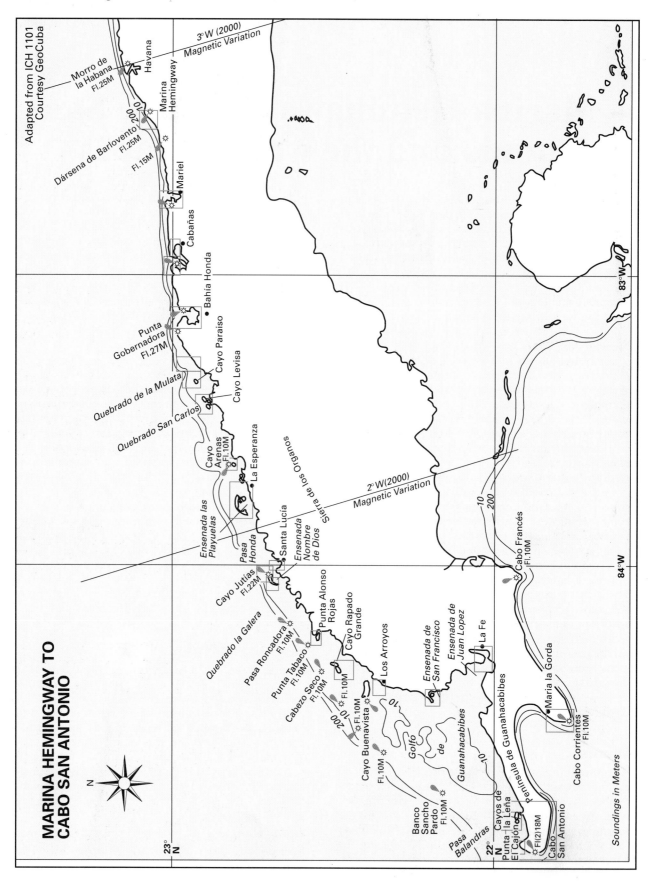

MARINA HEMINGWAY TO CABO SAN ANTONIO

Adapted from ICH 1101
Courtesy GeoCuba

Morro de la Habana
Fl.25M

Havana

3°W (2000)
Magnetic Variation

Marina Hemingway

Dársena de Barlovento
Fl.25M

Fl.15M

Mariel

Cabañas

Bahía Honda

Punta Gobernadora
Fl.27M

Cayo Paraiso

Cayo Levisa

Quebrado de la Mulata

Cayo Arenas
Fl.10M

Quebrado San Carlos

La Esperanza

Sierra de los Órganos

Ensenada las Playuelas

2°W (2000)
Magnetic Variation

Pasa Honda

Santa Lucía

Ensenada Nombre de Dios

Cabo Francés
Fl.10M

Cayo Jutías
Fl.22M

Quebrado la Galera

Pasa Roncadora
Fl.10M

Punta Alonso Rojas

Cayo Rapado Grande

Punta Tabaco
Fl.10M

Cabezo Seco
Fl.10M

Fl.10M

Fl.10M

Los Arroyos

Ensenada de San Francisco

Ensenada de Juan Lopez

La Fe

Cabo Corrientes
Fl.10M

Maria la Gorda

200

10

10

Golfo de Guanahacabibes

Cayo Buenavista
Fl.10M

Península de Guanahacabibes

Banco Sancho Pardo
Fl.10M

Pasa Balandras

Cayos de Punta la Leña
El Cajón

Fl(2)18M

Cabo San Antonio

22°
N

23°
N

Soundings in Meters

N

in the day. By mid-afternoon you will probably be faced with an arduous beat into the wind and waves, with quite likely an adverse current to add to your difficulties!

Charts and magnetic variation

ICH *1124*, *1123* and *1122* cover the region from the Marina Hemingway to Cabo San Antonio, and around the western tip of the island to Cabo Corrientes. These charts are all at a scale of 1:150,000. The Golfo de Guanahacabibes has also been charted at both 1:100,000 and 1:50,000. In addition there are various detailed charts for the Bahía del Mariel, Bahía de Cabañas, Bahía Honda, and the port of Santa Lucía. Finally, the chart book (Region 1: Marina Hemingway to Cabo Corrientes) covers this whole region, with some useful 1:25,000 charts of sections of the Archipiélago de los Colorados.

Magnetic variation decreases from 2°50'W (January 2000) at the Marina Hemingway to 1°05'W at Cabo San Antonio. In all areas it is increasing annually at a rate of about 8'W.

North coast 'pocket bays'

Between the Marina Hemingway and the cays and reef of the Archipiélago de los Colorados lies a 50M stretch of coastline with no off-lying dangers in its eastern half, but with a reef which comes out progressively further offshore the further west you go. A number of rivers indent the coastline, several of which reportedly have more than 2m in their mouths, but all of which rapidly shoal as you move inland. In addition, there are three major 'pocket bays', Mariel, Cabañas and Honda.

The entrances to the three bays are straightforward in any conditions but it should be noted that tidal currents of up to 2·5 knots are possible, sometimes with a set across the channel, so careful attention needs to be paid to your track when entering or exiting these bays. When the ebb tide is running out against an onshore wind, conditions in the approaches to the channels can be quite rough, so it is best to time an arrival or departure for slack water.

The interiors of these pocket bays hold out the prospect of some interesting cruising, but currently the Guarda are not at all welcoming at the Bahía del Mariel, or at the Bahía de Cabañas, and severely limit the movement of boats inside the Bahía Honda. Because of this, most cruisers make an early morning start from the Marina Hemingway so as to make the Bahía Honda before dark. They then lay over the night without doing any exploring, leaving the next day for Cayo Paraíso in the Archipiélago de los Colorados (see below) where the welcome may be warmer. (In 1997 and 1998 the Guarda put Cayo Paraíso off-limits to most boats!)

Río Santa Ana

2½M SW of the Marina Hemingway (at approximately 23°03·8'N 82°32·0'W) lies the Río Santa Ana which is easily recognized by the mass of white buildings immediately to the west of its mouth and the conspicuous water tower. These buildings house the Cuban naval academy. The river has reportedly been dredged to a depth of 5m, and the channel is marked, but it is closed to all civilian traffic.

Río Baracoa

The Río Baracoa (at approximately 23°03·2'N 82°34·6'W) is a little more than 2M west of the Río Santa Ana. Reportedly, there is a channel with more than 2m through the shoals at the river mouth, after which the depth increases for a short distance, before gradually decreasing to shoal water.

To the west of the Río Baracoa is a very conspicuous chimney. This is part of the Havana Libre sugar refinery, which is a little under 2M inland (at approximately 23°00·8'N 82°36·7'W). Further inland still is a conspicuous, flat-topped range of hills (Loma Mesa de Mariel – 275m high) which can be seen from many miles to both the east and the west.

Río Banes

The Río Banes (at approximately 23°02·3'N 82°38·5'W) has a bridge approximately ½M inland from its mouth which is quite visible from 2–3M offshore. The river reportedly has 2m in the entry channel, but rapidly shoals.

Río Mosquito

The Río Mosquito (at approximately 23°01·4'N 82°43·2'W) reportedly has several exposed rocks in its mouth, with a narrow channel between the rocks with depths of over 2m for up to ½M inland.

Bahía del Mariel

The Bahía del Mariel (at approximately 23°01·7'N 82°45·4'W) is the first decent all-weather anchorage to the west of the Marina Hemingway. However, visiting boats are limited to anchoring off the Guarda dock just inside the mouth of the bay. Here the protection is not always the best.

The bay is conspicuous from many miles away because of its cement works (on the eastern shore of the bay) and the chimneys of an electricity

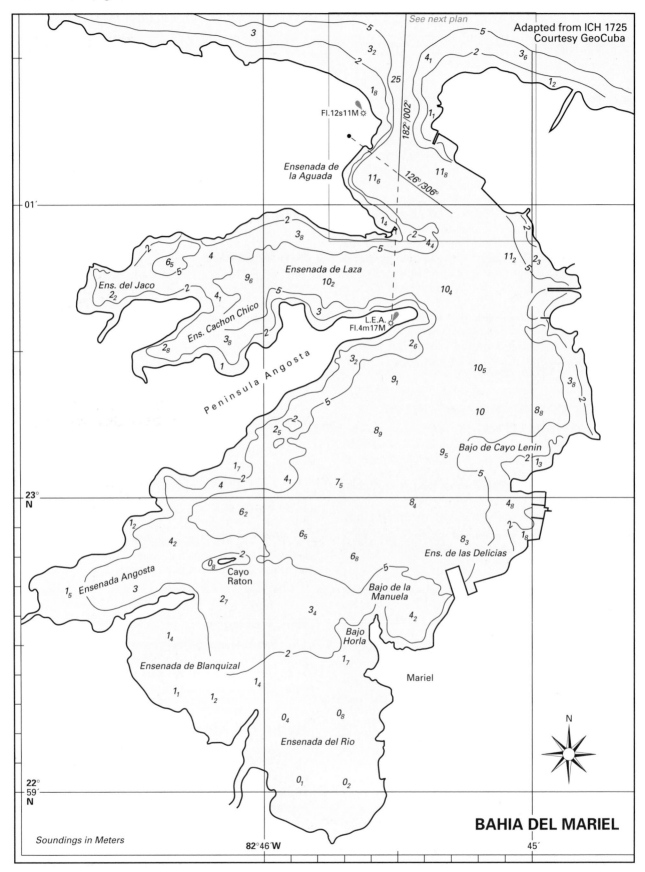

Adapted from ICH 1725
Courtesy GeoCuba

See next plan

Ensenada de
la Aguada

Fl.12s11M

182°/002°

126°/306°

Ensenada de Laza

L.E.A.
Fl.4m17M

P e n i n s u l a   A n g o s t a

Ens. del Jaco

Ens. Cachon Chico

Bajo de Cayo Lenin

Ens. de las Delicias

Ensenada Angosta

Cayo
Raton

Bajo de la
Manuela

Bajo
Horla

Mariel

Ensenada de Blanquizal

Ensenada del Rio

N

BAHIA DEL MARIEL

Soundings in Meters

82°46′W

45′

01′

23°
N

22°
59′
N

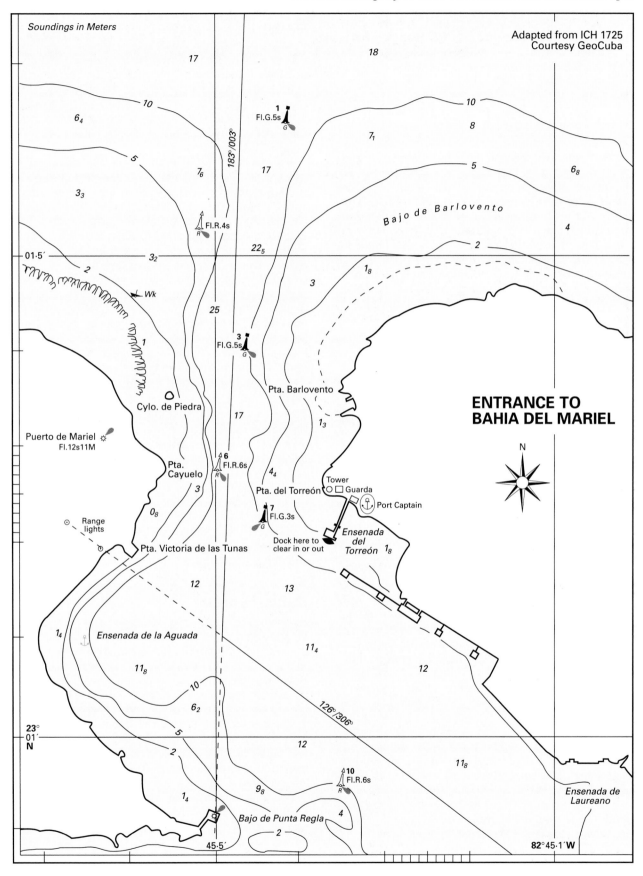

Soundings in Meters

Adapted from ICH 1725
Courtesy GeoCuba

17

18

10

6_4

10

8

1
Fl.G.5s
G

7_1

5

6_8

183°/003°

5

7_6

17

Bajo de Barlovento

3_3

4

Fl.R.4s
R

01·5′

3_2

22_5

2

1_8

25

3

Wk

1

3
Fl.G.5s
G

Pta. Barlovento

Cylo. de Piedra

17

1_3

Puerto de Mariel
Fl.12s11M

6
Fl.R.6s
R

Pta.
Cayuelo

3

4_4

Pta. del Torreón

Tower
Guarda
Port Captain

**ENTRANCE TO
BAHIA DEL MARIEL**

N

0_8

7
Fl.G.3s
G

Range
lights

Pta. Victoria de las Tunas

Dock here to
clear in or out

Ensenada
del
Torreón 1_8

12

13

11_4

12

1_4

Ensenada de la Aguada

11_8

126°/306°

**23°
01′
N**

10

6_2

5

12

2

11_8

1_4

9_8

10
Fl.R.6s
R

Ensenada de
Laureano

Bajo de Punta Regla

4

2

45·5′

82°45·1′W

43

generating plant (which is approximately ¼M SE of the eastern headland to the bay). As you approach within a mile or two, you will be able to pick out the 134ft high lattice-work tower of the Punta Cayuelo (Puerto de Mariel) light (Fl.12s) on the western headland.

Entry and anchorage

The entry channel is approximately midway between the two headlands. The channel is well marked (and lit) and can be traversed in all conditions, although during and after a norther large swells drive into it, making conditions rough. The channel itself narrows down to 100m just beyond the Punta Cayuelo light, although at this point you should be out of the worst of the seas. There is frequently a west-setting tidal current sweeping across the entrance to the bay for which allowance must be made. A conspicuous wreck on the west side of the channel serves as a warning to navigators who make a mistake (in spite of the lights, I would not make a night entry here, especially in rough conditions).

To enter the bay, locate the green sea buoy (at approximately 23°01·7'N 82°45·4'W, Fl.G.5s). Leave this to port (i.e. pass to the west of it), and then come in on a heading of 183°, making whatever allowance is necessary for the tide. The next buoy (red, Fl.R.4s) is almost at the northern edge of the western shoal (the charts show it a little further in than this). After this, the green *No. 3* buoy (Fl.G.5s) is left close to port (20m – the channel is narrow at this point), and then the red *No. 6* (Fl.R.6s) 30m to starboard and the green *No. 7* (Fl.G.3s) 30m to port, after which you should come onto the end of the dock immediately to the east in order to clear in with the Guarda (this dock has 3–4m alongside).

The Guarda are unlikely to allow any exploration of the bay, or even to give permission to go ashore. They will want to keep you on the dock, or will allow you to anchor out in the Ensenada de la Aguada immediately to the SW. This bay has deep water (9m or more) until close to shore, so a fair amount of scope is needed when anchoring. The holding is good. Depending on the wind direction, by morning the boat is likely to be covered in a layer of soot from the power station, and dust from the cement factory.

The eastern shore of the bay is heavily industrialized; the SW end is relatively pastoral and looks like it has several far more attractive anchorages, but currently it is all off-limits. In any event, if you are allowed into the bay, be sure to stay out of the Ensenada de Laza, and away from the south shore of the Península Angosta, since these are military areas strictly off-limits to civilians.

Bahía de Cabañas

Between the Bahía del Mariel and the Bahía de Cabañas there are no potential anchorages, with the possible exception of the Río Dominica (at approximately 23°01·4'N 82°50·1'W), but this contains a military base and is off-limits to tourists. Toward the Bahía de Cabañas the reef lies a little further offshore, but nowhere does it come out more than ½M.

The Bahía de Cabañas (at approximately 23°00·5'N 82°58·6'W) which is 12M west of Mariel, is a large bay with a deep-water, all-weather entry, and numerous protected anchorages. Unfortunately, much of the bay is reserved for military use and is strictly off-limits to tourists. The military zone includes the southern half of the entry channel to the (non-military) eastern half of the bay, and because of this the Guarda rarely allow visiting boats to enter (including us; our coverage is based solely on the Cuban charts and a close pass across the mouth of the bay). Should you be allowed in, once through the channel you need to keep to the north of 22°59·45'N until east of 82°57·5'W (which doesn't leave much of the bay!).

Entry

The entry channel is well marked and relatively wide (200m or more) with minimum depths of a little over 6m. It is approached from more or less due north and then transited on a heading of 173°, changing to 145° once past the green *No. 5* buoy (Fl.5s). This track leads into the eastern channel on the inside (Canal Cabañas). The channel is followed curving first to the east, and then to the NE after rounding Punta Mangle. This gets you out of the military zone, after which there are several potential anchorages, and the town of Cabañas itself.

Bahía Honda

Between the Bahía de Cabañas and the Bahía Honda there are no potential anchorages, while the further west you go, the further the reef extends offshore until it is 1M out on the approaches to the Bahía Honda. There are reportedly small breaks in the reef at approximately 23°00·5'N 83°01·4'W (off the town of San Pedro) and at approximately 23°00·4'N 83°05·0'W (off the Bahía Ortigosa), but with less than 2m in the channels and inside the reef. The latter passage, which gives access to a lagoon at the mouth of the Río Santiago, is narrow and winding.

The Bahía Honda (at approximately 22°59·6'N 83°09·7'W), some 23M west of Mariel, and 37M west of the Marina Hemingway, is another large pocket bay with a deep-water, all-weather entry, and numerous well protected anchorages once on the inside. It is a convenient overnight stop when

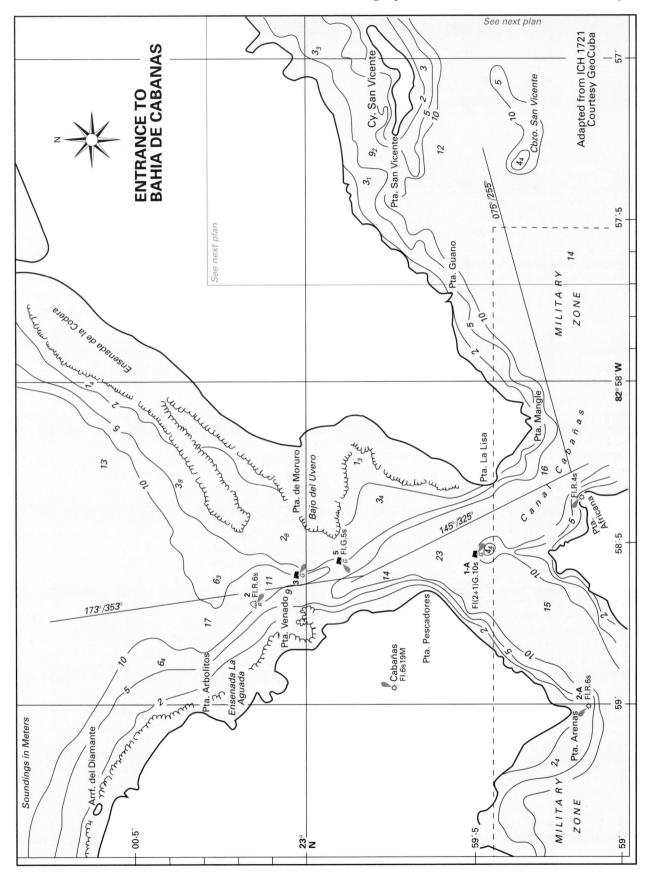

ENTRANCE TO
BAHIA DE CABAÑAS

N

See next plan

See next plan

Adapted from ICH 1721
Courtesy GeoCuba

Cy. San Vicente

Pta. San Vicente

Cbzo. San Vicente

075°/255°

MILITARY ZONE

Pta. Guano

Ensenada de la Codera

MILITARY ZONE

Pta. Mangle

82°58'W

Pta. La Lisa

Canal Cabañas

Fl.R.4s

Pta. Africana

Pta. de Moruro

Bajo del Uvero

145°/325°

Fl.G.5s 5

173°/353°

3 Fl.R.6s 11

Pta. Venado 9

2 Fl.R.6s

Pta. Arbolitos

Ensenada La Aguada

Arrf. del Diamante

Soundings in Meters

23 Fl(2+1)G.10s 1-A

4₄ 1

Cabañas Fl.6s19M

Pta. Pescadores

2-A Fl.R.6s

Pta. Arenas

MILITARY ZONE

23°N

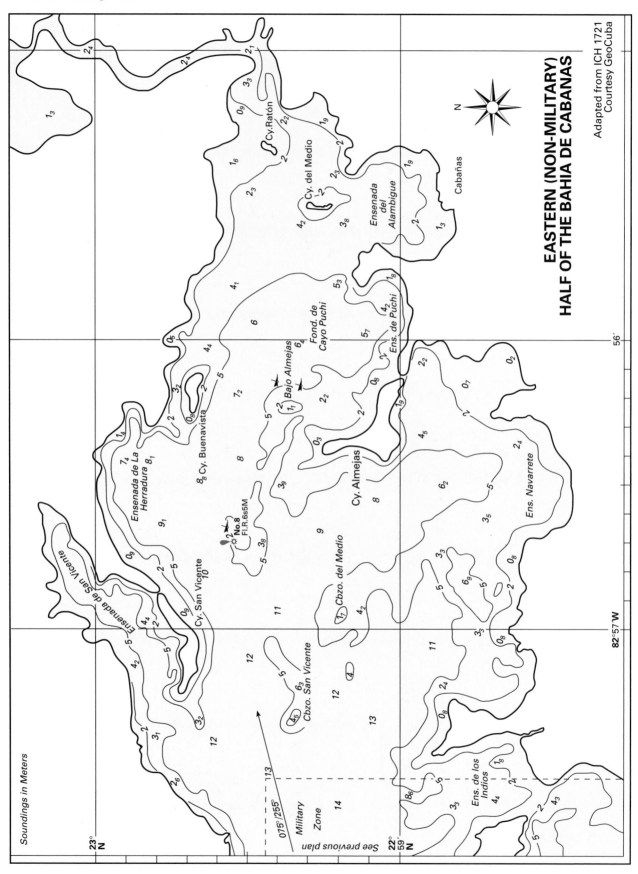

**EASTERN (NON-MILITARY)
HALF OF THE BAHIA DE CABANAS**

Adapted from ICH 1721
Courtesy GeoCuba

Soundings in Meters

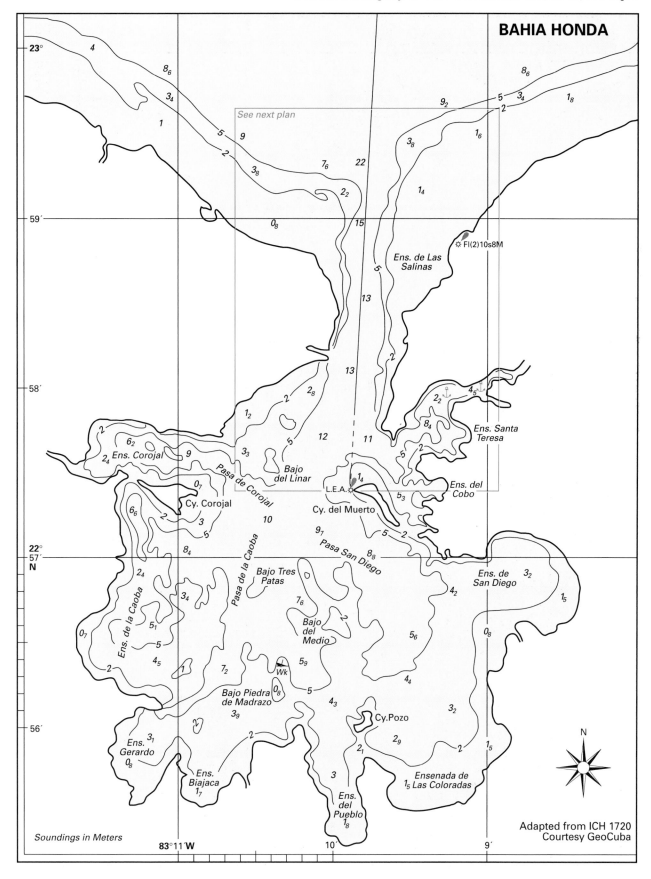

BAHIA HONDA

23°

4

8₆

3₄

1

8₆

5 3₄

1₈

9₂

See next plan

5 9

2

3₈

7₆ 22

2₂

15

0₈

59′

Ens. de Las
Salinas

✸ Fl(2)10s8M

5

13

13

2

58′

2₈

2

1₂

5

12

11

2₂

4₅

Ens. Santa
Teresa

6₂

2₄ Ens. Corojal

9

3₃

Bajo
del Linar

8₄

2 5

2₄

0₇

Cy. Corojal

3

5

1₄

L.E.A. ✸

Cy. del Muerto

5₃

Ens. del
Cobo

6₆

2

10

5

9₇

5 2

Pasa San Diego

8₈

22°

57′

8₄

Pasa de la Caoba

Bajo Tres
Patas

4₂

Ens. de
San Diego

3₂

N

2₄

3₄

7₆

2

5₆

0₈

1₅

0₇

5₁

5

Bajo
del Medio

4₄

4₅

1

7₂

5₉

Wk

5

Cy.Pozo

3₂

2

Bajo Piedra
de Madrazo

0₈

4₃

56′

3₉

2₉

2

1₅

Ens.
Gerardo

3₁

2₁

0₈

2

Ens.
Biajaca

1₇

3

Ensenada de
1₅ Las Coloradas

Ens.
del
Pueblo

1₈

N

Soundings in Meters

83°11′W

10′

9′

Adapted from ICH 1720
Courtesy GeoCuba

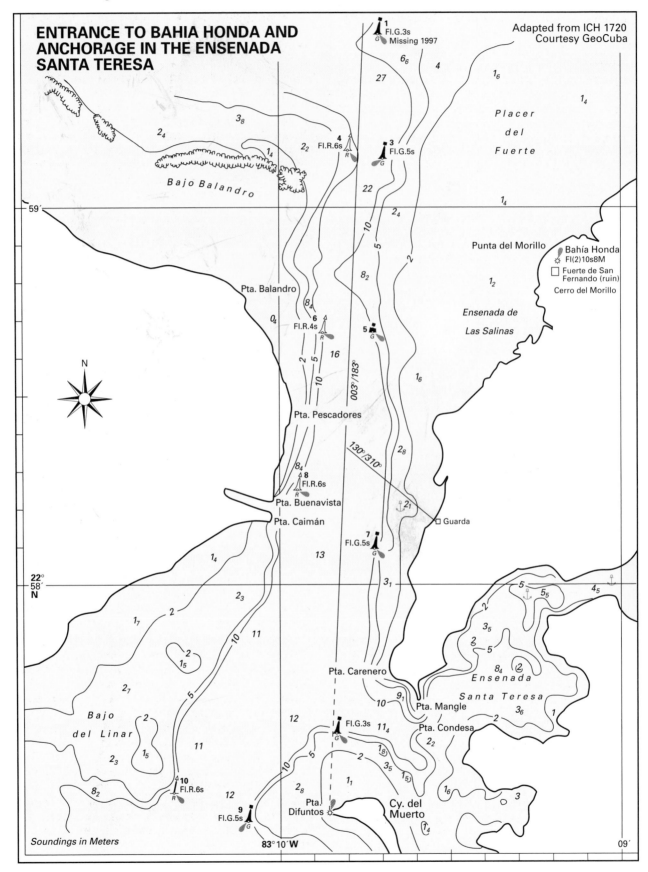

ENTRANCE TO BAHIA HONDA AND ANCHORAGE IN THE ENSENADA SANTA TERESA

Adapted from ICH 1720
Courtesy GeoCuba

1 Fl.G.3s
G Missing 1997

6₆   4

27   1₆   1₄

3₈   *Placer*

2₄   *del*

4 Fl.R.6s   **3** Fl.G.5s   *Fuerte*

1₄   2₂   R   G

Bajo Balandro   22

10   2₄

─59′─   1₄

8₂   Punta del Morillo   Bahía Honda
Fl(2)10s8M

Pta. Balandro   5   Fuerte de San Fernando (ruin)
1₂   Cerro del Morillo

0₄   8₄   2   *Ensenada de*
Las Salinas

6 Fl.R.4s   **5** Fl.G.5s
R   G

2   5   16   1₆

10

Pta. Pescadores

2₈

8₄   **8** Fl.R.6s
R

Pta. Buenavista   2₁

Pta. Caimán   □ Guarda

1₄   **7** Fl.G.5s
G

13

3₁

22°   5   5₅   4₅
58′
N   2₃   2   3₅

1₇   2   11   2   5

10   8₄   2

2   2   *Ensenada*
1₅

2₇   *Santa Teresa*

Bajo   2   9₁   Pta. Mangle   3₆   1

del Linar   5   10   2

1₅   12   **9** Fl.G.3s   11₄   Pta. Condesa
G   2₂

2₃   11   5   1₈

10   2   3₅   1₅

10 Fl.R.6s   2₈   1₁
R

8₂   12   1₆   3

9 Fl.G.5s   Pta.   Cy. del   1₄
G   Difuntos   Muerto

Soundings in Meters

83°10′W   09′

passaging to and from the Marina Hemingway along the north coast.

Approaches

Approaching the bay, the Punta Gobernadora lighthouse (at approximately 22°59·6'N 83°13·0'W; Fl.5s), a large red and white masonry light, is visible from many miles away. However, it should be noted that this lighthouse is 3M west of the entrance to the bay, and almost 1M inside the reef, so it should be used for orientation only, and not for a landfall.

From the east, a crane at Punta Buenavista (on the west side of the entrance) is also visible from a number of miles off. As the bay is closed, a small hill on the east headland (Cerro del Morillo, 18m) is quite conspicuous, with the Bahía Honda light (Fl(2)10s) on its top (partly hidden by trees).

From the west Once the reef off the Punta Gobernadora lighthouse has been rounded, an eastward course should be held for another ½M, after which a course of 120° *or more* toward the Cerro del Morillo – the conspicuous hill on the east headland, on top of which is the Bahía Honda light (Fl(2)10s) – will keep you off the reef and bring you within sight of the entrance buoy (pay close attention to the bearing, since the current will tend to sweep you onto the reef).

Entry

The outer buoy, shown at approximately 22°59·5'N 83°09·7'W on the charts (green *No. 1*, Fl.G.3s), was missing in 1997. This meant that the first buoys that were visible were a red (*No. 4*, Fl.R.6s) and green (*No. 3*, Fl.G.5s) pair at a point where the channel narrows to less than 200m.

From the west, these buoys can be approached directly, staying ½M off the coast.

From the east, a direct approach cuts across a reef – *it is essential to approach the bay ¼M to the north of the two buoys, and not to turn south until these are more or less due south.*

From these buoys, the bay is entered on a heading of 183°, making whatever allowance is necessary for the tide. The channel is more than 200m wide with another pair of buoys ½M further in (the red *No. 6* has a light, Fl.R.4s, but the green *No. 5* is unlit), and a red and green pair (*No. 8* Fl.R.6s and *No. 7*, Fl.G.5s) ½M beyond these. At night a pair of range lights (Q and Fl.6s) indicate the 183° bearing down the channel. Once inside the bay there are a number of other buoys and markers.

Checking in

The Guarda post is on a rickety wooden dock on the eastern shore a little more than ½M south of the Cerro del Morillo, and opposite a graveyard for old ships located on the western shore. The Guarda dock is in shallow water. To approach it, you should stay in the main channel until the dock bears 130°, and then come straight in for the north side of the dock. Approaching the dock, the water shoals quite rapidly down to 2m (a series of mooring buoys is set more or less on the 2m line), after which it shoals to 1·8m on the tip of the dock and along the outer end of the north side of the dock (the inner end is very shoal). Immediately north of the dock (10m) there is no more than a meter all the way out to a point parallel with the end of the dock, so when coming in come straight in on a course parallel to the dock, and just a meter or so off, and don't try any maneuvering in this area.

Boats with a deeper draft should pick up one of the moorings, or anchor out in the vicinity of the moorings, and wait for the Guarda to row out.

Anchorages

If the wind is at all out of the north, slight residual swells can make the vicinity of the Guarda dock somewhat rolly. A number of far more comfortable locations can be found in the bay.

An extremely well protected all-weather anchorage will be found by sailing around the point to the south of the Guarda post (Punta Carenero) into the Ensenada Santa Teresa. Punta Carenero is left 200m to port. Immediately to the SE, fronted by a sand beach, is Punta Mangle, at which point the channel becomes quite narrow. A clearly visible sandy shoal runs south from the tip of Punta Mangle, then deepens into a darker, grassy patch, after which there is another clearly visible patch of sand. The channel is immediately to the south of this (10m or so) and is 10m deep at this point. South of this, there is a moderately wide, gradually shoaling shelf, so if in doubt as to where you are, favor the south side of the channel rather than the north. Once past Punta Mangle a generally NE heading up the center of the bay clears all shoals. 2m can be carried to the north end of the bay and then up the canal to the east.

Note We tried anchoring in the Ensenada Santa Teresa, but at 2130 hours a siren went off, a spotlight picked us out, and a gunboat came alongside with orders to escort us back to the Guarda dock so that they could keep an eye on us. I hope you have better luck!

In recent months we have had reports that the Guarda are allowing boats to enter the bay and anchor at the southern end in 3m off a motel. The anchorage is at approximately 22°55·8'N 83°10·1'W. The motel has a bar and water, and offers access to town. The final approach to the anchorage passes between the Bajo del Medio (it will be to the east) and a wreck (it will be to the west).

Archipiélago de los Colorados

The Archipiélago de los Colorados, and its associated reef, the Arrecifes Colorados, stretches in a broad arc for almost 120M between Punta Gobernadora (3M to the west of Bahía Honda) and Cabo San Antonio (the western tip of Cuba). At Punta Gobernadora the reef is less than a mile offshore; at Cabo San Antonio it is almost 25M out from the town of La Fé. Behind the reef the coastline is indented by numerous bays, with the relatively shallow waters between the reef and the coastline containing numerous small cays, most of which consist of mangroves and are not very interesting, but one or two of which are lovely.

It is possible to enter and exit the reef at numerous breaks (*quebrados*) of which only a few of the more useful are covered in this guide. It is also possible to carry a 1·8m draft through the relatively sheltered waters behind the reef from the Quebrado de la Mulata, 13M to the west of Bahía Honda, all the way to Cabo San Antonio, with the exception of one short stretch (approximately 6M) around Cayo Jutías, where it is necessary to come outside the reef. This makes it possible to passage this stretch of the coastline in relative comfort in just about any conditions, with any number of secure anchorages along the way, although it should be noted that in many places the reef is partially submerged and as a result is an imperfect barrier to swells sweeping in from offshore.

Inland, the mountains of the Sierra de los Organos, although not particularly high, present an ever-present spectacular vista, with beautiful pastoral scenes on the lower slopes. The further west you progress the sparser and poorer the population. Aside from fish and lobster, you will find little in the way of supplies.

Morrillo

The small fishing town of Morrillo lies some 9M west of the Bahía Honda. Very deep water curves in to within a mile of the coastline at this point, with the reef on the one side heading offshore in a northeasterly direction, and on the other side running almost due west. Off Morrillo there is reportedly a passage through the reef which starts NW of Punta Morillo and runs in on a SE heading. Reportedly 2m can be carried in behind the reef. But from here a shoal obstructs the passage into the Ensenada de la Mulata, the bay to the west, so in order to enter the bay itself it is necessary to go back outside the reef and then come in again at the Quebrado de la Mulata.

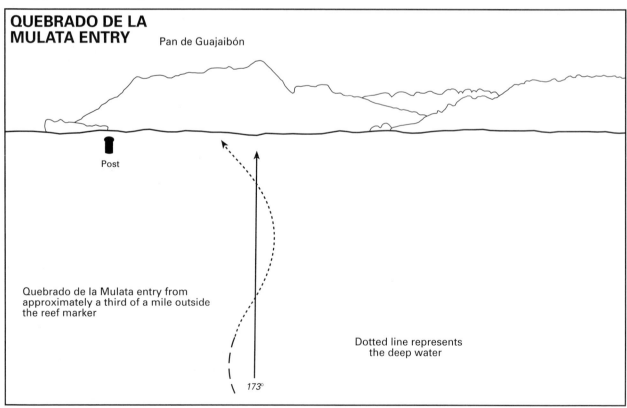

QUEBRADO DE LA MULATA ENTRY Pan de Guajaibón

Post

Quebrado de la Mulata entry from approximately a third of a mile outside the reef marker

Dotted line represents the deep water

173°

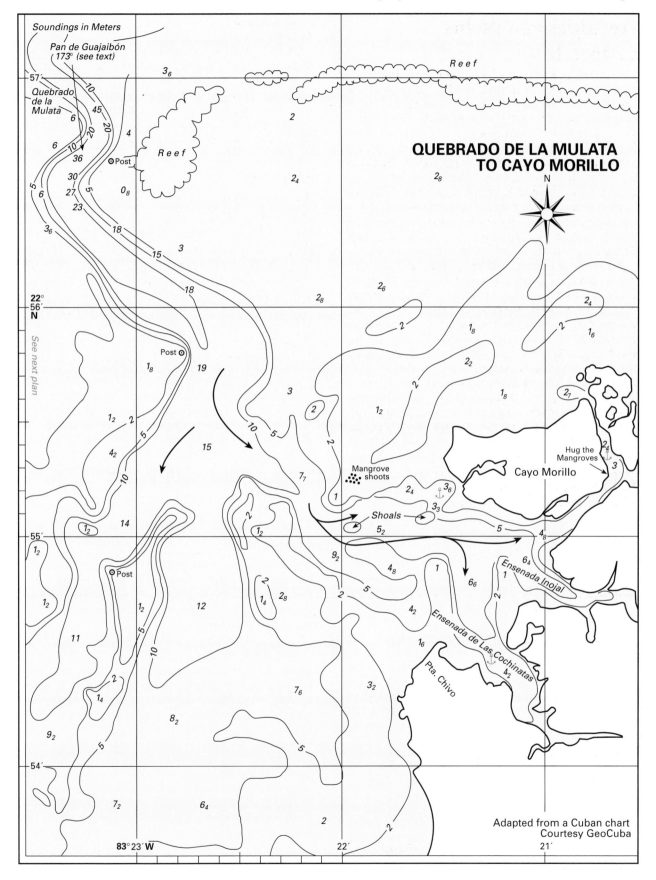

Soundings in Meters

Pan de Guajaibón
173° (see text)

Quebrado
de la
Mulata

Reef

Reef

⊙ Post

QUEBRADO DE LA MULATA
TO CAYO MORILLO

N

57'

22°
56'
N

See next plan

Post ⊙

⊙ Post

55'

54'

Mangrove
shoots

Shoals

Cayo Morillo

Hug the
Mangroves

Ensenada Inojal

Ensenada de Las Cochinatas

Pta. Chivo

Adapted from a Cuban chart
Courtesy GeoCuba

83°23'W

22'

21'

Quebrado de la Mulata

This is a straightforward, deep and wide, marked reef entry which can be transited in any conditions, and is preferable to the more popular unmarked Cayo Paraíso channel 2M to the west (which is relatively shoal and narrow, and can be extremely rough).

Passage through the reef

From the outside, you should take up a position at approximately 22°57·6'N 83°23·4'W which is about a mile north of the break in the reef. The western peak of the conspicuous Pan de Guajaibón mountain will be bearing approximately 173°. You should come in for this peak (173°) until you pick out a post on the reef (it will be off to port at 22°56·7'N 83°23·2'W). The deep-water channel (45m) actually makes a dogleg during the course of this mile in to the post, and on the 173° heading you will likely clip both sides of the channel, with the depths on each side rapidly shoaling to 6m but then leveling off. With the right light you can pick out the deep water and weave slightly to stay in center channel.

The post itself is in shoal water, with depths of less than 6m extending westward from it a good 50m, after which the channel rapidly deepens to over 30m. The channel itself is well over 100m wide, so leaving the post about 100m to port (i.e. you pass to the west of it) should put you in center channel. Once past the post, the main channel, which continues to be wide and deep (15–20m) curves gently around to the SE to leave another concrete post (approximately a mile inside the reef) to starboard (i.e. the channel passes to the east of the post). The channel forks at this point, with the SE fork leading to several excellent anchorages (see Cayo Morillo and Ensenada de las Cochinatas below) while the SW channel winds its way around to Cayo Paraíso (see Quebrado de la Mulata to Cayo Paraíso below).

From the inside, simply come north past the post on the reef, leaving it 100m to starboard (i.e. passing to the west of it) and then follow the deep-blue water. If the light is not adequate to eyeball the depths, take up a heading of 353° until 1M north of the reef (this will clip both sides of the deep-water channel, but minimum depths should be 6m or more).

Cayo Morillo and Ensenada de las Cochinatas

Excellent, protected anchorages can be found just to the west of Cayo Morillo; between Cayo Morillo and the cay immediately to its east; and in the Ensenada de las Cochinatas.

Approaches

To get to all three anchorages, after entering the reef via the Quebrado de la Mulata, follow the main channel down to the post 1M to the SE and then take the SE channel. After ½M or so you will be able to pick out a clump of mangrove shoots (currently just a few centimeters high) approximately ½M to the west of Cayo Morillo. These are close to the tip of a shoal that comes all the way out from Cayo Morillo. Leave these a minimum of 100m to port (i.e. pass to the west of them).

Anchorages

At this time you can curve around to the east into the lee of Cayo Morillo, or else head a little further south and then come due east, continuing either up the channel between Cayo Morillo and the mainland into the extremely sheltered anchorage shown on our plan, or else turning south into the Ensenada de las Cochinatas. In any event, note the extensive shoals extending northward almost ½M on either side of the Ensenada de las Cochinatas, and the couple of isolated shoal patches to the west of the southern edge of Cayo Morillo.

If going up the channel between Cayo Morillo and the mainland, note the extensive shoal that comes out from the north shore (it is marked with some stakes) about midway to the fork, and then at the point where the channel forks and you turn northward, hug the mangroves on the northern side of the channel to avoid an extensive shoal that comes out from the south shore.

Quebrado de la Mulata to Cayo Paraíso

There are numerous potential routes between the reef entry at Quebrado de la Mulata and Cayo Paraíso, but there are also numerous potential shoals and pitfalls. We have surveyed three routes which are as follows:

Along the reef

From the post at Quebrado de la Mulata, take up a heading of 242° directly to the southern tip of Cayo Paraíso. Minimum depths are 2·4m. There are isolated coral patches close to the Quebrado de la Mulata, but we found none near the surface. Nevertheless, keep a good bow watch. About halfway to Cayo Paraíso an extensive shoal area will be seen immediately to the south – stay north of this. Depending on the sea state outside the reef, the second half of this passage can be uncomfortable since substantial swells sometimes come in from the north.

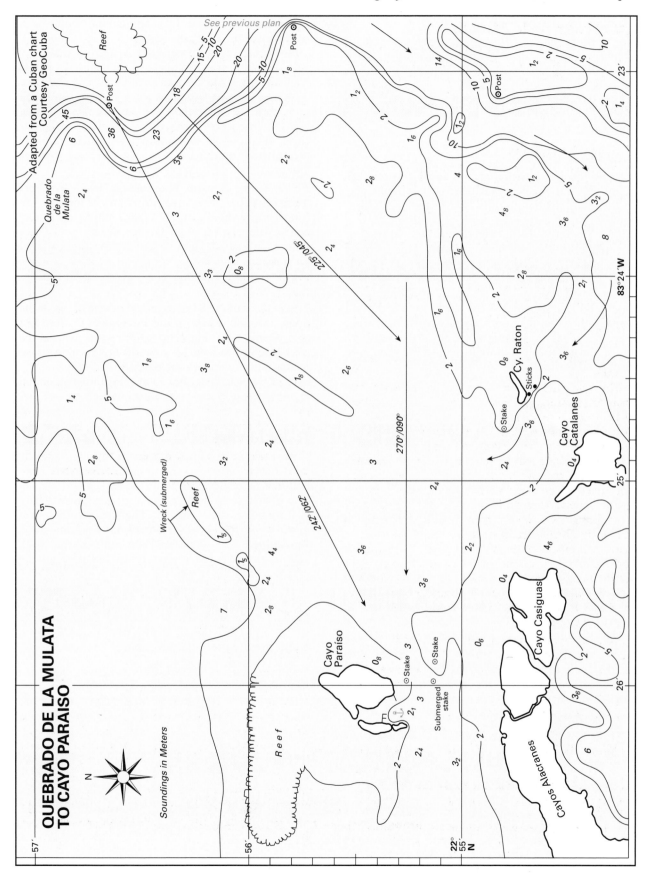

QUEBRADO DE LA MULATA
TO CAYO PARAISO

Soundings in Meters

N

Adapted from a Cuban chart
Courtesy GeoCuba

Reef

See previous plan

15—5
—10
—20
20
5—10
1₈
Post

Post

14

10
5
Post

10

1₂
2
5
10

23′

1₂

Quebrado
de la
Mulata

45
6
36
23
18
3₆
6
6
2₄

1₂
1₆

2₂

2₈
2
10
2

4

1₂
2
5

3₂

2₇

3

4₈
3₆
8

83°24′W

0₈
2

3₃

2₄

2

2₈

2₁

5

1₈

2₄

2₄
1₈
2₆

2
1₆

2

2

0₈
Cy. Raton
Sticks
⊙Stake
3₆

2
3₆

25′

Cayo
Catalanes

0₄

1₄

5
3₈

3

225°/045°

270°/090°

2₈
1₆
1
3₂
2₄
3

Wreck (submerged)

Reef

1₅

7

242°/062°

3₆

3₆

2₂

2₄

2

2

4₆

0₄

Cayo Casiguas

5
5
1₅
4₄
2₄
2₈

Cayo
Paraiso
0₈
⊙Stake 3
⊙Stake

Submerged
stake

0₆

2

3₆

26′

F

2₁ 3

2₄

2

3₂

6

Cayos Alacranes

Reef

57′

5′

56′

22°
55′
N

53

Further inside the reef

For a more protected passage, from the post at Quebrado de la Mulata continue ¼M south. Then head SW until the southern tip of Cayo Paraíso is more or less due west, after which you go straight to Cayo Paraíso. Minimum depths are once again 2·4m. About midway care will have to be taken to stay north of a shoal area.

Well inside the bay

This is the most sheltered and most complicated route. From the post at Quebrado de la Mulata, stay in the main channel until it forks at the post 1M to the SE. Now head to the north of another post that will be seen 1M to the SW. From here work your way to a point ¾M SE of Cayo Ratón. Once around the shoal that extends SE from this cay come NW leaving the two stakes off Cayo Ratón immediately to starboard (come 20m to the west of the stakes; keep a good bow watch – the depth here is a scant 2m and the channel is narrow). Leave the next stake also to starboard, coming north until the southern tip of Cayo Paraíso is more or less to the west, and then head for it.

Cayo Paraíso

Cayo Paraíso is a lovely little crescent-shaped cay with a protected anchorage, a gorgeous sand beach, and some interesting snorkeling in the surrounding waters. Ernest Hemingway used it as a base for anti-submarine patrols in the Second World War, and subsequently as a hideaway. For some reason, in 1997 and 1998 the Guarda intermittently banned boats from stopping here.

Approaches

From the east, the closest approach is from outside the reef via a break to the NE of the island. This is a north to south entry, starting at a spot at approximately 22°57·0'N 83°25·5'W and coming due south until due west of the northern tip of Cayo Paraíso, then heading SW to pass between the two stakes to the south of the island (note that the shoal off the southern tip of the island extends both south and west of the northern stake).

However, this is a potentially dangerous reef entry since breaking seas can occur in the 'channel' where it shoals to less than 3m. In addition, if you stray just a little to the east you hit a patch of hard sand with just 1·5m over it (it has been hit by a number of boats) while to the west is a great deal of shallow coral. If any seas are running, we would strongly recommend entering or exiting the reef via the Quebrado de la Mulata (see above).

From Cayo Levisa The passage inside the reef from Cayo Levisa is straightforward so long as you can clear the shoal patch (a scant 1·8m at low water) just to the east of Cayo Levisa (see below). Once clear of this shoal, simply head for the south side of Cayo Paraíso.

Anchorage

The water shoals to well under 2m well short of the dock, and also shoals on the east side of the bay, but it is deep (2·4m) right up to the sand spit on the west side of the bay. So you will not be able to get tucked up too far into the bay, and will need to stay over to the west side, but in any case the protection is pretty good in most circumstances.

Cayo Levisa

Cayo Levisa is mostly mangroves, but with a lovely sand beach on its northern shore which has been half-heartedly developed into a palapa-style beach and dive resort, with a bar and restaurant where visiting sailors are welcome. The water to the north of the cay is too shoal for boats (but has some good snorkeling), so a dock has been built on the south side of the cay and a short path cut through the mangroves to the resort.

This is another pleasant stop, with numerous potential spots in which to anchor and good protection in most circumstances, although once again in 1997 and 1998 the Guarda were intermittently putting it off-limits.

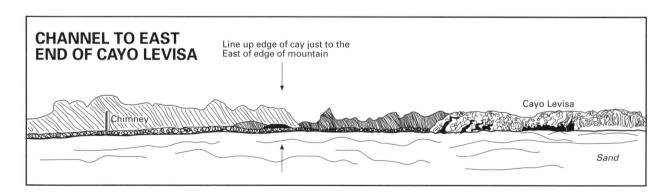

CHANNEL TO EAST END OF CAYO LEVISA

Line up edge of cay just to the East of edge of mountain

Chimney

Cayo Levisa

Sand

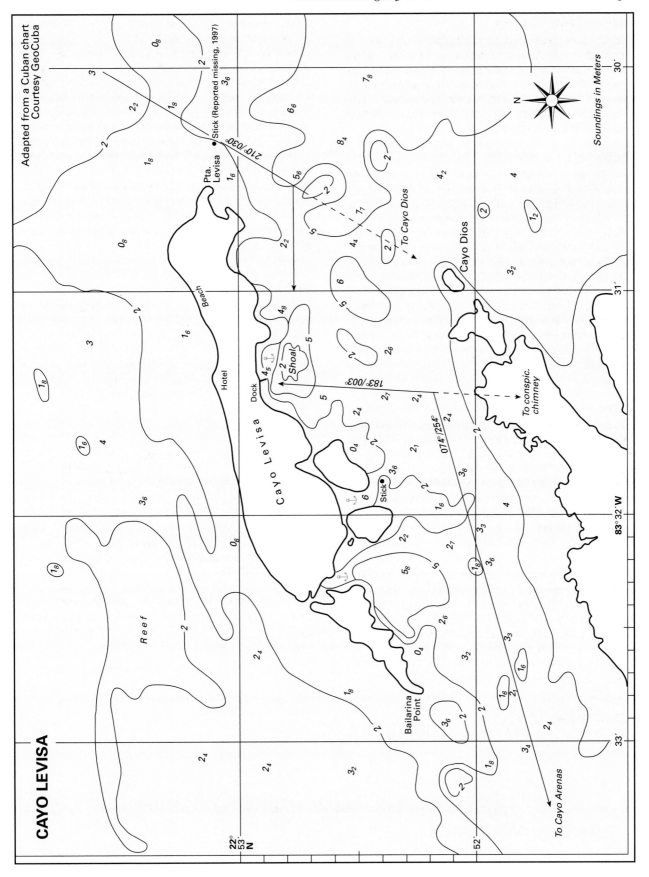

CAYO LEVISA

Adapted from a Cuban chart
Courtesy GeoCuba

Soundings in Meters

Pta. Levisa

Stick (Reported missing, 1997)

210°/030°

Beach

Hotel

Dock

Cayo Levisa

Shoal

Stick

074°/254°

183°/003°

To Cayo Dios

Cayo Dios

To conspic. chimney

Bailarina Point

To Cayo Arenas

Reef

22° 53' N

52'

83°32' W

30'

31'

33'

Approaches

From Cayo Paraíso, maintain a course to the WSW (246°) on a line between the southern tip of Cayo Paraíso and the northern tip of Cayo Levisa. The shallowest spot (2m) in the early stages will be found to the north of the western end of the Cayos Alacranes (you might need to jog north), after which you will find 3m or so until close to Cayo Levisa.

At Cayo Levisa there is an extensive shoal that comes ½M east from the tip of the cay, before deepening to about 1·8m at low water, and then shoaling again to form a distinctive white sand spit extending well to the east. As you approach the cay, you will be to the north of the white sand spit, but must turn SW where it ends in order to cross the 1·8m spot before finding deeper water once again.

You should make your turn to the SW at approximately 22°53·6'N 83°30·0'W when Cayo Dios (the nearest mangroves, which appear a little darker and higher than the rest) bears 210°. Head directly for Cayo Dios. At this time the western edge of Cayo Dios will be just to the east of an abrupt mountainside on the horizon (see sketch). You should keep Cayo Dios in this relationship to the mountain until ¼M south of the eastern tip of Cayo Levisa, and then head due west. Note that this course brings you down the edge of the shoal off Cayo Levisa; if you stray to the west you will clip this shoal. Note also that there are a couple of substantial shoals to watch out for as you enter the anchorage by the dock (see plan).

From the Quebrado San Carlos The Quebrado San Carlos is a straightforward, deep-water, all-weather reef entry. To find it come to a position at approximately 22°54·0'N 83°35·0'W, 1M outside the entrance, with the conspicuous peak shown in the sketch bearing approximately 175°, and then head toward the peak. After a bit you will pick out a buoy (at approximately 22°53·0'N 83°35·1'W) which is left 100m or more to starboard (i.e. you enter east of the buoy). From here, the channel is almost 200m wide, with 45m depths in the center, and runs more or less due south.

From the sea buoy head due south. You should be able to pick out some beacons 1½M to the south. There is one substantial one that is quite conspicuous, and another broken down one ⅓M to its west. Between the two is a shoal – you must pass *just to the west* of the broken down beacon. Once around this beacon, you will see another almost ⅓M to the south of the second beacon – the channel now runs between these two beacons and on to Cayo Levisa.

South of Cayo Levisa there are substantial fingers of shoal water extending up to ½M south of the island, while there are other shoals extending north from the mainland. To avoid these shoals, from a point midway between the last two beacons, head approximately 074° a little to the south of the center of the gap between Cayo Levisa and the mainland (the land immediately to the south of Cayo Levisa). Note that there is sometimes a tidal set across the channel, in which case an allowance will need to be made for it.

As you come south of the western tip of Cayo Levisa, you may clip a shoal extending out from the mainland, in which case make a short jog to the north. Another ⅔M further east you may clip a shoal extending south from Cayo Levisa, in which case make a short jog to the south. Finally, when the dock bears 003° come straight for it, making a slight jog to the west once inside the bay to avoid the edge of the shoal in the center of the bay.

Note There is another wide break in the reef to the

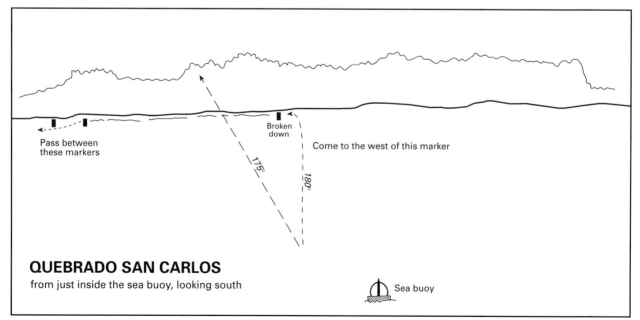

QUEBRADO SAN CARLOS
from just inside the sea buoy, looking south

Pass between these markers

Broken down

Come to the west of this marker

175° 180°

Sea buoy

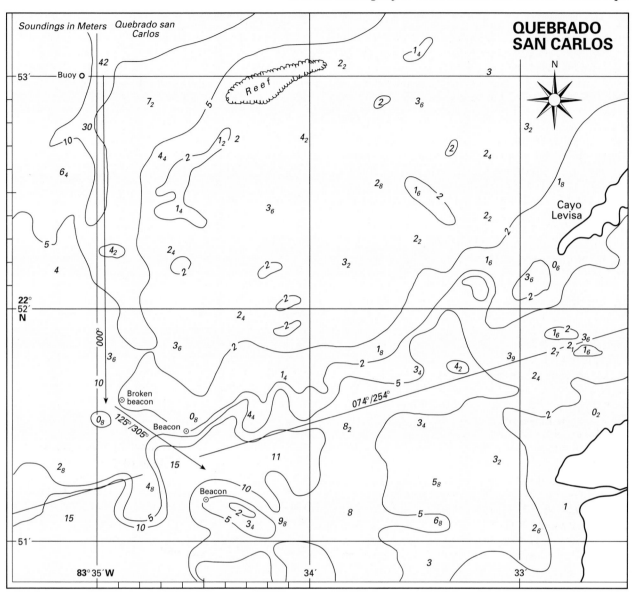

QUEBRADO SAN CARLOS

Soundings in Meters

Quebrado san Carlos

Adapted from a Cuban chart
Courtesy GeoCuba

CAYO ARENAS

Soundings in Meters

Adapted from a Cuban chart
Courtesy GeoCuba

west of the Quebrado San Carlos which is reportedly free of coral heads and easy to enter, but we have not checked it out.

From La Esperanza and Cayo Arenas Head north from La Esperanza across the Ensenada San Cayetano, watching for a shoal in the NE portion of the bay (at approximately 22°47·9'N 83°43·6'W). Note that the cay to the west of Punta Lavanaera extends ½M further east than is shown on the chart, with an additional ½M of shoal water to the east of this (the eastern tip of the shoal is at approximately 22°48·3'N 83°44·1'W). A course of 358° from La Esperanza to a position at approximately 22°48·0'N 83°43·8'W passes between these various shoal areas.

Leave Punta Lavanaera well to starboard (¼M or more – there are various shoals off the point), and

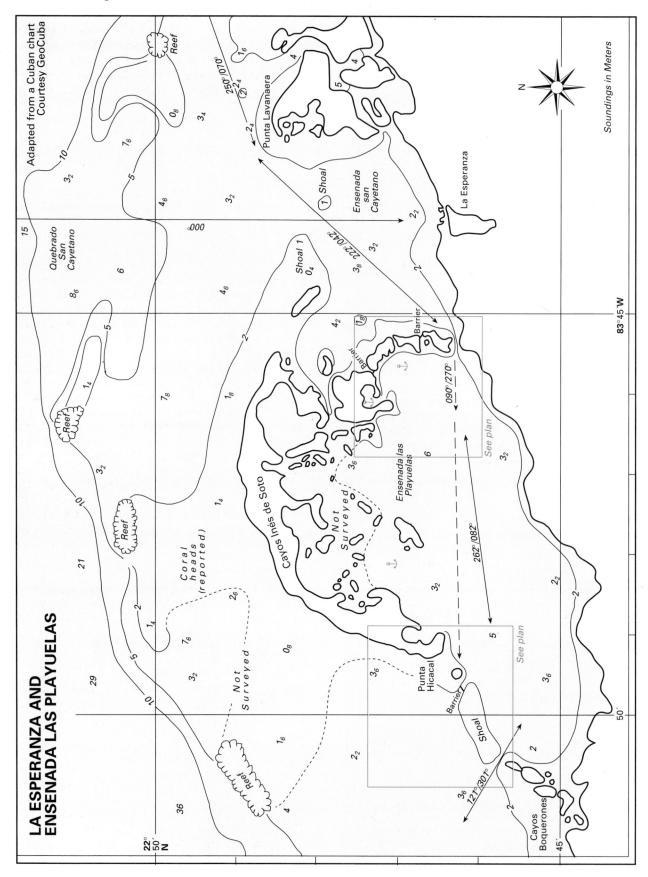

LA ESPERANZA AND ENSENADA LAS PLAYUELAS

Adapted from a Cuban chart
Courtesy GeoCuba

Soundings in Meters

then head directly for the southern tip of Cayo Arenas to pass south of the cay. South of Cayo Arenas there are extensive shoal areas but most seem to have 2m over them. However, you may have to pick your way through a little – we headed up into the bay on the south side of the cay and then back to the SE (to avoid the shoals at the eastern end of the island – see plan).

East of Cayo Arenas is another shoal area (clearly visible sand) which can be passed either to the north or south. After this head for the gap between Cayo Levisa and the mainland (the land immediately to the south of Cayo Levisa) until the inner channel beacons for the Quebrado San Carlos are visible, then continue as above (From the Quebrado San Carlos).

Anchorages

Most people anchor off the dock at Cayo Levisa. It is necessary to stay well off the shore since the depths are shoal out to the end of the dock and in a broad arc around the bay. You also need to watch out for the shoal in the center of the bay. However, 2m can be carried to the head of the dock. From the dock a boardwalk leads to the hotel.

An extremely well protected anchorage will be found around the headland to the west, in a deep bay with 6m depths. The entrance, however, is narrow and not marked, so you will need to feel your way inside. On the inside, it is deep almost everywhere right up to the mangroves.

La Esperanza

La Esperanza is a quiet little fishing town, now with several private restaurants, which is home to a small fleet of quite substantial fishing boats, and various service facilities (including a marine railway with adjacent workshops). It is possible to anchor north of the main dock (watch out for a couple of shoals in this area) and to dinghy in to the dock, but this location is wide open to the north. In unsettled weather a more comfortable anchorage will be found inside the Ensenada las Playuelas (see below), although this was another area intermittently put off limits in 1997 and 1998.

Approaches

From Cayo Levisa From the dock at Cayo Levisa take up a heading of 183° directly toward the conspicuous chimney on the mainland, making a slight jog to the west to clear the shoal south of the dock. Continue toward the chimney until the center of Cayo Arenas bears 254° (at which point you will be within ¼M of the mainland, and the water will be shoaling to 2·4m). Now head directly for Cayo Arenas, making whatever allowance is necessary to counteract any tide set.

After ½M this course clips a shoal extending south from Cayo Levisa – you may need to jog to the south – and then another ⅔M later it clips a shoal extending to the north from the mainland – you may need to jog to the north. By now you should be able to pick out two beacons ahead, with the south side of Cayo Arenas pretty much centered between them. Come straight for this south edge of Cayo Arenas until within ¾M of the cay. Here you will run into a sandy shoal which can be passed either to the north or the south.

Cayo Arenas is passed on its south side. The water is somewhat shoal – a certain amount of weaving may be necessary. After clearing the shoal to the south of the eastern tip of the island, we headed up into the bay on the south shore and then back out to the SW (to clear the shoal at the western end). From Cayo Arenas it is a clear run to a point ½M or so to the north of Punta Lavanaera (approximately 250°; Punta Lavanaera is not the northernmost point of land, but the first headland which can be picked out to the south of this northernmost point).

Give Punta Lavanaera a wide clearance since the bottom is very irregular well out to sea, with sudden shoal patches, and continue past it until almost due north of La Esperanza (at approximately 22°48·0'N 83°43·8'W). Then head for La Esperanza, or, for a sheltered anchorage, take up a heading of approximately 222° for the SW corner of the Ensenada San Cayetano and the east pass into the Ensenada Las Playuelas (see below). Note that there is a substantial shoal (at approximately 22°47·9'N 83°43·6'W) in the Ensenada San Cayetano which will have to be avoided, while the cay to the west of Punta Lavanaera extends almost ½M further east than is shown on the chart, with a shoal extending almost another ½M to the east of the cay (the east tip of the shoal is at 22°48·3'N 83°44·1'W).

From the Quebrado San Cayetano The Quebrado San Cayetano is ½M wide, with deep water on the approach shoaling rapidly to 6m and then very slowly shoaling as you work south. It is a straightforward reef entry, starting at a point at approximately 22°51·8'N 83°43·8'W and heading due south for La Esperanza, passing through a point at approximately 22°48·0'N 83°43·8'W. This is midway between the shoal extending from the cay to the west, and a shoal patch to the east.

From Santa Lucía It is not possible to pass inside the reef north of the Cayos Inés de Soto, so it is necessary to either go outside the reef, or to come through the Ensenada las Playuelas. If doing the latter, once clear of the entrance buoys to the dredged channel at Santa Lucía, simply come to the NE and then the east, more or less midway between the mainland and the reef (give the various headlands a wide clearance since there are some shoal spots well offshore), finally heading for the tip

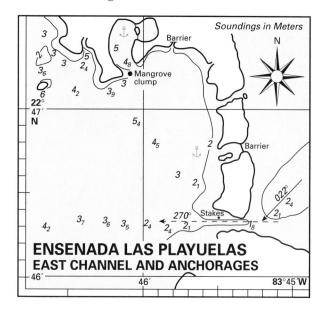

ENSENADA LAS PLAYUELAS
EAST CHANNEL AND ANCHORAGES

of the Cayos Boquerones and the west channel into the Ensenada las Playuelas (see below).

Ensenada las Playuelas

The Ensenada las Playuelas is an extremely sheltered bay enclosed on all sides with mangrove cays (the Cayos Inés de Soto), with narrow channels providing access at the SE and SW corners. Inside

there is much deep water with any number of potential anchorages. The controlling depth for transiting the bay is 1·8m at low water (the east end of the east channel).

Approaches

The east channel from the east Come SW across the Ensenada Cayetano into the corner of the bay (at approximately 22°46·3'N 83°45·2'W). You will appear to be running straight into the mangroves, but in the final stretch the channel will open up. The last 100m or so the depths will shoal to 1·8m at low water (the controlling depth). As the channel opens up, you will see an isolated cay on the horizon (which is actually an uncharted cay to the south of Punta Hicacal, see plan), and if you look carefully you will also see a couple of short stakes a little more than halfway through the channel. You should line up these stakes in front of the cay (a bearing of approximately 270° – see sketch) and then head directly for the cay, leaving the stakes 10–20m to starboard (i.e. passing to the south of them). The depths will go to 3 or 4m, and then shoal out once again to 2m beyond the stakes before deepening in the bay. Maintain the heading for the cay until well beyond the stakes (200m or more). After that, you are free to come north if simply looking for a place to anchor, or you can continue across the bay on a heading of 262° if going to Santa Lucía.

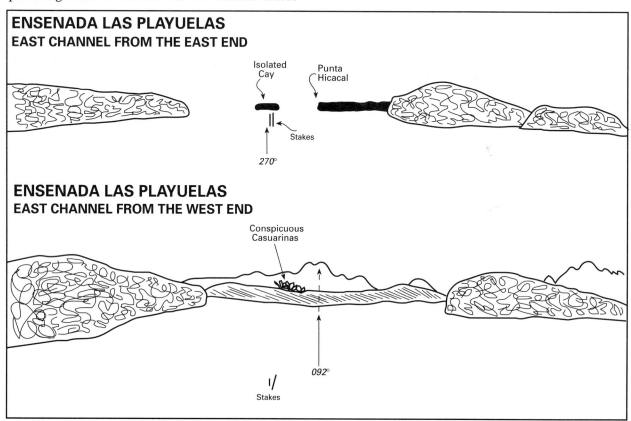

ENSENADA LAS PLAYUELAS
EAST CHANNEL FROM THE EAST END

ENSENADA LAS PLAYUELAS
EAST CHANNEL FROM THE WEST END

The east channel from the west Approach the channel from more or less due west on a heading of 092° toward the northernmost peak on the horizon (see sketch). As you close the channel you will be able to pick out a conspicuous clump of casuarinas (Australian pines) sticking out above the mangroves in the middle distance. Align these just to the left (north) of the peak, and then come through the channel headed for the casuarinas, leaving the stakes 10–20m to port (i.e. passing to the south of them). Once well past the mangroves that line the northern side of the channel, curve up to the NE (or you will run into quite shoal water).

The west channel from the east The west channel is 100m or so to the north of the Cayos Boquerones. It is marked with a stake more or less at its eastern end. To find the channel come to a position at approximately 22°45·7'N 83°50·5'W, and then pass through on a heading of 301°, leaving the stake 20m to starboard (i.e. passing south of the stake). If you look astern you will see a conspicuous escarpment in the mountains which will be on a back-bearing of 121°. You should keep it on this back-bearing until well out the other side (you may

need to compensate for a tidal set). Minimum depths are about 2·4m at both ends, rising to 6m in the center.

The west channel from the west You should approach the tip of the Cayos Boquerones more or less from the NW. You will see a conspicuous escarpment in the mountains. You should bring this onto a bearing of 121°, at which point you should be able to pick out a stake a little to the left (north) of the mountain (see plan). Come through the channel directly for the mountain (121°), leaving the stake 20m to port (i.e. passing to the south of it) and making any corrections necessary to compensate for leeway.

Anchorages

There is a great deal of deep water inside the Ensenada las Playuelas and innumerable potential anchorages. We have made no attempt to survey the whole bay, but have simply picked out a couple of likely spots.

On the eastern side, in prevailing easterly winds it is only necessary to curve to the north after clearing the channel, to come east until the water shoals, and then drop the hook (soft grassy bottom). For the ultimate in protection, once at 83°46·0'W come due north until you can pick out an isolated mangrove clump. Maintain the north heading to clear the mangrove clump by 100m (passing to the east of it), continue until 50m or so past the clump, and then head WNW into the bay. This channel leads between substantial shoals into a totally enclosed bay with deep water (5m or more) over all of it.

On the western side, excellent protection can be found by simply coming inside the arc of the mangrove cays to the north. An especially protected bay with an easy entry and 3m inside lies immediately to the NNE of Punta Hicacal.

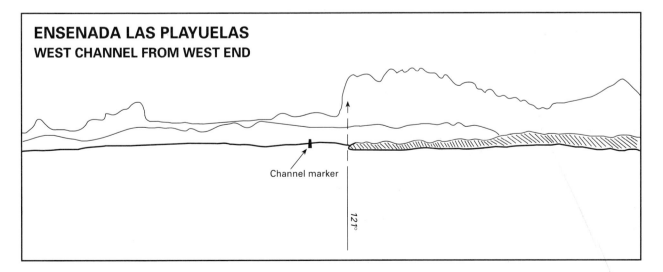

61

Santa Lucía

Santa Lucía is tucked into the south side of the Bahía de Santa Lucía. It is an industrial town, one of whose specialties is the manufacture of sulfuric acid which is shipped out from a small run-down terminal. Every once in a while the chimneys in the acid factory let out a burst of acid fumes. If you happen to be downwind, within five minutes you will be coughing and hacking like a bronchial old man. Asthmatics are likely to suffer an instant attack (this is no exaggeration).

The town is the most westerly port of entry on the north coast of Cuba, which is about the only conceivable reason you could have for going there. However, the officials have had little experience with yachts so the process may be quite protracted. Boats have to check in with the Guarda post, and can probably tie to their dock. From here it is possible to walk to 'town' which, in the area of the port, is small and decrepit. However, a turn to the left immediately after leaving the Guarda dock takes you into a street of picturesque houses, and then into the open countryside, with a Soviet-style new town on the horizon, backed by dramatic mountains. A short way along this road another road to the left takes you up a small escarpment to a second Guarda post with a great view over the surrounding mangroves and cays, and out to sea.

Approaches

From the east (Ensenada las Playuelas) Once clear of the west channel at the Ensenada las Playuelas, simply leave the various headlands well to port (½M or more). Note that when the wind is in the north, conditions can be quite rough since there is little offshore reef to break the seas (the middle bay that is passed through is aptly named the 'Ensenada Malas Aguas' – 'Bad Waters Bay'). After clearing Punta Tingo, the last major headland before Santa Lucía, you will be able to pick out two buoys to the SW. These mark the entrance to a dredged channel through an extensive shoal to seaward of Santa Lucía. If going to Santa Lucía, you need to approach these buoys on their north side in order to avoid this shoal, and then turn south down the channel (which is extremely well marked).

From the west (Pasa Honda) The relatively shallow and convoluted passage (Pasa Jutías) that used to exist between the Bahía de Santa Lucía, and the Ensenada Nombre de Dios (the next bay to the west) has now been blocked by a road so that the only way of getting to Santa Lucía from the west is to go outside the reef.

The two easiest reef passages to use to take you in and out are the Quebrado la Galera (see below) and the Pasa Honda. The Pasa Honda is well marked, but when heavy seas are running outside the reef, it can be extremely rough, with breakers running clear

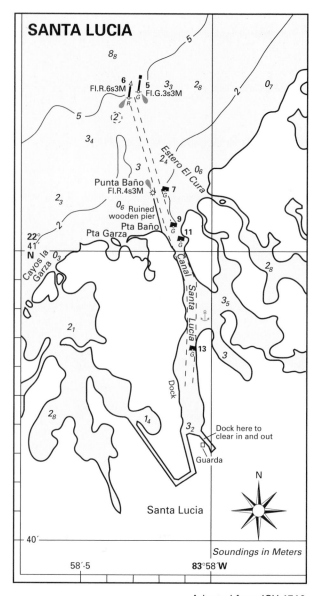

Adapted from ICH 1716
Courtesy GeoCuba

across the passage. It should therefore be considered a fair-weather pass. On its eastern side the reef extends well out to sea (to a point at approximately 22°46·5'N 83°57·8'W, which is 1½M NE of the outer channel marker, which in turn is at approximately 22°45·6'N 83°59·1'W). *If coming from the east on the outside be sure to clear the reef before turning south for the pass.*

To enter, come to a position at approximately 22°45·0'N 83°59·0'W. This is ½M south of the outer channel marker, and 2M NE of Cayo Restinga del Palo (which is not shown on chart ICH *1123*, but which is conspicuous). Head due south for 1M to pass between the two buoys marking the passage through the reef (red *No. 2* Fl.R.6s and green *No. 3* Fl.G.5s). Once inside, you will be able to pick up another buoy a little more than 1M to the SSE. This is left to starboard (i.e. you pass to the east of it). From here the two buoys marking the entry to the dredged channel into Santa Lucía will be clearly visible (another mile more or less to the south).

Note that there is another break in the reef between Cayo Jutías and Cayo Restinga del Palo (see plan). This is used by local fishermen. However, it is not marked and is relatively narrow. Except in calm conditions and good light, it is advisable to use the clearly marked Pasa Honda.

Entry

The channel into Santa Lucía is exceedingly well marked. After passing through the coastal shoal, you will see a couple of beat up docks (on the west side of the channel). Next comes a shoal on the west bank – at this point you hug the mangroves to the east (5m off). The channel then forks. You take the western fork, leaving another buoy to port, passing the loading dock for the sulfuric acid ships (on the west side of the channel), and arriving at a turning basin. The Guarda dock is immediately ahead as you reach the turning basin (down a short cul-de-sac; there will probably be a gun boat moored alongside). The dock has substantial rubber fenders, but take care since the outermost ones have various bits of steel sticking out!

Anchorages

Given the paucity of ship traffic in the port of Santa Lucía, the Guarda do not seem to mind people anchoring in the turning basin. Alternatively, there is plenty of deep water up the east fork of the channel into the port. The big problems in both locations are the mosquitoes and 'no-see-ums' (*jejenes* – biting insects which are small enough to pass through a mosquito net). We should know: Santa Lucía is where we were detained for 9 days by the Guarda!

Cayo Restinga del Palo

This cay is not shown on chart ICH *1123*, but is clearly visible from Santa Lucía, lying about a mile east of the east point of Cayo Jutías. The southern end of the cay consists of a lovely sand spit. In settled conditions you can anchor on either the east or west side of the cay, and snorkel the coral to the north.

Approaches and anchorages

A long, narrow shoal extends ½M due south of Cayo Restinga del Palo. In addition, there are extensive shoals to the NE and NW of the island. From Santa Lucía, the island is approached on a NW heading.

To anchor on the east side, simply leave the southern shoal, which in its later stages is quite

conspicuous white sand, to port. You can anchor 100m or so to the east of the southern tip of the island in a little over 2m.

To anchor on the west side, be sure to clear the southern end of the island by a ½M or more before heading north. The coastal shoal extends well out on this side of the island so you will not be able to get much closer than 200m off the beach.

Cayo Jutías

Cayo Jutías is home to the yellow-and-black striped Cayo Jutías lighthouse (Fl.15s), which is well worth a visit, with great views from the top (163 steps!) over the surrounding cays. The north side of the cay has a long beach.

Extensive shoals extend eastward from the NE tip of Cayo Jutías, and also line the eastern side of the cay a little further south. However, immediately to the SE of the tip of the cay, relatively deep water reaches almost in to the beach, forming a reasonably well protected anchorage off the beach, with the lighthouse just around the corner. The anchorage is approached on a heading of 302° for the lighthouse. A ¼M or so from the beach this course runs straight up on a conspicuous white sand patch. Just before this, turn to the west and anchor in something over 2m when 100m off the beach.

To get to the lighthouse you will need to take the dinghy, making a broad arc well offshore (200m or more) to avoid very shallow water, and then picking your way in directly toward the tip of the remnants of a steel jetty in front of the lighthouse. Note that although the anchorage is moderately protected in a norther, it will not be safe to take the dinghy to the lighthouse (the waves sometimes wash into the lighthouse keeper's house). However, you can walk around along a road behind the beach adjacent to the anchorage.

Ensenada Nombre de Dios to Cayo Buenavista

In this 25–30M stretch of coastline there is not a great deal of interest. Navigation is straightforward more or less dead center between the reef and the various cays or headlands jutting out from the coastline. The reef can be entered or exited at numerous breaks, of which the only two we cover are the Quebrado la Galera and the Pasa Roncadora (because both are clearly marked). There are plenty of potential anchorages amongst the mangroves – once again, in what follows we have just selected a few.

Reef entries

Quebrado la Galera A straightforward reef entry clearly marked with a buoy. To enter, come to a

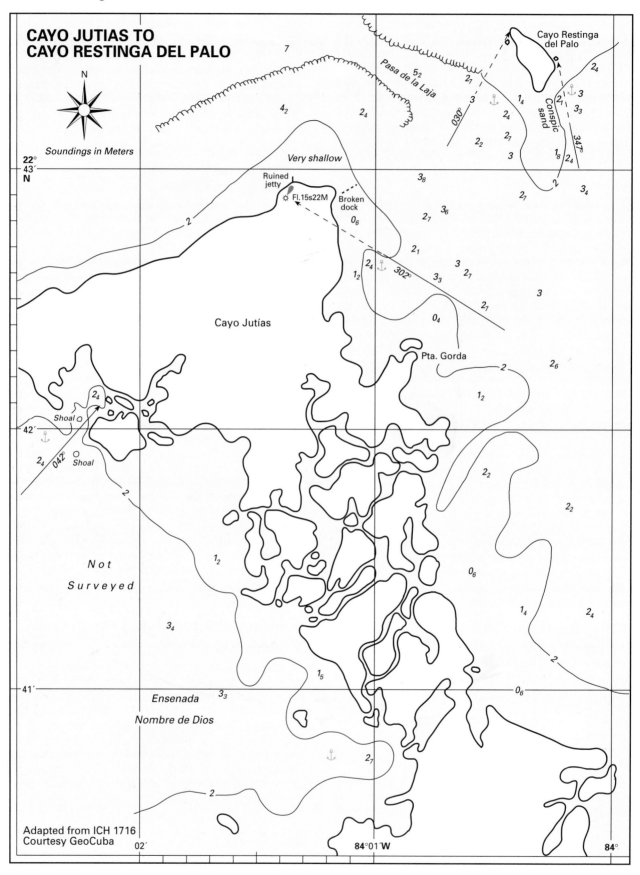

**CAYO JUTIAS TO
CAYO RESTINGA DEL PALO**

N

Soundings in Meters

22°
43′
N

Cayo Restinga
del Palo

Pasa de la Laja

*Conspic
sand*

Very shallow

Ruined
jetty

Fl.15s22M

Broken
dock

030°

347°

302°

Cayo Jutías

Pta. Gorda

Shoal

042°

Shoal

42′

*N o t
S u r v e y e d*

41′

Ensenada

Nombre de Dios

Adapted from ICH 1716
Courtesy GeoCuba

02′

84°01′W

84°

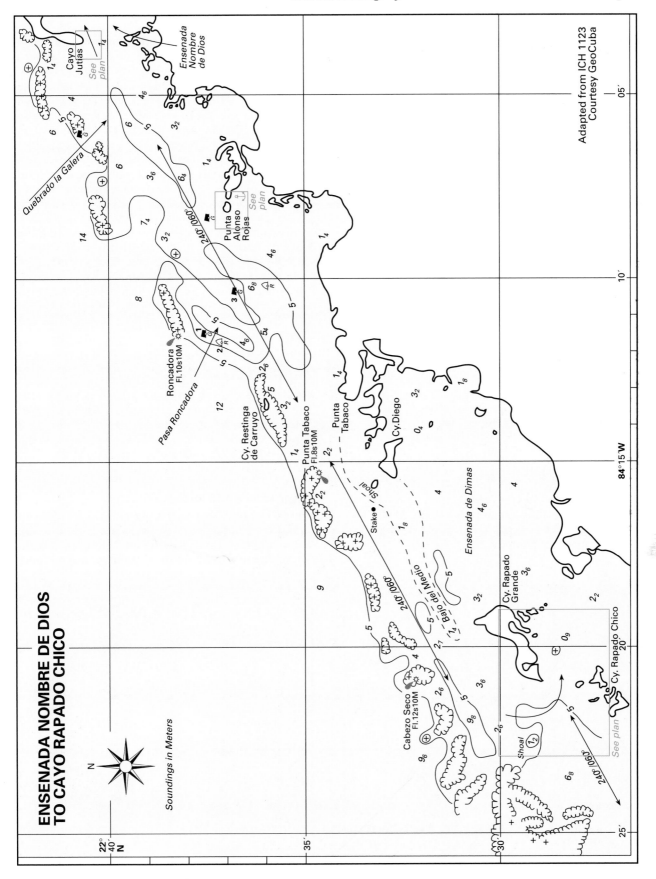

ENSENADA NOMBRE DE DIOS TO CAYO RAPADO CHICO

Soundings in Meters

N

Adapted from ICH 1123
Courtesy GeoCuba

position at approximately 22°41·4'N 84°06·7'W and sail in a southeasterly direction to leave the buoy at least 50m to port (i.e. pass to the west of it). Note that the buoy is toward the south side of the reef, on the eastern side of the entrance. If coming from the east, to avoid clipping the corner of the reef do not cut down toward the buoy until it bears 160° *or less*.

In settled conditions you can anchor behind the reef, which has some excellent snorkeling, but at night you would want to retreat to one of the anchorages described below.

Pasa Roncadora An exceptionally easy and well marked reef entry. Come to a position at approximately 22°37·8'N 84°12·6'W with the Roncadora light (Fl.10s) 1M off bearing approximately 060°. Proceed for 1M on a heading of 115° to pass midway between the two buoys (green *No. 1* and red *No. 2*). There is another buoy well inside the reef, but once through the two reef buoys there is plenty of water in just about any direction.

Ensenada Nombre de Dios

The Ensenada Nombre de Dios is a large bay, almost totally enclosed by mangrove cays. Since the construction of the causeway to Cayo Jutías, it can only be entered from the west.

Entry

Entry is straightforward, aiming for the southwestern tip of Cayo Jutías (easily distinguished by its white sand beach), and then continuing in on an easterly heading (at approximately 22°40·7'N) just to the south of the conspicuous sandy shoal which comes out from the tip of the cay.

Anchorages

The bay looks like it would have numerous well protected anchorages, but in fact most of the eastern shore is lined by a very extensive shoal, making it difficult to get close enough inshore to get out of the chop that sometimes builds up in late afternoon. We headed for the lighthouse after entering the bay (042° from the entrance), and found we could carry 2m almost into the mangroves, but the channel was narrow, somewhat tortuous, completely unmarked, and beset by shoals (not all of which are shown on our plan). We ran aground twice getting in, and then twice more coming out (even with the benefit of our plan!). It definitely wasn't worth the effort.

A better bet is to head due east after entering the bay, anchoring just before you run out of water – this will put you almost in the mangroves at the easternmost point of the bay. Alternatively, an easier anchorage to enter, with excellent protection, which is also more convenient for the Quebrado la Galera and Pasa Roncadora, is that behind Punta Alonso Rojas (see next entry).

Punta Alonso Rojas

At Punta Alonso Rojas a spit of land comes out to the west and then hooks to the south, creating a well protected anchorage within its arc. The point, however, is beset with shoals a good ¼M to the NW, with an additional isolated shoal ½M out. This latter spot is marked by a red buoy.

Approaches and anchorage

From the east, pass north of the buoy, or between it and the coastal shoal, and then arc around to the south and east, slowly closing the land until you are approximately 150m off the mangroves as you come

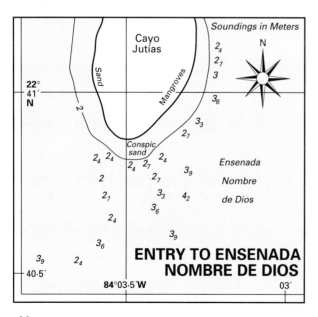

south of the cay. Then come to the NE and anchor in a little over 2m.

From the west, simply come due east, leaving the tip of the point 150m off, and then hooking to the NE to anchor.

Punta Alonso Rojas to Cayo Rapado Grande

The key to passaging through this stretch is to keep up toward the reef side of the channel. In the process you will come across a new cay (Cayo Restinga de Carruyo) developing out on the reef itself, a couple of miles SW of the Pasa Roncadora. This is worth a visit in settled conditions, heading directly toward the mangroves and anchoring when abeam of the startlingly white sand shoal immediately to the east.

A series of shoals extend well out from the mainland opposite Punta Tabaco light, including a cay which is incorrectly charted (it is a good ¼M SE of its charted position). Once again, stay well up toward the reef. In any case, Punta Tabaco light is another pleasant lunch stop worth a visit in settled conditions, in spite of the fact that there is nothing here but an exceptionally white sand bank and some lovely water colors. It is possible to come quite close to the light, but beware of an iron stake just sticking up above the water 50–100m to the west of the light.

Between Punta Tabaco and Cayo Rapado Grande there is a long shoal running parallel to the channel with depths of a little under, or a little over, a meter from time to time (Bajo del Medio). To avoid it, keep over toward the reef (on a line drawn from a point approximately ½M inside Punta Tabaco light to a point approximately 1M inside Cabezo Seco light).

Cayo Rapado Grande

The south coast of Cayo Rapado Grande offers protection in all conditions. On the SW tip there is a fishing station built on piles, but aside from this there is nothing to see but mangroves.

Approaches

From Punta Tabaco and the NE, the anchorages are approached by rounding the western end of the cay. You need to stay more than a mile to the north of the northern tip of Cayo Rapado Grande, since there is a very extensive shoal in this area. Once past this shoal, head SW. Another very extensive shoal extends almost ¾M to the SW of the cay so you will have to work down toward the northern tip of Cayo Rapado Chico in order to clear it. Note also the isolated shoal just over a mile to the west of Cayo Rapado Grande (Bajo la Vinagrera) – your track

should carry you between this shoal and the one coming out from the cay.

From Cayo Buenavista and the SW, Cayo Rapado Chico can be left either to port or starboard. In the latter case, when rounding the northern tip of Cayo Rapado Chico, stay over toward this cay in order to avoid the extensive shoal to the SW of Cayo Rapado Grande.

Entering the anchorage

The Cubans got the charting of the shoals on the southern side of Cayo Rapado Grande a little wrong. There is a mile-long shoal that extends almost from the western tip of the cay to the SE. The southern end of this shoal dries at low water. To get around it, you will have to come almost a mile south of the cay, hooking north once around the southern tip of the shoal. Alternatively, after rounding the shoal to the SW of Cayo Rapado Grande you can make a broad arc back up toward the fishing station, and then follow the coastline around to the east, staying approximately 100m off the mangroves. This will take you through a deep-water channel into a couple of very sheltered anchorages, protected in all conditions. At one point the channel narrows to a little more than 50m, with the tip of the shoal to the south marked by a stake. You should come past the stake about 10m to its north.

Cayo Rapado Chico

Cayo Rapado Chico is actually composed of several distinct cays. If approached from the western side, it is possible to work up between the cays in a number of places, providing excellent protection in most conditions. We have not, however, made a detailed survey of this cay – it will have to wait until a future edition.

Cayo Buenavista

Cayo Buenavista, so far as we could tell, does not have any fully protected anchorages. However, in settled conditions the south coast provides more than adequate protection from the prevailing NE and east winds.

The channel between Cayo Buenavista and the reef is relatively narrow (1M wide) but contains no hazards – you should simply keep ¼ to ½M off the cay. There is another passage (Pasa Santa María) between the east end of Cayo Buenavista and the mainland, but this is obstructed by a narrow shoal in its center part with just a meter of water over it.

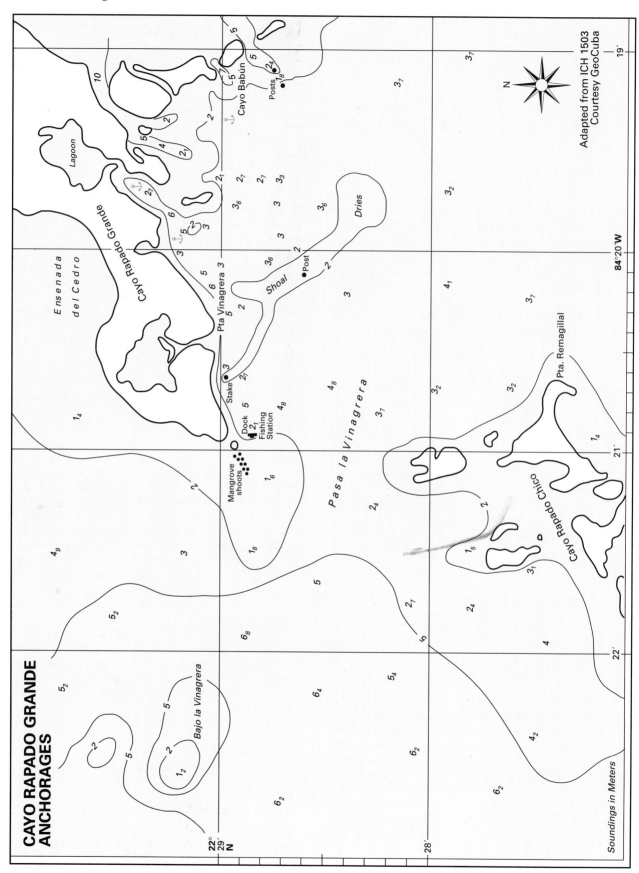

CAYO RAPADO GRANDE ANCHORAGES

Adapted from ICH 1503
Courtesy GeoCuba

Soundings in Meters

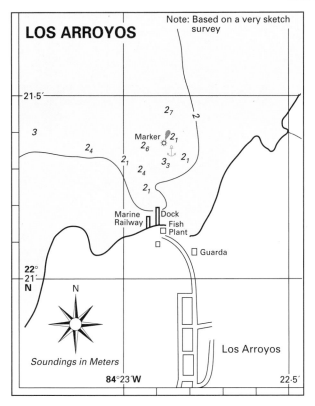

LOS ARROYOS

Note: Based on a very sketch survey

21·5′

3

2₇

2

Marker 2₁
2₆

2₄

2₁
2₄

3₃ 2₁

2₁

2₁

Marine
Railway   Dock
Fish
Plant

Guarda

22°
21′
N

N

Los Arroyos

Soundings in Meters

84°23′W   22·5′

Los Arroyos

Los Arroyos is a pretty little fishing town on the mainland, to the SE of Cayo Buenavista. It is worth at least a short visit, and an amble up the main street and back (which may take longer than you think since you will probably be stopped and engaged in conversation by a number of very friendly people!). Although the anchorage off the town is for all intents and purposes an open roadstead, it is well protected in prevailing NE and easterly winds, but is wide open to northers.

The approach should be made on an easterly heading for a point about ½M to the north of the town, with the final approach made on a southerly heading past the green channel marker (leave it to port) toward the dock. This is a busy fishing port with many boats at anchor and others coming and going at all hours of the day. Although 2m can just about be carried onto the dock, it would be better to anchor out in a convenient spot between the moored boats and then dinghy ashore. Note that some of the moored boats are in considerably less than 2m, while the bottom is somewhat irregular, so motor around slowly with a close eye on the depth sounder until anchored.

Golfo de Guanahacabibes

The Golfo de Guanahacabibes stretches from Cayo Buenavista to Cabo San Antonio. The coastline progressively recedes further from the reef, the further south you go, while the depths between the reef and the mainland gradually increase, so that the gulf encloses a substantial area which is almost completely free of hazards (with the exception of the Cabezos de Plumaje, more or less in the center of the southern half of the Gulf at approximately 22°05·7′N 84°30·4′W).

The outer perimeter of the reef is exceptionally well marked with a whole series of light structures generally no more than 5 or 6M apart. The reef itself is partially submerged for much of its length, with a number of distinct breaks which provide passages to and from the Gulf of Mexico. However, these passes are, for the most part, somewhat tortuous and narrow and have no aids to navigation. For this reason, since there is little need for anyone to enter and exit the reef in this stretch, we have ignored them (all but the wide-open entry at the southern end of the reef, by Cabo San Antonio).

On the inner edge of the reef there are numerous drying shoals, notably to the SW of Cayo Buenavista, some of which provide a fair measure of protection for snorkeling and diving trips, which are well worth making. These are, however, fair-weather, good-light anchorages. Fully protected anchorages are only to be found on the mainland, and these are few and far between – basically just the Ensenada de Anita, the Ensenada de Juan López (with the town of La Fé), and the Cayos de la Leña. All are covered below.

The mainland is mostly mangroves, although there are substantial stretches of beach from time to time. Inland are extensive stands of deciduous forest. The countryside is almost entirely deserted, with the scanty population concentrated in one or two small and isolated towns – this is very much the end of the road in Cuba.

Note that because of the somewhat confusing convention used to denote submerged coral, chart ICH *1122* shows numerous areas of apparently shallow coral throughout the center of the Golfo de Guanahacabibes. According to the Cuban pilot, however, there is at least 5m over everything, with the exception of the Cabezos de Plumaje already mentioned. But since we have not checked the central area of the Gulf, if sailing through this region, proceed with caution.

Ensenada de Anita

The Ensenada de Anita is a substantial bay at the north end of the larger Ensenada de San Francisco. A string of almost-connected cays, of which the

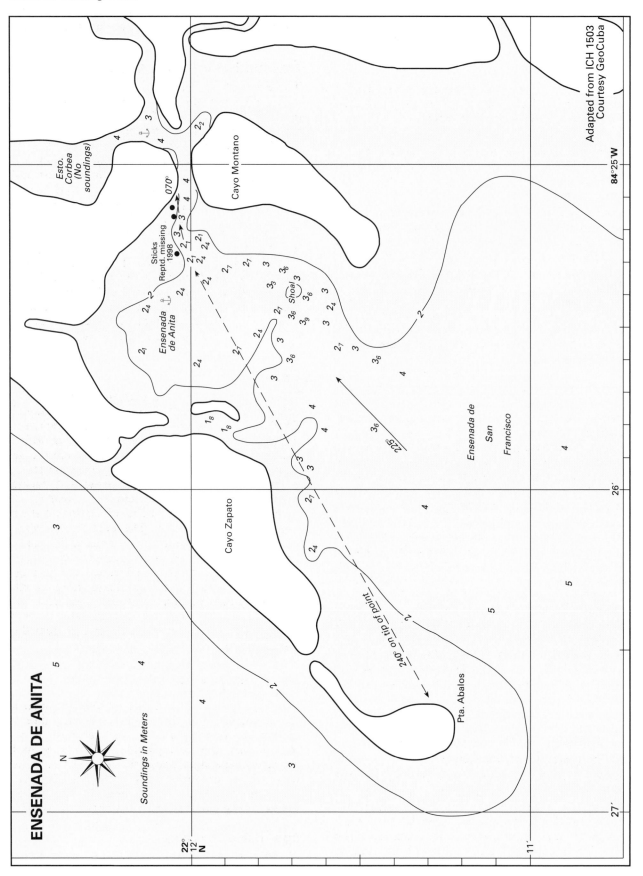

ENSENADA DE ANITA

Soundings in Meters

22°
12'
N

N

Esto.
Corbea
(No
soundings)

Cayo Montano

Sticks
Reptd. missing
1998

070°

Ensenada
de Anita

Shoal

Cayo Zapato

Ensenada de
San
Francisco

240° on tip of point

225°

Pta. Abalos

Adapted from ICH 1503
Courtesy GeoCuba

84°25'W

26'

27'

11'

largest is called Cayo Zapato, project toward the SW from the coastline, forming a funnel-shaped bay which is well protected from all but the SW.

Entry

From the north, clear Punta Abalos, at the southern tip of Cayo Zapato, by a little more than ¼M to avoid the shoal that extends to the west, south and east of the point.

From the south, entry is initially straightforward, up the middle of the bay, with no off-lying hazards.

Anchorage

Once past the southern tip of Cayo Montano you run into a series of shoals (not properly shown on the Cuban charts). There are no obvious landmarks to guide you around them. The best bet is to hook in toward Cayo Montano until the water shoals to about 2·5m, and to then curve to the north – this should carry you inside the mid-channel shoal (which already has several keel marks on it, including ours). You can anchor anywhere in the main body of the bay with excellent protection in most circumstances.

For total protection it is possible to carry 2m into the Estuario Corbea, a substantial land-locked lagoon, although the channel is narrow, poorly marked, and not straight. A certain amount of cautious feeling around will have to be done to get in. The procedure is as follows: once past the shoals at the mouth of the Ensenada de Anita, take up a position with the tip of the peninsula at the mouth of the Ensenada de San Francisco on a back-bearing of 240°. Head for the mangroves on the reciprocal course of 060°. As the depths shoal to just over 2m you should be able to pick out a stick (to call it a stake would be to exaggerate considerably!). This is left 20m or so to port (i.e. you pass to the south of it) at which point you arc around to a heading of 070° and should be able to pick out a couple more sticks dead ahead. Keep arcing around to also leave these 20m to port, at which point the depth will rapidly increase to first 3m and then 4m. From here you simply stay in mid-channel, curving around to the north. Since there is plenty of room to anchor in the entrance to the Estuario Corbea, we have not investigated further.

Ensenada de San Francisco to Ensenada de Juan López

In this stretch, a couple of shoals extend 1M offshore, notably immediately south of the Ensenada de San Francisco, and another 2M further south (south of Punta Pinalillo). A track outside of these shoals is free of all dangers. The coastline is almost all mangroves, with the notable exception of a sizable sandy beach, backed by coconut palms and casuarinas, at Punta Colorada.

Ensenada de Juan López

The Ensenada de Juan López is a substantial inlet which offers protection in all conditions and is also home to the tiny town of La Fé. The entrance is marked by a red and white buoy (at approximately 22°01·2'N 84°19·9'W), but in truth this is completely unnecessary since there are no hazards – you simply stay at least ½M off either coast and head in. The Bahía de Palencia, a cove to the south of the entrance buoy, offers good protection in prevailing winds, with 2m to within ¼M of the shore (except on the eastern side, where you should stay a little further off).

Once inside the Ensenada de Juan López, you should stay out of the bay to the south of La Fé (it is all shoal), and should avoid the shoal that comes out almost ½M from the western shore ½M or so south of La Fé (Bajo Algodonal). 2m can be carried 1½M past La Fé; you can anchor anywhere.

La Fé

There is not much to recommend about La Fé, unless you wish to see Cuban life at its poorest and simplest. The town was formerly an export point for timber, and has a substantial cement dock which was built for this trade, but currently there are no signs of activity. There is essentially one short street of tiny Cuban houses which soon peter out leaving you in the open countryside, and that's about it!

2m can be carried onto the tip of the dock, but we would not recommend it. The dock is very high, with a substantial steel fender running its entire length from which various bits of metal protrude at just the right height to foul lifelines and rigging. Much better to anchor off and dinghy in (although it will be quite a scramble to get out of the dinghy).

At night, unless you want friendly and curious visitors, it is best to move a mile or two from the town to anchor.

Cayos de la Leña

The Cayos de la Leña form an arc which encloses a sizable lagoon, but the lagoon is mostly pretty shallow and not suitable as an anchorage. Nevertheless, the cays provide a couple of well protected anchorages, one to the east and one to the west, just a few miles from Cabo San Antonio. These are excellent spots in which to prepare to round the cape, or rest up after a difficult passage.

Approaches and entry

On the east side of the cays the anchorage is in a

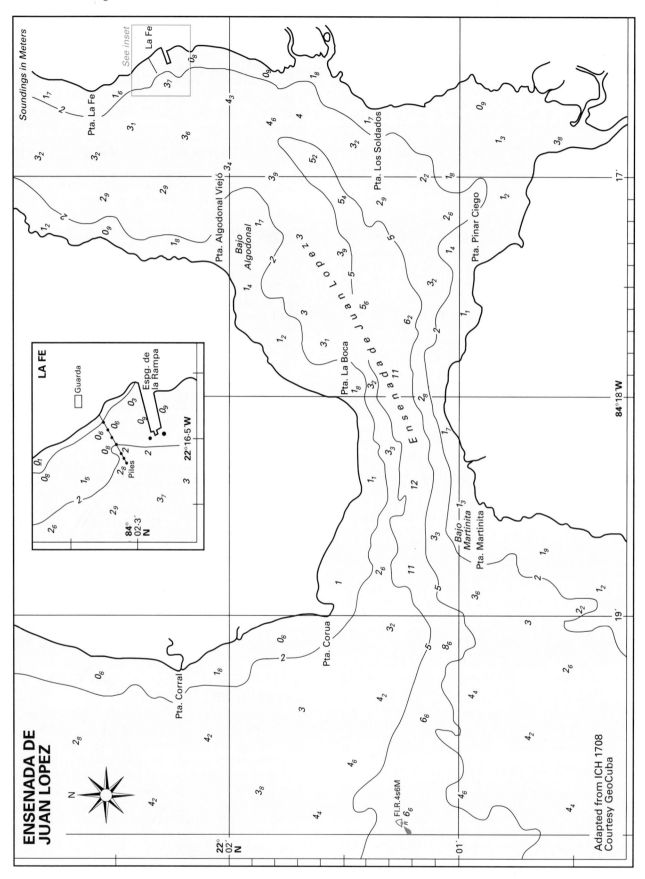

ENSENADA DE
JUAN LOPEZ

Soundings in Meters

LA FE

Guarda

Espg. de
la Rampa

Piles

84°
02·3'
N

22°16·5'W

Pta. La Fe

Pta. Algodonal Viejó

Bajo
Algodonal

Pta. La Boca

E n s e n a d a   d e   J u a n   L o p e z

Pta. Los Soldados

Pta. Pinar Ciego

Bajo
Martinita
Pta. Martinita

Pta. Corua

Pta. Corral

Fl.R.4s6M
R

Adapted from ICH 1708
Courtesy GeoCuba

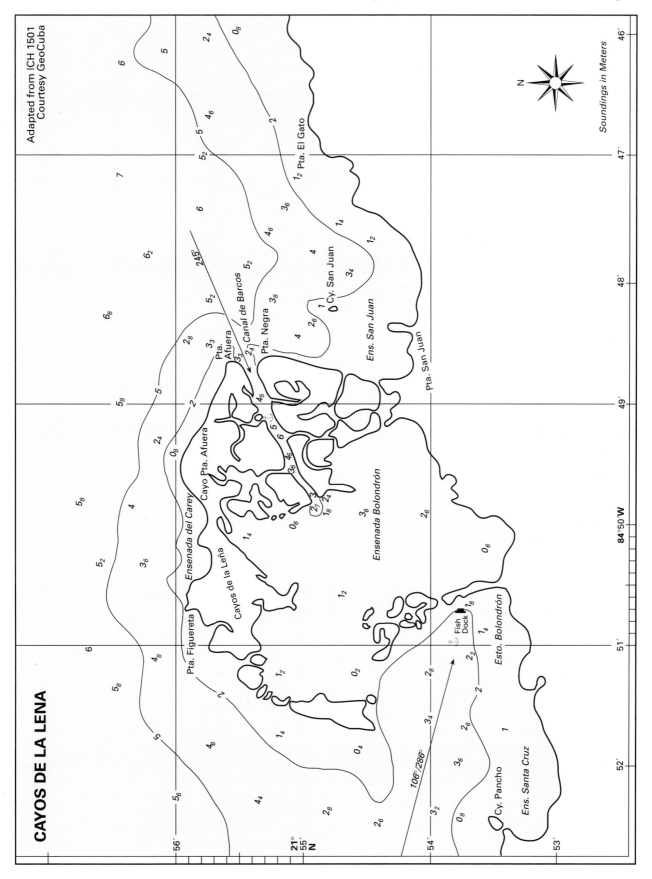

CAYOS DE LA LEÑA

Adapted from ICH 1501
Courtesy GeoCuba

Soundings in Meters

N

Pta. El Gato

Cy. San Juan

Ens. San Juan

Pta. San Juan

Canal de Barcos

Pta. Negra

Pta. Afuera

Cayo Pta. Afuera

Ensenada del Carey

Ensenada Bolondrón

Cayos de la Leña

Pta. Figuereta

Fish Dock

Esto. Bolondrón

106°/286°

Cy. Pancho

Ens. Santa Cruz

substantial (almost 200m wide) deep-water channel (the Canal de Barcos) which cuts through the mangroves to the lagoon. The canal has deep water along its entire length, with an easy, deep-water entry. It provides complete protection in any conditions.

On account of its width, the entrance to the canal (which is at approximately 21°55·5'N 84°48·5'W) is easy to see from some distance out. The canal is entered on a heading of 245°, aiming for a point a little to the south of center channel. Once inside, you can anchor anywhere.

On the west side of the Cayos de la Leña 2m can be carried all the way down to a fishing station built on piles in the SE corner of the bay. The dock itself has a scant 2m alongside. Protection is excellent in prevailing winds, but the bay is wide open to northers.

The dock is approached on a heading of 106°, directly on a line drawn between it and Punta Cajón, the furthermost tip of land to the west (i.e. Punta Cajón is on a back-bearing of 286°). This track avoids substantial shoals both to the north and the south. As you near the dock aim for its south end to avoid shoal water immediately to the north. The fishermen, who are based in Los Arroyos, are exceptionally friendly.

Punta Morros de Piedra

Punta Morros de Piedra is a small, rocky outcrop at approximately 21°54·0'N 84°54·3'W. At the present time there is nothing here, but the Cubans have plans to develop a marina to act as a point of departure or arrival for boats traveling between the NW Caribbean and the southern United States. To the west there are lovely sand beaches stretching up to Punta Cajón and around toward Cabo San Antonio.

Pasa Balandras

The Pasa Balandras is a 5M wide break at the southern end of the Los Colorados reef, with its midpoint at approximately 22°02·5'N 84°55·0'W. The pass is free of all hazards, with minimum depths of about 7m. The entire area to the south of the pass all the way down to Punta Cajón (5M to the south) is also wide open to small boats, with the exception of a couple of isolated shoal patches 1·4M north of Punta Cajón (at approximately 21°56·2'N 84°56·3'W and 21°56·4'N 84°55·5'W – see the next section).

Rounding the capes

At the western end of Cuba the land drops precipitously into an immense trench which is more than 3,000m deep in some places. Through this trench the Gulf Stream, one of the most powerful ocean currents in the world, surges northward. Typically, the Stream attains a speed of 3–4 knots between Cabo San Antonio and Cabo Catoche (at the tip of the Yucatan peninsula), but at times it has been clocked at speeds of up to 7 knots. Along its edges, the Stream spawns eddies and countercurrents.

The combination of this powerful current, the eddies and countercurrents, and the dramatic changes in underwater relief close to shore, can result in extremely rough conditions off Cabo San Antonio and the three headlands to its SE (Punta del Holandés, Cabo Corrientes, and Cabo Francés). In the main body of the stream, some miles offshore, the situation is exacerbated any time the wind blows out of the north, but along the margins of the Stream where there is often a southward-flowing countercurrent, it is a south wind that really stirs things up.

The optimum conditions in which to round the capes (going either north or south) occur with a moderate NE breeze, since this helps to flatten out the seas close inshore, and puts the boat on a reach or run in either direction. However, failing a NE wind, so long as you are confident in your navigational skills, the best thing to do is to sail this stretch at night when the winds tend to be at their lightest. Since each of the capes has a powerful lighthouse, there are adequate reference points for orientation, but careful attention must be paid to the potential effects of the currents which vary considerably over time.

In general, any time the wind is blowing off the land, the closer inshore you can sail the more likely you are to find smoother waters. However this does not necessarily apply to the relatively shoal water off one or two of the headlands (see below) where confused cross seas are likely in almost any conditions.

Cape by cape

In calm conditions, Punta Cajón, to the north of Cabo San Antonio, can be rounded ¼M off the beach in depths of 2–3m. In rough conditions it would be better to seek the deeper water 2M to the north of the point. In any event, you need to avoid the two shallow patches 1·4M north of Punta Cajón (at approximately 21°56·2'N 84°56·3'W and 21°56·4'N 84°55·5'W). To the west of Punta Cajón, the 5m line is almost 2M offshore. It runs almost due south to close the coastline off Cabo San Antonio.

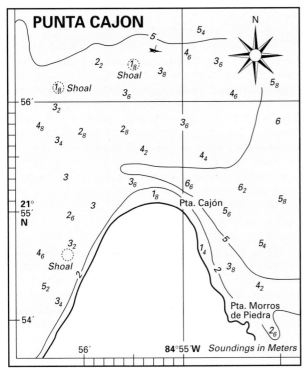

PUNTA CAJON

Adapted from ICH 1501
Courtesy GeoCuba

In calm conditions the stretch between Punta Cajón and Cabo San Antonio can also be taken close inshore, keeping ¼M or more off the beach with minimum depths of a little under 3m. Between Cabo San Antonio and Punta Perpetua, 2½M to the SE, the coastal shelf once again gradually extends further offshore until at Punta Perpetua it is 1M wide, with the remains of a shipwreck ⅓M off the beach. The shallow waters off Punta Perpetua are almost always confused – it is generally best to clear the point by 1M.

Between Punta Perpetua and Punta del Holandés deep water runs almost to the beach, but at Punta del Holandés another shoal extends almost ¾M to the SE, once again with confused seas on the shelf – the point should be given a wide berth.

The direct course between Punta del Holandés and Cabo Corrientes is 104°/284° straight across the mouth of the Bahía de Corrientes. This entire stretch can be quite unpleasant if the wind is in the south. At Cabo Corrientes the 10m line is ¾M off-shore, while at Cabo Francés it extends a good mile to the SSW of the cape; although the 2m line runs fairly close inshore, there are likely to be confused seas on the shelf – it is advisable to stay out in deeper water.

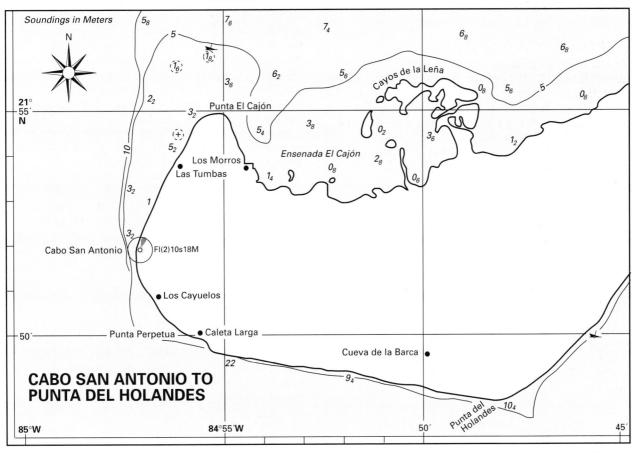

CABO SAN ANTONIO TO PUNTA DEL HOLANDES

Adapted from ICH 1122
Courtesy GeoCuba

Anchorages

Between the Cayos de la Leña and Puerto Cortés (Chapter 5), a distance of approximately 80M, there is not a single all-weather anchorage, although in prevailing easterlies and northeasterlies more or less the entire Bahía de Corrientes provides reasonable protection so long as you come close inshore (which you must do anyway to find water shallow enough in which to anchor). Within the Bahía de Corrientes, María la Gorda is by far the most attractive place in which to lay over for a night or two.

María la Gorda

María la Gorda is a dive resort tucked into the SE corner of the Bahía de Corrientes (at approximately 21°49·0'N 84°30·0'W). In 1998 it was made into an official Port of Entry, with a resident port captain, guarda, customs and medical doctor. However, the immigration officials may have to come from Pinar del Río (a long drive over bad roads) so clearance is likely to take from 5 hours on up and, in fact, because of this in 1999 some boats were refused clearance. At María la Gorda a series of lovely sand beaches are broken up by low-lying rocky headlands. A coastal shelf almost ⅓M wide slowly descends down to about 40m, and then ends abruptly in an underwater cliff – one moment the depth

sounder is showing 40–50m, the next moment it is off soundings with nothing in between!

The coastal shelf is alive with gorgeous coral in easy snorkeling depths; the wall provides world-class diving. The resort is quite happy to take qualified sailors out for a dive ($37 per dive), and to welcome visitors to its bar and restaurant (with highly variable buffet-style meals at $15 a piece). If conditions are right, a layover at María la Gorda is the ideal way to break the trip between the Cayos de la Leña and Puerto Cortés into two manageable distances (a midnight start for each leg will generally keep you in relatively calm conditions and have you anchored soon after dawn).

We have bought diesel at María la Gorda (siphoned from the generator tank), and hauled water in jerry cans, but in reality apart from the restaurant and bar, and an intermittently functioning international telephone, there are no services, although a few supplies may be available in the hotel store, and bread can be bought most days at about 1530 hours.

Anchorage

There is no protected anchorage at María la Gorda – this is an open roadstead. A small yacht basin was at one time constructed approximately ½M to the south of the resort, but this has now silted in (with depths of only a little over 0·5m). There is no choice but to anchor on the shelf in front of the resort, in depths of 4–20m (depending on how comfortable you are with being close in). The bottom is mostly coral, though without major heads. You have to hunt around for a patch of sand (both to get the anchor to hold and to avoid damaging the coral) and even then will find that the sand is thin with rock beneath it. We would not recommend using the dock (which has 2m on its outer end) since it can be subject to quite strong surges.

Any time the wind is south of SE, uncomfortable swells hook around Cabo Corrientes and sweep through the anchorage. During the NW phase of a norther, the anchorage is wide open and potentially dangerous – the local boats move up to La Bajada, 6 or 7M to the NNE (it can be picked out from María la Gorda on account of the conspicuous white radar dome immediately to the east).

La Furnia

La Furnia is a small settlement ½M to the NW of Cabo Francés. There is a beach here running toward the lighthouse. Reportedly, this is an attractive spot in which to anchor during settled NE conditions, but we haven't checked it out.

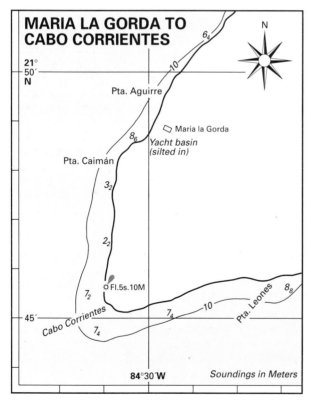

MARIA LA GORDA TO CABO CORRIENTES

N

21° 50' N

Pta. Aguirre

Maria la Gorda
Yacht basin (silted in)

Pta. Caimán

Cabo Corrientes

Fl.5s.10M

Pta. Leones

45'

84°30'W

Soundings in Meters

Adapted from ICH 1167
Courtesy GeoCuba

5. Cabo Francés to Casilda, including the Golfo de Batabano

Between Cabo Francés, the westernmost extension of the Golfo de Batabano, and Casilda, on the eastern fringes of the Golfo de Cazones (broadly defined) the south coast of Cuba makes an arc some 240M long. The predominant feature is the Golfo de Batabano, an enormous gulf, approximately 150M wide at its mouth, and 75M deep in its central part.

More or less in the center of the mouth of the gulf lies the Isla de la Juventud (Isle of Youth, formerly called the Isle of Pines), Cuba's largest island (approximately 30M in diameter). Between the Isla de la Juventud and the western and eastern extremities of the gulf lie a couple of island chains (the Cayos de San Felipe and Cayos los Indios in the western part of the gulf, the Archipiélago de los Canarreos in the eastern part), while within the body of the gulf itself are numerous scattered groups of cays. Most of the gulf is navigable by small craft, with depths, in places, of up to 10m.

Much of the mainland coast of the Golfo de Batabano is fringed by mangroves, although periodically there are substantial stretches of beach. The islands within the body of the gulf are also mostly mangroves and as such are not particularly interesting, but those in the fringing barrier intersperse mangroves with mile after mile of superb beach fronted by gorgeous crystal-clear waters and lovely coral reefs – some of the finest in the Caribbean.

The Isla de la Juventud contains a great deal of variegated scenery, from mangrove swamps to steep-sided and relatively dramatic hills, with acres of coconut palms, citrus orchards and pastureland between the two. The capital city, Nueva Gerona, though not large, is attractive and a better source of supplies at the present time than most Cuban cities. The south and west coasts of the Isla de la Juventud have some lovely beaches.

East of the Golfo de Batabano lies the Golfo de Cazones, a deep-water trench thrusting up toward the mainland. On its western side the Golfo de Cazones is defined by the same low-lying mangrove cays that form the eastern margin of the Golfo de Batabano, but on its eastern side the shoreline consists of inhospitable low, rocky cliffs with few opportunities to anchor. Inland, the terrain rises abruptly to the mountains of Trinidad. The principal feature here is the Bahía de Cienfuegos, a large pocket bay with the city of Cienfuegos on its eastern shore. At the head of the Golfo de Cazones is the infamous Bay of Pigs, an area which is still, to this day, off-limits to cruising sailors.

In short, there is much variety in this region. And although a good bit of the region is not particularly interesting, a leisurely cruise along the islands and cays across the mouth of the Golfo de Batabano can be a delightful experience. In particular, the stretch from the Isla de la Juventud to Cayo Largo is, without question, one of the finest cruising grounds in Cuba.

Winds

Winds tend to be lighter on the south coast than on the north coast. Typically, the wind is from the NE to the SE at speeds from 6 to 9 knots. Within these averages there is a marked daily pattern with the wind steadily increasing in intensity from the early hours of the morning (well before dawn) and building into the late afternoon (by which time it may be up to 20 knots) and then dying overnight. During the course of the day it tends to veer from north of east to south of east.

This pattern is broken by northers in the wintertime, although the effects are far more muted than on the north shore, and calms or the effects of tropical depressions in the summertime (Chapter 2). In addition, in late March and April there are sometimes strong SE winds (20 knots or so) blowing for days on end, creating large swells out in the Caribbean and quite substantial seas even in the relatively enclosed waters of the Golfo de Batabano.

Currents and tides

Although the Caribbean Current flows in a generally NW direction off the south coast of Cuba it is well out to sea and has little or no significance for this guide. Closer inshore the currents are variable, although there is a general tendency to flow toward the SE along the coastline and the outer reaches of the Golfo de Batabano. At times this SE current can get quite strong (up to 2·0 knots). At other times it

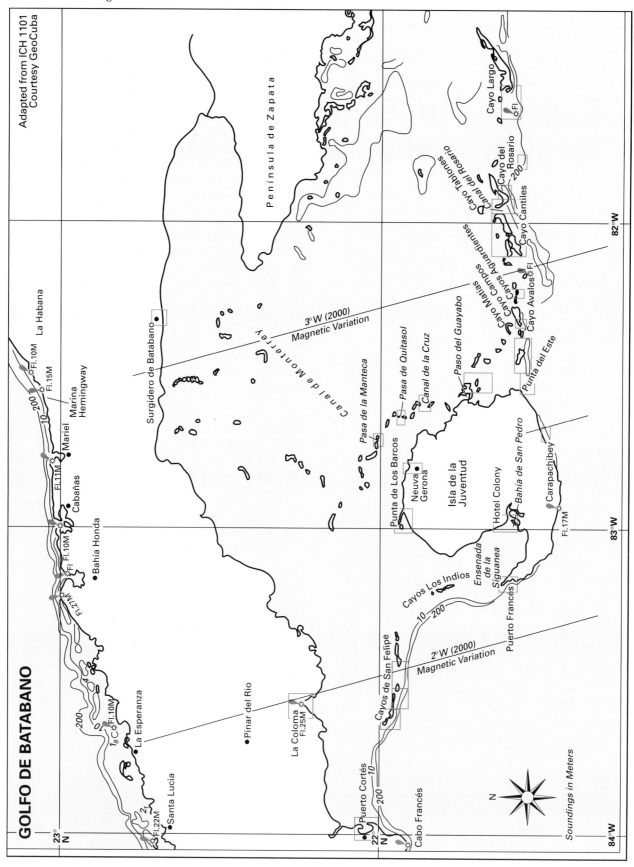

GOLFO DE BATABANO

Adapted from ICH 1101
Courtesy GeoCuba

La Habana

☆ Fl.10M
☆ Fl.15M
Fl.11M
Marina Hemingway
Mariel
Cabañas
• Bahía Honda
Fl.10M
Fl
☆ Fl.27M

• La Esperanza
☆ Fl.10M
1₈ C
• Santa Lucia
☆ Fl.22M

200
10
200
4

• Pinar del Río

Surgidero de Batabano

Península de Zapata

Canal de Monterrey

3° W (2000)
Magnetic Variation

La Coloma
☆ Fl.25M

Puerto Cortés
22° N

Cabo Francés

Cayos de San Felipe

Cayos Los Indios

10
200

2° W (2000)
Magnetic Variation

Puerto Francés

Punta de Los Barcos
Neuva Gerona
Isla de la Juventud
Hotel Colony
Bahía de San Pedro
Ensenada de la Siguanea
Carapachibey
☆ Fl.17M

Punta del Este

Pasa de la Manteca
Pasa de Quitasol
Canal de la Cruz
Paso del Guayabo

Cayo Matías
Cayos Campos
Canal de los Aguardientes
☆ Fl
Cayo Avalos
☆ Fl
Cayo Cantiles
Cayo del Rosario
Canal del Rosario
Cayo Tablones
200
☆ Fl
Cayo Largo

82° W
83° W
84° W

23° N

N

Soundings in Meters

78

disappears altogether and in fact may be replaced with a contrary current.

Tides are generally small, increasing from about 0·2m (8in) in the Archipiélago de los Canarreos to 0·4m (a little over a foot) in the vicinity of Casilda, but with as little as 0·1m (about 4in) in the interior areas of the Golfo de Batabano. Where there is the greater amplitude (essentially, Cienfuegos to Casilda) the flood tide tends to flow to the west, and the ebb to the east, but with no great force. In the Golfo de Batabano the flood is to the north, and the ebb to the south, but since the tides are so small the wind has a greater influence on the direction of flow. There are, however, moderate tidal currents in some of the channels between the cays, and in the entrance to the Bahía de Cienfuegos (up to 2·0 knots). The tides along the outside of the Archipiélago de los Canarreos and the coastline to Casilda are semi-diurnal (i.e. twice daily); within the Golfo de Batabano they are extremely irregular.

Sailing strategies

Going east If the earlier suggestion of sailing the south coast in the winter months (Chapter 2) is followed, the predominant winds should be from north of east. Combined with generally favorable currents, this should make it reasonably easy to work from west to east along this stretch of coast. In addition, much of the sailing can be done in the relatively protected waters of the Golfo de Batabano. Early morning starts will benefit from the somewhat lighter and more northerly winds than those found later in the afternoon.

Of course, these kinds of generalizations don't always apply. The great size of the Golfo de Batabano allows considerable seas to build at times, while the Golfo de Cazones is open ocean. With strong winds (notably northers, or persistent winds from the SE) the relatively shoal nature of much of the Golfo de Batabano has a tendency to produce short, steep and uncomfortable waves, while the Golfo de Cazones can produce some very large seas indeed – sailing these waters requires as much attention to the weather as sailing in other Cuban waters (we have more to say on strategies for crossing the Golfo de Cazones toward the end of this chapter).

Finally, the strong SE winds often found toward the end of March and in April can make any passage from west to east a tough slog to windward. We found out the hard way. This is the time to be on the north shore.

Going west should be a downwind romp just about any time of the year.

Charts and magnetic variation

ICH *1147*, *1146*, *1145*, *1144*, *1143*, *1142* and *1141* cover the region from Cabo Francés to Casilda at a scale of 1:150,000. Of these, if our advice to ignore the interior areas of the Golfo de Batabano is followed (see below), ICH *1146* and *1144* are not needed. In addition to these charts, the Golfo de Batabano has been charted at both 1:100,000 and 1:50,000, so you can really spend a fortune if you want to. There are then detailed charts of the ports of La Coloma, Surgidero de Batabano, Nueva Gerona and the Bahía de Cienfuegos (and Casilda, but this is dealt with in the next chapter). Finally, there is the chart book (Region 2: Cabo Corrientes to Casilda) which covers this region.

Magnetic variation (January 2000) increases from just over 1°30'W at Cabo Francés, to 3°30'W at Cayo Largo and almost 4°30'W at Casilda. In all areas it is increasing annually at a rate of about 9'W.

Important note The soundings on most Cuban charts are based on a theoretical low water, and as such are quite conservative. Those in the Golfo de Batabano, however, are based on some concept of mid-tide. In the interior areas of the gulf, where there is very little tide, the soundings are pretty reliable, but toward the outer edges of the gulf (i.e. along the fringing islands and reefs) the tidal range is up to 0·4m, which means that at low tide the soundings on the charts consistently exaggerate the depth by about 0·2m (sometimes more). This may not sound like much, but it is enough to make the difference between grounding, and not grounding, in many of the relatively shoal waters. We would recommend that, to be on the safe side, all soundings are reduced by a minimum of 0·2m (this does not apply to the soundings on our plans).

The mainland coast of the Golfo de Batabano

The coastline of the Golfo de Batabano stretches from Cabo Francés in the west to the Bahía de Cochinos (the Bay of Pigs) in the east. In the western part there are a couple of accessible towns with well protected anchorages (Puerto Cortés and La Coloma). Thereafter in the entire sweep of the gulf there are few protected anchorages with a 2m depth, and in any case almost nothing of interest ashore (that is, unless you are not yet tired of mangroves and mosquitoes).

We can see little reason why anyone would want to cruise most of this coastline, or the interior islands of the Golfo de Batabano, and so have simply omitted them from this guide, with the exception of the port of Surgidero de Batabano which lies at the northernmost extremity of the gulf.

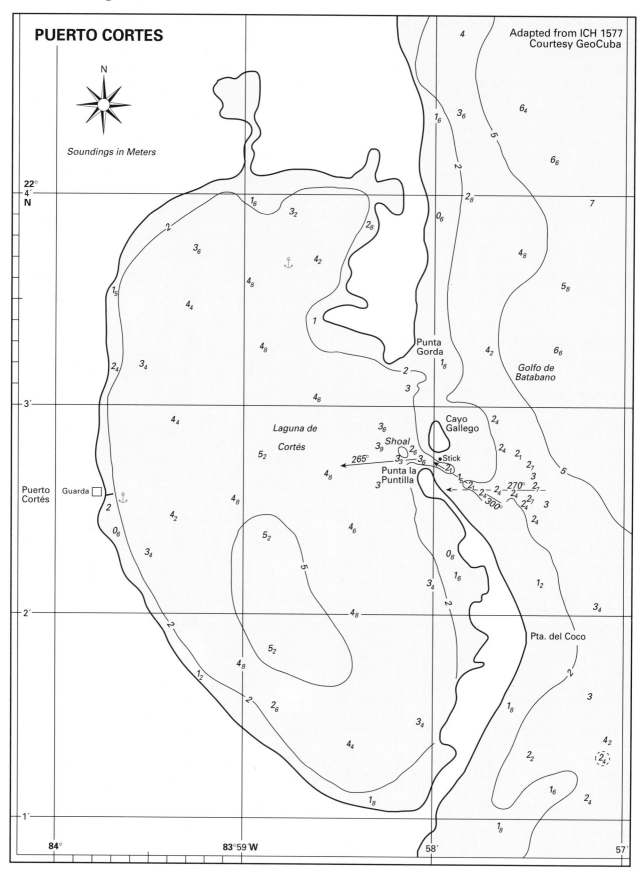

PUERTO CORTES

N

Soundings in Meters

Adapted from ICH 1577
Courtesy GeoCuba

22°
4′
N

4

3₆
6₄

1₆

5
2
6₆

1₆
3₂
2₈
0₆
2₈
7

3₆
4₂
4₈
5₈

4₄
1₅

Punta
Gorda
1₈
4₂
6₆

*Golfo de
Batabano*

3′

2₄
3₄

4₆
2
3

Laguna de
Cortés

3₆
Cayo
Gallego
2₄

4₄
3₉ Shoal
2₆
2₄
2₁
2₇
5

265°
3₃
3₆
Stick
2₇
3

Puerto
Cortés
Guarda
5₂
4₈
Punta la
Puntilla
3
1₅
2₄
270°
2₇

2
300°
2₄
2₇
2₄

0₆
4₂
4₆
4₈
5₂

3₄
5₂
5
0₈

1₆
1₂

2′
4₈
3₄
2
Pta. del Coco

5₂
3₄

1₂
4₈
2₆
3₄
1₈
2
3

3₄
4₂
2₄

4₄
2₂
1₆
2₄

1′
1₈
1₈

84°
83°59′W
58′
57′

80

This is a commercial port without tourist facilities, but since it has good communications with Havana, just 40 miles to the north, we have included it. (Nevertheless, a far easier way to get to and from Havana is to dock at Nueva Gerona on the Isla de la Juventud and to catch the high-speed ferry to Surgidero de Batabano.)

Note I have copies of a couple of articles from the June 1953 issue of *Yachting* magazine in which the author describes a trip up the Río Hatiguanico, which empties into the Ensenada de Broa, which in turn is in the NE corner of the Golfo de Batabano. He writes of the fabulous tarpon fishing in the river, so maybe this region deserves some exploration after all.

Puerto Cortés

Puerto Cortés is a small fishing town 10M to the north of Cabo Francés. It is on the western shore of the relatively deep, land-locked Laguna de Cortés. The lagoon provides excellent protection in any conditions and as such is a useful layover before or after rounding the capes to the west. However, the controlling depth at the entry to the lagoon is 1·8m at low water, and the entry itself is tricky, so entry and exit is limited to reasonably settled conditions. The town has almost nothing in the way of supplies.

Approaches

The lagoon is entered via a narrow, curving channel to the south of a small cay (Cayo Gallego) which lies in the center of the lagoon entrance. The break between this cay and the mangroves to the south is clearly visible from several miles to the east.

From the south To the SE of the channel entrance there are shoal patches with less than 2m over them, so any approach should be made at least a mile offshore until Cayo Gallego bears 310° *or less*, at which point you can head straight for the cay.

From the north There are no off-lying dangers – any track ⅓M or more offshore will clear all coastal shoals.

Entry

The entry channel is tricky. Not only is it narrow and curving, but it also shoals to 1·8m, and in fact is only kept open by the large fishing boats going in and coming out (these boats have cleaned the weed off the bottom, leaving a relatively clear sand channel which can be picked up in the right light). Just to complicate matters, there is often a tidal flow both through, and across, the channel, for which compensation must be made when following the directions below. In prevailing easterlies and northeasterlies there may be quite a chop on the approach to the channel – not the kind of conditions in which you want to run aground on a lee shore!

From offshore, come to a position at approximately 22°02·6'N 83°57·5'W, and take up station about ⅓M out from, and approximately 200m to the south of, the sandy spit on the south side of the channel (Punta la Puntilla). Then head due west toward the shore (i.e. aiming at a spot 200m south of Punta la Puntilla). The depths will shoal to a little over 2m.

When about 200m off the beach, come onto a heading of 300°, directly for a small stake which is just to the north of Punta la Puntilla (this stake is not easy to see). The depths will shoal to 1·8m.

Immediately before the stake, start a curve to the west, leaving the stake just 5m to starboard (i.e. passing to the south of it). You will be just 30m or so off Punta la Puntilla.

Past the point, the depth increases to 3m, but then there is a mid-channel shoal which can be left on either side. Once past the mid-channel shoal, it is a clear shot to Puerto Cortés on the western side of the lagoon.

When leaving the lagoon, a course from Puerto Cortés more or less for the center of the gap between Cayo Gallego and Punta la Puntilla just clears both the mid-channel shoal and the shoal on the south side of the channel. As you come to an imaginary line drawn between the western tips of Cayo Gallego and Punta la Puntilla, turn to a course of 120°, leaving the stake just 5m to port, and maintaining this heading until outside the lagoon and 150m south of Punta la Puntilla, at which time you head due east into deeper water.

Anchorage

Anchor off the town dock, amongst the assembled fishing boats, and dinghy in to the dock (a dilapidated steel-frame affair). Well out along the length of the dock the bottom is shallow and foul with debris so it would be best not to take the dinghy in too far. The Guarda post is at the head of the dock.

In strong easterlies, you may want to retreat to the east side of the lagoon for a quiet night.

Ensenada de Cortés

The Ensenada de Cortés is the large bay which encompasses the waters between Puerto Cortés and La Coloma. Along the coast, the mangroves are intermittently broken up by considerable stretches of sandy beach, on which various small tourist towns have developed (aimed more at Cubans than foreigners). The most notable of these are Playa de Bailén, 5M to the north of Puerto Cortés, and Playa Boca de Galafre another 5M to the NE. Neither are suitable as a stopover since in prevailing easterlies and northeasterlies, both are on a lee shore with no protection.

On the north side of the bay, anchoring anywhere off the coast offers reasonable protection in both northers and also northeasterly winds, but will be wide open any time the wind is east or south of east. A particularly attractive anchorage for bird lovers is at the eastern end of Cayo Guanito (at approximately 22°10·0'N 83°47·6'W) where the Estuario Cayuelo empties out into the bay. The mouth of the estuary is completely obstructed by shoals, so you will have to anchor off. The surrounding mangroves are home to a couple of egret rookeries, while at low tide the numerous drying mudflats are covered with hundreds of birds.

La Coloma

La Coloma is a large fishing town and small commercial port about 30M NE of Puerto Cortés. The waterfront area is quite run down, while immediately behind it is a large housing estate of incredibly ugly cement-block apartment buildings. This is not one of the more attractive Cuban

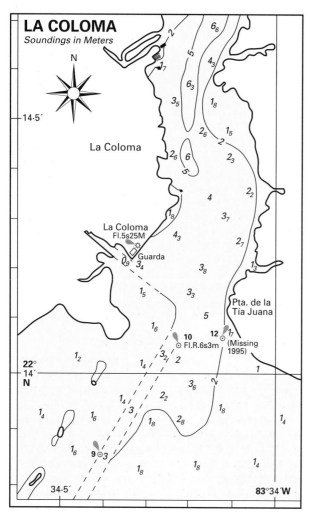

LA COLOMA
Soundings in Meters

Adapted from ICH 1860
Courtesy GeoCuba

locations! However, it is a port of entry, and the town is large enough to provide some modest supplies, as well as being connected by a good road to Pinar del Río, the capital of the province (the drive alone is worth making, through lush, flat countryside with extensive rice paddies, herds of cattle, and tobacco fields). The anchorage within the port area is well protected from all but a strong southerly wind, and even then provides a fair amount of protection. Water is available on the Guarda dock and diesel can be obtained.

Approaches

The initial landfall for La Coloma is the Santo Domingo beacon at approximately 22°09·5'N 83°36·5'W.

From the southwest (Puerto Cortés) the approach to the Santo Domingo light is free of all off-lying hazards.

From the Isla de la Juventud

1. The rhumb line course (approximately 290°/ 110°) from Nueva Gerona runs across a substantial shoal (Bajo Dios) which lies between 21°58·8'N and 22°03·5'N along a north/south axis at 83°11·0'W. This shoal can be taken on either side.

2. The rhumb line course (approximately 295°/ 115°) from the mouth of the Ensenada de Barcos at the NW tip of the Isla de la Juventud clips the southern tip of the Bajo Dios shoal. A heading of 290° for the first 10M will keep you clear.

3. The rhumb line course from the Hotel Colony runs slap into the Cayos los Indios. To avoid these islands and the shoals to their NW, come north up the coast of the Isla de la Juventud to Punta Buenavista, then head 310° *or more* to pass at least 2M north of the east end of the Cayos de San Felipe. This will keep you parallel to, and just to the north of, the long shoal that runs between the Cayos los Indios and the Cayos de San Felipe. It will also keep you out of isolated shoal patches that extend almost 2M to the north of the easternmost of the Cayos de San Felipe. Be sure to compensate for any southward set in your track. Once north of the Cayos de San Felipe, it is a clear shot of approximately 305° to the Santo Domingo beacon.

Entry

La Coloma is at the head of a funnel-shaped bay, almost 10M across at its mouth. A long shoal extends from the eastern shore to halfway across the mouth of the bay. The channel between the shoal and the western shore is indicated by the Santo Domingo beacon. The beacon can be passed on either side, up to ½M off. From the light, a course of 018° for 2½M brings you to a dredged channel which runs straight into La Coloma on a heading of

031°. The mouth of the channel is indicated by green and red channel markers (green *No. 1*, red *No. 2*), and thereafter there are paired markers about every ½M – this is a very straightforward entry. Just note that the dredgings from the channel have been dumped on spoil heaps to the west, so be sure not to get swept out this side of the channel.

Anchorage

The last marker (red *No. 10*) is left to starboard, at which point the small commercial harbor opens up to port, with the Guarda dock on the north side. The dock has over 2m alongside and is reasonably well fendered with rubber tires, so you can come alongside to check in. Thereafter the Guarda will probably ask you to anchor just off the dock in the company of the assembled fishing boats. The bottom is extremely soft; an anchor sets easily but the holding is none too good. The La Coloma river is navigable for some distance upstream of the town.

Surgidero de Batabano

Surgidero de Batabano is at the northern limit of the Golfo de Batabano, more or less due south of Havana. It is the main port in this area, and the principal connection between the mainland and the Isla de la Juventud (the port of Nueva Gerona). The anchorage off the port is an open roadstead which can get quite rough when the wind is out of the south, but there is a dredged channel, reportedly with a controlling depth of 2·5m, to a couple of fully protected basins. As we said earlier, we have not been there. We include a harbor chart, and sailing directions derived from the Cuban charts, in case you should need to get close to Havana.

Approaches

The approaches to Surgidero de Batabano are obstructed by a series of cays and shoals which form a broad arc from the mainland west of the town all the way around to the Península de Zapata in the east. These cays are cut by several channels, the most important of which are the Canal de Hacha, and the Canal de Monterrey, both of which are marked with beacons.

The Canal de Monterrey, which is the main ship channel to Nueva Gerona, is by far the easier to use, since it has a series of lit beacons on a 223°/043° axis, at 7M intervals, all the way from the Pasa de la Manteca (see below), north of Nueva Gerona, to a point 13M south of Surgidero de Batabano. From the last beacon (*No. 5*, at approximately 22°28·1'N 82°15·0'W) it is a straight shot to the port on a heading of 350° (the main channel makes a dogleg to the east, but there is sufficient water for smaller craft to go direct to Surgidero de Batabano).

From the west Unless you have adequate charts of the interior region of the Golfo de Batabano, you should make your way to the north shore of the Isla de la Juventud and then follow the Pasa de la Manteca and Canal de Monterrey to Surgidero de Batabano.

From the east Enter the Golfo de Batabano via the Canal del Rosario (see below). Once clear of the shoals surrounding Cayo Tablones it is a clear shot on a NNE heading to a position at approximately 22°18·0'N 82°25·0'W, where you will intersect the Canal de Monterrey (at beacon *No. 3*). Turn to the NE (043°) and follow the canal to the last beacon (*No. 5*), and then head directly to Surgidero de Batabano.

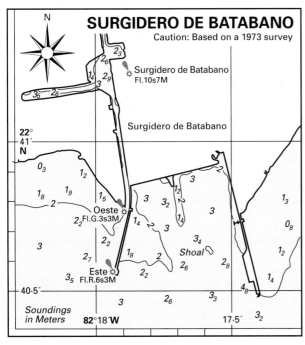

Adapted from ICH 1855
Courtesy GeoCuba

The Cayos de San Felipe and Cayos los Indios

Although the Cayos de San Felipe consist of one long line of mangroves when viewed from the north, from the south you see many miles of pristine, uninhabited, beach. A great variety of vegetation is found on the narrow strip between the two. Offshore are numerous coral patches. You can happily spend several days here beach-combing, snorkeling, and relaxing. In contrast, the Cayos los Indios are almost entirely mangroves and apart from some interesting bird life on drying mudflats, have little to excite the cruiser – we intend to pretty well ignore them in this guide.

The Cayos de San Felipe and Cayos los Indios are set upon a common shoal which extends several miles to the west of the Cayos de San Felipe (called the Bajo de Cucaña at this point) and also a mile or so to the south of the Cayos los Indios. At its southern end there is a 5M gap between this shoal and the Isla de la Juventud. In other words, the shoal, and its associated cays, forms a substantial barrier between the open ocean and the western half of the Golfo de Batabano. South of the shoal the bottom drops away into abyssal depths – in just a few miles you are over the 1,000m line.

Looking at the charts you get the impression that the Cayos de San Felipe and the section of the shoal between these cays and the Cayos los Indios, are cut by a number of passages, making it possible to move between the north and south sides of the cays, enabling sheltered anchorages to be found to suit more or less any weather conditions and sea states. However, in the interval since the surveys on which the charts are based were made, all of the channels through the Cayos de San Felipe have silted in – the controlling depth for passaging between the north and south shores of the cays is now down to 1·5m – while the shallow passes through the shoal between the Cayos de San Felipe and the Cayos los Indios tend to shift with time and so have to be considered good light, calm weather, passes (and still may not accommodate a 2m draft). What this means in practice is that once you have made a choice to pass to the north or the south of either end of either the Cayos de San Felipe or the Cayos los Indios, the die may well be cast until you get to the other end – a distance of close to 40M.

Deciding on which side to take the cays is not easy. The choice is complicated by the fact that the prevailing wind is out of the east. There are few spots in the Cayos de San Felipe, the more attractive of the cays, that are well protected from this direction. If the wind is out of the NE, the south coasts of the cays are the more sheltered, but then there may be substantial swells rolling in from the Caribbean. If the wind is out of the SE, the north coasts are more sheltered. On balance, the north coasts are preferable, since on the south coasts you could find yourself trapped on a dangerous lee shore in heavy seas.

Approaches to the Cayos de San Felipe

From the west (Cabo Francés and Puerto Cortés) and the north The shoal (Bajo de la Cucaña) to the NW of the Cayos de San Felipe extends intermittently for more than 5M. Where it connects with the Cayos de San Felipe considerable mangrove growth has occurred since the Cuban charts were made, so that the NW tip of Cayo Juan Garcia is now 1M further NW than charted, with isolated clumps of mangroves occurring for another ¾M all the way to an old fish station (now just a mass of piles) indicated on the charts by a black square.

Depending on whether you are headed for the north or south side of the cays, you may need to cross this shoal. There are a number of passes. By far the easiest to use is the Pasa de la Cucaña. This is identified by a large, relatively new, fishing station built on a shoal at approximately 22°01·9'N 83°39·7'W. The pass is transited on a heading of 225°/045°, passing some 100m or so to the south of the fishing station. Although the depths are very variable, changing from as little as 2·2m to 11m in a matter of meters, there are no hazards.

From the Isla de la Juventud: north coast A direct course between the north coast of the Isla de la Juventud (Nueva Gerona or the Ensenada de los Barcos) and the north coast of the Cayos de San Felipe passes just to the south of the Bajo Dios shoal. To be sure of clearing this shoal, you must stay south of 21°58·5'N (the southern tip of the shoal is at approximately 21°58·8'N 83°10·6'W). Aside from this shoal, there are no off-lying dangers until you close the east end of the Cayos de San Felipe, at which point there are isolated rocks with less than 2m over them. These extend up to 2M north of Cayo la Cucaña, the easternmost cay in the Cayos de San Felipe – this area should either be transited with a bow watch in good light, or avoided altogether.

From the Isla de la Juventud: Hotel Colony If approaching the north side of the Cayos de San Felipe from the Hotel Colony, it is necessary to skirt the Cayos los Indios and the shoal that extends from these cays all the way to the Cayos de San Felipe (making sure to compensate for any leeway or tidal set), and to then avoid the rocks off Cayo la Cucaña (see paragraph above).

Note About midway along the north coast of the Cayos de San Felipe a shoal area extends 2½M to the north (off Cayo Cocos). Its north end is easily identified by another of the Cuban fishing stations (at approximately 21°59·4'N 83°28·9'W). This shoal can be passed by simply swinging around to the north of the fishing station, but if you don't want to go this far out of your way there is a channel with controlling depths of more than 2m across the middle of the shoal. The channel is marked by a couple of substantial stakes which are left 20–50m to the north (i.e. you go south of them) when passing through. It is a straight shot on a heading of approximately 100°/280°. The west end of the channel is at approximately 21°57·9'N 83°29·0'W. The east end is at approximately 21°57·8'N 83°28·4'W.

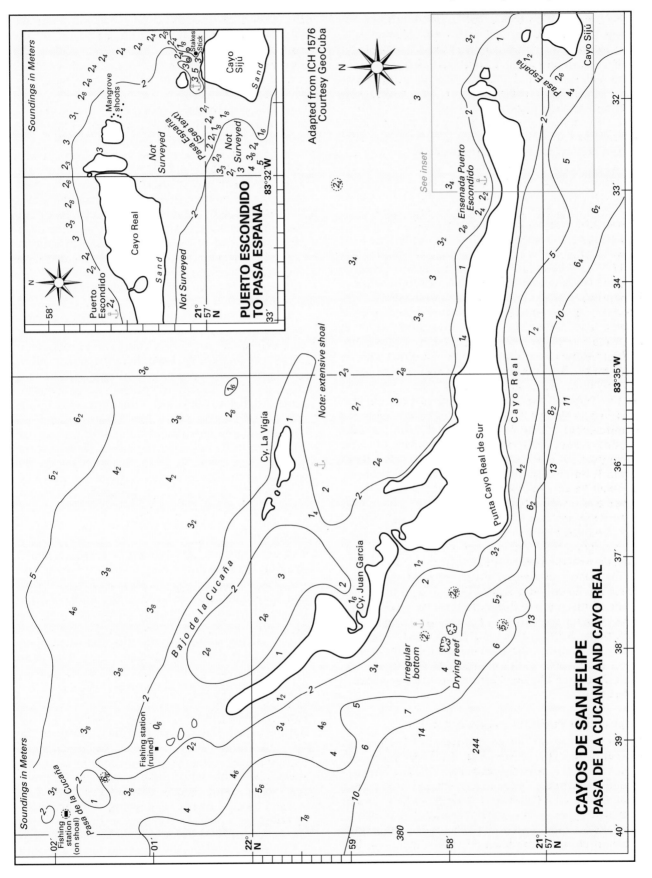

Soundings in Meters

**PUERTO ESCONDIDO
TO PASA ESPANA**

Adapted from ICH 1576
Courtesy GeoCuba

Mangrove
shoots

Stakes
Stick

Cayo
Sijú

Sand

*pasa España
(See text)*

Not
Surveyed

Cayo Real

Sand

Not Surveyed

Puerto
Escondido

*Not
Surveyed*

83°32'W

Ensenada Puerto
Escondido

pasa España

Cayo Sijú

See inset

Soundings in Meters

Fishing
station
(on shoal)

pasa de la Cucaña

Note: extensive shoal

Cy. La Vigía

Bajo de la Cucaña

Cy. Juan Garcia

Fishing station
(ruined)

Irregular
bottom

Drying reef

Punta Cayo Real de Sur

Cayo Real

**CAYOS DE SAN FELIPE
PASA DE LA CUCANA AND CAYO REAL**

Deep water passages between the north and the south coasts of the Cayos de San Felipe

You will have to use either the Pasa de la Cucaña at the western end of the Cayos de San Felipe, or else the wide pass some 40M away between the south end of the Cayos los Indios and the southwestern tip of the Isla de la Juventud.

Anchorages and shoal-draft passages

West end of Cayo Real

In settled easterlies and northeasterlies a calm and attractive anchorage will be found in the lee of the west end of Cayo Real. But if the wind moves into the SE, swells will hook around Punta Cayo Real de Sur, making this an uncomfortable location, while in a norther you will be on a dangerous lee shore. This is a fair-weather anchorage that should be entered in good light. Given these conditions, simply come in toward the mangroves, or the beach, until the water shoals and then drop the hook. You will be rewarded with a pretty beach and some good snorkeling.

Note that on the approach to the west end of Cayo Real there are two substantial reef patches 1M to the west of the cay (normally identifiable by breaking waves, but in any case with some bits of coral sticking up). There are one or two scattered rocks with less than 2m over them that are shown on the Cuban charts (although we could not find them – however, the bottom is very irregular, with numerous patches which have less water than shown in the Cuban soundings).

South side of Cayo La Vigía

This is one of the few spots in the Cayos de San Felipe with good protection in a norther. It has few other redeeming features being wide open to the east and in the middle of nowhere. To enter the anchorage, simply come in from the east. If coming from the north, note that the shoal at the eastern end of Cayo la Vigía extends ½M further than is shown on the Cuban charts, so give this cay a wide berth.

Ensenada Puerto Escondido

This is a bay on the northern side of Cayo Real, more or less at its eastern tip (which has grown for ½M beyond its charted position). This anchorage is wide open to the north and to the east, but has good protection when the wind is in the SE or south. Simply come in toward the mangroves until the water shoals and then drop the hook. If coming from the north, once again note that the shoal off the eastern tip of Cayo la Vigía extends ½M further east

than charted, so give this cay a wide berth. From the anchorage, a dinghy ride through one of the mangrove canals just to the east will bring you to the lovely south shore.

Pasa España

The Pasa España lies between Cayo Real and Cayo Sijú. The pass itself is full of shoal patches and is not suitable for vessels with a draft of more than 1m (it might be possible to pick your way through with 1·8m in good light and calm conditions, but then again it might not...). Also, the mangroves have grown considerably in recent years, extending ½M to the east of the charted tip of Cayo Real, and forming a small cay on the sand patch to the north of the west end of Cayo Sijú. Tucked in between this new cay and Cayo Sijú is a secluded little anchorage which provides excellent protection from southeasterly winds, and reasonable protection from both the north and the east.

The anchorage is entered via a narrow channel marked by a couple of very tall stakes. To find the channel, come to a position at approximately 21°57·5'N 83°31·0'W. From here the stakes will be clearly visible. Proceed on a heading of 220° leaving the first stake 15m to port, and the second about the same distance to starboard – this track will clip the east side of the channel (which has a slight curve to it) with minimum depths of about 1·9m – 2·2m can be carried in by following the curve. Once past the second stake there is deep water down to the mangroves and over to the south of the new cay. Immediately to the south of this anchorage are the beaches of Cayo Sijú.

Cayo Cocos

You can tuck in close to the mangroves at the junction between Cayo Sijú and Cayo Cocos with the cays providing excellent protection from the SE and the south, and the shoal to the north of Cayo Cocos providing reasonable protection from the east. Although this anchorage looks to be wide open, it has better protection to the east than most anchorages in the Cayos de San Felipe. The south coast of the cays is a dinghy ride away through various channels in the mangroves.

Pasa dos Hermanos

Between Cayo Cocos and the Cayos del Perro the Cuban charts show a clear, deep channel. Unfortunately, it has shoaled in both to the north and to the south, while the mangroves have grown considerably on both sides of the channel. The pass can still be used by vessels drawing 1·5m or less, in addition to which it contains a fully protected anchorage (the best in the cays for vessels that draw 1·5m or less) with dinghy access to the south coast of the cays.

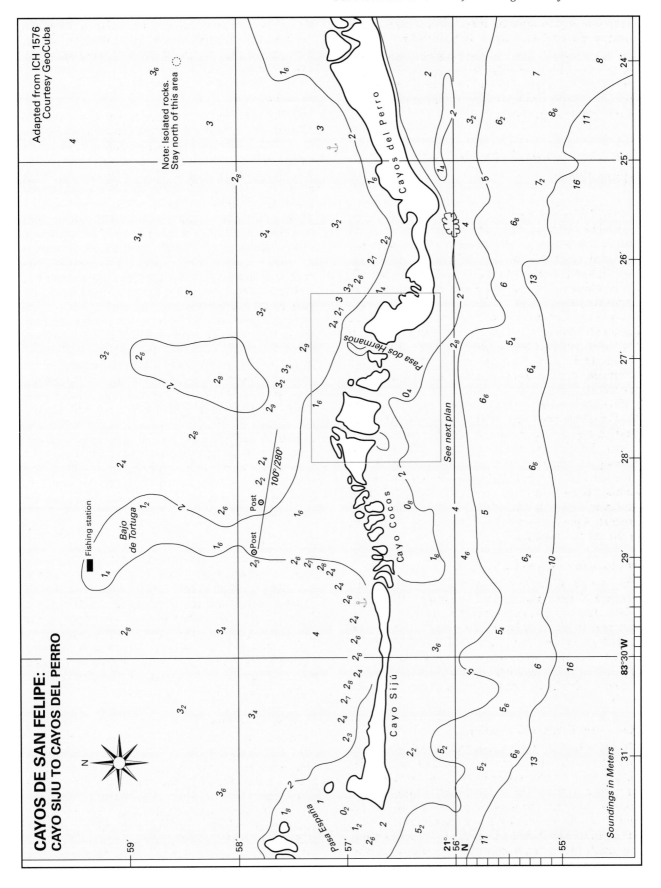

CAYOS DE SAN FELIPE:
CAYO SIJU TO CAYOS DEL PERRO

Adapted from ICH 1576
Courtesy GeoCuba

Note: Isolated rocks.
Stay north of this area

Soundings in Meters

From the north, to enter the anchorage come to a position at approximately 21°57·1'N 83°26·7'W, at which point you will be able to pick out a large stake. Line this stake up with the taller mangroves on the west side of the channel (220°) and then come in on this heading to leave the stake 10–15m to starboard (i.e. pass to the east of it). The controlling depth of 1·5m is in this first stretch; beyond the stake the channel steadily deepens until there is better than 3m between the various cays.

From the south, there is a shifting sand bar between Cayo Cocos and the Cayos del Perro. Although there is a substantial stake south of Cayo Cocos this does not now delineate a channel. Currently, entering the Pasa dos Hermanos is simply a matter of picking your way in, and should not be attempted in any but the calmest conditions (note that if the wind has been blowing from the SE the bottom will be stirred up and the water depths impossible to eyeball).

Cayos del Perro

At the western end of the Cayos del Perro it is possible to tuck in reasonably closely to the man-groves on the north shore, once again providing good protection when the wind is in the SE or south, but leaving you wide open to the east and north. The south coast of the cay is a long dinghy ride away through the Pasa dos Hermanos.

Cayos los Indios

There is not a single, decently protected, anchorage in the Cayos los Indios for vessels that draw more than 1·5m. In prevailing winds the entire west shore provides a lee, although there may be residual swells rolling in from the Caribbean, and there is the problem of how to regain the east shore (see introductory notes). There is a channel between the east and west shores around the north end of the cays, with depths through most of its length of 2·5–4m, but it shoals to a little over 1·6m at each end (you could get 1·8m through, but not easily), and in any case it is quite long and not straight. If you should attempt it, *coming from the west* pass 20m or so to the south of all the stakes except the final two at the east end, between which you pass; *coming from the east*, pass between the first two stakes and then pass 20m or so to the south of the rest.

Several of the cuts between the cays contain deep

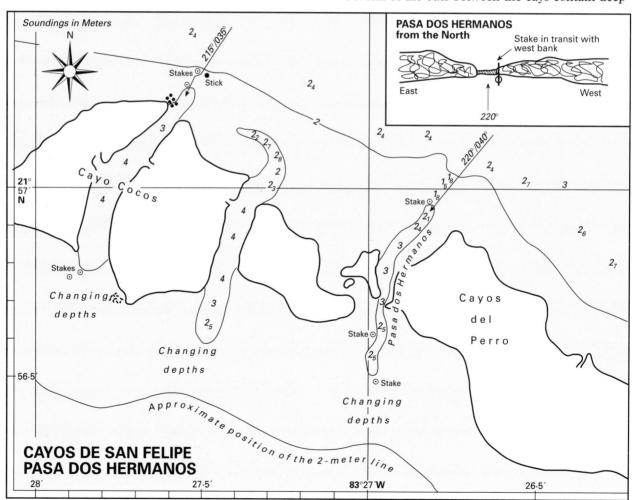

(up to 6m), well protected water, but all have shoals barring their entrances. 1·5m can be carried into both ends of the wide cut between the northernmost two cays, coming in from either end directly for the center of the cut on a heading of approximately 055°/235°. Inside there is plenty of deep water. The local fishing boats use the west end of the Canalizo de la Guasa (about midway down the cays) for shelter – the channel is narrow but can be picked out by the clear-sand stripe that the fishermen have cut through the eel grass with their keels. Inside there is deep water once again, but with little room to maneuver.

And that's about it. There is no reason to go to the Cayos los Indios and even less incentive to stay there if you do!

Isla de la Juventud

The Isla de la Juventud was discovered by Columbus, but largely ignored for centuries. As late as the Batista regime it was primarily a prison island, with an enormous 'model' prison (capable of housing up to 5,000 prisoners) on the north coast. Since the revolution it has been developed as a major agrarian region, with huge citrus orchards around the hills in the center of the island, and many other crops grown on the fertile lands in the northern half of the island. The southern half of the island is still almost completely undeveloped, and in fact much of it has been set aside as a nature preserve. The island is surprisingly picturesque: it is well worth renting a car for a day (from the Hotel Colony – see below) simply to drive through the countryside and enjoy the scenery.

Sailing strategies

Most cruisers will not wish to circumnavigate the island. The choice then lies in whether to make a pass along the northern or southern coast. The northern coast offers more protection from the prevailing winds and as such is particularly attractive if sailing from west to east (against the prevailing winds – if the wind is out of the east or the SE a passage along the south coast is a hard slog). The northern route also enables you to visit Nueva Gerona, which may be the first opportunity in some time to stock up on supplies (although, it may be easier to leave the boat in the Marina Siguanea, rent a car from the Hotel Colony, and do your shopping as part of a day's touring around the island – see below). Apart from the protection, there are few attractions on the north coast since it is almost entirely fringed with mangroves (there are, however, attractive vistas inland of acres of coconut palms interspersed with pastureland, backed by some quite dramatic hills).

The south coast of the Isla de la Juventud does not have a single, decently protected anchorage in 40M, but it does have attractive anchorages at the southwestern and southeastern tips of the island. However, it would not be worth braving the often substantial seas just to see these two spots, if it were not for the fact that the south coast route also leads along the south coast of the Archipiélago de los Canarreos, with some lovely beaches and gorgeous coral. So where does this leave us?

From west to east in prevailing winds we would choose the north coast route for its protection. We would come down from the Cayos de San Felipe to Caleta Puerto Francés and the Marina Siguanea, rent a car for the day to see the island and go shopping in Nueva Gerona, and then pass around the north coast to either the Canal de la Cruz (continuing to the Canalizo Aguardiente), or else the Pasa Quitasol (continuing to the Canal del Rosario). The choice of which set of passes to use would depend on the wind direction (all the passes are described below).

From the Canalizo Aguardiente or Canal del Rosario we would continue along the south shore of the Archipiélago de los Canarreos – this way we would avoid the slog along the south coast of the Isla de la Juventud without missing much of the Archipiélago de los Canarreos.

From east to west we would probably follow the south coast route all the way, perhaps making an overnighter of the stretch from Cayo Matías to Caleta Puerto Francés. Note, however, that the south coast of the Isla de la Juventud has only one lighthouse (at Carapachibey), and by the time you are on soundings you are almost on the reef or the shore, so nighttime sailing requires careful navigation if sailing close inshore.

In terms of our coverage of the island, we will do a clockwise circumnavigation (west to east on the north shore; east to west on the south shore) beginning at the NW corner of the island (the Ensenada de los Barcos).

Ensenada de los Barcos

The Ensenada de los Barcos is a large mangrove-lined bay with an extensive shoal closing off much of its mouth. It is easy to enter and once inside provides excellent protection from all directions.

Approaches

There are no off-lying hazards in the vicinity of the bay.

From the west, be sure to stay south of the Bajo Dios shoal (whose southern point is at approximately 21°58·8'N 83°10·6'W). Nearing the bay, you will be able to pick out various markers off

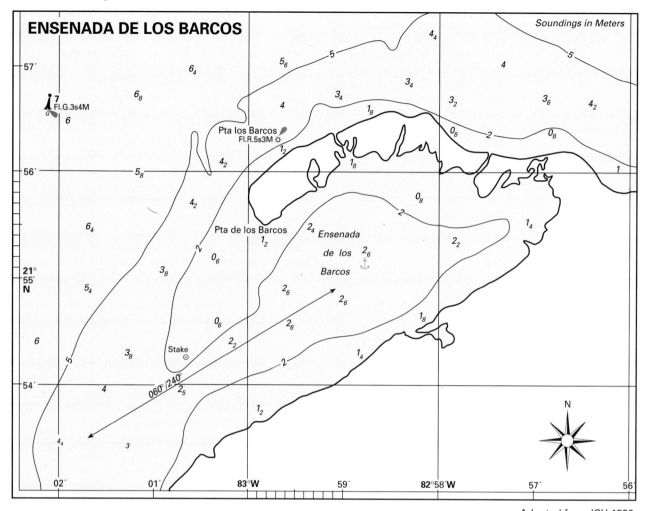

ENSENADA DE LOS BARCOS

Adapted from ICH 1590
Courtesy GeoCuba

Punta de los Barcos – you will need to lay a course 2–3M to the south of them.

From the east, simply stay ½M or more off the northern coast of the Isla de la Juventud, continuing in a southwesterly direction for the better part of 2M past Punta de los Barcos (if you try to turn in too soon you will run aground for sure!).

From the south (Hotel Colony), once again simply stay at least ½M off the coast, which will lead you directly into the bay.

Entry

Come to a position at approximately 21°53·8'N 83°01·2'W and head 060° for the better part of 2M into the bay. After about ½M you will leave a stake ¼M to port (i.e. you will pass to the south of it). The channel, which is ⅓M wide, has minimum depths of about 2·5m, with about the same amount of water over much of the interior of the bay. We have entered it at night, using a GPS, without problems.

Anchorage

Head toward the mangroves until the water shoals and then drop the hook.

Nueva Gerona

Nueva Gerona is the capital of the Isla de la Juventud. The approaches from seaward are unattractive (through a small commercial port area) but the city itself is pretty and less run down than most Cuban cities, with one or two fine colonial homes and a lovely little church on the central plaza. What is more, within easy walking distance of the dock the city has a group of dollar stores (including a reasonably stocked supermarket), ice cream (the first the children had seen in a month), gas and diesel, a farmers' market (the *agromercado*), and various other facilities and supplies. Water is available on the dock used by visiting boats. Propane can be obtained (with difficulty – it involves talking one office into issuing the paperwork, and then traveling several miles out of

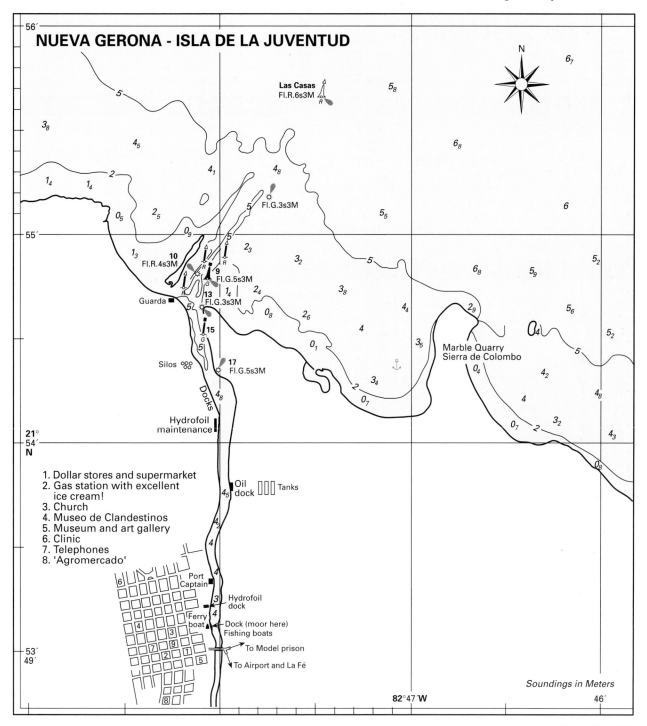

NUEVA GERONA - ISLA DE LA JUVENTUD

Las Casas
Fl.R.6s3M

Fl.G.3s3M

10
Fl.R.4s3M

9
Fl.G.5s3M

Guarda

13
Fl.G.3s3M

15

Silos

17
Fl.G.5s3M

Docks

Marble Quarry
Sierra de Colombo

Hydrofoil
maintenance

1. Dollar stores and supermarket
2. Gas station with excellent
   ice cream!
3. Church
4. Museo de Clandestinos
5. Museum and art gallery
6. Clinic
7. Telephones
8. 'Agromercado'

Oil
dock   Tanks

Port
Captain

Hydrofoil
dock

Ferry
boat

Dock (moor here)
Fishing boats

To Model prison

To Airport and La Fé

Soundings in Meters

82°47'W   46'

Adapted from ICH 1867
Courtesy GeoCuba

town to get the bottles filled). The city is also a port of entry for Cuba.

The Museo de los Clandestinos contains exhibits concerning the early days of the revolution; a walk of about a mile south from the central plaza, continuing past the *agromercado*, brings you to El Abbra, an old plantation home in some gorgeous countryside; while further out of town (to the east)

is the prison (Presidio Modelo – now another museum) in which Castro was held for a while; this is surprisingly interesting. Cars can be rented to tour the island.

There is no anchorage close to the city. In 1997 a dock was set aside for visiting boats close to the center of town but there is room for only a few boats and it is on a first-come, first-serve basis. There is a fence with tight security. However it may be easier to visit the city in a rented car from the Hotel Colony (see below), particularly since we have received reports that cruising boats are intermittently not allowed to enter the river and sail to Nueva Gerona.

Approaches and entry

Come to the sea buoy at approximately 21°55·6'N 82°47·4'W. This is a mile or so offshore in 5m and can be taken on any side.

The city is a couple of miles up the Las Casas river. The entry to the river is up a well marked, dredged channel. From the sea buoy, a course of approximately 214° will bring you into the channel, leaving a green marker (a lit post) to port (i.e. passing to the west of it), and then continuing between the numerous markers into the mouth of the river.

At the mouth of the river (on the west bank) is a Guarda post, but simply sail by. Inside the river you will find 4 or 5m. ½M in, on the west bank, are some silos, followed by a small commercial port and then a maintenance depot for the Soviet-built hydrofoils that provide a rapid service between Nueva Gerona and Surgidero de Batabano on the mainland. Next comes an oil and LPG (propane) unloading facility on the east bank. Another ½M further south you come to the port captain's office (a white house) on the west bank.

Clearance procedures

There is no dock in front of the port captain's office – simply some rotten (coconut) pilings and nasty looking bits of rusting steel. You should continue upstream to an excellent concrete dock alongside an old ferry boat that has been hauled ashore and mounted as a museum piece on a substantial steel cradle (it is the boat in which Castro and his comrades made the crossing to jail on the island after the failed assault on the Moncada barracks in 1953). Note, however, that there are one or two pieces of iron sticking out of the dock wall, so come in carefully with adequate fenders. Clearance is relatively formal (Guarda, customs, immigration, and perhaps others, depending on where you have come from). Currently, dockage fees if up to $0.45 per foot per day are being charged.

Anchorages

There is nowhere to anchor in the Las Casas river (it is too narrow). However, just to the east of the entrance to the river are a couple of bays with dramatic headlands which offer excellent protection from all directions except the NW and north (i.e. in all but northers). These are, in fact, the most dramatic anchorages in this part of Cuba. The water is deep and free of hazards until fairly close to the

shore, so simply come into the lee of the headlands and then drop the hook. The bay nearest to Nuevo Gerona (in the lee of the Sierra de Colombo) has a small beach at its south end. Its only drawback is the fact that the hills above it are being actively quarried for marble, which may produce a certain amount of dust at times, depending on the wind direction.

Passes to the north and east of the Isla de la Juventud

The islands of the Archipiélago de los Canarreos extend from the northeastern tip of the Isla de la Juventud in an arc to the SE and east; another string of cays extends away to the north, much of the way to the mainland. Collectively, they form a barrier to navigation down the middle of the Golfo de Batabano. This barrier, however, is cut by several navigable passes. From our perspective the most important are the Pasa de la Manteca, which allows navigation to the north up to Surgidero de Batabano; the Pasa de Quitasol, which is generally used when passaging between the north coast of the Isla de la Juventud and Cayo Largo; and the Canal de la Cruz, which is also useful for passaging to and from Cayo Largo, and is the most convenient pass for navigating around the east coast of the Isla de la Juventud.

South of the Canal de la Cruz, the Archipiélago de los Canarreos still obstructs any passage down the east coast of the Isla de la Juventud. There is a tricky inside passage (Paso del Guayabo) threading through the cays immediately to the east of the Isla de la Juventud, but the channel has a controlling depth of 1·6m (we got 1·8m through it at close to low tide, but ploughed a groove for a good part of the way, and stuck hard a couple of times, getting towed off by the masthead on the second occasion). The next pass closest to the east coast of the Isla de la Juventud is the Canalizo Aguardiente (see below), 16M to the east of Punta del Este (the SE tip of the island) – in other words, unless you can use the Pasa del Guayabo, a major detour is needed to passage from the north coast of the Isla de la Juventud to the south coast, via the east coast.

Pasa de la Manteca

We have not transited this pass. However, according to the Cuban charts and pilot it is a straight shot, with substantial markers at each end, numerous intermediate markers, and minimum depths of 4m. It lies on the principal commercial route between Nuevo Gerona and Surgidero de Batabano, and as a result sees a fair amount of traffic.

From the south, come to a position at approximately 21°59·6'N 82°43·3'W and pass through on a heading of 030°.

From the north, come to a position at approximately 22°01·3'N 82°42·3'W and pass through on a heading of 210°.

Pasa de Quitasol

The Pasa de Quitasol is the principal pass for commercial traffic coming to Nueva Gerona from the east. It is once again a substantial, well marked pass with a lighted beacon at both ends (both red) and another in the center (green), with various intermediate markers. The eastern end also has a lighted green marker, but at the time we passed through this was not working. The channel is to the north of the red beacons, and south of the green beacons. When passing through, you may need to compensate for a tidal set.

From the west, come to a position at approximately 21°55·8'N 82°39·4'W and pass

Adapted from ICH 1589
Courtesy GeoCuba

through on a heading of 080°.

From the east, come to a position at approximately 21°56·1'N 82°37·5'W and pass through on a heading of 260°.

Note Ned and Kate Phillips report a dangerous, unmarked wreck to the SW of the pass at approximately 21°55·3'N 82°39·7'W

Canal de la Cruz

The Canal de la Cruz cuts through the Cayos de los Inglesitos just to the east of the Isla de la Juventud. The canal is narrow in places, and not straight, but it is marked by numerous stakes and as a result is reasonably easy to transit. However, when you get there these stakes may not be as described. Note that the white square topmarks are almost all on the north side of the channel. The controlling depth, which occurs at the extreme west end, is 1·9m.

From the west, come to a position at approximately 21°52·1'N 82°36·7'W. You will be able to see a fair number of stakes. Try to pick out the westernmost one, and maneuver until this is in line with the tip of the land on the SE side of the canal (the two will be on a bearing of approximately 123°). Come into the canal on this heading, leaving the first stake about 30–50m to port (i.e. pass to the south of the stake) and then come onto a heading of approximately 140° down the channel, with most of the stakes to port, but one or two to starboard. After ½M you leave a large stake immediately to port (a couple of meters will do), and then arc around to the east (085°), coming almost down to the mangroves in the process. Continue out to the east, watching out for a piece of almost-submerged steel re-bar which forms the last stake and is left to starboard (you pass to the north of it).

From the east, come to a position at approximately 21°51·6'N 82°35·5'W and then enter the canal on a heading of 265° leaving the first stake with a square top to port (pass to the north of it) and the second one to starboard (pass to the south of it). In the process, watch out for an almost-submerged piece of steel re-bar on the run in to the canal. Once inside, come in toward the mangroves just before the large stake, leaving the stake to starboard (pass to the south of it), at which point you come to a heading of 320°, leaving most of the stakes to starboard. As you

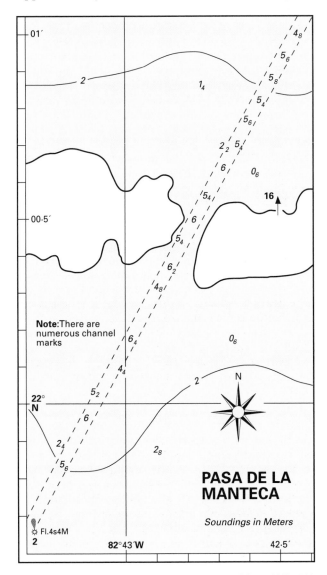

Note: There are numerous channel marks

PASA DE LA MANTECA

Soundings in Meters

Adapted from ICH 1589
Courtesy GeoCuba

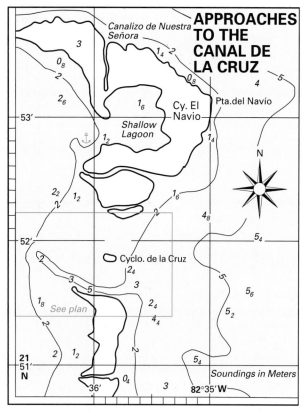

APPROACHES TO THE CANAL DE LA CRUZ

Adapted from ICH 1586
Courtesy GeoCuba

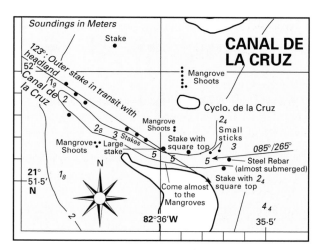

CANAL DE LA CRUZ

Adapted from ICH 1586
Courtesy GeoCuba

pass the last stake (stay 30–50m south of it), curve a little more to the west (300°) and continue out.

Anchorage Behind the headland a little more than a mile to the north of the pass, on the west side of the cays, there is an anchorage off the mouth of a shallow lagoon. This anchorage is well protected from all but the west and NW, and provides a convenient spot in which to layover before or after transiting the canal.

Paso del Guayabo

This is not one for the faint hearted except in a shoal-draft vessel. The pass is long (almost 5M), shallow (long stretches at 1·7m), and almost completely without markers! It does, however, avoid a major diversion to the east for those cruisers wishing to passage between the north and south coasts of the Isla de la Juventud, via the east coast, and it is well protected at almost all times so if you run into trouble it will be an inconvenience rather than life-threatening. We were lead through by a fishing boat (which helped to tow us off a couple of times). We can do little more than refer you to the track we took (see plan), and to augment this with a few notes.

From the north, come to a position at approximately 21°45·8'N 82°34·7'W. The first stretch of the canal is a mile or so, leading toward an area of deeper water (point '1' on our plan) on a heading of approximately 205° with minimum depths of more than 2m. The heading then changes to approximately 145°, toward the tip of the land on the west side of the channel (point '2'). The mangroves are passed a couple of hundred meters off, 50–100m to the east of several small stakes. Next you aim for a point midway between a small cay and the land to the east (point '3'), after which you maintain a north/south heading between points '3' and '4' which brings you about 70m off the mangroves at point '4'. Between points '4' and '5' the heading is 150°. At point '5' you come 50–100m to the west of a stake, which in turn is to the west of a newly developing cay. From point '5' you simply continue on the 150° heading until in deeper water.

From the south, come north between Cayo Guayabo and Cayo Ratones on a heading of approximately 330° to a position at approximately 21°41·4'N 82°33·3'W (note that there is an extensive shoal to the south of Cayo Ratones – you should hold a course over toward Cayo Guayabo). Continue on the heading of 330° to pass ¼M to the west of a small (uncharted) cay (point '5'), staying to the west of a stake that marks the end of a shoal coming out from the cay. Continue on the 330° heading to pass immediately to the west (70m or so) of the headland at point '4', and then change course to pass midway between the small cay and the land to the east at point '3'. From here it is a little west of north to pass close to the mangroves at point '2' (just to the east of a line of sticks), and then 325° to the deeper water at point '1', after which it is a straightforward run to the NNE (025°) and deeper water.

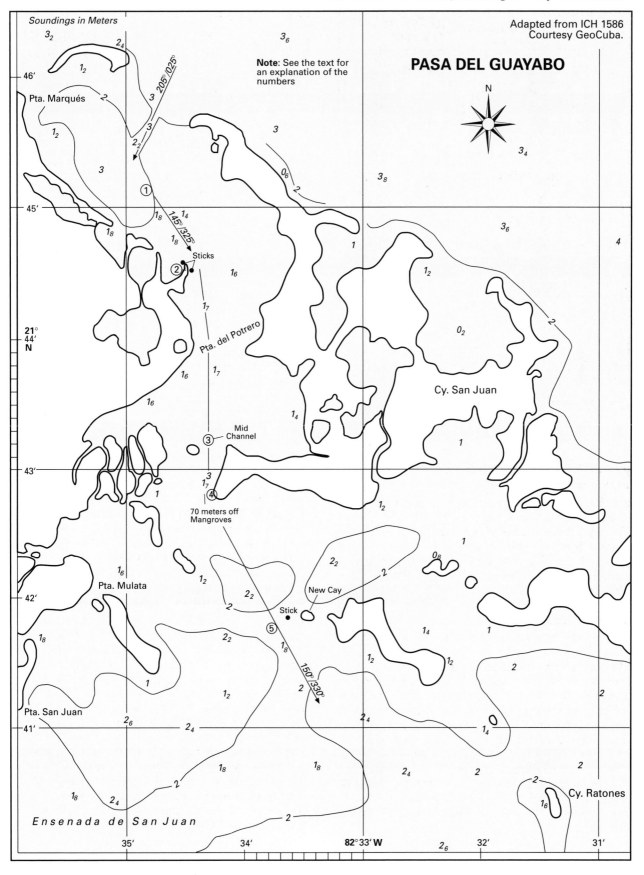

Soundings in Meters

Note: See the text for an explanation of the numbers

Adapted from ICH 1586
Courtesy GeoCuba.

PASA DEL GUAYABO

N

Pta. Marqués

Sticks

Pta. del Potrero

Mid Channel

Cy. San Juan

70 meters off Mangroves

Pta. Mulata

New Cay

Stick

Pta. San Juan

Cy. Ratones

Ensenada de San Juan

82°33' W

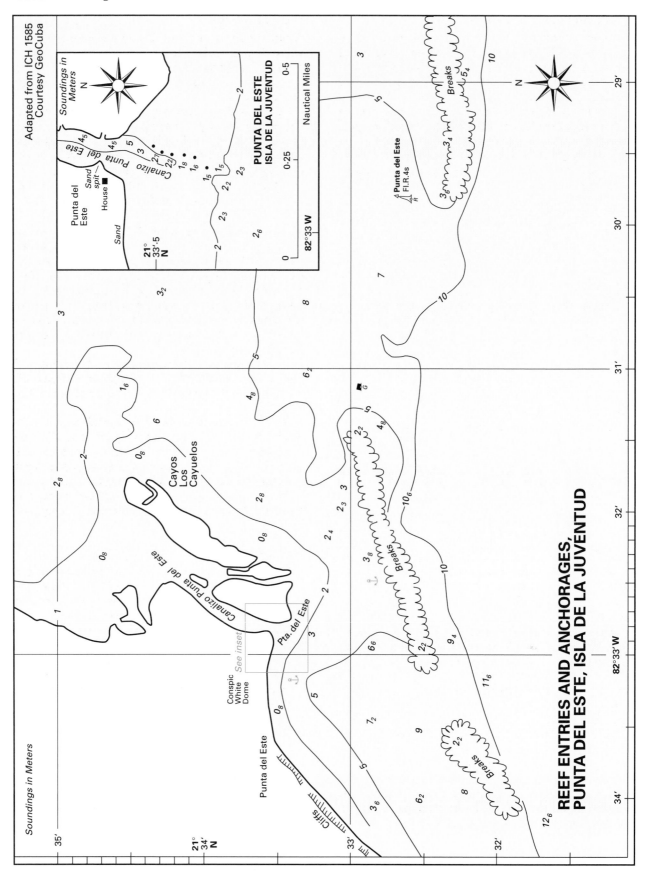

REEF ENTRIES AND ANCHORAGES, PUNTA DEL ESTE, ISLA DE LA JUVENTUD

Main channel at Punta del Este

A fringing reef runs along much of the south coast of the Isla de la Juventud, extending eastward to the south of the Archipiélago do los Canarreos. It is broken by a 1½M wide passage to the SE of Punta del Este, itself the southeastern tip of the Isla de la Juventud. The pass is free of all hazards, with a green can buoy marking the western edge of the pass (note that this is much closer to the reef than is shown on the Cuban charts, so don't attempt to come between it and the reef!), and a red lighted buoy (Fl.4s) marking the eastern edge of the pass.

South coast of the Isla de la Juventud

The eastern half of the south coast of the Isla de la Juventud has mile after mile of undeveloped beaches, interspersed with sections of low, rocky coastline. A fringing reef parallels the coast from Punta del Este all the way to Punta Guanal (more or less midway along the coast). At Punta del Este the reef is ¾M offshore with a couple of substantial, navigable, breaks, but by Punta Guanal it is close inshore with few breaks.

At Punta del Este you can sail around the eastern end of the reef, or pass through the breaks, to anchor in the lee of the reef. West from Punta del Este there is only one other break which is navigable (close to Punta de Curazao), and here the entry is not easy and is only suitable in good light and calm conditions. What is more, neither of these reef anchorages (Punta del Este and Punta Curazao) provides more than modest protection – if heavy seas are running outside the reef the anchorages will be relatively uncomfortable. To find a secure, well protected anchorage at the eastern end of the south coast, it is necessary to go to Cayo Matías (see below).

Between Punta Guanal and Punta Francés (at the western tip of the south coast) the coastline becomes more severe, with extensive stretches of low-lying rocky shoreline and fewer beaches. Although there are several substantial inlets, all are exposed to the south. Until close to Punta Francés none are suitable as overnight anchorages, and none are suitable even as lunch stops unless the conditions are particularly calm.

This lack of good anchorages on the south coast of the Isla de la Juventud makes it necessary to transit the entire coast in a single 40–50M passage. If traveling upwind (west to east) it might be just as well to head offshore and make this an overnighter; if traveling downwind, a daylight passage will benefit from the stronger winds as the day wears on.

Punta del Este

A mile or so inland from Punta del Este there is a white-domed radar building at a meteorological station. This is visible from many miles away from just about any direction, forming an excellent reference point.

At Punta del Este there is a deep-water channel between the sandy point and a couple of mangrove cays immediately to the SE. At the south end of this channel there is a well protected anchorage adjacent to a lovely beach. The only problem is that the controlling depth on entering the channel is 1·5m. Nevertheless, we have included a plan for shoal-draft vessels.

To enter, stay in the strip of light green water just off the white sand lining the shore, and inside the darker turtle grass. A number of stakes delineate the east side of the channel. The trickiest part is the first bit, after which the channel steadily deepens to 4m. Once inside, hug the mangroves on the east side of the channel, and if anchoring set an anchor fore-and-aft to avoid swinging onto the shoals to the west when the tide changes.

In prevailing easterlies, deeper draft vessels will find a fair measure of protection anchored just off the mouth of the channel, or in the lee of the reef to the south.

On the beach at the point is a small tourist villa which can be rented quite cheaply (☎ 2 3356). The caretakers have a substantial fishing boat to take people on day trips. Nearby there are some caves with the finest aboriginal paintings in Cuba, but unfortunately the caves are in a military zone; the best way to see them is from the Hotel Colony (see below).

Punta de Curazao

In calm conditions it is possible to slip through a break in the reef just to the east of Punta de Curazao, and to then hook around to the east and anchor in the lee of the reef off a white-sand beach backed by a large stand of casuarina trees.

The problem is, the reef on both sides of the entrance is more or less submerged, so that there is no clear line of breakers to guide you in, added to which the entry channel shoals to 2·5m with a fair amount of coral scattered around. This is a good light, calm conditions entry. Once inside, the protection is only modest – with heavy seas outside the reef the anchorage is somewhat rolly. We made the mistake of spending the night in here, anticipating the usual calm in the morning in which to make our exit. Instead, we got a southeaster in excess of 20 knots and had a nerve-wracking time getting out!

To enter, come to a position at approximately 21°27·6'N 82°44·5'W, from where you will be able to see the large stand of casuarinas more or less to

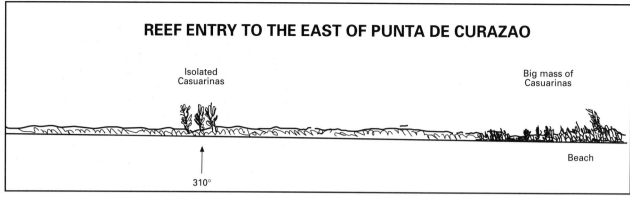

REEF ENTRY TO THE EAST OF PUNTA DE CURAZAO

Isolated Casuarinas

Big mass of Casuarinas

Beach

310°

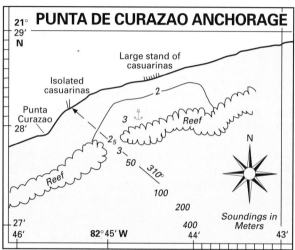

PUNTA DE CURAZAO ANCHORAGE

Large stand of casuarinas

Isolated casuarinas

Punta Curazao

Reef

Reef

Soundings in Meters

the north, and then a couple of isolated casuarinas about ½M further west. Come in on a heading of 310° for these isolated casuarinas, watching for coral heads, and then curve around to the north as you come inside the line of the reef itself. Once inside, hook to the east, keeping a good watch for coral patches, and anchor when out of the worst of the swells.

The south coast between Punta de Curazao and the Caleta Puerto Francés

This near 30M stretch of coastline has several inlets which look like they ought to provide reasonable shelter. They include the Caleta de Agustin Jol, the Caleta de Carapachibey, the Caleta Grande at Cocodrillo, and the Caleta Lugo at Punta Lugo. However, although some have enough water to permit entering, none provide protection from the SE and south, and all are potentially dangerous if the wind kicks up from these directions, so we have ignored them.

Caleta Puerto Francés

This is a large, wide-open bay on the west side of the Península de Siguanea. It contains some lovely beaches and gorgeous coral. At its northern end is a restaurant built on piles. The bay has extremely

deep water in its mouth, and then something of a wall on the inside. (The 200m line runs across the mouth of the bay, after which the bottom suddenly comes up to 40m or so, and then shoals gradually as you work further inshore.) The bay is used as a dive location by the Hotel Colony (see below), and has a whole series of mooring buoys just inside the wall – these are used by the dive boats.

In spite of its open nature the bay provides good protection in an east wind, and reasonable protection (off a beach in the SE corner) in a southeaster. It is, however, wide open to northers.

Note Recent reports suggest that the Cubans have now prohibited cruising boats from anchoring in this bay.

From the south, the approach is free of all dangers, with the exception of shallow coral close in to Punta Pedernales, the southern headland to Caleta Puerto Francés. 100m or so out from Punta Pedernales the coral is well submerged. If you should happen to cut across it you will see the depths suddenly reduce to 20m or less, and then just as suddenly drop away as you come into the outer reaches of the bay.

From the north, you must be sure to clear the shoal to the north of Punta Francés. Relatively shallow water extends to the north and west of the beacon that is ¾M north of the point. This shoal then connects with a reef ½M to the west of Punta Francés – the entire area should be given a wide berth. A little more than a mile south of Punta Francés the reef hooks in toward the beach, with a substantial restaurant built on piles at its southern end. Southeast of the restaurant deep water extends in almost to the beach, but then another shoal, culminating in a tiny, low-lying cay, extends ⅓M out from the northern tip of Caleta Puerto Francés – this shoal must be rounded in order to enter the bay itself.

Anchorage Close to the shoreline is a gorgeous, light blue channel with a sand bottom, 5–7m deep. This makes a good spot in which to drop the hook (a Danforth type will bite best – the sand is not very thick). Otherwise, there is a great deal of coral and it is hard to find a suitable spot in which to anchor.

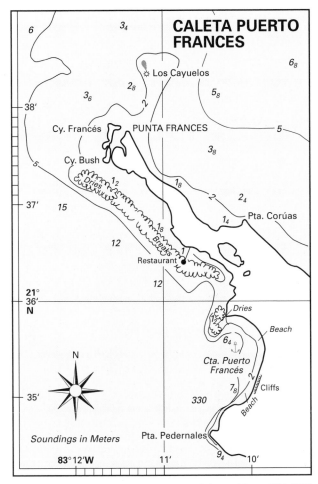

CALETA PUERTO FRANCES

Adapted from ICH 1590
Courtesy GeoCuba

With the 100 kilometers you can make it to Nueva Gerona and back, through some lovely countryside, seeing the most attractive part of the island and stocking up on supplies at the same time. Along the way, if you stop and ask at the various orchards you can obtain grapefruit and other citrus products.

The hotel staff can arrange a visit to the aboriginal cave paintings at Punta del Este, but generally two days' notice is required since the caves are in a military zone and various permits have to be obtained.

There is an excellent all-weather anchorage 2M south of the hotel in the Bahía de San Pedro, or better still, if leaving the boat, a small marina (the Marina Siguanea) just a mile south of the hotel.

Bahía de San Pedro

On the entire west coast, this is the only well protected anchorage between Punta Francés and the Ensenada de los Barcos. The bay has a straightforward entry, and once inside provides excellent protection from all directions.

From the south, give the shoals around Punta Francés a wide berth, and then beware of the isolated, and unmarked, shoal directly on the approach to the Bahía de San Pedro (at

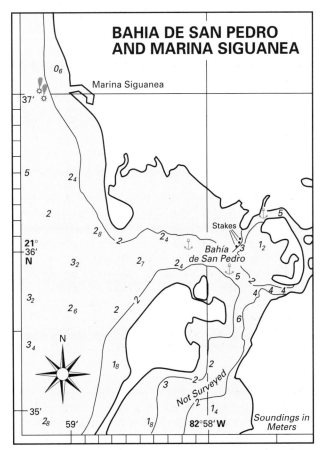

BAHIA DE SAN PEDRO AND MARINA SIGUANEA

Adapted from ICH 1590
Courtesy GeoCuba

In settled easterlies, anchor off the beach in the northeastern corner of the bay, but if a southeaster is driving swells into the bay, head down to the small beach in the SE corner.

In settled easterlies a comfortable anchorage can also be found SE of the restaurant, but in a southeasterly the swells drive up into this part of the bay, making it not only uncomfortable but also a potentially dangerous lee shore. Reportedly, 1·8m can be carried inside the south end of the reef and up toward the restaurant, but we have not checked this out. The channel, if it exists, must be right along the edge of the beach.

West coast of the Isla de la Juventud

The big attraction here is the Hotel Colony, a resort hotel originally developed as an American enclave prior to the revolution, but now catering mostly to European divers. The hotel welcomes sailors to its restaurant (buffet-style food at very reasonable prices), bar and pool. From the hotel a jeep can be rented for a 12-hour day at a cost of $32 (1997), which includes insurance and 100 free kilometers.

approximately 21°35·2'N 83°01·6'W – it has 2·2m over it).

From the Cayos de San Felipe and the Cayos los Indios, stay well clear of the shoals around and between these cays, noting the isolated shoal to the south of the Cayos los Indios (at approximately 21°43·3'N 83°10·0'W – it has a beacon).

From the north, simply stay ¼M or more off the coast.

Entry and anchorage Come into the bay on an easterly heading, 100m or more to the south of the north headland into the bay. The deep water (up to 6m) is in the center of the bay, gradually shoaling to 3m on either side, after which the bottom comes up very suddenly – if you go over the 3m line you will be aground soon afterward. The center of the bay provides good protection in prevailing winds.

For total protection it is possible to follow a rather narrow channel down to the south into a largish lagoon, or else to work up either of the two channels leading out of the bay to the east. The northernmost of these two channels has a line of stakes on its western side (i.e. you pass to the east of them) – you should approach the first stake on a heading of approximately 050°, leaving the stakes 10m or so to port. The southern channel has no markers. With both channels, once into the mangroves, keep over to the north side.

Marina Siguanea

The Marina Siguanea is a small marina catering primarily to the needs of the dive boats serving the Hotel Colony. Nevertheless, the marina welcomes visiting boats with good docks, water, and electricity (the usual dubious hookup – see Chapter 1) at $0.45 per foot per day. The marina has a fuel dock with 2m alongside, but only diesel is available ($0.46 per liter). The marina is an intermittent port of entry to Cuba, although procedures may take some time since the officials must come from Nueva Gerona (if already cleared into Cuba, clearance procedures are rapid). There are no nearby towns or facilities except for the Hotel Colony, which is a mile away up a good road – a pleasant walk, or you may be lucky enough to catch a ride. Some supplies (bread, meat, eggs, fruit and vegetables) can sometimes be bought from the hotel kitchen, with wine and spirits available in the hotel store.

Entry Come to a position at approximately 21°37·0'N 82°59·3'W and run straight up the clearly marked channel on a heading of 073° for the white leading mark ashore (a cross between a corkscrew and a unicorn's horn, or maybe it's a giant ice cream cone!). The depths shoal to a scant 1·8m about midway in, and then deepen again to 3m on the inside. The Guarda dock is just inside the marina on the northern side. Note: in 1999 the center of the channel had reportedly shoaled to 1·5m

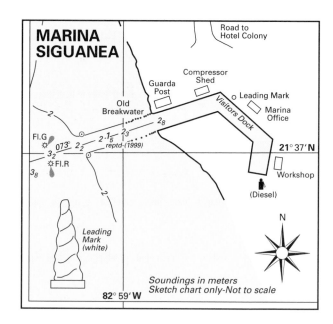

Archipiélago de los Canarreos

The Archipiélago de los Canarreos is a string of cays arcing down from the northeastern tip of the Isla de la Juventud and continuing well to the east. Most of the cays are mangroves once again, but a number of those to the south and east have lovely beaches, particularly the tourist island of Cayo Largo. The waters around the northern cays in the *archipiélago* are the usual green and dark waters of the Golfo de Batabano, but those along the southern edge are the most glorious hues of blue – some of the most beautiful water colors we have seen anywhere. A fringing reef runs along much of the south coast of the *archipiélago*. It contains a great deal of unspoiled, pristine coral (the finest we have seen in some time) with a fair amount of fish life and many lobster (the largest we have ever seen!). All-in-all this is a beautiful area in which to cruise and should definitely not be missed.

Note The reef is by no means continuous or uniform. In places it is miles offshore, in others it connects with the cays. Some of it is well submerged and navigable while other sections thrust up above the surface of the ocean. As a result, the protection afforded is very variable, while navigation can be quite complex – it is essential to have good charts if cruising in this area.

Ensenada Cayo Matías

Cayo Matías is just off the southeastern extremity of the Isla de la Juventud. From Cayo Matías a string of cays extends to the east and then in a broad arc to the north and back to the west. Between these cays

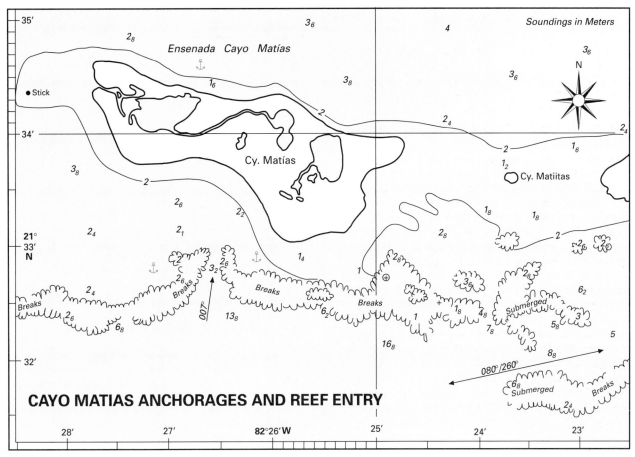

CAYO MATIAS ANCHORAGES AND REEF ENTRY

Adapted from ICH 1585
Courtesy GeoCuba

are very shallow banks. To the west is the Isla de la Juventud. The large bay thus formed, some 3M from north to south, and 10M from east to west, provides protection in more or less any conditions. The bay can only be entered by the Paso del Guayabo (see above), or by the more-than-a-mile-wide, marked, channel to the SE of Punta de Este (see above again) which leads in from the open ocean.

Cayo Matías

Cayo Matías is the largest of the cays bordering the Ensenada Cayo Matías. On its northern side it is all mangroves, but on its south coast it has substantial areas of beach, while just to the south is an almost continuous barrier reef which is 2M off the coast at the west end of the island, but closes the coast at the east end (making it impossible to navigate further east inside the reef – it is necessary to come outside for 3M and then re-enter south of tiny Cayo Matiitas).

Anchorages

The north shore of Cayo Matías provides protection in all but northers, but is uninteresting (mangroves).

The waters between the south shore of the cay and the reef are navigable, with minimum depths of just over 2m. Tucked up behind the reef at the east end of the island are a couple of lovely anchorages with beaches behind, and excellent snorkeling on the reef apron out front. The reef breaks all but the heaviest seas, so that the protection is good in all but strong southerly conditions.

Reef passage

Between the two anchorages is a straightforward reef entry/exit, although this should only be attempted in good light and calm conditions since the pass has no channel markers.

To enter the reef, come to a position at approximately 21°32·3'N 82°26·7'W and proceed on a heading of approximately 007°, midway between the two sections of breaking reef. Minimum depths going in are about 3m in the final stretch.

To exit, simply head south down the center of the channel.

Cayo Matiitas reef passage

The reef entry/exit south of Cayo Matiitas is between two well submerged areas of reef which do not appear to contain any dangerous coral heads, but nevertheless it would be better to stay in the charted channel which ranges from approximately 21°31·9'N 82°24·0'W to 21°32·1'N 82°22·8'W on an axis of 080°/260°. Once inside, the waters are protected by an almost continuous line of breaking reef which runs from 2M south of Cayo Matiitas eastward to close the western end of Cayo Campos.

The water inside the reef is navigable almost to the west end of Cayo Campos, but the navigable channel gradually narrows until south of the gap between Cayo Hicacos and Cayo Campos you run into a series of (beautiful) coral heads that almost entirely obstruct the channel. It is possible to thread through these in good light, or to skirt them immediately to the north (maximum of 1·8m), but then the channel finally closes the reef just 100m short of the basin inside the Cayo Campos reef passage (see below). 1·6m can be carried through this last shoal stretch, but only by staying just a couple of meters off the back of the coral on the reef apron (we took 1·8m through at close to low tide but touched lightly).

Cayo Campos

Cayo Campos has mile after mile of unspoiled white sand beach on its south coast. The cay is a protected area which is home to a considerable number of monkeys. The reef apron contains some gorgeous coral in protected waters at shallow snorkeling depths. There are lobster crawling around all over the place!

Unfortunately, there is shoal water between the cay and the reef along almost all of the southern shore, with the reef itself being submerged sufficiently to allow the swells to sweep in – with any kind of a sea running, there is just no way to approach close to the coastline, and no place to anchor if you could. There is, however, a reef entry at the western tip of the island, with a basin on the inside, which makes a reasonably protected anchorage. From here the western end of the cay is a ½M dinghy ride away, but the rest of the southern shore is a mile or two (you will want a planing dinghy).

Note that if you should happen to be approaching from the north side of Cayo Campos, a channel leads down to the SW tip of the island where you can anchor with a dock bearing 100°. However, a shoal blocks all passage south to the anchorage described below, although we have had reports of a channel leading to the SW which is used by local fishing boats.

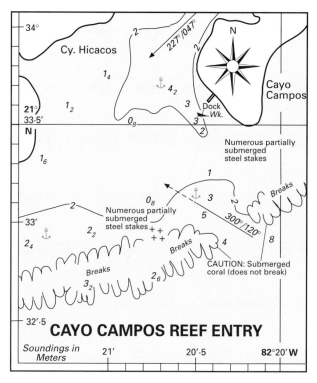

CAYO CAMPOS REEF ENTRY

Soundings in Meters

Adapted from ICH 1585
Courtesy GeoCuba

Reef passage

The reef entry/exit must be treated with caution since the break is set at an axis to the reef (it is not a straightforward north/south shot), with a considerable number of dangerous coral heads lining both sides of the passage well out from the breaking areas. There is also coral in the passage itself, although we found nothing with less than 4m over it. Nevertheless, this is a good light, calm conditions, passage.

To enter, come to a position at approximately 21°32·9'N 82°20·1'W and proceed on a heading of 300°, aiming just east of the breaking reef on the west side of the channel. Once abeam of the breaking reef on the east side of the channel, curve around toward the north.

To exit, maintain a heading of 120° down the center of the channel until well out to sea (in at least 8m).

Anchorage

Once inside the basin you must be extremely watchful because this area is used to construct pens to hold grouper during the April mating season. The pens are made from lengths of steel re-bar, hammered into the bottom on 10ft centers. The entire area is littered with these stakes, some of which are submerged. However, between the staked areas there is plenty of room to anchor on sand or turtle grass in 2–3m.

Cayos Aquardiente

The Cayos Aquardiente are mostly mangroves, and have little of interest. However, there is a straightforward pass – the Canalizo Aquardiente – which cuts through the cays, and which is the first decent passage through the Archipiélago de los Canarreos between here and the Isla de la Juventud. South of the cays, the reef is well offshore (up to 5M) with no apparent hazards between it and the cays, apart from the shoal water mentioned below.

Approaches on the south side

From the west, the waters inside the reef can be entered by staying south of a drying reef patch at approximately 21°33·1'N 82°17·7'W.

From the east, follow the channel between the various cays and the reef until south of Cayo Avalos (see below), after which it is a clear run to the west.

Canalizo Aguardiente

Owing to a slight curve to the channel, there is no visible break through the cays, so the north and south entrances are not easy to pick out from a distance. However, as you close either end of the pass you see various substantial channel markers and buoys which make the passage a straightforward matter (we've done it at night with a full moon, although I would not recommend this). Minimum depths are 2m at both ends, with up to 6m in between.

There are sometimes quite strong tidal currents in the pass, so you will need to watch your back-bearing when passing through, adjusting your heading as necessary to compensate for any tidal set.

The south end of the pass leads into a large bay with the Cayos Aguardiente to the north, and the fringing reef some miles to the south. The bay looks like it would be well protected. However, the reef is well submerged in many places, and has substantial breaks, so that it does not serve as a complete barrier to swells sweeping in from the south – the bay can get quite choppy. Just to compound problems, the charted depths in the bay tend to be rather optimistic. In particular, there is a shoal that extends all the way from the Canalizo los Ajos (a shoal-draft pass 1½M to the west of the Canalizo Aguardiente) to a point 1M to the SSW of the entrance to the Canalizo Aguardiente. The 3m that the detailed Cuban chart shows around the NW tip of this shoal does not exist (there is a scant 1·8m). To avoid a potentially uncomfortable grounding, the Canalizo Aguardiente should be approached from at least 1M due south of the entrance, or exited due south for at least 1M.

From the north, come to a position at approximately 21°35·4'N 82°14·6'W from where the outer channel marker, a post with a triangle on top,

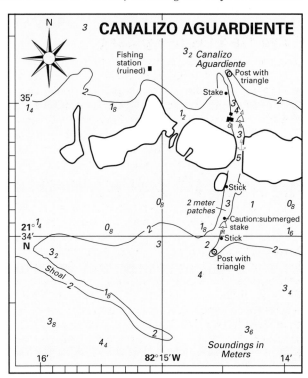

Adapted from ICH 1584
Courtesy GeoCuba

will be clearly visible. Enter the channel on a heading of approximately 160° leaving the post 15m or so to port (i.e. pass to the west of it), leaving the next post about the same distance to starboard, and passing between the two buoys. Aim for midway between the mangroves. At the other end of the mangroves come out in center channel and take up a heading to leave the red buoy just to port (a meter or two). There is a stick more or less midway between the buoy and the outer channel marker – you hold a course to leave the stick close to port, and then change your heading to leave the outer channel marker (which in 1997 was lying over and almost submerged) 30m to port (i.e. pass to the west of it). If you come too close to the final marker you will probably run aground, so watch out!

From the south, come to a position at approximately 21°33·8'N 82°14·7'W from where the outer channel marker (a post with a triangle on top which, in 1997, was laying over and almost submerged), and a buoy further in, will be clearly visible. Enter the channel on a heading of approximately 015°, aiming for a stick which is midway between the outer marker and the buoy, and leaving the outer marker 30m to starboard (i.e. pass to the west of it). You will see what appear to be two clear sand channels that converge off the stick, but the one closest to the outer marker has in fact been made by boats that have run aground – you need the one further from the marker. Leave the stick close to starboard, and then leave the buoy just a meter or

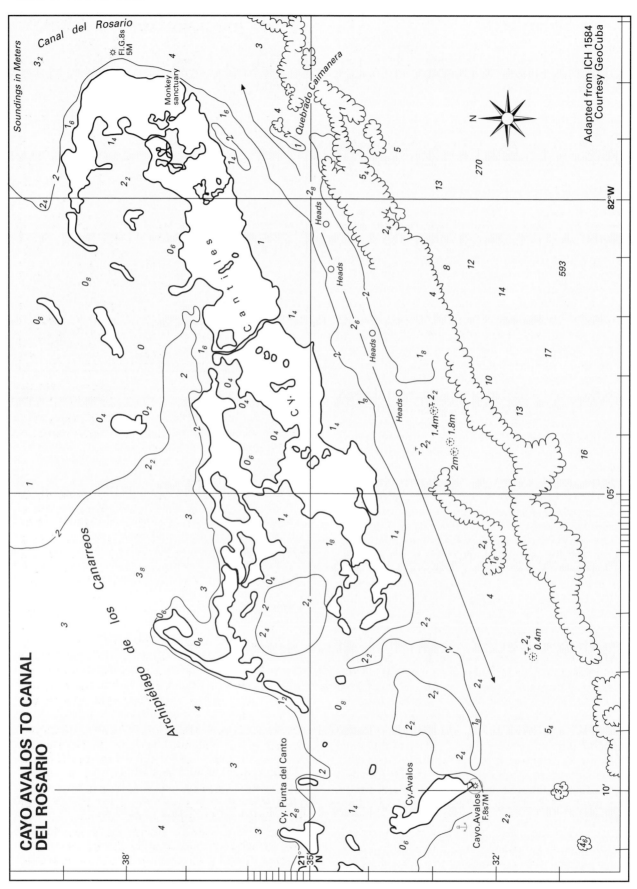

CAYO AVALOS TO CANAL DEL ROSARIO

two to starboard, after which you aim for the center of the channel up the mangroves. At the other end of the mangroves simply pass between the two buoys, and set a course to leave the outer marker 15m to starboard (i.e. pass to the west of it). This course will leave a midpoint post to port.

Anchorage

The stretch between the mangroves halfway through the canal provides protection from all directions and has more than enough width to provide adequate swinging room. Most of the time you will lie to the current rather than the wind.

Inside the reef between the Canalizo Aguardiente and the Canal del Rosario

After closing the shore at the east end of Cayo Campos (to the west of the Canalizo Aguardiente) the reef temporarily terminates and then begins again to the south of the Canalizo Aguardiente, but 6M offshore with one or two breaking stretches separated by submerged reef. Between here and the Canal del Rosario, 15M to the east, the reef has less water over it and is wider. Once again, it closes the shoreline until the navigable channel between the reef and the coastal shoals is down to about ½M, with depths of as little as 2m. In the stretch to the south of Cayo Cantiles a number of coral heads will be found in the channel itself (some excellent snorkeling) so good light and a bow watch are needed when sailing through this area.

5M to the east of the Canalizo Aguardiente a reasonable anchorage will be found in the lee of Cayo Avalos (anchoring ½M to the west of the light at the southern end of the cay), and then once into the narrower channel between the cays and the reef you can anchor just about anywhere with reasonable protection in most conditions, although there may be some residual swells working over the reef in strong southerly conditions, and a bit of a chop in a strong easterly. The cays themselves in this stretch are uninteresting: Cayo Avalos is a low-lying coral cay with a fair mixture of vegetation; the rest of the cays are primarily mangroves.

Canal del Rosario

The Canal del Rosario is the principal channel through the Archipiélago de los Canarreos into the eastern half of the Golfo de Batabano. It is wide, deep, well marked and easy to use in any conditions.

Cayo Cantiles, on the west side of the canal, is a monkey sanctuary which also has large iguanas, *jutías* (a mammal about the size of a small dog) and crocodiles. The resident staff are very friendly. The

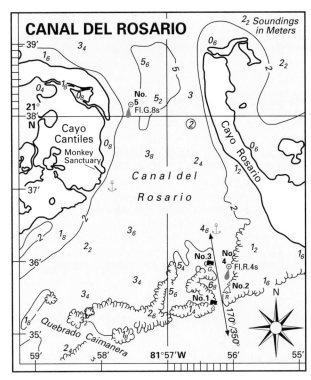

Adapted from ICH 1584
Courtesy GeoCuba

sanctuary is at 21°37·3'N 81°57·9'W. Watch out for lines of fish stakes off the monkey station and also the NW tip of Cayo Cantiles.

Approaches and transit

From the Pasa de Quitasol or the Canal de la Cruz, come to the north of Cayo Tablones (to a position at approximately 21°44·5'N 82°04·5'W). The course from the Pasa de Quitasol is 112°; that from the Canal de la Cruz is 104°. In prevailing easterlies, the west side of Cayo Tablones, which can be approached quite closely, provides adequate protection for a comfortable anchorage.

North of Cayo Tablones you must continue east for a mile or so in order to clear the extensive shoals that line this cay. After rounding the shoals, the next position is a beacon at approximately 21°41·0'N 81°58·6'W, 1M to the west of the southern end of Cayo del Pasaje – the water to the west of the beacon is relatively shoal (approximately 2m); while that just to the east is a little deeper.

From the beacon you head 155° midway between the cays to the SSE and continue on this heading until you reach the markers for the channel through the reef. You will see a lighted (red) beacon paired with a green can, and further out a red nun buoy paired with another green can. The channel is up the middle, leaving the red markers to port (i.e. passing to the west of them), on a heading of approximately 170°, *continuing well out to sea on this heading* (until in 8m or more) before changing course to the east or the west.

From outside, come to a position at approximately 21°35·3'N 81°56·1'W, to the south of the channel markers (don't cut the corner) and then come in midway between the red and green markers (red nun buoy to starboard) on a heading of approximately 350°.

Once past the second pair of markers, you can head west into the channel between Cayo Cantiles and the reef, or else continue northward toward the Pasa de Quitasol or the Canal de la Cruz. To reach these passes, change to a heading of 335° to pass midway between the cays to the NNW, and continue on this heading as far as the beacon 1M to the west of the southern end of Cayo del Pasaje, leaving the beacon to port (i.e. passing to the east of it) to find the deeper water. Beyond the beacon, a heading of 315° will keep you clear of the shoals to the east of Cayo Tablones, after which you can sail directly to the passes (on a heading of approximately 284° for the Canal de la Cruz, and 292° for the Pasa de Quitasol).

Anchorages

In prevailing easterlies the western end of Cayo del Rosario provides an excellent lee, while to the SW of the cay a considerable amount of reef breaks up any swells coming in from the SE – a comfortable anchorage will be found by approaching the SW corner of the cay and anchoring when the water shoals to 2–3m (go slowly – the bottom comes up rapidly in places).

In a norther the eastern end of Cayo Cantiles creates a good lee, with deep water relatively close in – simply come in until the bottom shoals to 2–3m and then anchor.

In both locations you may well lie to the tide rather than the wind, so this should be taken into account when dropping the hook.

Various sections of breaking reef in the vicinity of the canal also create a reasonable lee in which to anchor, with some lovely snorkeling around the coral.

Cayo del Rosario

Cayo del Rosario has miles of unspoiled sandy beaches. The interior of the cay is dry with scrubby vegetation that is home to some large iguanas. Much of the cay is a protected nature preserve, with a well marked nature trail leading away from the beach at the western end (close to the anchorage – see below). The off-lying reef has some reasonable snorkeling.

The fringing reef closes the shoreline at the SW tip of the cay – it is necessary to come outside the reef at this point. To the east of this there is a substantial break in the reef giving access to a reasonably sheltered anchorage, but it is not possible to continue eastward inside the reef from the anchorage because a band of coral intersects a sandy shoal coming out from the shore, reducing the depth to a little over 1·6m.

About midway along the south coast of Cayo del Rosario the reef ends, beginning again approximately 6M to the SE in a rather intermittent fashion as it runs in toward the coast at Cayo Largo. This lack of reef in the vicinity of the east end of Cayo del Rosario means that there are no protected anchorages in this area, although in calm conditions it is possible to anchor right off the beach, retreating to a more secure anchorage at night.

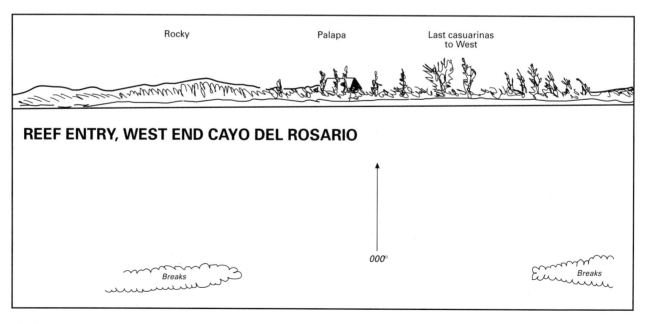

REEF ENTRY, WEST END CAYO DEL ROSARIO

Rocky   Palapa   Last casuarinas to West

000°

Breaks   *Breaks*

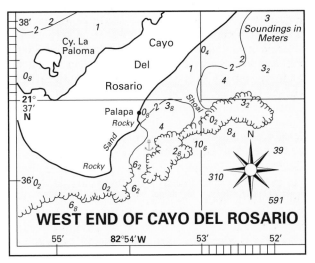

WEST END OF CAYO DEL ROSARIO

Adapted from ICH 1584
Courtesy GeoCuba

Reef entry and anchorage

The reef entry at the SW tip of Cayo del Rosario is straightforward. On both sides of the channel the reef is shallow enough to break in all but the calmest conditions, clearly identifying the channel. The channel itself is wide (200m), with minimum depths of 3m, and so far as we could tell no isolated coral heads.

To enter, come to a position at approximately 21°35·7'N 81°53·9'W and head more or less due north, midway between the two sections of breaking reef, for the conspicuous casuarinas ashore (the westernmost of the casuarinas; nestled beneath, and just to the west of them, is a largish palm-thatched *palapa*). Once abeam of the breaking reef to the west, begin a gentle curve to the east to come in behind the reef and anchor. You won't be able to get far to the east (less than ¼M) before running into a series of coral heads that intersect with shoal water coming out from the beach, closing off this end of the anchorage.

Cays and reef between Cayo del Rosario and Cayo Largo

The cays between Cayo del Rosario and Cayo Largo have some spectacularly beautiful beaches and shallow canals which are a delight to explore in a dinghy. In particular, Cayo Rico, and the canals through the Cayos Pareses, are gems. Unfortunately, there are no protected anchorages along the coastline in this entire stretch. The best way to enjoy these cays is to anchor off in the daytime (which may be quite uncomfortable if the wind is strongly out of the SE or south), and to retreat to Cayo Largo or one of the reef anchorages at night (see below).

The reef, which begins again 5M offshore south of Cayo Estopita, progressively works its way into the western end of Cayo Largo. It is partially submerged for much of its length, and as such forms a very incomplete barrier to the swells which frequently sweep in from the Caribbean – the waters between the cays and the reef can be quite choppy, particularly when the wind is in the SE. There are, however, one or two sections of reef which protrude sufficiently to form a reasonable lee in southeasterlies, and to a certain extent easterlies, and these create the best opportunities for anchoring in this area.

Navigating between the reef and the cays is straightforward so long as particular care is taken to avoid the various shoal patches clearly shown on the Cuban charts (and one or two not shown!), and so long as you remember that the soundings frequently exaggerate the depth by 0·2m. The local fishermen tend to transit this area on an east/west axis at latitude 21°35·8'N which reportedly stays clear of all shoals (we zigzagged too much to be able to confirm this with confidence; Mike Stanfield on *Janetta Emily* reports running aground in less than 1·8m where the chart showed 4·2m just north of this track at 21°35·95'N 81°41·91'W).

Anchorage south of Cayo Estopita

At the point where the reef begins again south of Cayo Estopita, a substantial section, about ⅓M in length, comes all the way to the surface. This provides an effective barrier to swells sweeping in from the SE and south, and is long enough to create an area which, even in a strong southeaster, is out of reach of the swells hooking around either end of the reef.

The anchorage is approached from the north, heading for the center of the breaking reef (to a point at approximately 21°33·8'N 81°45·8'W), taking care to avoid the shoal patch 1M to the NNW. As you close the reef, immediately to the east you will see a large sandy shoal (with depths of 2–3m) which is clearly visible in the right light, and which also runs all the way up to the reef. You should make your final approach just to the west of this shoal, with the depths decreasing to 3m ½M off the reef, then increasing to 5 or 6m, and finally steadily shoaling as you approach the reef apron. You should anchor in a patch of sand, in 3–4m, 200m behind the reef. Although it is possible to work in closer, if you do you will find a number of isolated coral heads which are likely to get you into trouble.

The reef has some good coral and fish life in shallow snorkeling depths.

Cayo Estopita to the Ballenatos lighthouse

In the 5M between the reef anchorage described above, and the lighthouse on Cayo Ballenatos, there are several more stretches of breaking reef, culminating in a small rocky cay on which the lighthouse sits. Looking at the chart you would think that at least one of these bits of reef would provide a sufficient lee to create a calm anchorage when the wind is in the SE or east, but in fact in all instances if more than minor swells are sweeping in from the Caribbean they find their way around one, or both, ends of the reef, resulting in a rolly and uncomfortable night. Consequently, it is preferable to use the anchorage described above, or the one described below.

Anchorage at Cayo Hijo de los Ballenatos

2–3M to the east of the Cayo Ballenatos lighthouse a couple of rocky islets are linked by partly submerged reef, with more breaking reef extending both to the west and the east, forming a substantial barrier of about a mile in length. This breaks all seas from the south. The presence of Cayo Largo to the east moderates the influence of even relatively strong winds from this direction. The result is a reasonably comfortable anchorage in all but northers.

At both ends of this section of reef there is a pass leading to Cayo Largo (see below). From outside, simply come around the ends of the reef into its lee. From inside the reef, there are no hazards to the north of the anchorage, so the approach is simply a matter of heading up into the lee of the cays.

The area to the north of the smaller cay (the easternmost of the two) has a substantial amount of submerged coral, and as a result is not suitable as an anchorage (although you may wish to pick up the mooring set by Joey Roussell of Cuba Nautica – at his own expense – in order to protect the coral). The area to the north of the gap between the two cays is subject to swells coming in through the gap. Then there is more coral extending to the north of the

larger cay (Cayo Hijo de los Ballenatos). To the west of this coral there is a considerable area with a sandy bottom which runs up close to the reef. Here you will find the best protection (and also two more of Joey Roussell's moorings, although one is a little too close to the reef to be used overnight). If you drop an anchor, the sand is thin, so the holding is none too good (a Danforth type sets the best) but at least you will not be tearing up the coral (which has some gorgeous snorkeling).

Cayo Largo

Cayo Largo is one of Cuba's premier tourist resorts. The island has some spectacular beaches at the west end (Playa Sirena) and along the south coast. An airport at the west end brings tourists into a cluster of hotels on the SW corner of the island. There are all the usual attractions – bars, discos, restaurants, watersports, etc. – at high prices (dollars only), but little that would attract most cruisers.

Nevertheless, the island is worth visiting just to enjoy the beaches and fabulous water colors, and maybe to visit the turtle and crocodile farm, and also to do a little exploring in the dinghy away from the tourist areas. On the NW tip of the island, for example, there are extensive drying mudflats with some lovely birdlife (even a few flamingos). Cayo Largo is, in any case, likely to be a more or less required stop on any cruising *despacho*.

The destination for visiting boats is the Marina PuertoSol, which is also a port of entry to Cuba. The marina has to be approached from the south since the entire area north of Cayo Largo is obstructed by numerous extensive shoals.

Approaches and entry

The marina is up a dredged canal close to the NW tip of the island. The canal itself cannot be picked out from any distance, but nevertheless it is easy to find.

Note: Considerable development is taking place at Cayo Largo. The buoyage and channels may change. In addition, there have been reports of shoal areas to the SW of the marina entrance channel.

From the west, you can approach either inside the reef, or outside the reef.

If inside, an easterly heading along latitude 21°35·8'N should stay clear of isolated shoals (see above). You continue until you come across a couple of yellow buoys (at approximately 21°35·5'N 81°36·7'W) and then head 060° for 2½M to the dredged channel into the marina.

If outside, you pass the Faro los Ballenatos (Ballenatos light house) at approximately 21°34·7'N 81°38·3'W, and then 1½M later come through the reef between the lighthouse and the next section of reef at Cayo Hijo de los Ballenatos. The channel is

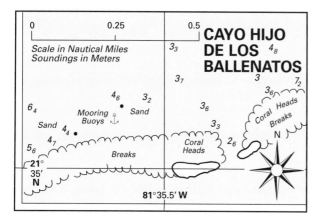

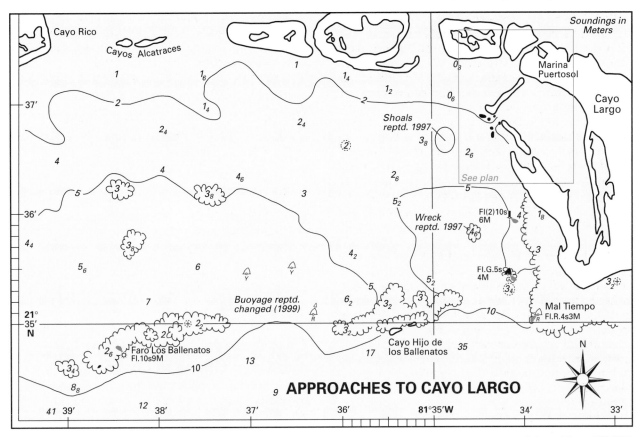

9 **APPROACHES TO CAYO LARGO**

Adapted from ICH 1583
Courtesy GeoCuba

entered on a northerly heading from a position at approximately 21°34·5'N 81°36·7'W, leaving the red buoy several hundred meters to starboard (i.e. passing to the west of it), and aiming midway between the two yellow buoys about a mile to the north. This is a very easy entry, 1M wide, and free of hazards. From the yellow buoys you head 060° to the dredged channel into the marina.

From the east, you must round the southwestern tip of Cayo Largo, staying the better part of ½M off the coast to avoid shoals at the tip of the island (marked by a red buoy). Come to a position at approximately 21°34·7'N 81°34·3'W and head 342° for a couple of miles. This is another relatively wide (½M) and uncomplicated reef entry, but you must beware the isolated coral patch (at approximately 21°35·5'N 81°34·2'W) ½M to the NNW of the entrance buoy. (In 1997, it was given a green buoy Fl.G.5s4M.)

The dredged channel into the marina is just to the north of the highly conspicuous white sand beach (Playa Sirena). The channel has a couple of substantial concrete beacons at its mouth, located at approximately 21°36·9'N 81°34·4'W – it runs midway between these, on a heading of 040°. Note that there is a clearly visible, white sand, shoal patch (1·8m) on the approach to the beacons, but

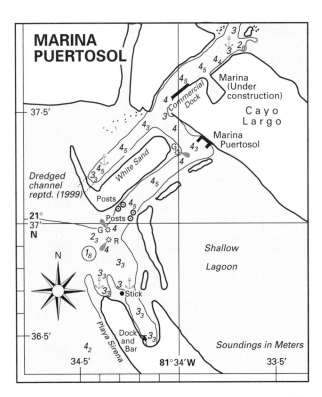

109

immediately to the south of this there is 3m between the shoal and the highly visible white sand spit extending northward from the tip of Playa Sirena. Once inside the channel there is 3–4m all the way to the marina. You should favor the north side of the channel since there is quite a bit of shoal water on the south side.

Marina PuertoSol

The marina is dead ahead as you come up the channel. It monitors channels 16 and 06 on the VHF. As marinas go, it is a small affair with only one dock and two finger piers but nevertheless it is a port of entry to Cuba. You will normally be directed to tie up to the eastern pier which is well built and fendered, and has 4m alongside. Clearance procedures are likely to be fast and straightforward.

There is water on the dock, which is potable but has a bit of a flavor (some consider it unpotable), and the usual dubious electrical hookup (see Chapter 1). Ashore there are showers and toilets. The marina charges $0.45 per foot per day; it accepts European credit cards. There is a diesel pump at the head of the dock ($1.00 a liter – the worst price for many miles!) and gasoline can be obtained (also expensive). In the vicinity of the marina there are a number of dollar stores with some groceries (including butter, cheese, canned meats, etc. but at pretty steep prices), an international phone, a post office, a medical clinic, and various bars and restaurants. The hotel strip is 5M away; a free ride can generally be hitched on one of the tourist buses running back and forth. The hotels have a number of different dollar stores. The Playa Sirena is a dinghy ride away, just outside the marina entry channel.

The marina is right alongside the airport, which has regular services to Havana and other Cuban cities, and also Cancun, the Cayman Islands and Canada – this is one of the easiest places in which to pick up, or drop off, crew or guests, and since it is in the middle of some lovely cruising grounds it is also an excellent spot at which to do this.

Address Marina PuertoSol, Cayo Largo, Archipiélago de los Canarreos, Isla de la Juventud, Cuba. ☎ and fax (53) 95 2204.

Anchorages

Having checked in, there is little reason to suffer the mosquitoes and lack of breeze at dockside since there are several excellent anchorages in the vicinity of the marina.

On the inside, a newly dredged channel (4m or more) leads to the NW and then forks. One branch leads to the SW, ending up behind a sand dune and some low-lying mangroves; the other branch goes to the NE past a marina under construction (so far, only the basin has been dredged) and up into a fairly open area of mudflats with a pleasant breeze and some great birdlife.

Note We have had reports that the Cubans are now charging boats to anchor in these locations.

On the outside, immediately south of the beacons at the entrance to the marina channel there are a couple of conspicuous white sand shoals projecting northward from the beach. It is possible to anchor in 3m or so in the area north of these, or between the two, with good protection from the east and SE, or else to go inside both of them and anchor close to the shore (in 2–3m). The latter spot has great protection, but suffers from a fair amount of boat traffic since a dock at the south end of this bay is the principal point of disembarkation and embarkation for the tourists from the hotel zone (you should not anchor in the narrow bay itself since you will be very much in the way).

Cays and reef between Cayo Largo and Cayo Guano del Este

It is a little more than 25M from the southwestern tip of Cayo Largo to Cayo Guano del Este. The reef, which closes the southwestern tip of Cayo Largo, runs more or less due east/west, while Cayo Largo hooks away to the north, opening up a substantial sound with navigable water between the two. The reef itself is partially submerged for much of its length, with substantial breaks, so that it creates a very imperfect barrier, but nevertheless when the wind is in the SE, and heavy seas are sweeping in from the Caribbean, it is far more comfortable to sail north of the reef than in the open waters to the south.

It is a simple matter to move between the north and south sides of the reef through most of the clearly charted breaks. We cover only one, close to Cayo Largo.

At its eastern end the reef terminates at the Golfo de Cazones, where the bottom drops away to depths of up to 1,700m. Along the reef there are several rocky cays, which provide a partial lee creating potential anchorages, culminating in Cayo Guano del Este. There is then no place in which to stop between Cayo Guano del Este and Cienfuegos, 40M to the NE, since this entire stretch of coastline (which includes the Bahía de Cochinos – the Bay of Pigs) has been declared a prohibited zone by the Cuban government.

Reef entry/exit

The western half of the southern shore of Cayo Largo is beset with a number of shoal spots, but more or less midway along this southern shore the

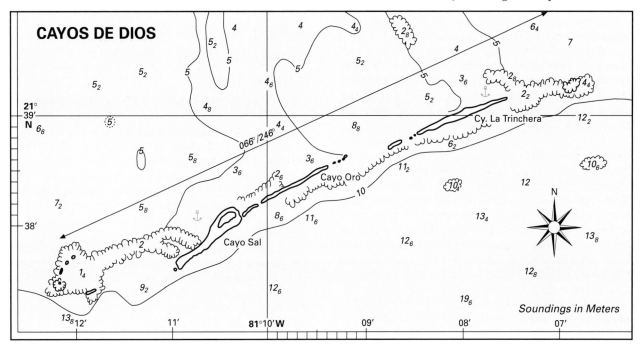

CAYOS DE DIOS

Cy. La Trinchera

Cayo Oro

Cayo Sal

N

Soundings in Meters

Adapted from ICH 1582
Courtesy GeoCuba

reef gets itself organized, while the area behind the reef is almost completely free of shoals. Rather conveniently, there is a substantial break in the reef at this point which creates an easy entrance/exit.

From the Marina PuertoSol, to come behind the reef you will want to take the eastern channel out to sea, between Cayo Hijo de los Ballenatos and Cayo Largo. Leave the red buoy, ¾M off the SW tip of Cayo Largo, to port (i.e. pass to the west of it). Once south of this buoy, head east, paralleling the hotel strip, in 15–20m to approximately 81°30·0'W. Next head ENE to a position at approximately 21°36·3'N 81°25·0'W, at which point you come north through a ¾M wide break in the reef, with minimum depths of 7m. When north of 21°37·5'N head more or less due east (086°), ½M or so inside the reef, with minimum depths of 4–5m.

From the west, we assume you will already be behind the reef. Come to a position at approximately 21°37·5'N 81°25·0'W and simply head south for ¾M until in 15–20m.

Anchorages

Cayos de Dios consist of several rocky cays more or less linked by reef. The cays and reef break all seas from the SE, but are not completely effective in breaking seas from the east. Nevertheless, in both southeasterlies and easterlies a fair measure of protection can be found either by coming in almost to the shoreline in the central part of Cayo Sal, or else by tucking up behind the reef at the northeastern tip of Cayo la Trinchera. In the former

case, the approach is made from the NW, aiming for the middle of the island, taking care not to stray onto the reef area to the west of the cay; deep water will be found almost to the shoreline. In the latter case, the approach is made from the west to close

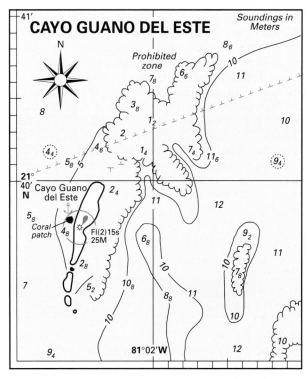

CAYO GUANO DEL ESTE

Soundings in Meters

N

Prohibited zone

Cayo Guano del Este

Coral patch

Fl(2)15s 25M

81°02'W

Adapted from ICH 1582
Courtesy GeoCuba

the northeastern tip of the cay, dropping the hook when the bottom shoals to 2–3m.

Cayo Sal, Cayo Oro immediately to its north, and Cayo la Trinchera have some pretty sections of beach and some good snorkeling on the surrounding coral.

Cayo Guano del Este is home to a powerful lighthouse, visible from many miles away (Fl(2)15s). The island is on a north/south axis, with several little rocky cays to its south and an extensive reef area to the north. It looks like it would create an excellent lee in easterlies and southeasterlies. However, it has a rather curved shape and when heavy seas are running the swells tend to hook around from both ends, so that there is a certain amount of rolling at anchor. Nevertheless, this is not a bad spot in which to rest up before or after making the passage to and from Cienfuegos or Casilda.

The cay is deep-to all along its western shore with the exception of a substantial patch of very shallow coral immediately in front of the ruined lighthouse (a heap of rusty iron). You can anchor to the south or the north of this coral patch. The north anchorage (just a little south of the northern tip of the island) tends to be the calmer, since swells come through the small gap between the southern end of Guano del Este and the small cay to its south, disrupting the southern anchorage.

The island is worth a visit, if only to climb the lighthouse (completed in 1972; looking like a rocket ship, 45m high, with 234 steps to climb and a great view) but there is no good place to land a dinghy since the shoreline consists of jagged limestone (eroded coral). However, immediately to the south of the lighthouse there is a substantial steel girder laid across two outcroppings of rock to which you can attach a dinghy without it swinging into the rocks. Just around the corner to the south, the rocks have been worn smooth – here you can first land crew members who do not want to walk the girder.

The island has numerous dry-stone ruins of unknown antiquity, a variety of low-lying vegetation, and a lovely little beach at its north end. The coral head in front of the ruined light has some good snorkeling; the reefs to the north a fair amount of fish life and lobster.

Cayo Guano del Este to Casilda, including Cienfuegos

As a result of the prohibited zone around the Bahía de Cochinos, there are no anchorages open to cruising sailors between Cayo Guano del Este and Cienfuegos, and then as a result of the steep mountainous coastline between Cienfuegos and Casilda there are no suitable anchorages in this stretch either. The cruiser must go from Guano del Este to either Cienfuegos or Casilda, or, if coming the other way, from Casilda to either Cienfuegos or Cayo Guano del Este.

These passages cross the deep water of the Golfo de Cazones, which on occasion can get quite rough and unpleasant. The boat needs to be well prepared before any passage. Beyond this, there are certain weather factors that should be taken into consideration.

Passage-planning

Going east is generally the tougher proposition, since the prevailing winds are from the east or SE, sometimes at a steady 20 knots or more – it can be a hard beat from Cayo Guano del Este to either Cienfuegos or Casilda. In particular, as mentioned earlier, during the last two weeks of March, and throughout April, there is a good possibility of being faced with strong SE winds, in which case it is just about possible to lay Cienfuegos in one tack, but quite out of the question to lay Casilda.

We found marked differences in the impact of the katabatic effect (the influence of a land mass on the daily wind patterns) at Guano del Este, as compared to Cienfuegos and Casilda. With a typical easterly or southeasterly, at Guano del Este the wind tends to die in mid to late afternoon, perhaps swinging briefly into the south and SW soon after dark, but then it returns at full strength between 0300 and 0500, continuing like this until the afternoon. At Cienfuegos and Casilda, the wind tends to build all day, but then dies in late afternoon. During the night there may be an offshore breeze. In the morning it is calm, with the wind once again slowly building up strength during the course of the day. This pattern, however, does not extend more than a few miles out to sea.

The rhumb line course between a point just to the north of the reef at Guano del Este, and a point just to the south of the channel into Cienfuegos is approximately 060°/240°. However, this passes through the prohibited zone for almost the entire passage. We simply don't know to what extent the Cubans are offended by boats sailing just inside the margins of the prohibited zone – we have done it without problem, and would do it again if the winds dictated this as the best option, but we can't recommend it. Otherwise, the only way to keep outside the prohibited zone is to leave Guano del Este to the south, and to hold a course of approximately 070° (which is not possible much of the time, given the prevailing wind direction), until up to latitude 21°50·0'N, at which point you head approximately 022° for Cienfuegos; from Cienfuegos the course is approximately 202° to latitude 21°50·0'N, and then 250° to a point a little south of Guano del Este: this should be no problem in prevailing winds.

The rhumb line course between a point just to the south of Guano del Este and the north entry channel into Casilda is approximately 088°/268°. This skirts the north side of the Banco de Jagua. This bank is a relatively shoal area (with as little as 3m in places) which comes straight up from the depths of the ocean. It is reportedly subject to extremely nasty seas, and is considered to be very dangerous by the Cuban pilot – regardless of what course the winds dictate, it should be given a wide berth.

Going east

Guano del Este to Cienfuegos or Casilda In stronger east and SE winds you want to time your departure from Guano del Este in such a way as to take advantage of the calm period in this area, arriving at the entrance channel to Cienfuegos or Casilda when the winds are calm in these areas. To do this you have to leave Guano del Este some time after the late afternoon, arriving in the vicinity of Cienfuegos or Casilda sometime around 0300. This then necessitates a night entry, or heaving-to until dawn. Cienfuegos is easy to enter at night, at least as far as the Guarda dock, and the Guarda will likely allow you to rest up on their dock until dawn. Casilda is not quite so easy: although there is a lit channel, it is somewhat convoluted; rather than try a night entry, it would be better to heave-to until dawn.

Cienfuegos to Casilda If the wind is in the east, the entire trip is in the lee of the mountains between the two cities. Remaining close inshore, a daytime sail should ensure reasonably flat seas and light winds. But if the wind is at all in the SE (as it commonly is), substantial swells tend to sweep up the Golfo de Cazones, while the wind will be on the nose, often packing quite a punch in the afternoon. In this case, a night sail close inshore will take advantage of the night breeze coming down off the mountains, which will also flatten the seas. However, to benefit from this you must stay close inshore, and even so the seas can still be unpleasantly uncomfortable until south of the Río Hondo, after which you begin to find more of a lee. The later your departure in the evening, the calmer

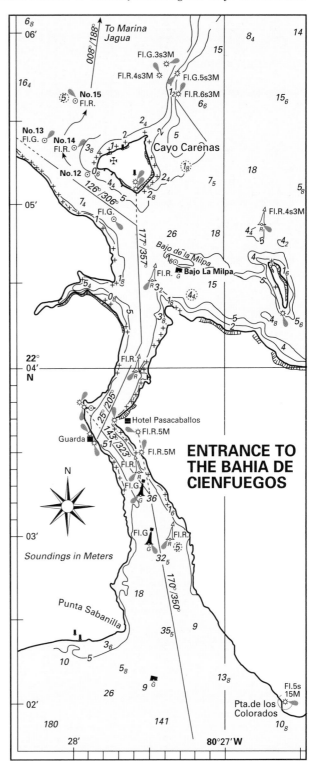

ENTRANCE TO THE BAHIA DE CIENFUEGOS

Adopted from ICH 1840
Courtesy GeoCuba

the seas are likely to be – leaving the Marina Jagua (at Cienfuegos) some time between 2200 and 0000 hours should put you at the entrance to the channel into Casilda around dawn.

Going west

This is generally straightforward. In prevailing conditions a morning departure from Casilda to Cienfuegos or Guano del Este, or from Cienfuegos to Guano del Este, should ensure favorable winds. There should be no problems in avoiding both the prohibited zone and the Banco de Jagua.

Cienfuegos

Cienfuegos is one of Cuba's larger cities and is also a port of entry. It sits on a peninsula jutting into the eastern side of the Bahía de Cienfuegos, a magnificent 'pocket bay' with a narrow entrance from the Golfo de Cazones.

The entry channel runs between cliffs, with the modern Hotel Pasacaballos on the eastern shore, and the imposing Spanish Castillo on the western shore (built in 1745 to protect Spanish shipping from pirates and privateers). It is an especially impressive sight early in the morning, lit up by the sun. Beneath the Castillo are some wonderful, if somewhat run-down, colonial houses. Following this great introduction, the cruiser sails across the southern half of the bay to the Marina Jagua (VHF Ch 19), with more (beautifully restored) colonial mansions and the modern Hotel Jagua as a backdrop behind the shabby marina offices.

From just outside the marina, the broad avenue of the Malecón leads into the city itself. A ride on a horse-drawn buggy (for one peso in 1995), and then a short walk of a few blocks, brings you to the Central Plaza (Parque José Martí), surely one of the finest in Cuba with delightful gardens, a colonial cathedral, and the imposing edifice of 'city hall'. With all this to see, it is possible to push the huge cement works, the naval base, and the other ugly industrial developments just outside the city, to the back of your mind – some cruisers come to Cienfuegos, intending to stop a day or two, and end up staying for weeks.

In town, you will find a number of dollar stores, including a reasonable supermarket, and a couple of *agromercados* for fresh fruit and vegetables (pesos only). In addition, there are a number of rather better-stocked peso stores than in most other Cuban cities, and a fair number of restaurants, bars, discos and so on. The Hotel Jagua (next to the marina) has a buffet-style dinner at a reasonable price.

Cienfuegos has an airport with direct connections to Toronto and Montreal, in Canada, but no regular domestic services! To get to any Cuban city, you have to hire an (expensive) aerotaxi.

The bay itself, outside of the industrial areas, has some interesting possibilities, but is currently off-limits to cruisers (especially the western shore in the vicinity of the unfinished nuclear power plant, which can just be glimpsed through a gap in the hills).

Approaches

The entry into the Bahía de Cienfuegos is uncomplicated by day or night. The main ship channel lies on a bearing of 350°/170°; to come in on this heading you will need to come to a position at approximately 22°02·0'N 80°27·3'W, a little more than ½M west of the Punta de los Colorados lighthouse (Fl.5s, visible from many miles out). Smaller vessels, of course, do not have to sail in the ship channel, but if approaching the bay from the west you must not cut the western corner too close; if you do you will run afoul of an extensive shallower area with isolated hazards which comes out from Punta Sabanilla on the western shore. To avoid it, you will probably need to counteract a westward setting current and should aim to be in the channel by the time you reach the first buoy (at approximately 22°02·1'N 80°27·5'W), since this is more or less at the tip of the shoal. Also, at night beware numerous small fishing boats, most of which have bright white lights to attract the fish, but some of which are not lit at all.

The channel

The channel is well buoyed, leaving the green buoys to port on entering (i.e. passing to the east of them), and compensating for any tidal set (sometimes quite pronounced). Note that the lights on the green buoys are more or less white. At night you will also be able to pick out two fixed-red range lights (350°/170°), mounted on the eastern shore, SSE of the Hotel Pasacaballos. Approaching the Hotel Pasacaballos, you will see the Guarda dock on the western shore, more or less at the point where the channel hooks to the NNE. At night the dock is not well lit, but you will know where it is as soon as the searchlight hits you!

Although the Guarda do not deal with the paperwork at this post, you may be required to stop at their dock (3m alongside; the dock is in reasonable condition but has some ironwork sticking out so be careful when coming alongside. In the past couple of years the Guarda have been allowing boats to proceed to Cienfuegos without stopping here). In the mornings it is generally calm alongside, but by late afternoon there may be a troublesome surge.

The Guarda may want to call a pilot ($30). You should tell them this is not necessary since you have good charts and instructions to the Marina Jagua at Punta Gorda. They may, in any case, escort you to the marina themselves (no charge). From the Guarda dock the course is initially approximately 030°, curving northward as you go. You will see a substantial cove open up to the west, and then after this a gap will appear between the western shore and an island (Cayo Carenas) in the Bahía de Cienfuegos. The channel runs between the shoreline and this island, curving first to the NW to leave *No. 12* red beacon to starboard (i.e. passing to the west of it), and then coming north between *No. 13* (green) and *No. 14* (red). Ahead is *No. 15* (green) which is left to port, after which you strike out across the bay on a heading of 008° for the tall apartment blocks on the horizon (a little to the east of the chimneys).

In about 1½M you will be abreast of the Hotel Jagua and the marina, on the tip of Punta Gorda peninsula, with another red beacon (*No. 18*) a little ahead. You can come in directly for the marina docks, with the depths shoaling to 4m. The staff will direct you to a vacant berth; the paperwork is dealt with promptly.

Marina Jagua

The Marina Jagua has several well-constructed docks, although there is the odd piece of ironwork sticking out a few centimeters, so good fenders are needed. The outer docks have 3m alongside; the inner docks at least 2m. Given the size of the Bahía de Cienfuegos, when the wind is from the south or SW (common in the afternoons) or the NW (northers) substantial swells can develop, so it is important to lay out breast lines to hold you off the dock, or a side anchor if breast lines are not possible.

Facilities The marina has potable water and electricity (the usual dubious hookup – see Chapter 1). Do not be fooled by the apparently good-looking electrical outlets; we found 230 volts on the 120-volt outlet, and it was still 230-volts after the electrician assured me he had corrected the problem! The slip rent is currently $0.25 per-foot per day.

Diesel is available dockside ($0.50 to $0.60 per liter) while gas can be bought at a gas station three blocks down the road (on the Malécon – $0.90 per liter for 'especial'; diesel is also available here at $0.35 per liter). The marina can fill propane bottles at dockside by decanting gas from one of their bottles. The marina will also supply fresh vegetables, other groceries, and ice on request; other supplies can be obtained from SUMARPO, a Cuban ship chandlery. The Hotel Jagua across the way has international phone and fax connections (☎ and fax (53) 7 335056). There is a post office in the hotel (dollar rates), and another downtown (peso rates). Across the street from the marina is an international medical clinic (dollars only), while down the road is a car rental agency.

A local shipyard with a marine railway has the capability to haul any cruising boat, and reportedly does good work. The marina can arrange a haul-out if necessary.

Address Marina Jagua, Calle 35, entre 6 y 8, Cienfuegos, Cuba. ☎ and fax 8195 (Cuba only; not international). The marina does not accept credit cards, and neither do any of the banks in town (although this is supposed to change soon).

The coastline between Cienfuegos and Casilda

This section of coastline is mostly rocky, with low cliffs (a couple of meters) backed by the Trinidad mountain range which contains a series of peaks just over 1,000m high. The coast is penetrated by a large bay (Ensenada Barreras) immediately to the SE of the entry channel into the Bahía de Cienfuegos (it is too deep and not sufficiently protected to make a good anchorage), and a number of rivers (the mouths of which are blocked by shoals, bridges, and power lines). At its southern end the mountains recede, and the rocky foreshore gives way to miles of sandy beaches, with first the Playa la Boca, frequented by Cubans, and then the Hotel Ancon, a major tourist center.

There are no off-lying dangers along this entire coast as far south as Punta María Aguilar – it is possible to sail ½M or less offshore, and in fact at times we sailed a good deal closer than this when trying to take advantage of the offshore breeze at night. South of Punta Aguilar an intermittent line of shoal water and reef extends further offshore until it is 1½M out abreast of Punta Casilda – it is necessary to keep well offshore to avoid these hazards.

There are no protected anchorages in this entire stretch, although in settled conditions it would be possible to find a certain amount of protection off the mouths of one or two of the rivers, and in the bay to the north of the Playa la Boca.

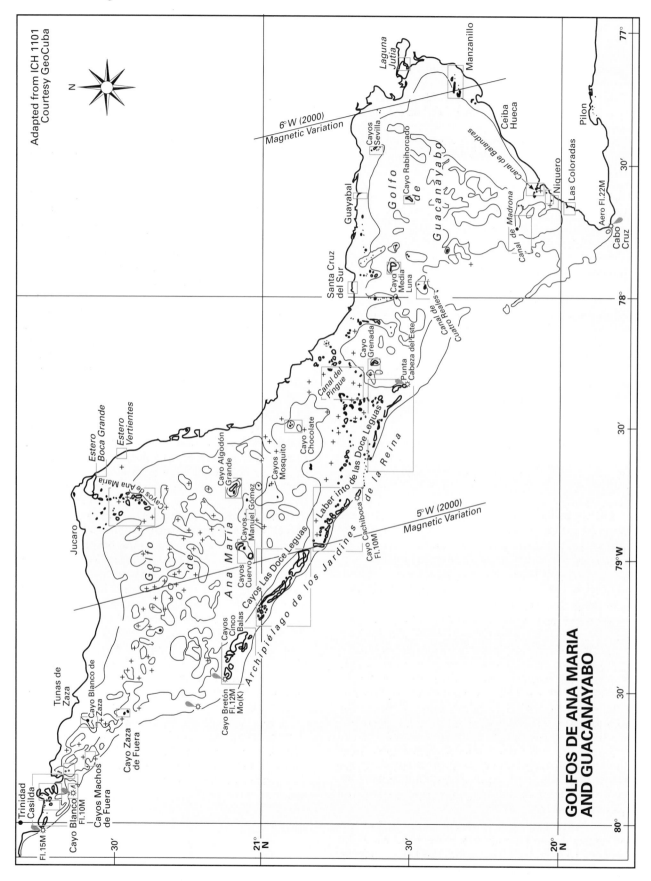

Adapted from ICH 1101
Courtesy GeoCuba

**GOLFOS DE ANA MARIA
AND GUACANAYABO**

6. Golfo de Ana María and Golfo de Guacanayabo south to Cabo Cruz

Together the Golfo de Ana María and the Golfo de Guacanayabo form a huge, relatively sheltered bay almost 200M long and up to 40M deep. The seaward perimeter of the Golfo de Ana María is defined by a long chain of cays and shoals known collectively as the Jardines de la Reina (the Gardens of the Queen). At its south end this barrier curves eastward to intersect the mainland, forming the dividing line between the Golfo de Ana María and the Golfo de Guacanayabo to the SE. The seaward side of the Golfo de Guacanayabo is then defined by a series of shoals extending from the southern end of the Jardines de la Reina to the mainland a little north of Cabo Cruz.

With the exceptions of a new low-key resort development on Cayo Caguama, at the south end of the Jardines de la Reina, and Cayo Campos in the NE corner of the Golfo de Ana María, not a single one of the hundreds of cays within the two gulfs is inhabited! The only signs of human activity are the numerous ferro-cement fishing boats, and the occasional fishing station built on piles in the lee of a cay. There are almost no shoreside sources of supplies on the mainland. Currently, very few cruisers come this way. You will be very much on your own to enjoy at your leisure the unspoiled beaches, the peaceful, secluded anchorages, and the pristine reef – there are few areas in the Caribbean as untouched as this.

In spite of the many cays and shoals, the two gulfs are navigable by small craft almost everywhere. The cays and shoals themselves are divided by numerous navigable passes. At first glance the navigator would seem to be faced with a bewildering array of possibilities for transiting this general area, making choices a little difficult. In practice, however, the matter is simplified by the fact that there are no navigable passes through the southern 40M of the Jardines de la Reina, and only one substantial pass through the cays and shoals that divide the Golfo de Ana María and the Golfo de Guacanayabo – you must either go 'inside' or 'outside' the cays for this entire stretch.

The 'inside' passage is the more protected but less interesting (mostly mangroves: taken as a whole the coasts of the Golfo de Ana María and the Golfo de Guacanayabo comprise Cuba's largest littoral swamp); the 'outside' passage runs along mile after mile of sandy beaches fronted by coral reef, but with few opportunities to stop and enjoy them unless the weather is particularly calm. Perhaps the best choice is a bit of both – to sail the northern half of the Jardines de la Reina, where there are plenty of passes making it possible to seek the most sheltered route on either side of the cays, but to head inside before the southern end of the Jardines de la Reina is reached, passing through a lovely group of inner cays (Cayos Cuervo, Cayos Manuel Gómez, and Cayo Algodón Grande) en route to or from the Canal del Pingue (between the Golfo de Ana María and the Golfo de Guacanayabo).

So far as the Golfo de Guacanayabo is concerned, its outer rim is somewhat hazardous and lacks secure anchorages. This leads most sailors to simply by-pass the Golfo de Guacanayabo altogether, or else to work around its mainland coast, stopping at one or more of the fishing ports along the way.

We would suggest taking in at least some of the following (starting from Casilda and heading SE): Casilda, Cayo Blanco de Zaza, Cayo Zaza de Fuera, Cayo Bretón, Cayos Cinco Balas, Cayos Cuervo, Cayos Manuel Gómez, Cayo Algodón Grande, and perhaps Cayo Chocolate (which we have not surveyed, but which is reported to have a good anchorage, where the fishing boats hang out, on its west side; we include notes provided by Geoffrey and Susanna Nockolds), followed by the Canal del Pingue into the Golfo de Guacanayabo.

In terms of our coverage, we have started at Casilda in the NW extremity of the Golfo de Ana María, making a swing along the north coast of this gulf and then down through the interior cays. We then begin again at Casilda to pass southward down the chain of the Jardines de la Reina to the Golfo de Guacanayabo. In the Golfo de Guacanayabo we make a broad arc from the Canal del Este in the NW around the coastline and off-lying cays, to Manzanillo in the east, and on to Niquero in the south.

Winds

The average wind speed in the two gulfs is quite light (6–10 knots), mostly from the east. These averages, however, disguise some quite marked seasonal and daily variations.

In seasonal terms, as elsewhere there is a tendency for the winds to be north of east in the winter, and south of east in the summer. In the wintertime there is the odd norther, but these occur with less frequency than in areas further to the west – only 50% of those that reach the northern coast penetrate this far – and the results are relatively muted. Of more concern are the strong to violent thunderstorms, with winds of up to 60 knots from the south, that occur in the summertime, especially in the Golfo de Guacanayabo (where these storms are known as *bayamas*; in a typical summer there are 14 in all).

In terms of the daily wind pattern, there is a pronounced katabatic effect (daytime/nighttime). Typically (if there is such a thing when it comes to the wind!) the wind comes up quite suddenly and strongly from the NE in the very early hours of the morning, and then gradually shifts to the south and eases until by noon it is well in the south, and often quite light. It continues to clock around, but building in strength once again until it may well be up to 20 knots from the SW or even the west by mid to late afternoon, after which it dies in the early hours of the evening.

Currents and tides

The northwesterly setting Caribbean Current is far enough offshore along this part of the coast to have little or no effect. Along the outside of the cays and reef of the Jardines de la Reina there is quite frequently a moderate countercurrent setting toward the SE, but this is easily upset, or even reversed, by the wind. In the interior regions of the two gulfs, there are no predictable currents, with the exception of tidal currents through some of the narrow passages and channels.

The tidal range is moderate, varying from as little as 0·2m (8in) at Casilda to an average of 0·4m (15in) around Cabo Cruz. Surprisingly, it is higher along the interior coastlines of the gulfs than it is along the margins, with the highest tides occurring at Manzanillo (0·5m; 20in). The tides are classified as irregular semi-diurnal (twice a day, but influenced by the weather).

Sailing strategies

On account of the thunderstorm activity in the Golfo de Guacanayabo, there is even more reason to be on this coastline in the wintertime, and clear of it in the summer months, than in some other areas.

From west to east, given the NW to SE axis of the two gulfs, so long as the wind is at all north of east (the winter months), it should be relatively easy to lay most courses. If, in addition, an early morning start is made, you will benefit from the generally NE slant of the wind. As the day progresses, and the wind shifts into the south, you can end up with a moderately hard beat to windward.

From east to west, it should not be a problem laying any course at any time of the year.

Charts and magnetic variation

ICH *1139* and *1138* basically cover the Golfo de Ana María and the Golfo de Guacanayabo with the exception of the southern end of the Jardines de la Reina, which is covered on ICH *1140* (the rest of which covers open ocean). If the inside route is taken between the two gulfs as suggested above, you can get by without ICH *1140*. Also missing from ICH *1139* and *1138* is Cabo Cruz and the southern coastline to Pilón, which are covered on ICH *1137* (together with another large area of open ocean). Between this guide and a general passage chart for Cuba, it should also be possible to eliminate ICH *1137*.

There is then a series of charts covering most of this region at a scale of 1:75,000, and detailed harbor charts for Jucaro, Manzanillo, Guayabal and Niquero. In what follows, we sometimes refer to errors or omissions on various Cuban charts – they all belong to these more detailed series, which were our primary charts. Finally, there is the chart book (Region 3: Casilda to Cabo Cruz) which covers this region.

Magnetic variation (January 2000) increases from almost 4°30'W at Casilda, to 5°30'W on a line from Santa Cruz del Sur to Cabo Cruz, and 6°00'W at Manzanillo. In all areas it is increasing annually at a rate of 9'W.

Golfo de Ana María: mainland coast and inner cays

Casilda and Trinidad

Casilda has little to recommend it, being a small port and commercial fishing town with few facilities of interest to cruisers. However, it is a port of entry to Cuba, and it is also the gateway to Trinidad. For this latter reason alone, it should be a stop on everyone's itinerary.

Trinidad and Casilda are a couple of the oldest cities in the New World (Trinidad was first settled in 1514; Hernán Cortés departed from Casilda to conquer Mexico). Trinidad is a fine colonial city

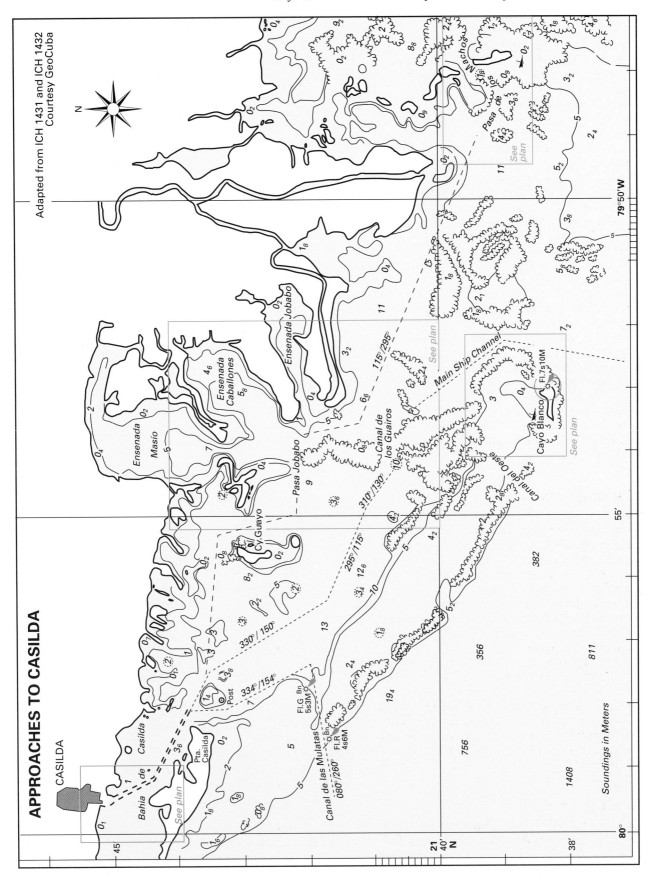

APPROACHES TO CASILDA

Adapted from ICH 1431 and ICH 1432
Courtesy GeoCuba

CASILDA

Bahía de Casilda

Pta. Casilda

Ensenada Masio

Ensenada Caballones

Ensenada Jobabo

Cy. Guayo

Pasa Jobabo

Canal de los Guairos

Main Ship Channel

Canal del Oeste

Cayo Blanco

Fl.7s10M

Post

Canal de las Mulatas

Fl.G Bn 5s3M

Fl.R 4s6M

Pasa de Machos

330°/150°
334°/154°
080°/260°
295°/115°
310°/130°
115°/295°

Soundings in Meters

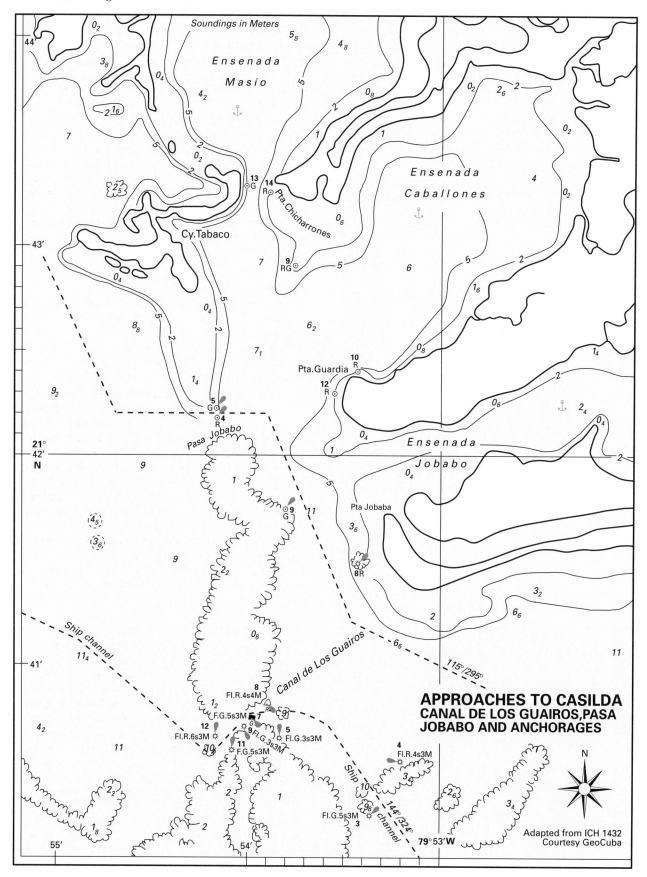

Soundings in Meters

E n s e n a d a
M a s í o

E n s e n a d a
C a b a l l o n e s

Cy.Tabaco

13
G

14
R
Pta.Chicharrones

9
RG

Pta.Guardia

10
R

12
R

E n s e n a d a

Pasa Jobabo

5
G

4
R

21°
42'
N

J o b a b o

Pta Jobaba

9
G

8R

11

Ship channel

Canal de Los Guairos

115°/295°

8
Fl.R.4s4M

F.G.5s3M
12
Fl.R.6s3M

5 7
G
9 Fl.G.3s3M

5
Fl.G.3s3M

11
F.G.5s3M

Ship

4
Fl.R.4s3M

144°/324°
channel

Fl.G.5s3M
3

APPROACHES TO CASILDA
CANAL DE LOS GUAIROS,PASA
JOBABO AND ANCHORAGES

N

Adapted from ICH 1432
Courtesy GeoCuba

79°53'W

which is on UNESCO's list of World Heritage sites. Over the centuries it prospered on the sugar industry but then suffered severely during the Cuban War of Independence (1895–8), and subsequently never really recovered – perhaps this is why there have been so few changes in the past century.

The city was declared a national monument by Fulgencio Batista, a status which it has retained under the Castro regime. But in spite of this recognition, like so much of Cuba today it is sadly run down. Nevertheless, the core remains intact, with some buildings tastefully restored, several of which have been converted to museums. It is well worth half-a-day's ramble. In particular, the view from the top of the steeple in the Museo de la Lucha Contra Bandidos, looking toward the Escambray mountains, is truly beautiful.

Since Trinidad is a few miles inland, to see it you must park the boat and find shoreside transportation. This is done at Casilda, using the Hotel Ancon as a base of operations.

Approaches

Casilda is tucked up on the north side of a sheltered lagoon. The lagoon is entered via a well-marked channel. This channel is in turn reached by one of several different channels, the most important of which are the Canal de las Mulatas (used if coming from the west or north), the main ship channel (used if coming from the south), and the Pasa de los Machos (leading to the Pasa Jobabo or the Canal de los Guairos) if coming from Tunas de Zaza in the east.

Canal de las Mulatas The Canal de las Mulatas leads through the reef a couple of miles south of the Hotel Ancon.

To enter, come to a position at approximately 21°41·7'N 79°59·0'W. From here you will see that the pass is marked with a red beacon at its entrance, and a green one on the inside. It is transited on a heading of 080°/260° passing to the north of the red beacon and to the south of the green one (with less than 3m draft, you could actually cross the shoals to the north of the pass at any point up to 1M further north).

A substantial shoal extends ¾M to the south of Punta Casilda. In order to avoid this, once inside the green beacon you have to work almost ½M further east before heading for the tip of the mangroves at Punta Casilda. As you close Punta Casilda, you will see a considerable number of buoys and beacons, the closest being a red post with a triangle on top – this is left to starboard (i.e. you pass to the west of it) after which you head more or less due north for the red and green markers of the main ship channel.

Once into the ship channel, you follow the markers on a heading of 299° until past small Cayo Ratón, at which point the channel turns NNW directly for the docks.

Main ship channel For those coming from the south, the main ship channel is the most convenient route to Casilda (see the plan later in this chapter). The well buoyed channel starts outside the reef (at approximately 21°38·0'N 79°52·4'W) close to Cayo Blanco, and comes through the reef on an axis of 010°/190°. Inside the reef, it runs on an axis of 324°/144° for 2½M to the Canal de los Guairos (at which point it can be picked up by those coming from Tunas de Zaza). At the Canal de los Guairos the channel passes through a narrow cut in another reef on a NE/SW axis, before continuing in a generally northwesterly direction for a further 4–5M to the Bahía de Casilda. The channel is extremely well marked, so following it is no problem at all.

Pasa de los Machos See below.

Pasa Jobabo The Pasa Jobabo is about 6M east of Casilda. The channel, which is transited on a more or less east/west axis, is clearly marked with a couple of beacons (green *No. 5* on the north side, red *No. 4* on the south side) – you simply pass midway between them with minimum depths of 6m.

Note The red and green beacons at the Pasa Jobabo are reversed when compared to those in the Pasa de los Machos to the east, and those delineating the channel between the Pasa de los Machos and the Pasa Jobabo: if sailing from the Pasa de los Machos you will leave the red beacons to starboard until the Pasa Jobabo, at which time the red is left to port: if sailing from Casilda, you will leave the red marker at the Pasa Jobabo to starboard, but then leave all the reds delineating the channel to the Pasa de los Machos to port (we have brought this anomaly to the attention of the hydrographic department, so by the time this is published the color of the beacons at the Pasa Jobabo may be reversed to match those in the Pasa de los Machos).

Clearance procedures

To clear in or out of Casilda you must go to the rickety fishermen's dock, which is normally crowded with fishing boats. This dock is to the west of the big-ship dock, pretty much straight ahead as you come into the port area. You should approach it on its eastern side, watching out for a line of partly submerged piles that extends south of it. The dock itself is in a very bad state of repair, so even if there is free space you might find it better to tie off alongside one of the fishing boats that are already there, or else anchor to the south and dinghy in.

Regardless of where you have come from, in Casilda you are likely to be visited by the full range of officials (Port Captain, Guarda Frontera, immigration, customs, and perhaps agriculture, transport and medical!). These officials can, on occasion, be extremely bureaucratic. Since several

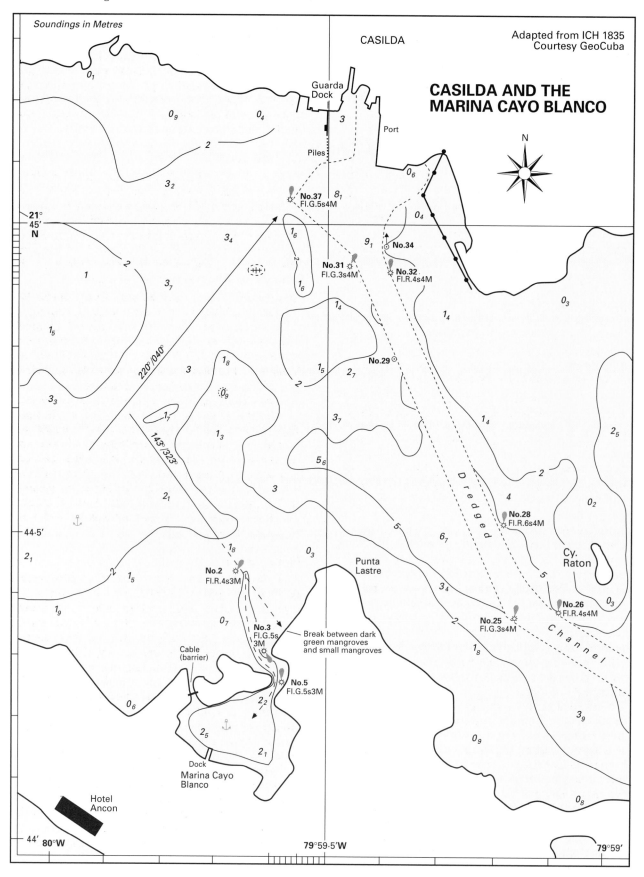

Soundings in Metres

CASILDA

Adapted from ICH 1835
Courtesy GeoCuba

CASILDA AND THE MARINA CAYO BLANCO

Guarda
Dock

Port

Piles

No.37
Fl.G.5s4M

No.34

No.31
Fl.G.3s4M

No.32
Fl.R.4s4M

No.29

Dredged

No.28
Fl.R.6s4M

Cy.
Raton

No.2
Fl.R.4s3M

No.3
Fl.G.5s
3M

Break between dark
green mangroves
and small mangroves

No.25
Fl.G.3s4M

No.26
Fl.R.4s4M

Channel

Punta
Lastre

Cable
(barrier)

No.5
Fl.G.5s3M

Dock
Marina Cayo
Blanco

Hotel
Ancon

21°
45′
N

44·5′

44′ 80°W

79°59·5′W

79°59′

of the officials have to come from Trinidad, they may take some time in arriving. Once cleared in, you will be advised to go to the 'Base Nautica' across the bay – this is the local 'marina' (called the Marina Cayo Blanco), which is situated in the mangroves immediately to the south.

Marina Cayo Blanco

Whoever called this a marina was being a little optimistic. There is a shoal-draft dock with water and electricity, and a fuel line (diesel). By dropping an anchor out in the lagoon it is possible to get the stern of a vessel with a 1·8m draft pretty close to the dock, at which point you can bring the water and diesel hoses aboard, and also make the usual dubious electrical hookup (see Chapter 1). There is room for just two or three boats. The charge is currently $0.15 per foot per day.

Those wishing to take advantage of the security provided by the marina without mooring to the dock can anchor in the lagoon, but will find this a rather airless and bug-ridden location and will still have to pay the mooring fee. We preferred to anchor out in the Bahía de Casilda (see below), leaving our dinghy on the dock when we went ashore.

Entry The entrance to the marina lagoon is marked with three imposing beacons, all of which are lit (see plan). This gives the completely false impression that there is a substantial channel, and that all you have to do is to head for the entrance, leaving the red to starboard and the green to port. The reality is that there is no clear-cut channel to the beacons, and even once up to them the channel is very narrow in places.

To get to the marina from the Guarda dock in Casilda you need to locate the green *No. 37* beacon just to the SW of the dock (the beacon may be obscured by anchored boats) and to pass to the west of this beacon (which marks the northern tip of a north/south shoal). Once past the beacon, keep it on a back-bearing of 040°, which will take you between two shoal areas, continuing until the red beacon marking the entry channel into the marina bears 143° (at which point this beacon will be in transit with the western edge of some large, dark-green mangroves ashore).

Now head for the red beacon until 50m or so off, at which point you curve around it to the north and then to the east, progressively coming closer until you leave it about 15–20m to starboard as you head down toward the green (*No. 3*) beacon. The controlling depth for the channel, which is 1·6m at low tide (about 1·8m at high tide), occurs in the approach to, and when coming around, this beacon.

The next beacon (green *No. 3*) is left to port, after which you should favor the western side of the channel when passing the final beacon (green *No. 5*) – the beacon itself is in just 1·5m of water. Once inside the lagoon you will find pretty uniform depths of 2·2–2·5m, shoaling at the edges.

Note Ned and Kate Phillips entered the marina by leaving the main ship channel just south of the green *No. 29* post, and heading just to the east of the red beacon marking the channel to the marina. Thereafter, directions are as above. They report minimum depths of 2m.

Anchorages

Bahía de Casilda The Bahía de Casilda is generally shoal, but there is an area to the SW of the port with depths of 2·5–3m in which it is possible to anchor with pretty good protection from all directions. To get into the anchorage you must pass between a couple of shoals, heading 220° from the green *No. 37* beacon in the port area (see the instructions above for entering the marina).

Ensenadas Masío, Caballones and Jobabo 6M to the east of Casilda are three substantial bays with well marked entrances and deep water, all of which provide excellent protection in just about any conditions (see plan). The northernmost (Ensenada Masío) is the most attractive, with pleasant views toward the mountains behind Trinidad.

These anchorages are approached from the west via the Pasa Jobabo, from the south via the main ship canal into Casilda, and from the east via the Pasa de los Machos. Both the Ensenada Masío and Ensenada Caballones have red and green beacons marking their entrances, but the Ensenada de Jobabo, which has a rather narrow entry channel and is the most shoal of the three bays, does not. The red beacons are left to starboard on entering, the green to port.

Hotel Ancon

The Hotel Ancon is a tasteless 1960s-style development which nevertheless has a number of amenities, such as bars, restaurants and a swimming pool, which will be welcomed by many cruisers. In particular, the buffet-style breakfast, at $4 a head, is a pretty good deal (if you are hungry). The hotel has an international phone and fax, but note that this is at the main desk in the lobby, not in the communications center. The hotel organizes various tours to Trinidad and the Escambray mountains (worth taking) and can take you diving ($30 per dive). There is a car rental desk which offers a special 12-hour rate of $32 on a jeep. The price includes the insurance and 100 free kilometers; this is more than adequate for a day trip to Trinidad and then up into the mountains of the Topes de Collantes where terrific views are to be had over the city and out to sea. Taxis to Trinidad are $11.00 one way. There is a medical center in the hotel.

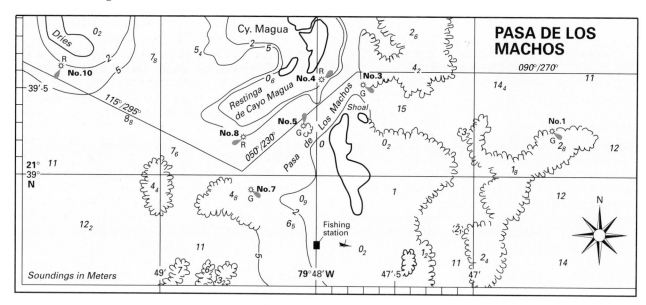

Adapted from ICH 1432
Courtesy GeoCuba

Pasa de los Machos

A string of cays and reefs cut off the northern part of the Golfo de Ana María from the Caribbean and Casilda. The Pasa de los Machos is the principal pass through this area, cutting through the Cayos Machos de Tierra. The pass has deep water the entire way (6m or more) and is relatively wide, but it is not a straight shot. However, it is well marked with a series of red and green beacons, many of which are lit, so passage is uncomplicated. It is assumed that the pass runs from east to west, so following the 'red, right returning' rule you pass north of the green beacons and south of the red beacons.

From the west, the approach to the Pasa de los Machos is made either through the Pasa Jobabo or the Canal de los Guairos, which will bring you to a point south of the red *No. 8* beacon which is south of the entrance to Ensenada Jobabo. The heading is then 115° for 6M leaving red *No. 14* to port, green *No. 11* to starboard, red *No. 10* to port, and ending up midway between another red *No. 8* and green *No. 7*. Here you come onto a heading of 050°, leaving green *No. 5* to starboard, and red *No. 4* to port, after which you change course to due east to leave green *No. 3* to starboard, continuing past green *No. 1* (note that this last stretch runs over an area shown as relatively shallow coral on ICH *1432*, whereas there is 10m; there is a shoal from green *No. 3* all the way to the cay to the south, in an area where the chart shows 15m – be sure to pass to the north of green *No. 3*).

From the east, you come to a position at approximately 21°39·5'N 79°46·5'W which puts you ¼M north of the first beacon (green *No. 1*). The next beacon (green *No. 3*) is more or less to the west

– you pass just to the north of it (note that this track leads over an area shown as relatively shallow coral on ICH *1432*, whereas there is in fact 10m or more; the charts show 15m between the *No. 3* beacon and the cay to the south, whereas a shoal obstructs this area – be sure to stay to the north of the beacon).

Beyond green *No. 3* you come onto a heading of 230° to leave red *No. 4* to starboard, green *No. 5* to port, and then pass midway between red *No. 8* and green *No. 7* (there is deep water just to the south of red *No. 8*, in spite of the fact that the Cuban chart shows shallow coral in this area). The heading now changes to 295° for 6M, leaving red *No. 10* to starboard, green *No. 11* to port, red *No. 14* to starboard, and ending up south of another red *No. 8*. From here you can continue either through the Canal de los Guairos or the Pasa Jobabo (see above).

Cayo Blanco de Zaza

Cayo Blanco de Zaza is a lovely little cay 3M to the SW of Tunas de Zaza. On its western side it has an attractive sand beach, while to the SE there is an extensive shoal area which, from time-to-time, is home to a substantial number of flamingos. The cay is well worth a visit if passing through this area, although the anchorage off its west coast is somewhat exposed – it is best considered a day stop.

Approaches

From the west The approach is either made through the Pasa de los Machos (after which the heading is 110° for 10M direct to the lighthouse in the middle of the cay), or else through the Canal de Tunas, a wide, marked reef entry to the SW of the island.

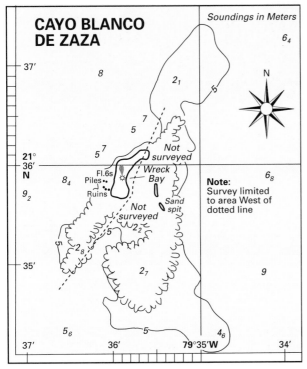

Adapted from ICH 1431
Courtesy GeoCuba

If coming through the Canal de Tunas, from the outer buoy (at approximately 21°30·9'N 79°41·5'W) head 033° *or less* until west of the lighthouse, and then head straight for the light. This will keep you clear of a couple of shoal patches, and an extensive shoal extending almost ½M to the SW of the cay.

From the east The eastern side of Cayo Blanco de Zaza is beset with shoals that extend almost ½M to the NE and more than 1M to the SE. While there is deep water between these shoals, it is better to simply give this entire area a wide berth, keeping ½M north of the island until due north of its northern tip, at which time you can head directly for the beach in front of the lighthouse.

Anchorage

The water is deep all the way into the beach in front of the lighthouse, and just around the sandy spit to the north (including north of this spit, where ICH *1431* shows 1·8m). However, it is shoal to the south of the lighthouse, with the shoals extending almost ½M to the SW. As a result, depending on the wind and swells, the best spots in which to anchor are in front of the lighthouse or just around the sand spit to the north. In both locations, in strong easterly or southeasterly winds there are likely to be some swells hooking around the island, creating a somewhat rolly anchorage.

On the east side of the island there is a small bay with deep water almost into the mangroves at its southern end. It is currently used as a graveyard for old ferro-cement fishing boats (at last count there were 7 in there). Although it looks as if it is completely exposed to the east and SE, this bay is in fact well protected by a small cay to the east, an off-lying sand spit to the SE, and other substantial areas of extremely shoal water. It makes a well protected anchorage in most conditions.

Unfortunately, we have not been able to do a thorough enough survey to provide a detailed harbor plan. The entry appears to be from the south, heading directly for the SE tip of Cayo Blanco de Zaza, and then curving around the mangroves, remaining 100m or more off, until in the bay. If any readers should work their way in here, we would like to hear from you!

Tunas de Zaza

Tunas de Zaza is a small, dirt-poor fishing village. There is little reason to go here. If you should choose to do so, simply come in from the SW for the large concrete pier, which has a fish, lobster and shrimp processing plant on it. The pier is set on beat-up concrete piles which are much too high to safely moor alongside, but at its tip there is a lower section with a solid wall to which one boat at a time can moor (3m can be carried alongside). Even here the dock is rather beat up, so good fenders are needed, and we would not want to be around in the presence of any swells. The Guarda post is on the dock; the 'town' consists of a couple of streets of tiny Cuban houses at the head of the dock.

Jucaro

Jucaro is a fishing town and small commercial port in the NE corner of the Golfo de Ana María which we have not visited – the following information is therefore second-hand. Both the commercial dock and the fishing dock (to the east) are in a bad state of repair. The port has a rather exposed anchorage, particularly if the wind is from the south or SW (which it often is in late afternoon), and as such is not recommended as an overnight stop. The town itself, in common with other small towns in the area, has little to offer the visiting cruiser.

The approach is made from the vicinity of Cayo Obispo (see below), but not from further east (there are extensive shoals around Cayo Encantado), heading for the port's outer beacon (at approximately 21°36·6'N 78°51·2'W). The area beyond the beacon is dredged – you can anchor fairly close in.

6M to the west of Jucaro is a large commercial port (Palo Alto) which appears to be abandoned, although we did see a ship in here so there must be some activity. Anyway, there is nothing here for the cruiser.

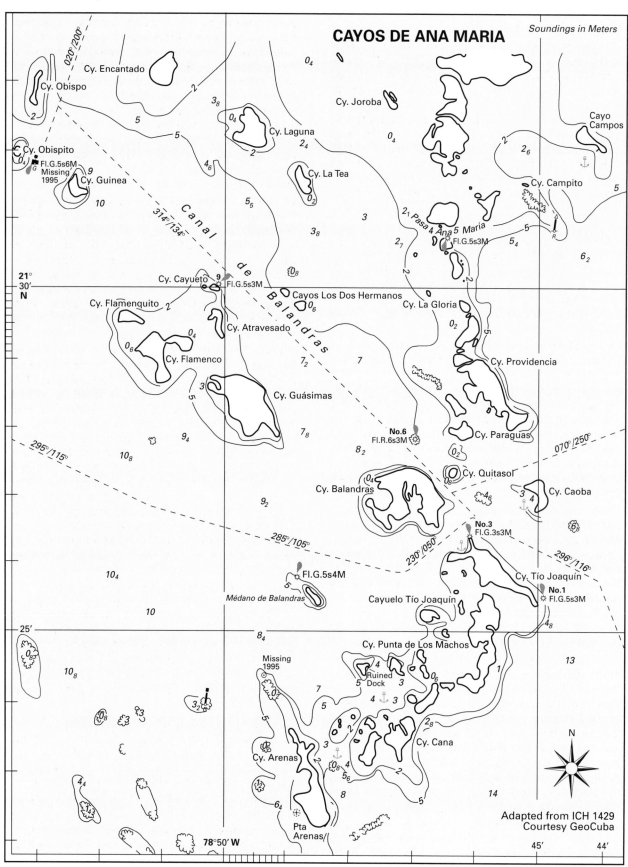

CAYOS DE ANA MARIA

Soundings in Meters

Cy. Encantado

Cy. Obispo

0_4

Cy. Joroba

$020°/200°$

Cayo Campos

3_8

0_4

Cy. Laguna

Cy. Obispito

Fl.G.5s6M
Missing
1995

Cy. Guinea

2_4

0_4

Cy. La Tea

2

Cy. Campito

2_6

Cy. Campito

$314°/134°$

Cy. Cayueto

Canal de Balandras

5_5

3

3_8

2_1 *Pasa* 4 *Ana* 5 *María*

Fl.G.5s3M

5_4

6_2

$21°$
$30'$
N

Fl.G.5s3M

Cayos Los Dos Hermanos

Cy. La Gloria

Cy. Flamenquito

2

0_6

Cy. Atravesado

0_2

5

Cy. Providencia

0_6

0_4

Cy. Flamenco

7_2

7

Cy. Guásimas

3

5

Cy. Paraguas

9_4

7_8

No.6
Fl.R.6s3M

8_2

$070°/250°$

10_8

0_2

Cy. Quitasol

$295°/115°$

0_4

4_6

3 4 Cy. Caoba

Cy. Balandras

0_8

6_8

9_2

No.3
Fl.G.3s3M

$285°/105°$

$230°/050°$

$296°/116°$

10_4

Fl.G.5s4M

Cy. Tío Joaquín

No.1
Fl.G.5s3M

5

Médano de Balandras

Cayuelo Tío Joaquín

4_8

10

$25'$

8_4

13

0_8

Missing
1995

Cy. Punta de Los Machos

10_8

0_7

7

4

5 Ruined 3
Dock

0_6

1

3_2

4

2_8

0_8

3

0_8

2

Cy. Cana

4_4

14_3

Cy. Arenas

3

0_8

4 5_6

2

5

1_2

8

78°50' W

6_4

Pta
Arenas

14

N

Adapted from ICH 1429
Courtesy GeoCuba

$45'$ $44'$

Cayos de Ana María

The Cayos de Ana María are a substantial group of cays tucked up into the NE corner of the Golfo de Ana María. While they consist mostly of mangroves, scattered around there are a number of small, attractive beaches. The cays themselves are uninhabited – there is nothing to do here but relax, go beach-combing for shells, catch some fish and lobster, and perhaps snorkel the scattered coral on the shelves around the cays. If nothing else, the cays create a number of protected anchorages for those sailing the inside route around the Golfo de Ana María.

Approaches

From Cayo Blanco de Zaza There is a 5M wide channel, deep (typically 8m) and free of hazards that runs parallel to the coast from Tunas de Zaza to the cays, terminating at Cayo Obispo (5M south of Jucaro). From here there are a number of clearly defined passages through the cays (see below).

From Cayo Algodón Grande There are various isolated shoals on the direct route between Cayo Algodón Grande and the Cayos de Ana María. It is easy to navigate around them. Otherwise, a course can be laid to pass between Cayo Santa María and the mainland (i.e. passing to the east of Cayo Santa María), after which it is a clear shot to the east side of the Cayos de Ana María (on a heading of 338°), but taking care not to get set to the west since this track passes close to the Cabezo Pipa and Cabezo Cornuda shoals.

Channels through the cays

Canal de Balandras The main shipping channel to Jucaro and the commercial dock of Palo Alto runs through the middle of the Cayos de Ana María. The channel is deep (10m or more) and well marked, including several lighted beacons.

From the south, you come to a position at approximately 21°25·4'N 78°44·5'W and pass through on a heading of 314°.

From the north, you come to a position at approximately 21°30·3'N 78°50·0'W and pass through on a heading of 134°.

East/west channel A deep-water channel cuts through the cays on an east/west axis, but this is not a straight shot. However, there is plenty of water, and navigation is straightforward enough.

Pasa Ana María The Pasa Ana María connects the northeastern extremity of the Golfo de Ana María to the Ensenada Sabanalamar to the north and west. The pass cuts between two unnamed cays. It is transited more or less in the middle of the gap between the cays, on an east/west axis, with minimum depths of a little more than 2m on the approaches on the western side, deepening to 3–5m

passing through and on the eastern side. The channel is marked with a green lighted beacon at the east end. This beacon is set down toward the cay to the south – you can pass well north of it, keeping just a little to the south of the midway point between the beacon and the cay to the north.

From the west, come to a position at approximately 21°30·8'N 78°46·9'W and head east.

From the east, come to a position at approximately 21°30·8'N 78°45·8'W and head west.

Anchorages

Canal de Balandras About midway through the Canal de Balandras there is a beacon on the tip of a conspicuous sand spit (the beacon is at approximately 21°26·5'N 78°46·1'W). Behind this sand spit is an anchorage, well protected in prevailing winds. Simply hook around to the west of the spit and come south toward the mangroves, dropping the hook when the water begins to shoal. It is deep (2m or more) fairly close into the sand and the mangroves.

Cayo Caoba Cayo Caoba is also about midway through the Canal de Balandras, this time to the east of the beacon mentioned above. The west side of the cay forms a bay with a couple of headlands projecting westward, and shoal water off both headlands. The net effect is to create a sheltered anchorage in prevailing conditions, and even when the wind is in the north. It is entered by simply coming around either headland, ¼M or so offshore (to avoid the shoals) and then heading toward the mangroves. At the southern end of the bay the water is deep (5m) until close to the mangroves; at the northern end it is a little shallower (3m) but nevertheless you can get quite close inshore. The most attractive spot is off a small sandy beach at the northern end of the bay.

Cayo Punta de los Machos There is a great deal of deep water between the cays in the southern region of the Cayos de Ana María. Here you could find a protected anchorage in just about any conditions. We could find no off-lying hazards with the exception of the ½M long shoal extending to the NNW of Cayo Arenas (note that the beacon which ICH *1429* shows at the tip of this shoal is currently missing).

Cayo Obispo This is a favorite with some cruisers, but we were not overly impressed! The cay sits on a shallow shelf, which drops off quite suddenly into 2 or 3m. It is possible to anchor just off this shelf on either the east or west side, but in both cases if any seas are running the swells are likely to hook around the island.

Cayo Guinea This cay, to the south of Cayo Obispo, has an attractive sand spit on its northern tip. Depending on the wind direction, a reasonably sheltered anchorage can be found on either side of the spit, but if rounding from one side to the other be sure to give the cay a good clearance since shoal water extends 200–300m to the north. Relatively deep water (2–3m) comes in fairly close to the sand both to the west and east, but note that on the east side in particular there is a very abrupt shelf with shallow water up to 100m off the beach. There are some lovely shells on the beach.

Cayo Campos We mention this cay because from a little distance it looks most beguiling with sandy beaches, coconut trees and a small settlement, including a beach restaurant and bar – in fact a most enticing sight after an extended diet of mangroves. Reality is a bit of a shock, with pigs and goats running around loose, dung everywhere, a soggy, muddy beach, and leeches in the water! If you still want to go there, you can approach within 100m of the tip of the dock on the western side, coming at it from the SW in order to avoid the shoal that extends ½M to the south of the island. Note also the shoal that extends ½M to the SE of Cayo Campito (its tip is marked with a stake surmounted by a triangle).

Mainland anchorages in the Golfo de Ana María

To the east of the Cayos de Ana María there are reportedly a couple of navigable estuaries (Estero Boca Grande and Estero Vertientes) which the local fishermen use as refuges (*refugios*) in bad weather. We have not investigated either (having had enough of mangroves) but include plans (supplied by the Cuban Ministry of Fisheries) for those who might need the shelter.

The minimum depth at the mouth of the Estero Boca Grande is reportedly 2·5m, increasing on the inside, while the Estero Vertientes has a controlling depth of 2·8m at its mouth (marked by a lighted beacon), once again increasing on the inside. At the mouth of the Estero Vertientes there is a beach and a small fishing community.

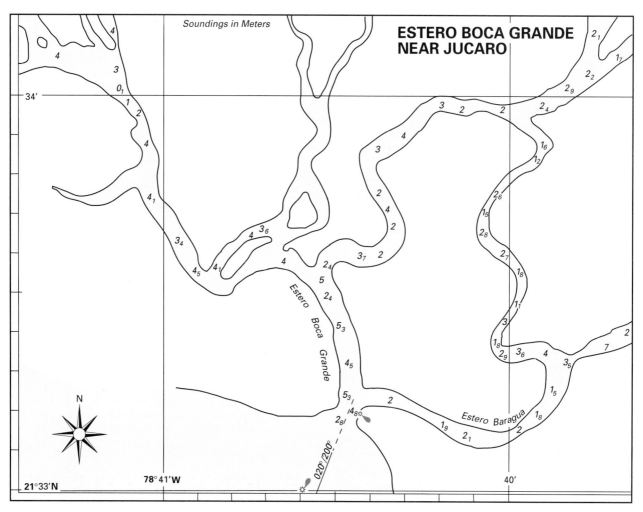

Courtesy Cuban Ministry of Fisheries

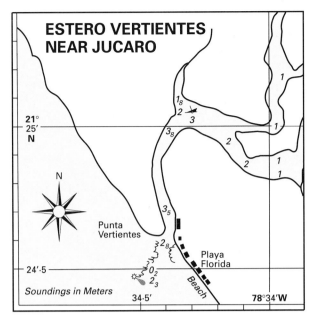

ESTERO VERTIENTES NEAR JUCARO

Punta Vertientes

Playa Florida

Beach

Soundings in Meters

Courtesy Cuban Ministry of Fisheries

Cayo Algodón Grande

Cayo Algodón Grande has that fine combination of an easy-to-enter, extremely well protected lagoon anchorage, some lovely coral heads for snorkeling, and a gorgeous beach. Unfortunately they are separated by a mile or two, but that's what the dinghy's for.... The anchorage is at the SW extremity of the island, the coral heads are just outside the line of the reef to the west, and the beach is on the north coast.

There is an abandoned resort development on the beach, with a dilapidated dock. In prevailing easterlies this coast is untenable as an anchorage, but very often even with strong easterlies at night and in the morning, by midday it is quite calm. In such conditions you can anchor in the lagoon overnight, take the big boat around to the coral on the west coast in the morning (which will still be in the lee of the island) and then anchor off the beach on the north coast in the afternoon. The reef arcs in

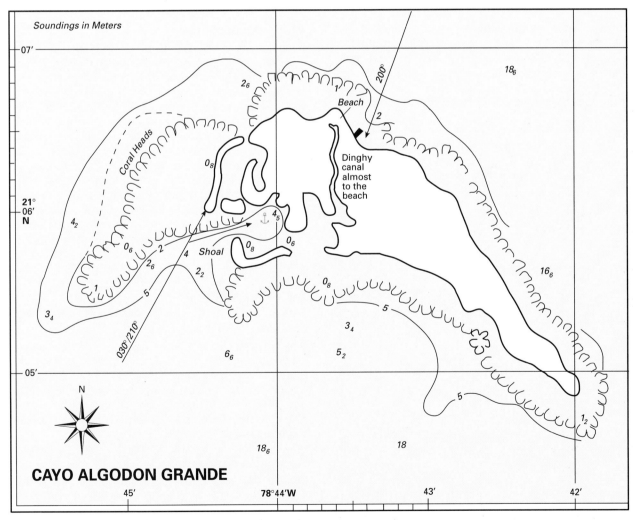

Soundings in Meters

Coral Heads

Beach

Dinghy canal almost to the beach

Shoal

CAYO ALGODON GRANDE

Adapted from ICH 1427
Courtesy GeoCuba

toward the beach on either side of the dock – if you come in for the tip of the dock on a heading of 200° you can carry 2m quite close inshore, although you will need to watch for isolated coral rocks in the final stages.

Entry and anchorage

The lagoon anchorage is approached from a position at approximately 21°05·7'N 78°44·7'W on a heading of 030° for the near tip of the westernmost mangroves. When due west of the mangroves on the east side of the lagoon entrance, come around to the east in a broad arc to enter the lagoon midway between the mangroves on either side. Note that there is an extensive shoal to the SW of the eastern mangroves, so do not cut this corner when curving around to come inside. Anchor anywhere in the center of the lagoon. Minimum depths going in are a little less than 3m, with 3–5m on the inside.

Cayos Manuel Gómez

The Cayos Manuel Gómez are a mass of small cays, mostly mangroves but with some lovely sandy shoals and small beaches, and a considerable amount of coral around the perimeter. On the western side there is a well protected anchorage within a broad arc of cays. This is a popular spot with the local fishing fleet – we have seen seven shrimpers in here

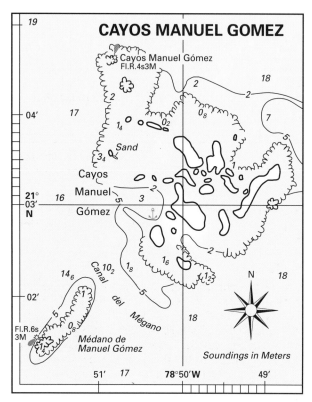

Adapted from ICH 1428
Courtesy GeoCuba

(one of whom obligingly pulled us off a shoal when we strayed a little too close during our survey).

Entry and anchorage

Come to a position at approximately 21°03·0'N 78°50·8'W and enter on an easterly heading. Watch out for the shoal to the south which projects ½M to the NW of the cay on the south side of the lagoon. The least buggy spot is likely to be in the SW corner tucked up behind this reef, more or less where it joins the cay. The anchorage is well protected from all but the west and NW, and even then reasonable protection could be found somewhere within the rim of cays.

Cayos Cuervo

The Cayos Cuervo is another group of numerous small cays which contain a number of lovely beaches (notably toward the southern end), some interesting reef on the perimeter, and an excellent, well protected anchorage in the center of the cays.

Entry and anchorage

The lagoon is entered from its western side (the Cuban charts give the impression there may be an entry from the east, but in fact all other channels between the cays are closed off with shoals). Come to a position at approximately 21°04·0'N 78°58·4'W and enter on a heading of 070° to pass 15–50m south of the green beacon. Once past the beacon the lagoon opens out all around with 6–7m over much of it, although there are some substantial shoal and coral patches toward the perimeter so take care in these areas. You can anchor in many places. A nice anchorage will be found at the north end of the lagoon, leaving the piles to port and the wrecked fishing boat to starboard, and anchoring off the beach in 3m.

Cayo Chocolate

The following notes were provided by Geoffrey and Susanna Nockolds.

The western side of Cayo Chocolate has a detached reef, running NW to SE about 1M west of the cay. This reef provides some protection from the west. The cay itself has narrow beaches on the NW side, with a shallow, mangrove-fringed bay to the south. On the southern end are three small detached mangrove cays.

Approaches and entry

Inside the reef If the light allows the reef to be seen, come to a position (at approximately 20°51·5'N 78°40·7W) at the NE end of the Canal de Cucaracha (this is the body of water between the

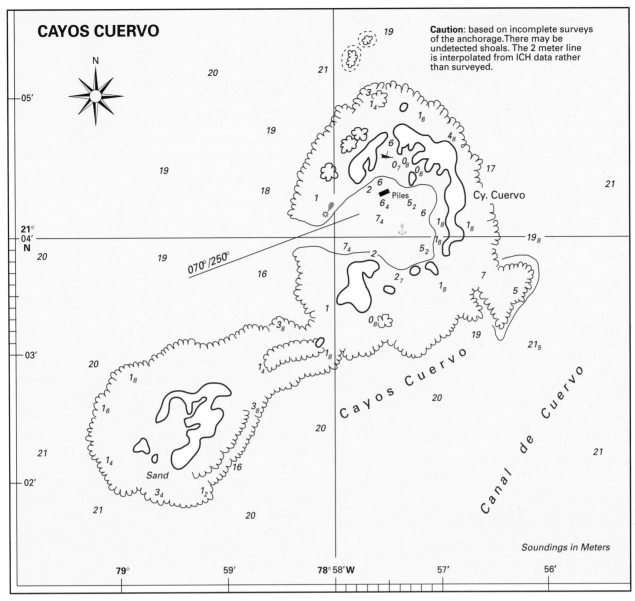

CAYOS CUERVO

Caution: based on incomplete surveys of the anchorage. There may be undetected shoals. The 2 meter line is interpolated from ICH data rather than surveyed.

070°/250°

Piles

Cy. Cuervo

Cayos Cuervo

Canal de Cuervo

Sand

Soundings in Meters

Adapted from ICH 1428
Courtesy GeoCuba

reef and the cay). The central cay of the three small cays to the south of Cayo Chocolate will be bearing 142°. Head for this cay, making good a track parallel to the reef (which will be quite close to starboard), until the southern point of the northern part of Cayo Chocolate bears 070°, with a least depth of 3m, then turn towards the cay and anchor.

Outside the reef If the sun is in the west it is easier to come down the outside of the reef, rounding its southern end. To do this, come to a position at approximately 20°51'N 78°41·8'W. Proceed on a heading of 142°, leaving the reef to port (i.e. passing to the west of it), until the left-hand edge of Cayo Chocolate (i.e. the north end) bears 050°, and then come onto a heading of 070° towards the anchorage.

Note that there is a stick towards the SE end of the reef, but that shoal water extends some 150m beyond it.

Anchorages

In settled conditions you can anchor 100m off the west-facing beach in 3m, or anywhere on the sand between the beach and the reef. Better protection will be found in about 2m, in the north end of the bay, with the western edge of Cayo Chocolate a quarter of a mile to the north. It may be possible to edge further in, but beware a shoal patch, with less than 1·5m over it, at approximately 20°49·6'N 78°38·8'W.

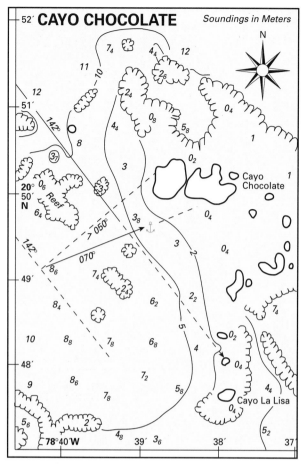

Adapted from ICH 1427
Courtesy GeoCuba

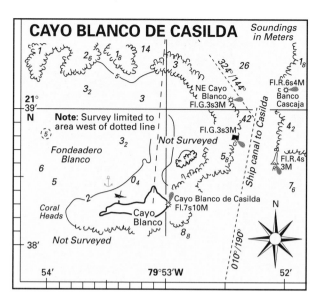

Adapted from ICH 1432
Courtesy GeoCuba

Golfo de Ana María: Jardines de la Reina

Cayo Blanco de Casilda

Cayo Blanco de Casilda is approximately 9M to the SE of Casilda. The cay has a small beach on its north coast, and some reasonable snorkeling on coral heads off its western tip. Otherwise it is not particularly attractive, but nevertheless it is a favorite stop for tour boats operating out of the Hotel Ancon. It does not have a decently protected anchorage, and is best considered a day stop only.

Approaches

From Casilda, you can follow the main ship channel through the Canal de los Guairos and then cut south for the eastern tip of the island until ½M off, at which point you head for the western tip. This brings you down the western edge of an extensive shoal extending out from the cay. The best spot to anchor is 200m to the west of the remains of the wreck (which is further inshore than shown on ICH 1432).

From the Pasa de los Machos, simply follow the 21°39·0'N line of latitude until ½M north of the cay, and then proceed as above. This track leads over a whole series of areas charted as rocky shoals but there seems to be at least 3m everywhere; nevertheless it would be advisable to keep a bow watch and a close eye on the depth sounder.

From the Cayos Machos de Fuera, you can head directly for Cayo Blanco, staying 300m off its south coast, and then rounding its western tip the same distance off (there are some substantial coral heads closer in to shore). Come north to anchor off the wreck.

Caution We have received reports of a 1m shoal close to this track at approximately 21°37·7'N 79°51·9'W.

Anchorage

In prevailing easterlies and southeasterlies, the most protected spot in which to anchor is just to the west of the wreck. This is, however, an exposed location. If the wind shifts into the SW (as it often does in the afternoon), or the NE (as it often does in the night), this will be an uncomfortable anchorage.

Cayos Machos de Fuera

Cayos Machos de Fuera is a group of mangrove caylets 6M to the SE of Cayo Blanco de Casilda. The cays are uninteresting, but to the NE is a reasonably well protected anchorage encircled by reef and a small sand cay, with extensive shallow flats extending to the east on which we have found hundreds of flamingos – a wonderful sight. If nothing else, this is an attractive spot in which to layover for a night when sailing between Casilda and Cayo Bretón.

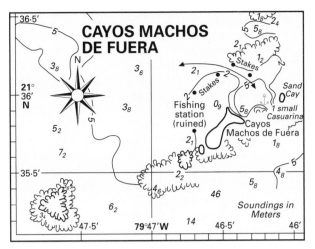

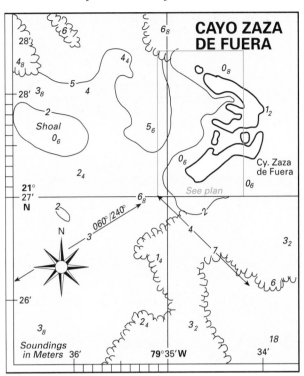

Adapted from ICH 1431
Courtesy GeoCuba

Approaches

The cays are beset with reef and shoals to the east, but wide open to the west and south, and reasonably accessible from the north (from the western side of the Pasa de los Machos, not the eastern side). As you close the cays, note the shoals extending almost ½M to the SW and the isolated near-drying shoal 1M to the SW.

Entry and anchorage

The anchorage is to the NE of the cays. To come into it you must skirt the edge of an extensive shoal to the north of the cay, and then come between this shoal and another further north, finally anchoring off a small sand cay not shown on ICH *1432*. The shoal immediately to the west of the cay has the remains of an old fishing station on its western edge, and then a couple of stakes delineating its northern edge (which is further north than shown on the chart). The shoal further to the north has a couple more stakes delineating its southern edge – these should be left just 20m or so to port on entering (i.e. you pass to the south of them). Then head SE, with the depths first increasing to 12m and then shoaling again, and anchor off the sand cay.

Note ICH *1432* shows a narrow pass through the reef immediately to the south of this anchorage. However, this pass has less than 2m and contains various rocks and small pieces of coral – it should not be attempted.

Cayo Zaza de Fuera

Cayo Zaza de Fuera has the best-protected anchorage between Casilda and Cayo Bretón. Otherwise, the island does not have much to recommend it (it is all mangroves) although there is a fair amount of bird life in the interior lagoon (providing a wonderful dawn chorus).

Approaches

From Casilda The easiest route is down the outside of the reef, heading directly for Cayo Zaza de Fuera once past the channel marker for the Canal de Tunas (at approximately 21°30·9'N 79°41·4'W), taking care not to stray south onto the shoal 1M or more to the west of the cay.

From Cayo Blanco de Zaza Once clear of the shoal to the SW of Cayo Blanco de Zaza, head for a point approximately ½M to the west of Cayo Zaza de Fuera.

From Cayo Bretón Depending on the wind and sea states, you can come either inside or outside the Medanos de la Vela, a 16M long shoal which can be crossed at various points, but nevertheless should be avoided because of its numerous extremely shallow areas. If on the outside, head for Cayo Zaza de Fuera when the south end of the cay bears approximately 060°. If on the inside, after skirting the eastern edge of the Medanos de la Vela you can head NW in deep water to a position at approximately 21°26·2'N 79°34·5'W, 1M to the south of the southern tip of the cay, continuing on a northwesterly heading for another mile, skirting an extensive shoal area off the cay, and then curving around into the lee of the cay.

Anchorage

The cay forms a broad arc, with extensive shoals to both the north and the south, so that in prevailing easterlies there is excellent protection to be had at

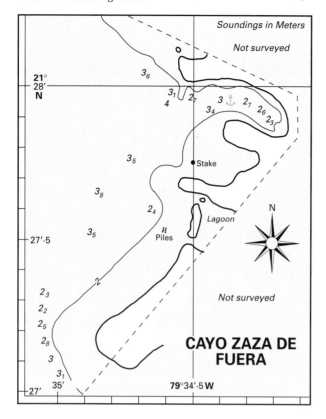

any point along the western side. The further north you go in the lee of the cay, the closer inshore it is possible to carry a 2m draft, until at the northern end you can go inside a substantial inlet which provides excellent protection from all but the west.

Cayo Bretón

Cayo Bretón is a substantial mangrove cay which is not particularly interesting. It is, however, the northernmost of the cays in the Jardines de la Reina, with a 25M jump between it and Cayo Zaza de Fuera (the next cay to the north). As a result it is a popular spot in which to rest a night either before or after sailing this stretch. It has several good anchorages.

Approaches

From Cayo Zaza de Fuera Depending on the wind and sea states, you can come either inside or outside the Medanos de la Vela, a 16M long shoal which can be crossed at various points, but nevertheless should be avoided because of its numerous extremely shallow areas.

If sailing on the outside, leave the south end of Cayo Zaza de Fuera on a back-bearing of approximately 060° until outside the line of the reef and then head SSE until you pick up the channel marker for the Canal de Bretón (at approximately 21°08·2'N 79°30·5'W) from where you can continue to your chosen anchorage (see below).

If sailing on the inside, you can skirt the shoal to the SW and south of Cayo Zaza de Fuera, working down to a position at approximately 21°26·8'N 79°35·0'W, and then heading SE toward a deep-water channel that runs down the east side of the Medanos de la Vela. At approximately 21°11·3'N 79°28·9'W you will pick up the inner channel markers for the Canal de Bretón from where you can continue to your chosen anchorage (see below).

From the south and east Whether approaching the cay from inside or outside the reef, you will arrive at either the Canal de Bretón or the Canal Boca Grande, both of which are wide, uncomplicated passes which will provide access to your chosen anchorage (see below).

Anchorages

Estero Bretón The western tip of Cayo Bretón is separated from the rest of the cay by a wide, 3–6m deep, channel (the Estero Bretón), which in turn is connected to a large lagoon with fairly uniform depths of 3–4m throughout its western end. Both the Estero Bretón and the lagoon form exceedingly well protected anchorages in just about any conditions, with the Estero Bretón opening out in front of the lighthouse to form a basin with plenty of swinging room.

From the north, beginning at a point at approximately 21°08·0'N 79°26·4'W, head 205° for the center of the channel into the mangroves. The depth will shoal to about 2m, and then increase. As you come within the line of the mangroves on either side, you should stay a little to the east of the centerline of the channel, but don't overdo it since there are shoals on both sides. Once inside, the water is mostly deep into the mangroves.

From the south, come to a position at approximately 21°07·0'N 79°27·5'W and then head 050° for a point just to the west of the lighthouse, leaving a stick about 20–30m to starboard (i.e. passing to the west of it). Minimum depths are approximately 2m, with the water on the inside deep into the mangroves.

The lagoon is entered via a channel which forks off to the east of the Estero Bretón about midway through. When turning into the lagoon channel, you should favor the north side, which is deep into the mangroves, in order to avoid a shoal coming out from the south side.

The lagoon channel has 3m going in, almost immediately deepening to 4m. After 200m or so the channel opens out, with 3 little cays ahead. There is deep water to the north of the center cay, staying in center channel to avoid minor shoals. Beyond the cays the channel continues the better part of ½M before opening out into the lagoon proper. There is plenty of water in the channel and more-than-enough swinging room to anchor; the lagoon itself we have not sounded.

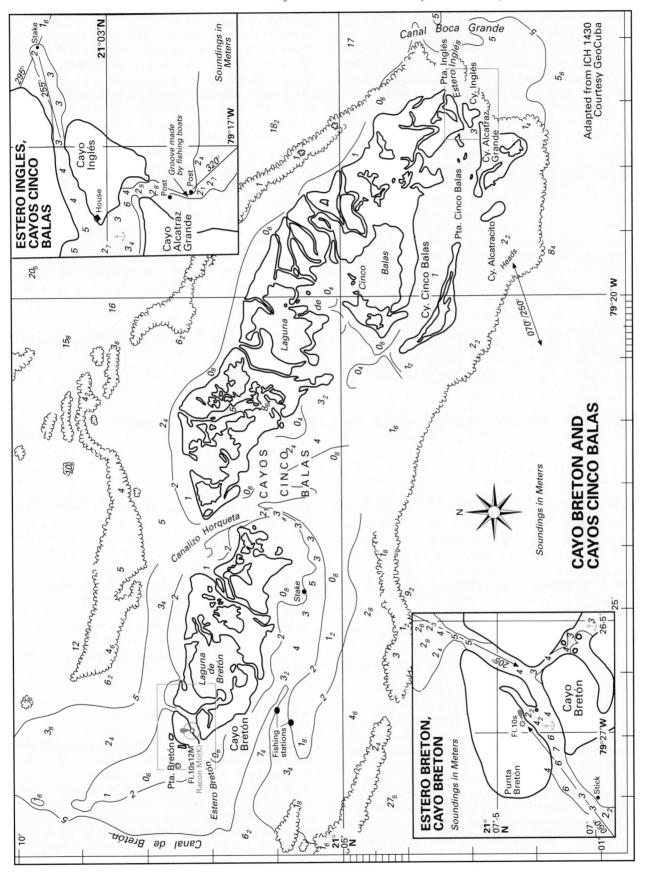

ESTERO INGLES, CAYOS CINCO BALAS

Soundings in Meters

CAYO BRETON AND CAYOS CINCO BALAS

Soundings in Meters

ESTERO BRETON, CAYO BRETON

Soundings in Meters

Adapted from ICH 1430
Courtesy GeoCuba

South of Cayo Bretón The anchorages above can be seriously bug infested! In prevailing winds it is better to simply anchor off the south coast of Cayo Bretón, somewhere to the NW of the two conspicuous fishing stations. Simply head toward the shore until the bottom shoals and then drop the hook. For added protection, follow the coastline around to the east, staying ¼M offshore and passing just to the north of the northernmost of the two fishing stations, and then anchor anywhere up to 1M to the east of the fishing stations – this will put you in an area surrounded by shallow water.

Canalizo Horqueta The Canalizo Horqueta is a relatively deep-water channel that separates Cayo Bretón from the Cayos Cinco Balas to the east. Deep water extends in a number of places into the mangroves on either side of the channel, enabling protection to be found in just about any conditions.

The channel is entered from the north from a position at approximately 21°07·5'N 79°24·0'W, heading 150°. It is also possible to come in around the south coast of Cayo Bretón, inside the reef, passing to the north of the fishing stations, but the channel is both narrow and twisting – this is very much a calm conditions/good light passage.

Cayos Cinco Balas

The northern and western coasts of this group of cays are simply mangroves, but the SE region has the hard-to-beat combination of sandy beaches, some excellent coral, and well protected anchorages. In particular, the south coasts of Cayo Alcatraz Grande, Cayo Alcatracito, and Cayo Cinco Balas contain miles of sandy beaches, which are nesting sites for turtles, fronted by an extensive barrier reef. Between the two is a reasonably well protected sound with an easy entrance and plenty of water in which to anchor.

Approaches

From inside or outside the reef, simply make for the Canal Boca Grande, a 2½M wide, 4m deep, passage between the Cayos Cinco Balas and the Cayos las Doce Leguas.

Anchorages

Estero Inglés The Estero Inglés provides access to an extremely well protected, deep-water lagoon surrounded by cays and shoals. There are two navigable entrances to this lagoon, one to the north and one to the south of Cayo Inglés.

The northern channel can only be entered after crossing a wide area of relatively shoal water. We found no clear channel at this point, but had no trouble carrying 1·8m inside at high tide by coming to a position at approximately 21°02·8'N 79°16·0'W and then heading 295° toward a stake just off the mouth of the channel, with minimum depths of 1·6m (1·9m at high water). We left this stake 5m to port (i.e. we passed to the east and north of it), and then immediately came onto a heading of 255° more or less for the center of the mouth of the channel. Once between the mangroves the channel widens and deepens.

The southern channel is approached from a position at approximately 21°02·5'N 79°17·0'W on a heading of 320° for a steel post. Just before the post the bottom shoals to less than 2m, and from here to the other side of another post to the north there is just a narrow 2m groove cut in the bottom by the keels of fishing boats going in and out. In the right light, this groove can be clearly seen as a light-green sandy stripe. In any case, leave the outer post about 10m to starboard (i.e. pass to the west of it) and then head due north to leave the inner post about 5m to port (i.e. pass to the east of it). Once past this second post stay about midway between the mangroves as you enter the channel, continuing on a northerly heading until almost into the mangroves to the north, and then hook around into the lagoon.

The eastern end of the lagoon has deep water almost into the mangroves on all sides, with plenty of swinging room all around. We have not sounded the western end.

Cayo Alcatracito To the SW of Cayo Alcatracito there is a substantial break in the reef through which it is possible to enter, anchoring in the lee of the cay.

To enter the reef come to a position at approximately 21°02·2'N 79°20·0'W and simply head 070° for the center of Cayo Alcatracito. The depths will decrease to 6m when approaching the line of the reef, and then gradually shoal all the way to the cay. When passing through the line of the reef you will need to maintain a bow watch since there is a fair amount of scattered coral – almost all of it is well submerged, but the odd head looks as if it might have less than 2m over it. You will not be able to get much closer than ½M to the cay, since it shoals well out. In prevailing easterlies there should be adequate protection; in a norther, however, this anchorage is wide open.

Cayos las Doce Leguas

The Cayos las Doce Leguas is a group of cays extending for almost 18M, with mile after mile of sandy beach on the seaward side, mangroves on the landward side (facing mainland Cuba), and a series of shallow lagoons in between. On the beach side there is a variety of interesting vegetation and all kinds of lizards and iguanas. A coral reef parallels the coast, breaking the surface for considerable distances, but then submerged elsewhere. On the landward side, another long reef parallels the coast,

Bahia de Mariel. In many bays in Cuba visiting boats are
obliged to tie to beat up docks such as this under the eye of the
local Guarda. Good fenders are essential. Mariel is the bay from
which the boat lift took place in 1978; 100,000 Cubans fled to
the States.

Cayo Paraiso, a favorite hang out of Ernest Hemingway.

Old colonial home in Havana.

Above Transportation, Cuban style. The island is dotted with fine old 1950's American cars, most of which are still running, sometimes with Chinese and Russian engines. *Below* The severe shortage of fuel means that any operating vehicle is loaded to the maximum.

Otherwise, the Cubans have been driven back to the middle ages. Ox and pony carts are a common sight in the countryside, in this case hauling in the sugar harvest.

Tobacco country in the western part of the island (Pinar del Rio).

The tobacco goes the cigar factory, where it is made into the finest cigars in the world.

The fishing in Cuba is the best we have found anywhere.

Below Cuban people, the friendliest we have met anywhere in the world.

The old Spanish church in Cienfuegos, more-or-less shut down during our visit, but active once again since the Pope's visit.

Below The beaches and sand spits off Cayo Largo.

One of hundreds of similar islands in the Jardines de la Reina, making for weeks of pleasurable gunk-holing and exploring.

Below The grandest lighthouse of them all, on Cayo Bahia de Cadiz. This one is 199 feet tall, and, as with all the others, needs to be wound up at least once a night.

Below One of the many spectacular lighthouses around the coast of Cuba, this one on Cayo Paredon Grande.

The entrance to the lagoon at Chivirico. The reef is funnel shaped. The channel runs almost onto the rocky shoreline and then hooks in behind the reef into an incredibly well-protected lagoon.

Below The old waterfront at Caimanera a the north end of Guantanamo Bay (outside the US zone).

North shore coastline near Baracoa. It is hard to imagine Columbus making his way up and down these coasts, year after year, with no windward ability, and hardly losing a single vessel.

Below Baracoa. It looks to be a wonderful anchorage but is, in fact, somewhat exposed to swells from the NE.

Revolutionary art in Baracoa.

Below The Cubans have plans for several large marinas, particularly on the north coast. Here we have the beginnings of such a venture on Cayo Coco.

Most of the waters around Cuba are spectacularly clear.

Below Another wonderful lighthouse, on Cayo Caiman Grande.

The old customs house at Caibarien, once a prosperous sugar port.

But now fallen on hard times.

The mangrove lagoons of the Bahia de Santa Clara are home to thousands of flamingoes.

Below The grassy flats in the Bahia de Santa Clara are home to innumerable lobsters which give the lobster boats busy, here seen unloading at an ice house. All the boats appear to have come out of the same mold. The older boats are all ferro-cement, the newer boats are fiberglass ('plastico').

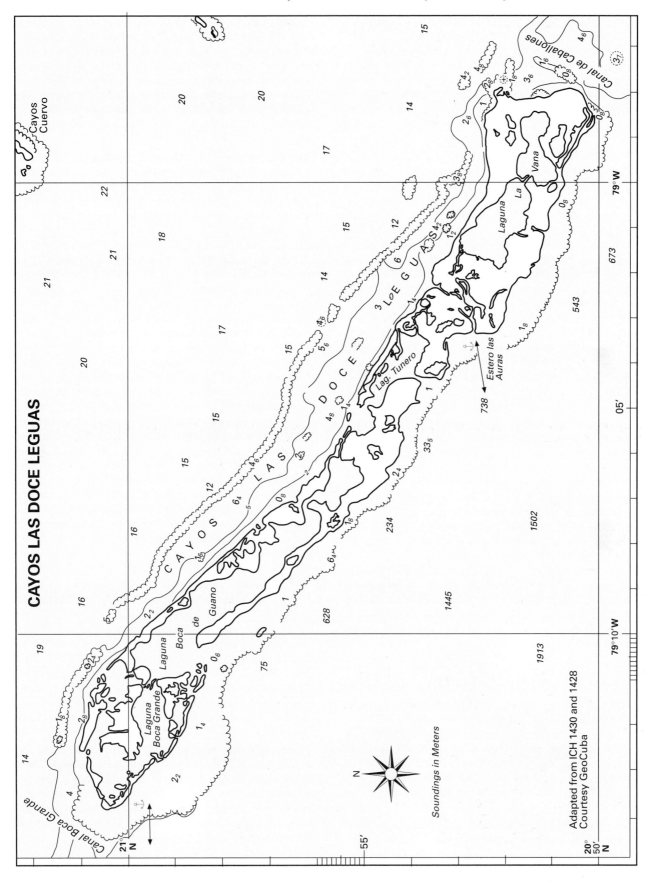

CAYOS LAS DOCE LEGUAS

Soundings in Meters

Adapted from ICH 1430 and 1428
Courtesy GeoCuba

but this is well submerged for most of its length and as a result provides little protection.

So far as we can see, there is not a single, decently protected all-weather anchorage in this entire stretch, although a couple of the submerged sections of reef on the seaward side enable the reef to be entered to find reasonable protection in settled easterly conditions.

Anchorages

Canal Boca Grande A submerged section of reef at the northwestern end of the cays allows boats with a draft of up to 2·5m to enter the reef. To do so, come to a position at approximately 20°59·5'N 79°14·2'W and head east toward a conspicuous stand of mangroves at the southeastern end of the beach ahead. The depths shoal fairly rapidly to 2·5–3m, with isolated coral rocks (but so far as we could see, no major heads – nevertheless, keep a good bow watch), and then gradually shoal toward the beach. You can carry 2m to within ¼M of the beach, although there are isolated patches en route with a little less depth than this. Between the cay to the east and the breaking reef to the south, there is quite good protection from all but the west and the NW.

Estero las Auras The Estero las Auras is a deep-water estuary toward the southern end of the Cayos las Doce Leguas, once again on the seaward side. In front of it, there is a substantial section of well submerged reef. Unfortunately, the bottom shoals to 1·5m in the approaches to the estuary, so for most boats the estuary is inaccessible and the only place to anchor is off the coast, inside the reef. The best location is to the NW of the estuary, off a sandy beach. Here the protection is good to the east, but not so good to the south and SW.

To enter, come to a position at approximately 20°52·5'N 79°04·0'W and head 080°. The bottom shoals rapidly to 2–3m, with isolated coral rocks, but no coral heads so far as we could see (nevertheless, keep a good bow watch), and then gradually shoals toward the estuary.

Cayos Laberinto de las Doce Leguas

The Cayos Laberinto de las Doce Leguas is a 40M long chain of cays and shoals extending in a NW to SE direction without a single navigable channel (for boats that draw more than a meter), from one side to the other. The sailor is faced with the choice of passing these cays on the inside or the outside, and must then stick with this choice until the other end is reached.

On the inside, the cays and shoals extend increasingly further eastward toward the southern end of the chain, until they finally close the mainland. Although there are various channels between these cays and shoals, in practice all boats use the Canal del Pingue, so eventually all choices are narrowed down to this canal. North of the canal there is a string of small mangrove cays on an east/west axis, many of which provide shelter, but none of which are covered in this guide since the canal is almost always approached or exited via Cayo Chocolate or Cayo Algodón Grande (see above).

On the outside, the Cayos Laberinto de las Doce Leguas offers few opportunities for shelter, and all of these are limited to boats drawing 2m or less. At the northern end protection can be found in prevailing winds by simply anchoring in the lee of Cayo Anclitas; 8M to the SE good protection can be found in the Pasa Piedra Grande; a further 6M to the SE there is good protection in a lovely anchorage in the Pasa Cachiboca; another 13M to the SE there is excellent protection in the Pasa Boca de Juan Grin; and finally at the very tip of the chain (Cabeza del Este), 14M further on, there is a tight anchorage in the mangroves. All are covered below.

The southernmost of the cays in the Cayos Laberinto de las Doce Leguas chain is Cayo Caguama. This has miles of beautiful sandy beach and has been selected by the Cuban government as a potential site for a major tourist development. Already a small airstrip has been cut in the brush, and a restaurant constructed. Next will come a number of *cabañas* (rustic cabins). It remains to be seen how far the project will go, but in the meantime if passing this way in calm conditions it is worth anchoring off and dropping in at the bar/restaurant, which has been very tastefully constructed and was occupied on our visit by half a dozen iguanas and two goats, with the iguanas fighting for scraps from our table!

Anchorages

Cayo Anclitas Cayo Anclitas is at the northwestern extremity of the Cayos Laberinto de las Doce Leguas. Its western shore forms a broad arc which creates excellent protection from all winds from the NE to the S, but is wide open from the SW to the NW. Shoal water extends ½M offshore, with the bottom coming up quite suddenly in many places. To anchor, simply come in toward the sandy beach until the depth shoals to about 2·5m and then drop the hook.

Pasa Piedra Grande A ½M wide channel separates Cayo Boca de Piedra Chiquita and Cayo Boca de la Piedra de Piloto. This channel is almost all shoal, but a narrow tongue of deeper water runs up its center, while another channel winds its way into a lagoon to the west where PuertoSol, one of the Cuban tourist companies, has a small floating hotel (complete with air-conditioned rooms, TV, a stereo, and a resident cook). The controlling depth

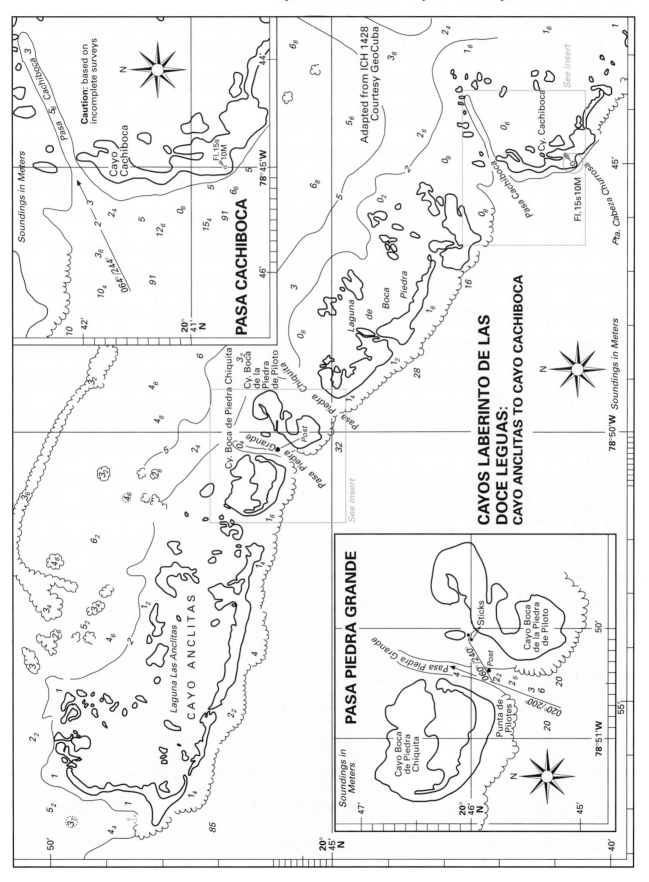

PASA CACHIBOCA

Caution: based on incomplete surveys

Soundings in Meters

Cayo Cachiboca

Fl.15s10M

78°45'W

CAYOS LABERINTO DE LAS DOCE LEGUAS: CAYO ANCLITAS TO CAYO CACHIBOCA

78°50'W Soundings in Meters

Adapted from ICH 1428 Courtesy GeoCuba

Cy. Cachiboca

Fl.15s10M

Pta. Cabeza Churrosa

Laguna de Boca Piedra

Pasa Piedra Chiquita

Cy. Boca de la Piedra de Piloto

Cy. Boca de Piedra Grande

Post

CAYO ANCLITAS

Laguna Las Anclitas

PASA PIEDRA GRANDE

Soundings in Meters

Cayo Boca de Piedra Chiquita

Sticks

Post

Punta de Pilotes

Cayo Boca de la Piedra de Piloto

Pasa Piedra Grande

78°51'W

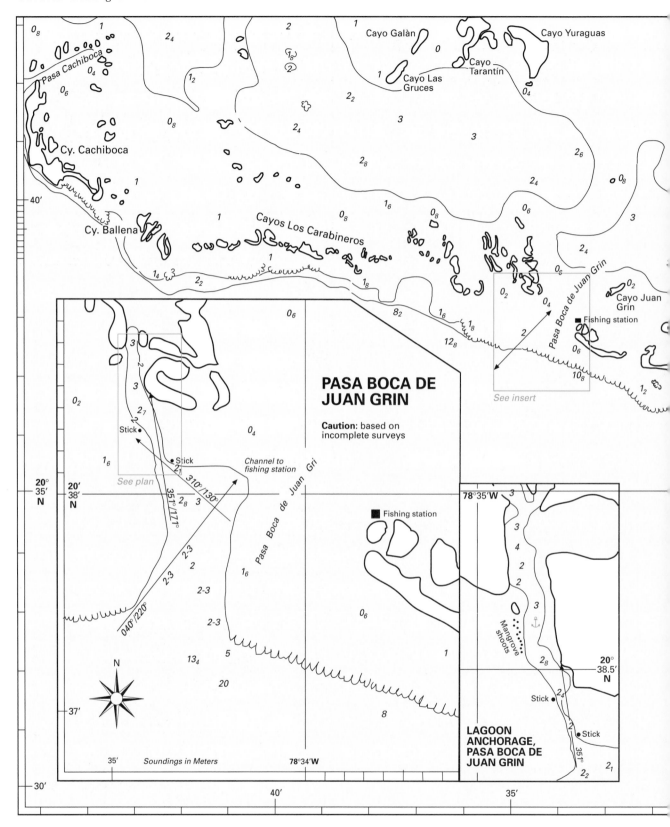

PASA BOCA DE JUAN GRIN

Caution: based on incomplete surveys

Channel to fishing station

Pasa Boca de Juan Grin

Stick

See plan

Stick

N

37'

35'   *Soundings in Meters*   78°34'W

Fishing station

LAGOON ANCHORAGE, PASA BOCA DE JUAN GRIN

Mangrove shoots

Stick

Stick

See insert

Cayo Galàn   Cayo Yuraguas

Cayo Tarantín

Cayo Las Gruces

Cayos Los Carabineros

Cy. Cachiboca

Cy. Ballena

Pasa Cachiboca

Pasa Boca de Juan Grin

Cayo Juan Grin

Fishing station

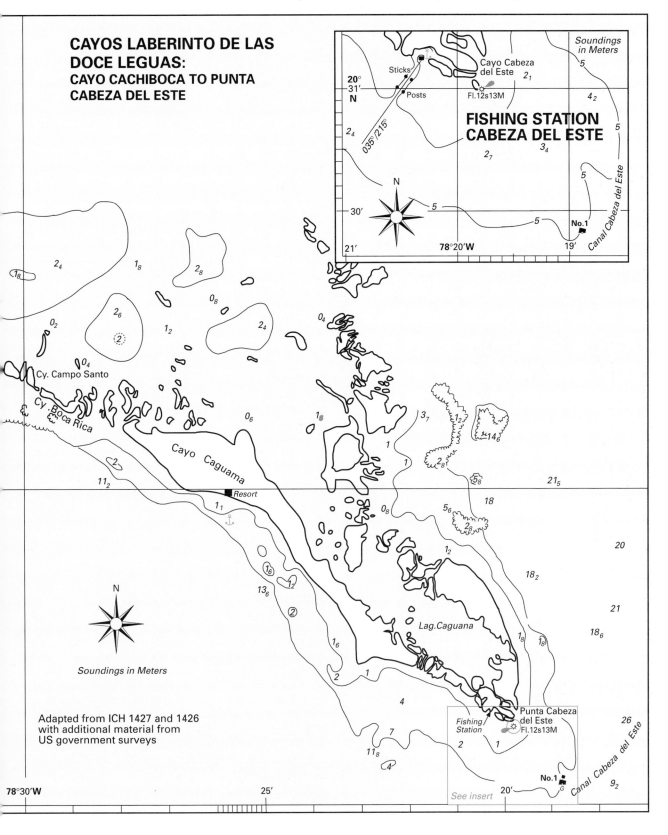

CAYOS LABERINTO DE LAS DOCE LEGUAS:
CAYO CACHIBOCA TO PUNTA CABEZA DEL ESTE

FISHING STATION CABEZA DEL ESTE

Soundings in Meters

Adapted from ICH 1427 and 1426
with additional material from
US government surveys

Soundings in Meters

for entering the tongue is about 2·2m (over an uneven bottom), deepening to 5m on the inside; the controlling depth for entering the lagoon is basically 1·6m, although the Cubans regularly take a 1·8m draft inside, and we did the same at close to high tide.

Despite the fact that the tongue is wide open in an arc from the NW to the east, it is reasonably well protected by shallow water in this direction. The bottom, however, has poor holding (rocky, with numerous small coral heads). The lagoon is exceedingly well protected, but as a result is plagued with the usual bugs; it has much better holding. In both locations the boat is likely to lie to the tide rather than the wind.

To enter the tongue, come to a position at approximately 20°45·5'N 78°50·6'W. Proceed on a heading of 020°, making whatever allowance is necessary for any tidal set. You will see a stake half knocked over – this is left 100m to starboard (i.e. you pass to the west of it). The channel around here is about 2·2m deep with numerous scattered rocks. Beyond this stake, the channel narrows but deepens, particularly on its western side. Somewhat further in is another stick which is also left about 100m to starboard, at which point you should anchor in 4–5m.

To enter the lagoon, pass about 15m to the west of the knocked-over stake (i.e. leave it just to starboard) and then head more or less 060° somewhat to the west side of the entrance to the lagoon. The depth in this stretch shoals to 1·6m with no particularly clear-cut channel. You will see a mangrove clump on the western side of the lagoon entrance – as you close it, curve to the east to pass about 60m south of it. Next you will see a stake on a shoal to the south (off to starboard), and another less-obvious stake on a shoal which will be just off to port. Pass midway between the stakes, continuing to curve around until on a heading of approximately 150° with the mangroves on the south side of the lagoon entrance dead ahead. Now curve back to the east, and then the NE, to come 50m or so to the north of these mangroves and anchor right here in a small basin with depths of up to 2·5m.

The PuertoSol boat works its way further into the lagoon to the floating hotel, but this is quite intricate and also unnecessary in terms of protection.

Pasa Cachiboca The Pasa Cachiboca is a narrow, deep-water channel that runs in to the north of Cayo Cachiboca (recognizable by the substantial steel-frame lighthouse, Fl.15s, on its southwestern tip).

To enter the pass, come to a position at approximately 20°41·8'N 78°45·8'W. Proceed on a heading of 064°, aiming for a point midway between the northern tip of Cayo Cachiboca and the small cay to the west of it. Be sure to make whatever course corrections are necessary to compensate for

any tidal set. As you approach the northern tip of Cayo Cachiboca, you should work over to this side of the channel to avoid extensive shoals to the west (on which there are the remains of old fish pens; the smaller shoal to the east also has similar remains).

The bottom shoals to a little over 2m, with scattered rocks quite soon after heading in toward the channel, and then gradually deepens until off the tip of Cayo Cachiboca it is about 5m. Beyond here the channel continues for another 2M in a more or less straight direction (020°), with shallow flats on either side, before petering out. A chain of small cays and shoals forms a protective rim around the whole area, creating excellent protection. There are lovely beaches on Cayo Cachiboca and the cay to the west. Altogether, a very pleasant spot.

Pasa Boca de Juan Grin The Pasa Boca de Juan Grin is a wide pass between the cays. It is generally quite shoal, but on its eastern side there is a large fishing station in sheltered water which is approached via a somewhat tortuous channel up which a 2m draft can reportedly be taken. There is an extremely sheltered lagoon, which is accessible to boats with a draft of up to 1·8m, in the mangroves to the east.

Both anchorages are approached by coming to a position at approximately 20°37·4'N 78°35·0'W and then proceeding on a heading of 040° across a generally shoal area (with variable depths of 2–3m and numerous small scattered rocks) to a position at approximately 20°38·0'N 78°34·5'W. From here various channel markers can be seen to the north and east which lead around to the fishing station on the tip of the cay to the east – we have not surveyed this channel. Instead, we headed approximately 310° for about ¼M, at which point the entrance to the lagoon can be clearly seen on a heading of about 340°. You need to continue toward the NW until the east side of the lagoon entrance bears 351° and then head directly for this east side.

You will soon come to a point at which the fishing boat keels have cut a clear light-green streak in the eel grass – you should center yourself in this stripe but then continue heading for the east side of the channel rather than following the light-green stripe as it curves off to the NW. As you near the mangroves to the east, curve somewhat to the west coming up center channel into the lagoon to anchor. The controlling depth is really 1·6m at low tide in the first part of the light-green stripe, but only for a few meters; by dragging the bottom, up to 2m can be taken inside.

Cayo Caguama There is no protected anchorage off the new resort development, which is located at approximately 20°35·0'N 78°25·8'W. However, in settled conditions it is possible to approach to within ½M of the beach, anchor off, and dinghy in. The bottom shoals very gradually from well out with patches of turtle grass and scattered rocks, but so far as we could tell no substantial bits of coral. We eased in slowly from the south until in 2m and then anchored.

Cabeza del Este There is a small fishing station tucked into the mangroves at Cabeza del Este. For a change, it is approached via a short and direct channel, with a minimum depth of 2m. On the inside, there are a couple of small basins in the mangroves with all-around protection but not much swinging room – a fore-and-aft mooring is needed.

To enter the basins, come to a position at approximately 20°30·8'N 78°20·7'W and head toward the east side of the fishing station (035°). You will be able to pick out two substantial posts between which you pass, favoring the east side of the channel (centered in the light-green stripe, with minimum depths of 2m). Continue toward the east side of the fishing station, passing midway between the next pair of sticks, and then curve somewhat toward the mangroves to the west in order to avoid a shoal in front of the station, after which you make a sharp turn to come in to the dock on the north side of the fishing station. 2½m can be carried alongside, with adequate room in which to anchor up either of the channels to the north of the dock.

Note In 1996, the stakes on the starboard side of the channel were reported to be missing.

Golfo de Guacanayabo

Northern passes

There are two principal passes into the northern end of the Golfo de Guacanayabo – the Canal del Pingue (connecting with the Canal Rancho Viejo at its southern end), which forms the inside passage from the Golfo de Ana María, and the Canal Cabeza del Este, the main pass out to sea.

There is then another pass, the Canal de Cuatro Reales, which leads in from the open ocean to Santa Cruz del Sur, but this one is not much used by cruising sailors.

Canal del Pingue

Note We did not transit either the Canal del Pingue or the Canal de Rancho Viejo. The following information is derived from a very detailed Cuban chart, the Cuban pilot, Syd Stapleton and local sources, but must nevertheless be treated with caution.

Between them the Canal del Pingue and the Canal de Rancho Viejo are approximately 7M long, but for much of this distance they pass through relatively open water. However, every once in a while the channel narrows down between shoals and

cays, but at all such spots it is well marked so passage appears to be uncomplicated.

From the north (Golfo de Ana María) The approach is generally made from just south of Cayo Malabrigo (12M to the NW of the entrance to the canal) on a heading of 123° to a position at approximately 20°47·2'N 78°19·3'W. This point is just north of a lit can buoy (green *No. 13*, Fl.5s), and ⅓M west of a post (*No. 14*) set on a shoal. (If coming from Cayo Chocolate, the course is due east for about 13M before picking up the 123° heading for the final 5M.)

The buoy is left reasonably close to *starboard* (i.e. you pass to the *east* of it; the channel is assumed to be running from south to north, so the 'red, right, returning' rule is reversed) on a heading of 155°, continuing past a red lighted beacon (*No. 12*, Fl.6s) and then a post (*No. 10*), both of which are left to port (i.e. you pass to the west of them).

Straight ahead, at a distance of 1½M, you will see a post (*No. 5*) and a red lit beacon (*No. 4*, Fl.4s). The channel runs between them, but instead of heading straight for them *you must make a slight dog-leg to the east* to avoid a shoal about halfway toward them. So, after passing the *No. 10* post you should come to 146° until the channel between *No. 5* and *No. 4* bears 170°, and then turn to this heading, continuing another 2½M south of *No. 4* beacon on the same heading.

By now you will be to the NW of a lit nun buoy (red *No. 6*, Fl.4s) which is left to port (i.e. you pass to the west of it) on a heading of 135°. This heading is maintained for the better part of 2M leaving first a post (*No. 4*) and then the final lit nun buoy (red *No. 2*, Fl.6s) to port. You are now in the Golfo de Guacanayabo.

From the south (Golfo de Guacanayabo) Come to a position at approximately 20°41·0'N 78°16·0'W, which is about 200m SSE of a nun buoy (red *No. 2*, Fl.6s). Leave the buoy to starboard (i.e. pass to the west of it), sailing up the channel on a heading of 315° leaving first a post (*No. 4*) and then another nun buoy (red *No. 6*, Fl.4s) to starboard.

After you are well clear of the buoy, head 350° toward a red beacon (*No. 4*, Fl.4s) a little more than 2M to the north. Leave the beacon to starboard (i.e. pass to the west of it) and then the next post (*No. 5*) to port.

Just off the port bow, at a distance of 1½M, you will see a post (*No. 10*) and beacon (red *No. 12*, Fl.6s). Before turning toward them you must maintain the 350° heading for another mile, at which time the post and beacon will be pretty much in transit on a bearing of approximately 335°. Now change course to leave both of them to starboard (i.e. you pass to the west of them), and then leave the final can buoy (green, *No. 13*, Fl.5s) to port.

You are now in the Golfo de Ana María, with

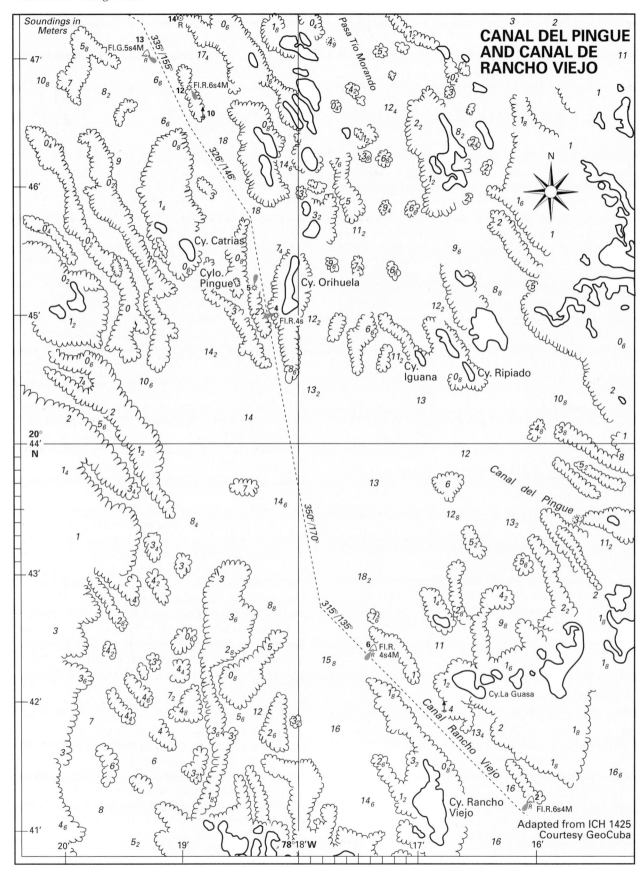

CANAL DEL PINGUE
AND CANAL DE
RANCHO VIEJO

Soundings in Meters

Cy. Catrias

Cylo. Pingue

Cy. Orihuela

Cy. Iguana

Cy. Ripiado

Canal del Pingue

Cy. La Guasa

Canal Rancho Viejo

Cy. Rancho Viejo

Pasa Tío Morando

Adapted from ICH 1425
Courtesy GeoCuba

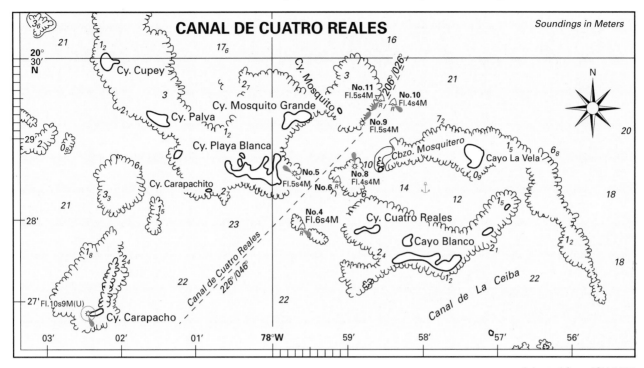

Adapted from ICH 1426
Courtesy GeoCuba

Cayo Malabrigo 12M distant on a heading of 303°, and Cayo Chocolate 18M away on an initial heading of 303° once again, but then turning due west after 5M.

Canal Cabeza del Este

The Canal Cabeza del Este is a more than 2M wide reef entry at the southeastern tip of Cayo Caguama. Passage is straightforward on a SW to NE axis, passing south of a green can buoy which is at approximately 20°29·8'N 78°18·8'W.

Canal de Cuatro Reales

This is another pass that we have not transited. It looks to be exceedingly well marked and without problems. We include a plan in case you should need it. We have been told that there is an excellent anchorage in the deep-water lagoon enclosed by the cays and reefs to the SE of the channel.

Cayo Grenada

Cayo Grenada consists entirely of mangroves and as such is uninteresting. However, the cay is crescent-shaped with shallow reef extending from its two tips, with the result that it has a well protected anchorage, sufficiently spacious to be able to anchor well away from the mangroves (and therefore the bugs), and with some good snorkeling on nearby reef patches. The cay forms a pleasant spot in which to rest up from, or prepare for, the 'outside' passage along the southern end of the Jardines de la Reina.

Note It is not clear from our notes whether the bearings we wrote down are true or magnetic. We have assumed they are magnetic, and have deducted 4° to convert them to true, but they may already have been converted so *it may be necessary to add 4° to get a correct true bearing.*

Approaches and entry

Come to a position at approximately 20°37·4'N 78°15·4'W and maneuver to place Cayo Sombrerito, the small cay in the center of the three cays to the west, on a back-bearing of 274°. Then sail into the anchorage on a heading of 106°, heading for the remains of the wrecked fishing vessel (identifiable by a couple of ferro-cement girders sticking up just above the surface of the water). Just to the north of the entry there is a very shallow coral patch which has some ironwork (somewhat like a tripod) more or less on its southern end (at approximately 20°37·5'N 78°15·3'W – it sticks up less than a meter and is not easy to see). The reef extends a few meters to the south of this ironwork – the iron should be left 100m to port (i.e. you pass to the south of it) at which point you will be in 6m. Further to the south the bottom shoals gradually with the 2m line reoccurring ¼M to the south of the coral patch, so the entry is quite wide. To the north of the coral patch there is another shallow entry (2·5m) and then a continuous reef all the way to the northern tip of the island.

Once inside anchor more or less in the center of the lagoon in 5 or 6m. Although deep water extends

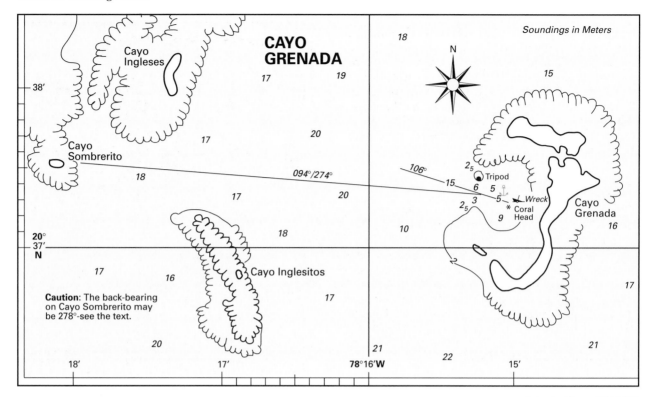

Caution: The back-bearing on Cayo Sombrerito may be 278°–see the text.

Adapted from ICH 1426
Courtesy GeoCuba

in toward the mangroves in many places, there is a good bit of scattered coral all around the perimeter of the lagoon, with one or two substantial coral heads. In particular, there is a head with just 2m over it immediately to the SW of the wrecked fishing vessel

Santa Cruz del Sur

Santa Cruz del Sur is an exceedingly busy fishing port with a medium-sized town nearby which has few facilities for cruisers (there is an *agromercado* and a post office, but not much else). The town has the rather dubious claim to fame of having been wiped out by a hurricane in the 1930s, with the loss of 3,000 lives.

The fishing fleet operates from a lagoon to the east of the town. The approach channel to the lagoon, and the lagoon itself, were dredged years ago to a controlling depth of 3·5m, but since then considerable silting has occurred so that today in places the channel is only kept open by the boat traffic. The lagoon has a controlling depth of 1·6m (immediately past the Guarda post at the entrance), although deeper draft vessels regularly plough their way in and out.

Approaches

There are two approach channels, one from the SE and the other from the west. Between the two is tiny Cayo Muerto, surrounded by an extensive shoal. Both channels are marked with substantial beacons as shown on our plan. 2m can be carried onto the Guarda dock, but no further. The dock itself is somewhat beat up, but quite well fendered. Alternatively, you can anchor out (the best spot probably

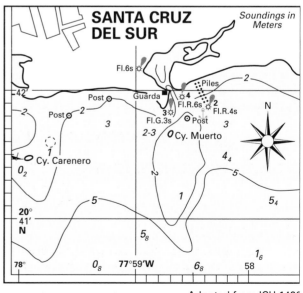

Adopted from ICH 1426
Courtesy GeoCuba

being just to the west of the tip of the line of piles coming out to the red *No. 2* beacon), and dinghy in to the dock. The Guarda will, in any case, probably ask you to anchor out (and will run a spotlight over you every hour, on the hour, throughout the night). When going to town, you can leave the dinghy on the Guarda dock and catch a ride on a horse-drawn buggy from just down the street (you will need pesos for the fare).

Cayo Media Luna

Cayo Media Luna is a crescent-shaped mangrove cay with reef and shoal extending to the west from both tips of the crescent. In between the arms of the cay is a large, uncomplicated anchorage which provides good protection in most conditions (including a norther, if tucked up toward the north end of the bay). To enter, simply come into the center of the bay on an easterly heading and anchor far enough off the mangroves to avoid the worst of the bugs. This is a relatively deep anchorage (5–7m) so you will need plenty of scope.

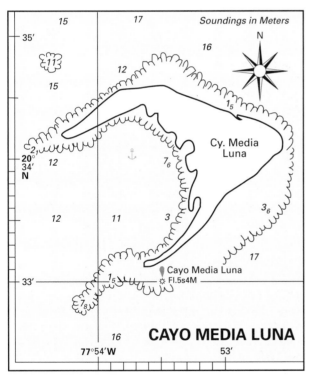

Adapted from ICH 1426
Courtesy GeoCuba

Cayo Rabihorcado

Cayo Rabihorcado has a fine mixture of mangroves, beach and coral with a reasonably well protected anchorage in prevailing conditions for deeper-draft vessels, and an extremely well protected lagoon anchorage for vessels drawing less than 1·6m.

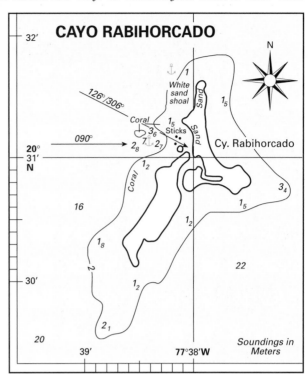

Adapted from ICH 1153
Courtesy GeoCuba

The southern end of the cay is entirely mangroves and not interesting; the northwestern side is mostly beach. In settled conditions the shrimp boats simply anchor to the west of the northern tip of the cay where there is a highly visible white sand shoal extending almost 200m off the beach. The 2m line runs along the outside edge of this shoal, so you can simply sail up to it and then drop the hook.

Anchorages

To the south of the white sand shoal at the northern end of the cay is an area of shallow coral, and then a relatively well protected bay with deep water to within 200m of the shoreline, at which point the bottom comes up very suddenly (from 4m to almost drying). To enter this bay, come to a position at approximately 20°31·2'N 77°38·5'W. Proceed in on an easterly heading, keeping a close watch for the substantial area of shallow coral immediately to the north of this entry track. Anchor 200m or more off the line of stakes that delineate a narrow channel into the lagoon (see below).

Lagoon The lagoon at Cayo Rabihorcado can be entered on a heading of 126° between the line of stakes. Once past the last of the stakes be sure to hug the mangroves on the south side of the channel since there are a couple of isolated coral heads on the north side. The controlling depth in the channel (very tight!) is 1·6m at low water. The lagoon itself has depths of 3m.

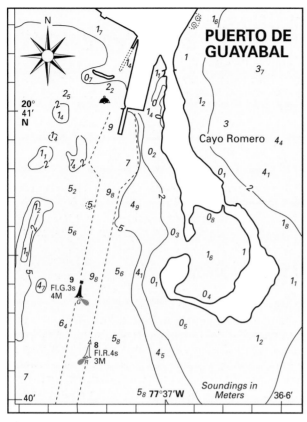

Adapted from ICH 1818
Courtesy GeoCuba

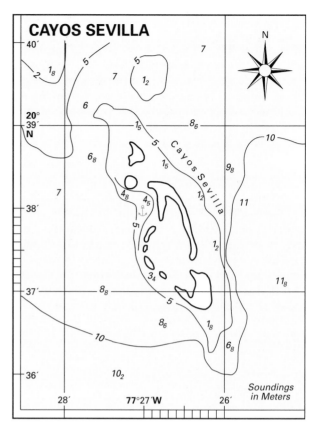

Adapted from ICH 1153
Courtesy GeoCuba

Guayabal

Guayabal is a commercial port from which sugar is exported. It has a well-buoyed channel to a large dock which is protected to the east by Cayo Romero, creating a calm anchorage in prevailing easterlies. But there is nothing of interest here for cruisers, added to which it is a ½-hour walk to town; when you get there, few supplies are to be found.

Cayos Sevilla

The Cayos Sevilla are a substantial group of mangrove cays of little interest except that they provide a reasonably protected anchorage for those sailing between the inner regions of the Golfo de Guacanayabo and Manzanillo.

Anchorage

The anchorage is in a broad bight on the west side of the cays. It is entered from a position at approximately 20°37·9'N 77°27·2'W on a northeasterly heading, coming in until 200m or so off the mangroves and then anchoring. 4–5m will be found in the center of the bay, shoaling to 2–3m toward the edges and then coming up quite abruptly. Protection is good from the prevailing easterlies, but the bay is wide open to the west (and

consequently often quite choppy in the late afternoon when the wind tends to be out of the west). Note that the cays to the south of this anchorage enclose a substantial lagoon which would make an excellent anchorage but this is shallow and without a deep-water access, so entry should not be attempted.

Laguna Jutía

We have not been to the Laguna Jutía, so what follows is a combination of hearsay and information from the Cuban pilot and Ministry of Fisheries. This lagoon is the primary small-vessel hurricane hole in this part of Cuba. It also provides access to the Río Cauto, Cuba's largest river, which reportedly is navigable with a 2m draft for 40M, and so might make for some interesting exploring.

The lagoon is entered from a position at approximately 20°31·4'N 77°10·0'W on a NNW heading up the center of the channel with minimum depths of 2–3m. Once inside the lagoon entrance you hug the east shore, curving around to the NNE, and then passing between the east bank and a small cay into the Estero Jutía, which runs to the ENE. Once again, there are 2–3m in the Estero Jutía.

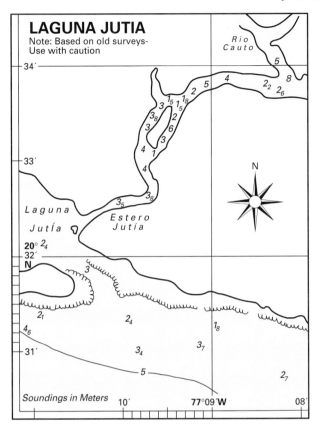

LAGUNA JUTIA
Note: Based on old surveys-
Use with caution

Laguna Jutía

Estero Jutía

N

Soundings in Meters

77°09'W

Adapted from ICH 1153
Courtesy GeoCuba
Additional information from
the Cuban Ministry of Fisheries

After 1½M the Estero Jutía divides around an island – both channels are navigable, but the north one is more frequently used. Another 1½M past the island a channel leads to the north into the Río Cauto. To enter this channel it is necessary to hook to the south side of the Estero Jutía (in order to avoid debris washed out of the Río Cauto), and then turn to the north into the channel. Once into the Río Cauto, the river can be navigated up to the railway bridge at Guano, 30M further upstream.

Manzanillo

Manzanillo is a somewhat faded colonial city which nevertheless retains a certain charm and in particular has a lovely central plaza. It is also a port of entry to Cuba, and a potential source of limited supplies (in addition to an *agromercado* and one or two poorly supplied dollar stores, there is an office of Mambisa (SUMARPO), a Cuban agency which arranges re-supply of commercial shipping; Mambisa, which can be contacted on VHF Ch 16, will supply diesel and gasoline, as well as groceries). The city has an airport with twice-weekly flights to Havana, and direct flights to Canada (Toronto). Water is available on the Guarda dock.

Approaches

The Canal Chinchorro, a wide, marked pass, links Manzanillo with Guayabal, Cayo Rabihorcado, and Cayo Media Luna to the NW.

The Canal de Balandras (see below) enables an inside passage to be made between Manzanillo and Niquero.

The Canal de Madrona (see below) leads in from the open ocean.

Entry and anchorages

The point of contact for cruisers is the Guarda dock (at approximately 20°19·8'N 77°09·3'W) at the mouth of a small enclosed basin (used by the fishing fleet). This basin is located at Punta Caimanera, to the SW of the town. Immediately to the NE of the Guarda dock are some conspicuous oil tanks and a large boathouse; to the south is a sizable beach. The dock is approached more or less from the north; simply come alongside and tie up.

2m can be carried onto the dock, which is well fendered. Here the formalities will be handled (the full range of officials, since this is a port of entry; the officials can be particularly bureaucratic). After processing the paperwork, the Guarda will probably ask you to anchor out just to the north where they can keep an eye on your boat; you can dinghy in, leaving the dinghy on the Guarda dock and catching a horse-drawn buggy (pesos needed) to town from a bus stop a couple of hundred meters down the road.

The problem with this scenario is that the wind often gets up quite strongly from the west in late afternoon, blowing from this direction until as late as midnight, which makes this an uncomfortable anchorage, added to which the bottom is exceedingly soft mud with very poor holding. Much better protection can be found in the cays to the west, with excellent holding, but it is a long dinghy ride to town. The Guarda used to be resistant to the idea of boats being out of their sight. However, in the interests of the safety of the boat and its crew we insisted on moving into the lee of the cays at night, telling the Guarda that if they didn't like it they could put a man aboard for the night to watch us (which they then declined to do, allowing us to go). We returned each morning to anchor off the Guarda dock and go to town.

Note that there is an oil pipeline that runs from the oil tanks (NE of the Guarda dock) to the four substantial buoys south of the cays, so when anchoring off the Guarda dock, do not stray into this area. Note also that at night the Guarda sometimes string a steel hawser across the mouth of the fishing harbor, so take care when coming in or out with the dinghy.

Note Recent reports indicate that the Guarda have got used to the idea of boats anchoring in the cays;

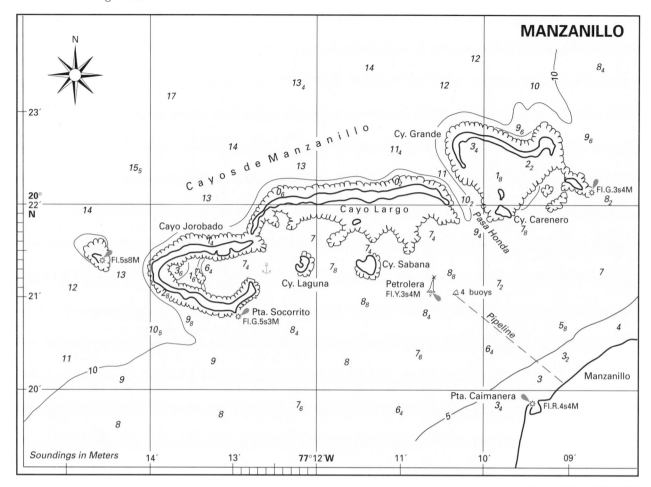

MANZANILLO

Adapted from ICH 1813
Courtesy GeoCuba

they have also taken to allowing boats to anchor off another Guarda dock at the NE end of town, next to which is the Port Captain's office, conveniently close to the center of town. It may prove best to try clearing in here rather than at Punta Caimanera. However, this is also a lee shore with mixed holding, so you may still want to retreat to the cays at night.

The Cayos de Manzanillo provide excellent protection in just about any conditions. The various small cays are set upon steep-sided shoals, as is the surrounding rim of mangroves, so a careful eye needs to be kept on the depth sounder when approaching any shoreline. Rather than tucking up in the westernmost bay, which offers the best protection but with the most bugs, we recommend anchoring in the spot indicated on the plan as there is more of a breeze and fewer mosquitoes. The holding is excellent (dense mud packed with shells).

Canal de Madrona

The Canal de Madrona is the main ship channel that links the southern end of the Bahía de Guacanayabo with the Caribbean. Once again, we have not transited it, but it looks straightforward enough – wide, deep and well marked, with numerous buoys and beacons which are shown on the accompanying plan.

Ceiba Hueca

Ceiba Hueca is a commercial port devoted to the export of sugar. It has no facilities for cruisers, and its exposed wharf provides little protection in many situations. There is no reason to go there.

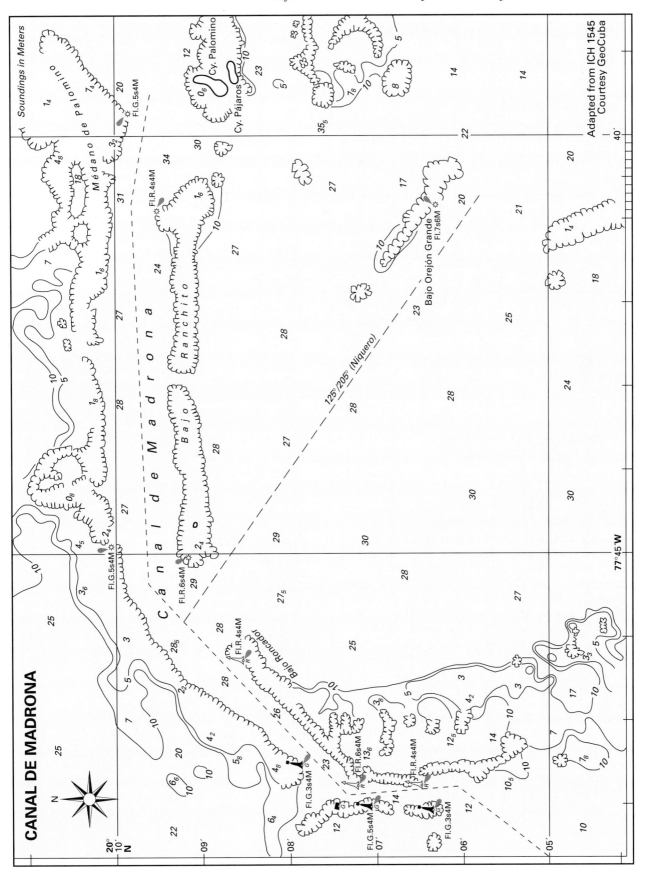

CANAL DE MADRONA

Soundings in Meters

Adapted from ICH 1545
Courtesy GeoCuba

125°/205° (Niquero)

Canal de Madrona

Bajo Ranchito

Médano de Palomino

Cy. Palomino

Cy. Pájaros

Bajo Orejón Grande

Bajo Romeador

Fl.G.5s4M
Fl.G.5s4M
Fl.R.4s4M
Fl.R.6s4M
Fl.R.4s4M
Fl.G.3s4M
Fl.G.5s4M
Fl.G.3s4M
Fl.R.6s4M
Fl.R.4s4M
Fl.7s6M

77°45'W

Golfo de Guacanayabo to Cabo Cruz

Canal de Balandras

The Canal de Balandras is the principal channel for coastal traffic between Manzanillo and Niquero. It is relatively wide and deep, and therefore easy to transit. However, at the southern end there is a shoal that must be skirted; since the canal is entirely unmarked and sometimes has quite strong tidal currents, it is important to keep a reasonably close track of your boat's position as you pass through this end. In addition, in a norther the north end of the canal can be rough enough to be considered hazardous to small craft.

From the north, come to a position at approximately 20°06·0'N 77°35·6'W and pass through the first part of the canal on a heading of 202° until due east of the southern tip of Cayo Cocos (the cay on the west side of the channel). At this time, come to a heading of 236° and hold this for another ½M.

From the south, come to a position at approximately 20°05·0'N 77°36·4'W and sail into the canal on a heading of 056° until due east of the southern tip of Cayo Cocos (the cay on the west side of the channel). Now come onto a heading of 022° and hold this until clear of the north end of the canal.

Anchorage

The margins of the canal provide a fair measure of protection in most circumstances. For all-around protection you only have to go around the corner into the Pasa Piragua.

Pasa Piragua Cayo Piragua forms the eastern side of the Canal de Balandras. Between Cayo Piragua and the next cay to the east there is another channel which is both relatively deep (5–6m) and extremely well protected. It can be entered from the north, but the channel here is narrow and beset with shoals on either side. It is far easier to enter from the south, either passing clear through the Canal de Balandras and then hooking around to the south of the shoal between the Canal de Balandras and the southern end of Cayo Piragua, or else heading directly for the southern tip of Cayo Piragua from the middle of the Canal de Balandras, and then passing either side of the small mangrove cay immediately to the SW of Cayo Piragua (minimum depths are 4m in mid-channel to the north of this cay, and 3m to the south of it).

4m will be found in mid-channel entering the Pasa Piragua, deepening to 6m on the inside, with plenty of swinging room (the boat will lie to the tide rather than the wind). Note, however, that there is an extensive shoal on the inside of the bend in the middle of the pass (i.e. on the west side), with shoal water on both sides of the channel to the north of this. Throughout, the shoal areas have very abrupt edges so at all times take care when approaching the margins of the channel.

Immediately to the SW of the entrance to the pass there is an attractive sand spit which is home to a substantial number of terns. Please stay away from this from March to June (nesting season – they simply lay their eggs in the sand).

Niquero

Niquero is home to a small fishing fleet and a large sugar refinery. The town is quite a bit larger than we expected and although relatively poor is attractive in its own way (lots of vegetable and flower gardens; one or two nice colonial buildings; and a general ambiance of being cared for despite being down-at-the-heel). It has an *agromercado* for fresh produce, and diesel and gasoline are available, although only from the ServiCenter gas station which is some distance from the dock area.

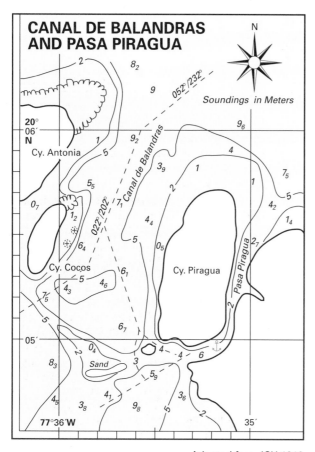

Adapted from ICH 1810
Courtesy GeoCuba

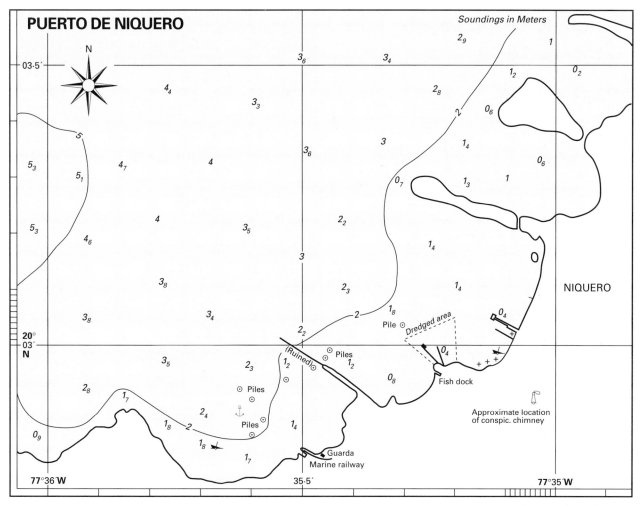

Adapted from ICH 1810
Courtesy GeoCuba

Approaches

From the Canal de Balandras The chimney of the sugar refinery is clearly visible; you should aim a little to the south of it. As you get closer, you will pick out a number of cays which can be passed relatively closely (3m or more depths almost everywhere), but there is one shoal that must be avoided, known as the Bajo Damian and located at approximately 20°04·0'N 77°35·9'W (it has a stake marking it).

From the Canal de Madrona There is no need to transit the full length of the canal. Instead, when halfway through (a position at approximately 20°09·2'N 77°45·8'W) come to a heading of 125°, leaving the red *No. 10* beacon almost ½M to port and continuing for 6M until 1M past the beacon on Bajo Oregon Grande (which is left ½M to port – i.e. you pass to the south of it). The sugar factory chimney should now be visible (approximately 116°) in transit with the northern edge of Cayo Niquero. You can head for the chimney, passing just to the north of Cayo Niquero.

On the inside from the south See Coastline between Niquero and Cabo Cruz below.

Entry and anchorage

As you close the coast you will be able to pick out a substantial concrete dock with a fish-processing station, and to the south of this the remains of a long dock (now just a mass of wooden piles). To the south of this ruined dock is a small marine railway and dock, and tucked in behind a palm tree at the head of this dock is the Guarda post. This is where you check in.

Between the ruined dock and the Guarda dock there are a number of substantial piles, some of them almost submerged at high water, to which local boats are likely to be moored. In any event, keep a close watch as you enter this area. The bottom shoals to less than 2m well out from the Guarda dock, so when 100–200m off you should drop the anchor and dinghy in. The protection is quite good, except in a norther when it would be advisable to retreat to the Pasa Piragua (see above) or the Bahía de los Cachones (see below).

153

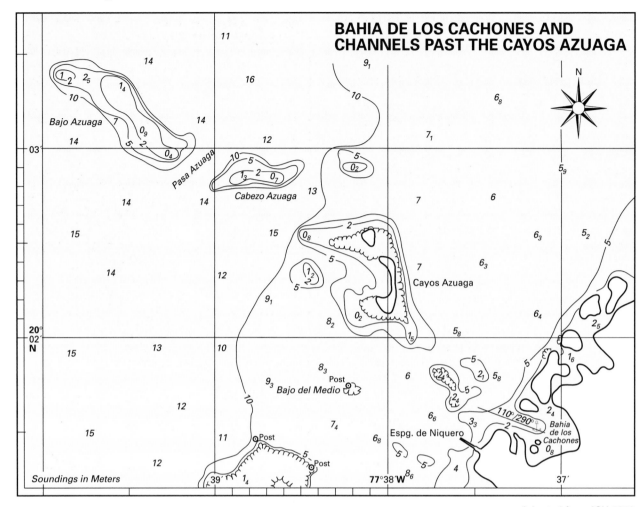

BAHIA DE LOS CACHONES AND CHANNELS PAST THE CAYOS AZUAGA

Adapted from ICH 1810
Courtesy GeoCuba

Bahía de los Cachones 2½M south of Niquero there is a substantial dock (conspicuous) built for the export of sugar. Immediately to the north of this there is a bay, the Bahía de los Cachones, with an easy entry which provides excellent shelter. To enter, approach from the north or the SW, but not the NW (there is a shoal barring the way), coming to a position at approximately 20°01·6'N 77°37·4'W and then sailing in on a heading of 110° midway between the mangroves on both sides. The depths will gradually shoal to about 3m in the center of the bay. You can carry 2·7m fairly close to the small cay inside the south side of the bay, and also up to the SE corner of the cay that forms the northern side of the entry. Further east of a line drawn between these two cays, the bay shoals to less than 2m.

Coastline between Niquero and Cabo Cruz

The 10M coastal stretch south of Niquero is potentially one of the more hazardous around the coast of Cuba since it contains numerous unmarked shoals and rocks with less than 2m over them, and must be transited through one or more unmarked passes. The principal hazards are in the vicinity of the Cayos Azuaga, the Bajo Arreola to the west of the Cayos Limones, and the Bajo Borlón de Tierra.

In the midst of these hazards there is a small settlement at Belic with a well protected anchorage, but with numerous hazards in the approaches.

South of these hazards there is a beach development at Las Coloradas. This is close to the site at which Castro and his comrades landed the *Granma* in 1956, starting the revolution.

At Cabo Cruz there is an excellent anchorage behind the reef, with the lighthouse and dramatic cliffs as a backdrop – one of the most picturesque anchorages in Cuba, and an excellent spot from which to prepare for, or rest up from, a passage of the south coast (see the next chapter).

Cayos Azuaga

The Cayos Azuaga can be passed to the west (via the Pasa Azuaga) or to the east. The eastern passage, which comes past the tip of the sugar-loading dock south of Niquero, is the easier to follow since there are a number of clearly identifiable marks.

From the north, if coming past the dock simply hug the coast (200–300m off) until at the dock, and then head west between the post on the Bajo del Medio (pass to the south of it) and the two posts on the shoal to the south (pass to the north of these), heading SW when past the second of these southerly posts.

If using the Pasa Azuaga, come to a position at approximately 20°03·1'N 77°39·0'W and sail through on a heading of 200°. Although the channel is unmarked, it is wide (300m) and deep (14m or more) – if the bottom starts to come up, you are running out one side or the other!

From the south, if coming past the dock, stay a couple of miles offshore until the tip of the dock bears 090° *or more*, and then head for it, leaving the first post to starboard (i.e. passing to the north of it), and then passing midway between the next two (widely spaced) posts. Come past the north side of the dock and then hug the coast (200–300m off), heading north.

If using the Pasa Azuaga, come to a position at approximately 20°02·7'N 77°39·2'W and sail through on a heading of 020°.

Bajo Arreola and the Cayos Limones

Shoal water (marked with a stake) extends ½M to the west of the Cayos Limones with a further, isolated, shoal patch just over ½M to the west of this. The unmarked channel runs between these shoals.

From the north, come to a position at approximately 19°59·6'N 77°40·4'W and sail through on a heading of 200°, leaving the stake on the shoal off the Cayos Limones well to port (i.e. passing to the west of it).

From the south, come to a position at approximately 19°59·3'N 77°40·5'W and sail through on a heading of 020°, leaving the stake on the shoal off the Cayos Limones well to starboard (i.e. passing to the west of it).

Belic

Having just had more than our fill of officialdom at both Manzanillo and Niquero, we could not face dealing with the Guarda yet again, so we by-passed Belic. The approaches to the town are littered with shallow coral heads, according to old DMA and BA charts, so if going there take care.

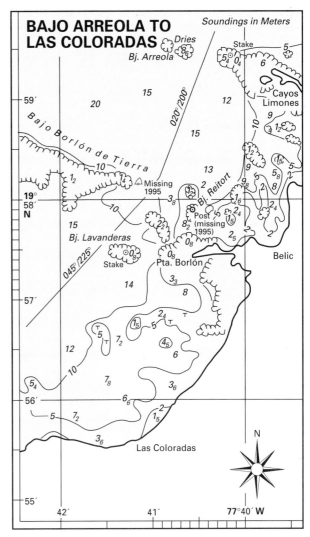

Adapted from ICH 1545
Courtesy GeoCuba

Bajo Borlón de Tierra

The channel passes between a series of shoal spots (Bajo Borlón de Tierra, Bajo Reitort, and the Bajo Lavanderas), none of which are marked, with the exception of a stake on the Bajo Lavanderas (ICH *1545* shows a buoy on the Bajo Borlón de Tierrra, but in 1995 this was missing, as was the post on Bájo Reitort).

From the north, come to a position at approximately 19°58·2'N 77°40·9'W and sail through on a heading of 225°, leaving the stake on the Bajo Lavanderas well to port (i.e. passing to the west of it).

From the south, come to a position at approximately 19°57·5'N 77°41·7'W and sail through on a heading of 045°, leaving the stake on the Bajo Lavanderas well to starboard (i.e. passing to the west of it).

Las Coloradas

A beach at Las Coloradas is being developed as a tourist site with a restaurant, bar and disco. By the time this is published it may be functional, but then again it may be yet another abandoned project.

From the north, you should only head in toward the beach when the buildings bear 140° or less (there are a considerable number of isolated shoals in the northern half of the bay).

From the south, you can follow the coast around, staying ⅓M or more off Punta Coloradas (the actual site of Castro's landing, in the mangroves, now marked by a small pier), and then head inshore.

Anchorage The water is deep relatively close inshore so you can anchor a couple of hundred meters off the beach. In prevailing conditions the land provides a good lee, although in the afternoons, depending on how strongly the westerly wind builds up, this may be an uncomfortable location and it may be hard to land a dinghy on the beach.

7. Cabo Cruz to Punta Maisí

The 200M stretch of coastline between Cabo Cruz and Punta Maisí is in many ways the most spectacular in Cuba, providing some of the most dramatic scenery in the Caribbean. To the east of Cabo Cruz the relatively low cliffs and hills steadily increase in height. By Portillo, some 35M away, there are sporadic sheer cliffs up to 70m in height, with the mountain chain of the Sierra Maestra rising to as high as 1,972m (Pico Turquino) immediately inland. Underwater, the topography is even more dramatic, with the bottom dropping into the abyssal depths of the Oriente trough (maximum depth 7,239m) and the Caimanes trough (maximum depth 7,680m). The change in elevation here from the tops of the mountains to the depths of the ocean is the greatest, in the shortest distance, on the surface of the earth.

Although there are no off-lying hazards, such a coastline is potentially quite dangerous. Year round, substantial swells sweep in from the Caribbean, pounding against the cliffs. Close inshore, and around every headland, there are frequently confused and unpleasant seas from deflected waves. Beyond the few natural harbors there is absolutely no shelter to be found – once you put to sea you are committed until the next haven is reached. Fortunately for the navigator, there are excellent sheltered anchorages spaced out along the coast, with the greatest distances between them being 48M (Portillo to Chivirico), and 75M (Baitiquiri to Baracoa on the north coast – the longest stretch without shelter around the entire island). The typical distance between anchorages is 30–40M – a comfortable day sail or a short overnighter.

Between these anchorages are a number of bays and river mouths which, on the chart, also look as if they might provide reasonable shelter, but for one reason or another none are suitable as an overnight anchorage (with the possible exception of the Ensenada Cabañas, 2M west of Santiago, an exceptionally well protected bay with a narrow entry which reportedly has a controlling depth of more than 2m but which, from a sailboat point of view, is barred by a 10m high cable across the entrance; it might, however, make a good haven for a powerboat).

Winds

The prevailing winds are the trades, which blow with some constancy from the east, tending toward the NE in the winter and the SE in the summer. Cold fronts have little effect in the wintertime since only a third of those reaching Cuba penetrate this far south, and when they do they are greatly weakened. Of more significance is the effect of tropical depressions in the summertime, bringing strong winds from a southerly direction.

The general flow of the trades is modified by the katabatic effect – the influence of a land mass on the daily wind pattern. This effect is most pronounced where the mountains are at their highest, and also closest to the sea – that is, in the central section of the coast from Portillo to east of Guantánamo. Near the two headlands, Cabo Cruz and Punta Maisí, the effect is less apparent, particularly at Punta Maisí where the winds are consistently out of the east to NE.

In the central section, during the night the winds steadily abate until it is nearly calm in the early hours of the morning; there may even be an offshore breeze which continues until daybreak. Soon after daybreak a gentle breeze reasserts itself from the east, or a little north of east, building in intensity and moving into the SE and even the south as the day wears on. By late afternoon it can easily be blowing a steady 20–25 knots, after which it gradually abates once again.

The katabatic effect is a factor only for a short distance out to sea, after which you once again run into the trades. So far as the seas are concerned, the effect is less pronounced. Most of the time the constancy of the trades, combined with the great fetch across the Caribbean, produces a considerable swell from the SE which rolls in to the coast continuously. The swell is, however, somewhat reduced at night, and often confused by an unpleasant wind-driven chop in the late afternoon.

Currents and tides

A branch of the Caribbean/Antilles Current rolls southward through the windward passage, hooking around Punta Maisí to the west. This, however, is relatively weak and frequently upset by wind- or tide-driven currents. For example, a strong south

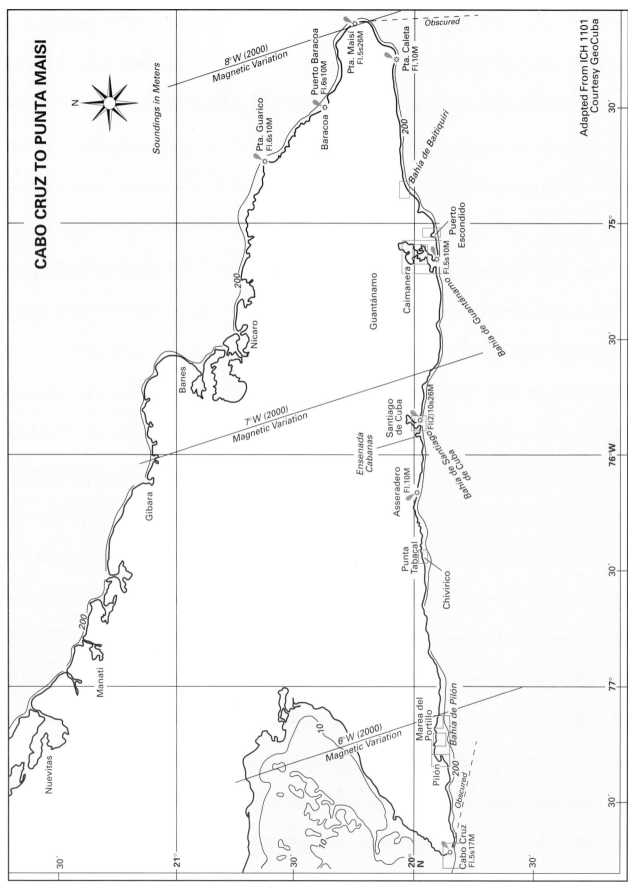

CABO CRUZ TO PUNTA MAISI

N

Soundings in Meters

8° W (2000)
Magnetic Variation

7° W (2000)
Magnetic Variation

6° W (2000)
Magnetic Variation

Obscured

Pta. Guarico
Fl.6s10M

Puerto Baracoa
Fl.6s10M

Baracoa

Pta. Maisi
Fl.5s26M

Pta. Caleta
Fl.10M

200

Bahía de Baitiquiri

Puerto
Escondido

Caimanera Fl.5s10M

Bahía de Guantánamo

Guantánamo

Nicaro

Banes

Gibara

Santiago
de Cuba

Ensenada
Cabanas

Fl(2)10s26M

Bahía de Santiago
de Cuba

Asseradero
Fl.10M

Punta
Tabacal

Chivirico

Manati

Nuevitas

Marea del
Portillo

Bahía de Pilón

Pilón

10

200

Obscured

Cabo Cruz
Fl.5s17M

N

Adapted From ICH 1101
Courtesy GeoCuba

30′

75°

30′

76° W

30′

77°

30′

21°

30′

30′

20°
N

wind (mostly summertime) will produce an eastward-setting current, whereas a north wind (wintertime) will reinforce the generally westward set.

The tidal range is about 0·4m (16 inches). The tide is semi-diurnal (i.e. twice daily).

Sailing strategies

While the wind and the waves are clearly the prime navigational considerations when passaging this coast, to these must be added the desire to enjoy as much of the mountains as is possible, which requires daylight passages.

Sailing from west to east is a challenge. When the trades are firmly in the NE (primarily the winter months and early in the day) an eastward passage can be quite comfortable, but as soon as the wind moves into the east or the SE (primarily the summer months and later in the day) the wind is close to dead on the nose, frequently with unpleasant seas.

The calmest winds and seas will be found at night, with a midnight or early morning departure bringing you to the next anchorage before noon to avoid the afternoon winds and chop. You will, however, miss much of the coastline. To take advantage of the katabatic effect you will also need to hug the coast which for the most part is completely unlit and extremely steep-to – the depth sounder will provide little if any warning if you stray dangerously close inshore. Precise navigation and constant vigilance are essential.

So when going east the choice of sailing time can only be decided in light of the sailing qualities of your vessel, the weather conditions at the time, your confidence in your navigational skills, and the strength of your desire to see the coastline. Since the individual mountains in the Sierra Maestra range, although dramatic, are essentially very similar (and, dare I say it, somewhat boring after a while – this is the rain-shadow side of the mountains and therefore rather brown and scrubby), we were not too concerned if we passed much of the range in the night. We gave precedence to comfort over sightseeing, but you will have to call this one for yourself.

Sailing from east to west is straightforward – a daybreak start from one secure anchorage will result in a fast and comfortable, though somewhat rolly, passage, arriving at another secure anchorage before dark.

Caution Note that if sailing at night, when going east Punta Maisí light is obscured by the coastline until it bears 358° *or less*; when going west, Cabo Cruz light is obscured until it bears 285° *or more*.

Charts and magnetic variation

ICH *1137, 1136, 1135* and *1134* cover this entire stretch at 1:150,000. In addition to these there are detailed charts of Pilón, and the Bahías de Santiago and Guantánamo. Finally, there is the chart book (Region 4: Cabo Cruz to Punta Maisí) which covers this region.

Magnetic variation increases steadily from 5°30'W (January 2000) at Cabo Cruz to 6°40'W at Chivirico, 6°45'W at Santiago de Cuba, and 8°00'W at Punta Maisí. In all areas it is increasing annually at a rate of 9'W.

Cabo Cruz

At Cabo Cruz a solid barrier of reef extends westward for 2M from cliffs at the southern tip of Cuba. Between the reef and the mainland there is a lovely, well protected anchorage, with a strong breeze coming in over the reef to keep the bugs at bay. A small fishing village nestled between the lighthouse and a dramatic cliff forms a picturesque backdrop.

Approaches

The region north of the reef is relatively free of hazards. It is possible to simply come around the reef's western tip, or to head down from any point to the north, into its lee. A beacon more or less marks the western end of the reef, although it is important to note that the reef extends almost another ⅓M to the west of this beacon. Behind the reef, a red beacon marks an isolated coral head, with more heads in the area between the beacon and the reef, while a green beacon marks the edge of a shoal that extends from the cays lining the mainland.

From the north Note that shoal water extends ½M offshore at Punta Casimbas, 2M to the north of Cabo Cruz. This shoal is covered in sticks and fishermen's nets. South of Punta Casimbas the shoal more or less parallels the coast, slowly closing it until at Cabo Cruz it is only about ¼M offshore. To the west of this shoal there are no off-lying hazards for small vessels. As Cabo Cruz is approached the green beacon will be clearly visible; this is left to port (i.e. you pass to the west of it) after which you curve around to the east to come between the mangroves to the north and the breaking reef to the south.

From the east You must come at least ⅓M to the west of the westernmost beacon before heading north and then east into the lee of the reef. Once around the tip of the reef, you leave the more easterly red beacon immediately to starboard (i.e. pass just to the north of it) and the green beacon to port (i.e. pass to the south of it) to come between the mangroves to the north and the breaking reef to the south.

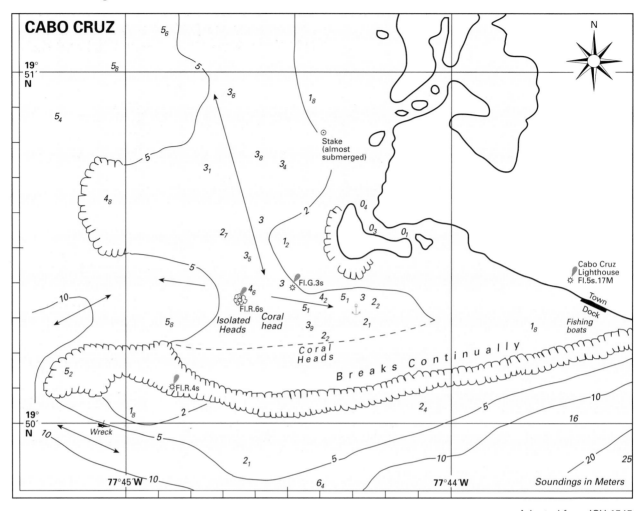

Adapted from ICH 1545
Courtesy GeoCuba
With additional information from
the Cuban Ministry of Fisheries

Anchorage

Although 1·8m can be carried all the way onto the fish docks by the lighthouse, your presence will not be appreciated, and in any case the channel is narrow with coral on one side and shoals on the other. It is best to anchor between the mangrove cays and the reef apron well to the west of the settlement. The further east you go, the more protection there is from the north, but the narrower the navigable channel and the more you will be in the way. In any case, in normal circumstances there is no need for protection from the north so it is best to drop the hook as soon as you are south of the mangroves, anchoring somewhat closer to the mangroves than the breaking reef in order to avoid isolated coral heads which extend some distance north of the reef. You will need to show an anchor light since there is a certain amount of nighttime traffic. The Guarda may or may not pay you a visit – they are exceptionally friendly here.

If you should go to the dock, the fishing boats follow a track toward the eastern edge of the houses, then curve north toward the water tower as they near the docks. You will need to clear in with the Guarda. The settlement is in any case worth a visit in the dinghy in order to climb the lovely stone lighthouse, to tour the well preserved colonial building at its base, to see the fish hatchery up the hill, and to walk around the town which is attractive and well cared for, with a pretty little beach and a pleasant walk to the nearby headland.

Note Following the downing of the American planes in February 1996, the Guarda were requiring boats to anchor close to town.

Bahía de Pilón

The Bahía de Pilón is a large bay protected by a fringing barrier of reef and cays, with the town of Pilón in its NW corner. Pilón itself is a run-down port with a small fishing fleet. It has little to offer in the way of supplies or services. The bay, however,

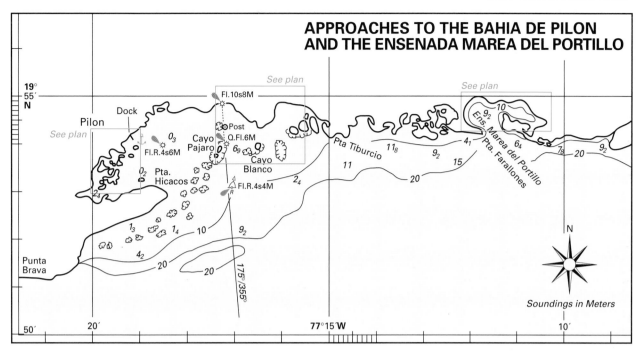

APPROACHES TO THE BAHIA DE PILON AND THE ENSENADA MAREA DEL PORTILLO

Adapted from ICH 1137
Courtesy Geocuba

provides excellent shelter, and also contains an attractive cay (Cayo Blanco) with some reasonable snorkeling on nearby coral reefs and coral heads. This is a good spot in which to layover before or after the passage to Cabo Cruz (35M by the time you have worked from one anchorage to the other).

Approaches

Although there are a number of breaks in the reef fringing the bay, only one is marked so this comprises the principal entry channel. This channel runs more or less up the center of the bay. To approach it from either the west or the east, *it is essential to stay well outside the reef until the outer channel buoy is visible*, and only then to make the turn in. This buoy (red, *No. 2*) is located at approximately 19°53·0'N 77°17·1'W.

From the west, once past Punta Brava, the headland preceding the Bahía de Pilón, maintain a heading of 085° or more until the buoy bears 025° *or less*, and then head for the buoy.

From the east, once past the cliffs on the west side of the entry into the Ensenada Marea del Portillo (see below) maintain a heading of 255° or less until the buoy bears 270° *or more*, and then head for the buoy. Note that it is also possible to enter the bay at its eastern extremity, between Punta Tiburcio and Cayo Blanco, holding over toward the mangroves around Punta Tiburcio in order to avoid extensive areas of reef which extend almost ½M to the east of Cayo Blanco. This is, however, a good light and calm seas entry (lots of coral if you get it wrong). Once past Punta Tiburcio, if going to Pilón, you

must continue on a NW heading toward the mangroves on the mainland to the north of Cayo Blanco before making the turn to the west (to avoid some very substantial coral heads to the NE of Cayo Blanco).

Entry

The main channel is 400m wide and 20m deep, so entry is pretty straightforward in any conditions, although it may well be rough since the seas and swells tend to drive right up the channel. At night, a couple of range lights can be picked up from some way out on a heading of 355°, but in the daytime the marks are not so easily seen (the front one is a green beacon which does not show up against the green mangroves ashore, while the rear one is just a small, white concrete patch in the midst of the mangroves). If you do follow the range, it will bring you pretty much to the outer channel buoy. This is left well to starboard (i.e. you pass to the west of it) and from here on you can ignore the range.

Once past the outer channel buoy continue on a heading of 005° to pass midway between the green beacon to the NE of Cayo Pajaro and the red beacon to the NW of Cayo Blanco. At this point you may decide to simply anchor off Cayo Blanco, or to head into the Ensenada Tiburcio (for both see below), but if continuing to Pilón or the anchorage at Cayo Redondo (see below) come around to the north of the beacon off Cayo Pajaro, leaving a red post to starboard (i.e. passing to the south of it) and then continue on a heading of 260°. You will see another red beacon ahead with a green buoy to the

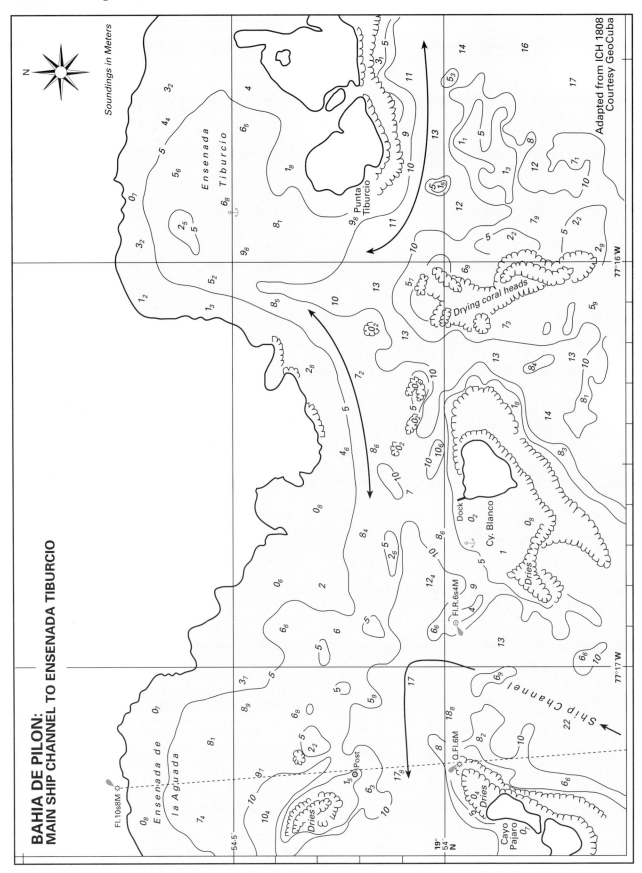

BAHIA DE PILON:
MAIN SHIP CHANNEL TO ENSENADA TIBURCIO

Adapted from ICH 1808
Courtesy GeoCuba

Soundings in Meters

N

Ensenada
Tiburcio

Punta
Tiburcio

Drying coral heads

Cy. Blanco

Dock

Dries

Ship Channel

Cayo
Pajaro

Dries

Post

Dries

Ensenada de
la Aguada

Fl.10s8M

Fl.R.6s4M

Q.Fl.6M

77°16'W

77°17'W

19°
54'
N

54·5'

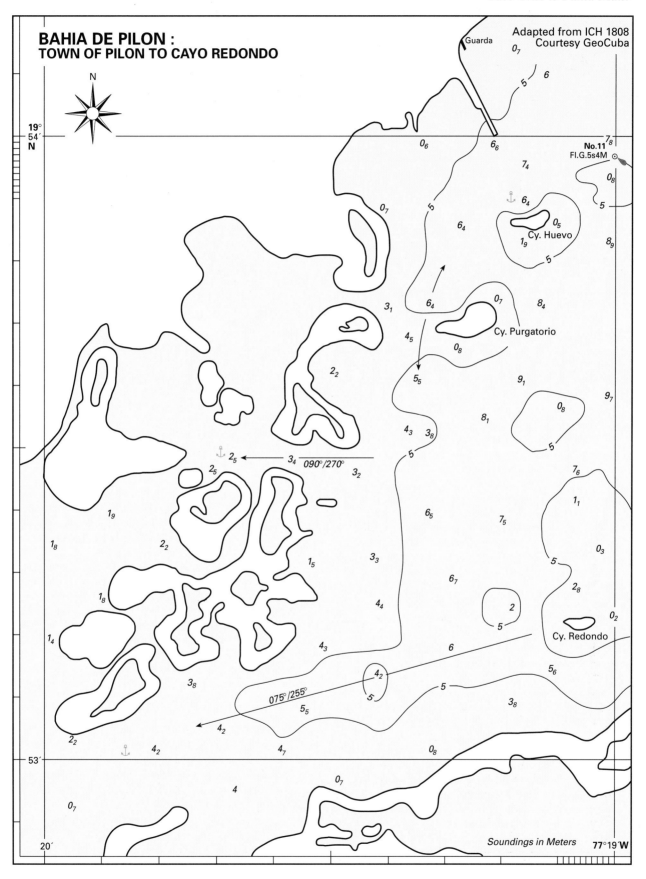

BAHIA DE PILON :
TOWN OF PILON TO CAYO REDONDO

N

Adapted from ICH 1808
Courtesy GeoCuba

Guarda

0_7

5 6

19°
54'
N

0_6 6_6 7_8

No.11
Fl.G.5s4M

7_4

0_8

0_7 5 6_4 5

6_4 0_5

Cy. Huevo

1_9 5 8_9

3_1 6_4 0_7 8_4

Cy. Purgatorio

4_5 0_8

2_2 5_5 9_1

8_1 0_8 9_7

4_3 3_8

2_5 3_4 090°/270° 3_2 5

2_5

1_9 7_6

1_1

1_8 2_2 1_5 3_3 6_5 7_5 0_3

1_8 6_7 5 2_8

1_4 4_4 2 0_2

5

Cy. Redondo

4_3 6

3_8 5_6

4_2 5 5

075°/255° 3_8

5_5

2_2 4_2

4_2 4_7 0_8

53'

0_7

4

0_7

20'

Soundings in Meters   **77°19'W**

163

south of it; you pass between these two, and then curve north toward the conspicuous sugar-mill chimney, leaving another green beacon (*No. 11*) to port (i.e. passing to the east of it).

Clearance

In front of the sugar mill there is a substantial concrete dock with an ironwork extension in poor repair. In calm conditions it is possible to come alongside the dock to clear in, but typically there are some small swells here so it would be better to anchor off. If necessary, some protection can be found by coming into the lee of tiny Cayo Huevo, where the bottom is deep almost into the mangroves. The Pilón Guarda post is at the head of the rickety dinghy dock, immediately to the east of the concrete dock. Further to the east, in the mangroves, is a wooden fishing dock with another Guarda post; 2m can just about be dragged in here, but you will be in the way.

Anchorages

Cayo Redondo This is one of the cays to the SW of Pilón. Between it and the mainland is an extremely well protected lagoon which the local fishermen use as a hurricane hole. We have not checked it out, so the following information and accompanying plan are based on second-hand information.

The anchorage is entered by sailing SW down the channel between the mainland and Cayos Huevo and Purgatorio (Purgatorio is the cay to the south of Cayo Huevo), continuing until a channel opens up to the west. This is entered in mid-channel on a westerly heading, anchoring once inside the mangroves, or working into one of the channels or lagoons on either side. Further south there is another sizable area of well protected water which is entered by keeping tiny Cayo Redondo on a back-bearing of 075°.

Cayo Blanco This is a lovely little cay which is used as a day trip by the Hotel Farralon at Marea del Portillo (see below). The guests are brought over to do a little snorkeling and enjoy a barbecue on the beach. If you happen to show up at the right time you may be allowed to join in.

To anchor, simply come around the red beacon to the NW of the cay and then work into the lee of the reef between the beacon and the cay, off the beach. Note that the bottom comes up from 5m very suddenly, so come in slowly and anchor once in 2–3m. Although the cay is beset by extensive reefs, looking as if this would be a very secure anchorage, in fact the circular nature of the reef allows small swells to swing around from both sides so on a windy day by late afternoon it can be quite rolly here, in addition to which the holding is poor. For an overnight anchorage it would be better to retreat to the Ensenada Tiburcio (see below).

Ensenada Tiburcio The Ensenada Tiburcio is a well protected bay at the easternmost extremity of the Bahía de Pilón. To enter it from the west (i.e. Pilón and Cayo Blanco), when north of Cayo Blanco it is essential to stay well over toward the mangroves on the mainland – this is to avoid several large, and very shallow, coral heads to the NE of Cayo Blanco (unmarked except for a couple of small, hard-to-see sticks, but clearly visible in the right light). The Ensenada de Tiburcio is otherwise free of hazards, with 5m or more in the center shoaling gently toward the edges (with the exception of a shoal in the center of the northern half of the bay). The bay can also be entered and exited directly from or to the outside by rounding Punta Tiburcio, but this is a good-light, calm-conditions-only passage, taking care to avoid the extensive coral areas to the east of Cayo Blanco.

Ensenada Marea del Portillo

The Ensenada Marea del Portillo is a substantial bay which contains an extremely well protected lagoon at its east end, and a couple of hotels at its west end (one of which is very nice). The anchorage end of the bay is surrounded by mangroves and not particularly interesting; the hotel end has a silty beach backed by coconuts and other cultivated vegetation. The entire bay is rimmed by mountains.

At the time of our visit one hotel (the lower one, hidden behind the palms) was closed for renovation, but the very conspicuous one (the Hotel Farralon) had just opened for business. It welcomed visiting sailors to its bars and restaurants (excellent buffet-style meals at $6 for breakfast, $10 for lunch, and $15 for dinner – a welcome change from onboard cooking), and, if buying a meal, to its other facilities (swimming pool, tennis courts, etc.). Cars could be rented from the hotel to tour the local mountains, and horseback trips arranged. Facilities for scuba diving and instruction (PADI) were planned. The hotel flies its guests into either Manzanillo (from Canada) or Holguin (Europe), bringing them the rest of the way by road (not too long a drive). This unlikely spot might make a good place for guests to join or leave the boat. The hotel's number (☎ and fax) is: (537) 335 301.

Approaches

The entrance to Marea del Portillo is wide (500m), deep, and well marked and can be attempted in any conditions, which is just as well since it is often quite rough, especially in late afternoon when the seas and swells drive straight up the channel.

From the west, the entrance is preceded by three conspicuous headlands, with small beaches between them. The first headland has a conspicuous hotel. Before the third headland is rounded, the outer

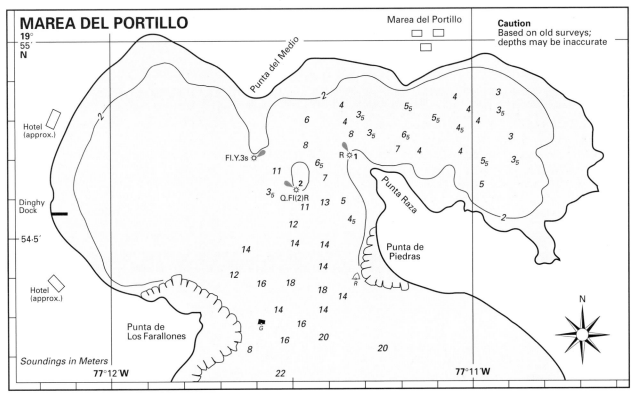

MAREA DEL PORTILLO

19° 55' N

Hotel (approx.)

Dinghy Dock

54·5'

Hotel (approx.)

Punta de Los Farallones

Punta del Medio

Fl.Y.3s

Q.Fl(2)R

Punta Raza

Punta de Piedras

Marea del Portillo

Caution
Based on old surveys; depths may be inaccurate

Soundings in Meters

77°12'W

77°11'W

N

Adapted from ICH 1137 and old DMA surveys
Courtesy GeoCuba and DMA

channel buoys will be visible. There are no off-lying hazards so long as you stay ¼M or more offshore. A point at approximately 19°54·0'N 77°11·4'W will put you in a good position to enter.

From the east, there are no off-lying hazards so long as you stay ¼M or more off the mangroves. The headland on the west side of the channel is quite conspicuous; later the outer channel buoys will be clearly visible. A point at approximately 19°54·0'N 77°11·4'W will put you in a good position to enter.

Entry

Reef extends up to 200m out from the headlands on either side of the bay, with the red and green buoys set pretty much on the end of the reefs, so give the buoys a good clearance, entering in center channel. On the inside you will see a red beacon to starboard (the east), a red beacon ahead, and a yellow beacon to port (the west). All three mark shoals. The eastern (red) beacon marks the northern tip of a shoal extending north from Punta Raza; the center (red) beacon marks the southern edge of an isolated shoal, and the western (yellow) beacon marks the southern edge of a shoal extending south from the mainland.

If going to the anchorage, come in on a northerly heading to pass between the two red beacons, and then when north of the eastern beacon simply hook around to the east into the sheltered bay and anchor

anywhere. If heading over to the hotels (not advisable in the afternoons – the swells roll straight up into this section of the bay) leave the center red beacon and the yellow beacon to starboard (i.e. pass to the south of them). The most protection will be found by tucking down into the SW corner of the bay.

Some time after you have anchored the Guarda will arrive in a rowing boat to check your papers.

Visiting the hotels

The prevailing swells roll right up the center of the bay and over to the NW in front of the hotels. During the mornings it is generally calm in the bay, but by late afternoon and into the evening it can be a wet and wild dinghy ride across the bay. A morning visit with a midday meal is recommended over an evening at the bar! The beach off the hotels shoals way out and there may be substantial little breakers, so landing a dinghy can be tricky. There is a decrepit concrete dinghy dock which has a foot or two (0·3–0·6m) at its outer end. This probably offers the best bet. If you choose not to use this, the best spot to beach a dinghy is to the south of the large hotel where the seas are most subdued and there is the least chance of a swamping.

165

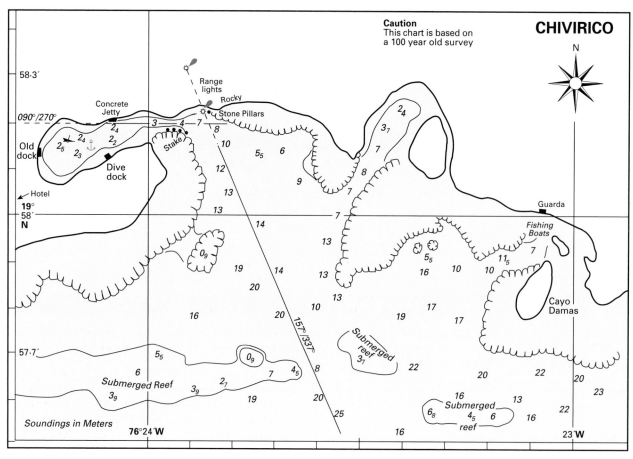

Adapted from an old DMA chart

Chivirico

Thank goodness for Chivirico, for without it there would not be a single secure anchorage for sailboats between the Marea del Portillo and Santiago de Cuba, a distance of more than 75M.

Chivirico is a small, well protected lagoon tucked in behind a substantial headland. It provides excellent protection in any conditions. A hotel (Hotel Galeones) on the headland welcomes visiting sailors to its bar, restaurant (expensive) and pool, and can arrange a rental car, while the town of Chivirico, a few hundred meters away, is a (very limited) source of supplies.

The Hotel Galeones is an excellent base from which to rent a car to explore Santiago de Cuba, rather than taking your boat there (for more on this, see Santiago de Cuba).

Note Chivirico was put off-limits in March 1996 after the Cubans shot down the two American planes. Recent reports indicate that this prohibition is not always enforced.

Approaches

The coastal shelf is wider at Chivirico than in most places along the southern coast. On this shelf, in the approaches to the lagoon, are numerous extremely dangerous areas of coral, many of which leap straight up from 5–10m of water to within centimeters of the surface. When the trade wind is from the SE or south, long swells roll in from the Caribbean and then hump up on the shallow water of the shelf, breaking heavily across the various reef areas.

The channel runs up between the reef areas almost to the (rocky) shoreline before making a sharp turn parallel to the coast to run through a narrow passage between a reef and the shoreline. When the seas are running, the swells drive up the channel and you are not free of them until after making the turn and getting tucked in behind the reef. Although the swells tend to abate as the shoreline is approached, in such conditions this entry is not one for the faint-hearted.

The situation is complicated by the fact that from offshore the entry to the lagoon is not visible; even close inshore the entry is difficult to see until the last minute. The temptation to 'come in and take a look' must be resisted until you are absolutely certain you are in the right spot; otherwise you run the risk of crashing into the coral.

With these thoughts in mind, it is best to make the initial approach to the bay to a point reasonably well

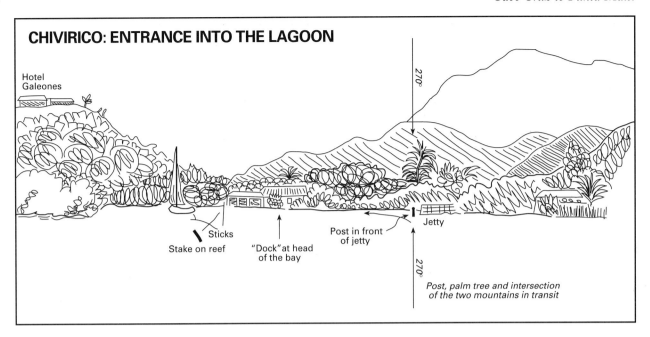

CHIVIRICO: ENTRANCE INTO THE LAGOON

Hotel
Galeones

270°

Sticks

Stake on reef

"Dock" at head
of the bay

Post in front
of jetty

Jetty

270°

*Post, palm tree and intersection
of the two mountains in transit*

offshore – certainly no closer than 19°57·0'N 76°23·6'W. From here you will be able to pick out the small metal framework (with a white box by its side) of the leading light of a set of range lights for the channel, but in the daytime you may not be able to pick out the rear light in the range since it is only visible through a narrow slot cut in the surrounding trees. You have to be right in line to see it. However, you will be able to see a conspicuous dark-green, bushy tree on the hillside above the leading light. You should manoever to keep this in transit with the leading light until you can pick out the rear half of the range. You need to come in for the range light and tree on a heading of 337°, taking constant bearings and adjusting your course for any tidal set.

At night you will be able to pick out both lights, although the sector of the rear light is extremely narrow in order to keep you off the reef! However, we would not attempt a night entry under any circumstances.

Entering the lagoon

You must keep coming in toward the leading light until almost onto the rocks. The reef closes in on both sides. As you get closer you will be able to pick out the rear half of the range which will enable you to hold to a tight 337° bearing which is especially necessary around latitude 19°57'·7N. Closer still, you will be able to see several stone pillars just in front of the leading light, and a rocky headland immediately to the east – these are the remnants of an old ore-loading pier. To the west you will be able to see a half-knocked-over stake, and to the west of this some sticks (reported missing in 1996). The stake marks the tip of the reef to port. You must curve to the west as you come within about 50m of

the leading light, coming about midway between the stake and the shoreline to get tucked in behind the reef.

At this time you will be able to pick out a concrete jetty, with a concrete handrail, on the north side of the lagoon. Immediately in front of this is a post in the water. Behind is a reasonably conspicuous palm tree, and behind this a range of hills backed by the edge of a mountain. You need to line up the post, the palm tree, and the crossover point of the hills and mountain, all on a bearing of 270° (see sketch). Come straight for the post, keeping everything in line, until almost at the jetty, at which point you ease around in front of it (it has 2·4m right off its tip), and then hook south into the center of the lagoon to anchor.

This last part of the channel, from the range light into the lagoon, narrows down to no more than 20m at the point where you come between the mangroves on both sides of the lagoon entrance, so you need to pay close attention to the transit. The depths shoal to 2·5–3m. Once in the lagoon, the depths are not much more than 2·5m in the center, shoaling toward the edges.

Some time after you have anchored the Guarda will come and seek you out to check your papers. However, it may be a while before they arrive since they might have to come across the bay from the fishermen's anchorage behind Cayo Damas (see plan).

Going ashore

Take your dinghy to the small dock on the south side of the bay. From here a track leads to the west end of the bay where one road runs up the hill to the hotel while another goes into town.

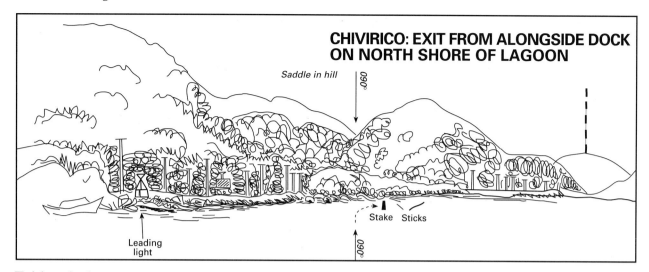

CHIVIRICO: EXIT FROM ALONGSIDE DOCK ON NORTH SHORE OF LAGOON

Saddle in hill 090°

Stake   Sticks

Leading light

090°

Exiting the lagoon

Come to a position immediately in front of (3–5m only) the concrete jetty and the post on the north side of the lagoon. From here, looking due east (090°) you will see a distinct saddle in the hills on the horizon (see sketch). Head straight for this saddle, leaving the sticks and stake on the reef to starboard (i.e. passing to the north of them), and then curving around to the final exit bearing of 157° as you come past the stake, at which time the leading light will be off to port and the rocky headland ahead. Get the leading light in transit with the rear light (and conspicuous tree) on the hillside (back-bearing of 337°), and keep these in transit until south of 19°57·0'N, at which time you can bear off in either direction along the coast.

Santiago de Cuba

Santiago de Cuba, which is a port of entry to Cuba, is second only to Havana in terms of size and importance, but every bit as illustrious in terms of its history. It was founded in 1514 by Diego de Velazquez, the first governor of Cuba; Hernán Cortés, the conquistador was the first mayor. Until 1553 it was the capital of Cuba.

The city has always been a major commercial center. Early prosperity produced some lovely colonial buildings, a few of which survive, and the powerful fortifications – El Morro – at the entrance to the bay. In more recent times, there has been a great deal of industrialization, with the factories and plants crowding in toward the city itself.

Santiago was a center of rebellion against Spain, and the site of Castro's failed assault on the Moncada barracks in 1953. Subsequently it played a major role in the successful fight to topple Batista. Many of the heroes of the various independence wars are buried in its principal cemetery, while throughout the streets and surrounding countryside there are numerous plaques and small monuments to commemorate those who fell in the 1956 to 1959 campaign.

Santiago clearly is a 'must' stop, but there are problems in visiting by boat. The city is built at the head of a large, enclosed bay, much of which is something of an industrial wasteland, some of which is still green and alluring, but all of which is currently off-limits to sailors! Arriving boats are met at the entrance to the bay and escorted to the 'Marina' at Punta Gorda, just inside the bay, where the boat must stay until it leaves.

The principal dock at the marina is a beat-up affair with bits of steel re-bar sticking out which threaten damage to your topsides every time the boat is hit by the wake of a passing vessel. A floating section has been added to the end which is kinder on the topsides but still subject to the wake of passing boats. Dock fees are $0.45/ft/day. Electricity can be jury rigged. To avoid damage, we chose to anchor off, for which we were charged the exorbitant sum of $0.30 per foot per day. We then discovered that the harbor is the filthiest in which we have ever been; during the day the onshore breeze drives all the muck up to the north end of the bay, but at night the offshore breeze brings it back, with great gobs of crude oil and tar floating by (we were told this only happens after a rain, but I suspect it is more common than this).

After three days our waterline had a solid ridge of tar, while the inflatable was plastered with it. When we left we had to cut the painter off and replace it, while the dinghy itself has never fully recovered. To add insult to injury, the marina is miles out of town, which necessitates at least one expensive ($10) taxi ride into the city. Once in town you can either rent a car or do business with the various hustlers who will rapidly surround you, making arrangements to be driven around, and picked up from the marina in the future by a private car at a much more reasonable price.

In spite of these problems, it is worth making

some effort to see Santiago, both because of what it has to offer culturally, and also in terms of the opportunity it affords for re-supplying the boat (the best for many miles in any direction). But in the future, until the harbor is cleaned up and the marina improved, we will leave the boat in Chivirico, rent a car from the Hotel Galeones, and drive to Santiago. (Note, however, the recent prohibition on Chivirico – see above.)

Sights to see

In the city, the magnet for tourists is the Parque Cespedes, with the cathedral on one side, the 'town hall' on the other side, and the Casa Velazquez (the home of Diego de Velazquez) on yet another side. The latter is reputed to be the oldest house in Cuba. It has been beautifully restored and filled with period furniture and should not be missed. A stroll through the streets surrounding the square will bring you past many more fine buildings, some crumbling, and some restored. The Bacardi Museum and Museo de las Clandestinidades are worth a visit.

A little further afield, en route to the Hotel Santiago and the Hotel Las Americas (Santiago's two leading tourist hotels – the Santiago, in particular, has good phones, a fax, a swimming pool, and various other facilities) you pass the striking monument to General Antonio Maceo, with a museum beneath it. Further still are the Moncada Barracks, the site of Castro's unsuccessful assault on July 26, 1953, pock-marked with bullet holes but essentially rather boring, and the far more interesting cemetery of Santa Ifigenia (we are generally not fans of cemeteries, but this one is well worth a visit).

Outside of town, the sanctuary of El Cobre, the most sacred spot for Cuban Catholics, is an impressive building looking down a lovely valley in front, but scarred by a strip-mining operation behind (copper, hence the name of the sanctuary). East of Santiago, a twisting road leads almost to the 1,200m summit of Gran Piedra, with mountain trails and great views. In the same general area, the Siboney farmhouse, in which Castro and company planned the assault on the Moncada barracks, is a revolutionary museum, while the Valle de la Pre Historia is peopled by enormous concrete dinosaurs.

Finally, not to be missed on any account are El Morro and the lighthouse. The impressive fortifications at El Morro provide great views up and down the coast and over the city; the lighthouse is yet another 19th-century gem (built in 1898 after the Americans destroyed the 1848 light during the Spanish-American war). The original French mechanism and lens are lovingly maintained by the resident light-keeper (if you ask at the house, he will happily take you up; as with other Cuban lighthouses, there is a $1 charge).

Supplies and services

Santiago has two or three *agromercados* and is quite the best source of fresh vegetables and fruits for some distance (which is not saying much). There are also two dollar supermarkets, the Cubalse near the tourist hotels, and the Diplotienda near the airport, but the contents are disappointing, considering the size of the city.

DHL operates a courier service in and out of Santiago (five days or more to get something from the US, and this is assuming customs officials don't tie it up); their office is next to the cathedral on the Parque Cespedes. The Hotel Santiago has excellent phones and a fax (and will hold fax messages for collection – fax 53 226 86105).

Santiago has an international airport, but currently the only direct flights overseas are charter flights to Toronto, Canada. However, there are regular internal connections to Havana and other Cuban cities – this might be a good place in which to pick up or drop off guests.

Approaches and entry

There are no off-lying hazards on the approaches to Santiago de Cuba. Whether coming from the west or the east you should make for a position at approximately 19°57·8'N 75°52·6'W from where the red and green buoys marking the entrance to the channel will be clearly visible (on a heading of 035°). The ancient fort, Castillo del Morro, with additional fortifications below it, will be conspicuous on the headland to the east of the entrance channel, making you reach for your camera as you head in. Whether or not you have notified the authorities of your impending arrival (VHF Ch 16 – call *Morro Santiago*), a patrol boat will come out to greet you.

The Guarda may require you to heave-to in the mouth of the channel while the officials get their act together at the marina. In their own good time you will be escorted to the marina dock, which is less than a mile to the north of the *castillo*. The marina is recognizable by its blue building and cement jetty with a red-roofed, open-air bar at the tip and the new floating dock beyond this. The jetty has a little over 2m on its outboard end, shoaling rapidly toward shore on both sides. It has a crumbling overhang, with various pieces of re-bar sticking out just below this ledge. So if you come alongside here you will need good fenders to avoid damage; a breast anchor is highly recommended to hold your boat off the dock.

If you elect to anchor out, the authorities will direct you to a spot immediately to the NW of the jetty. Note that the bottom shoals to less than 2m

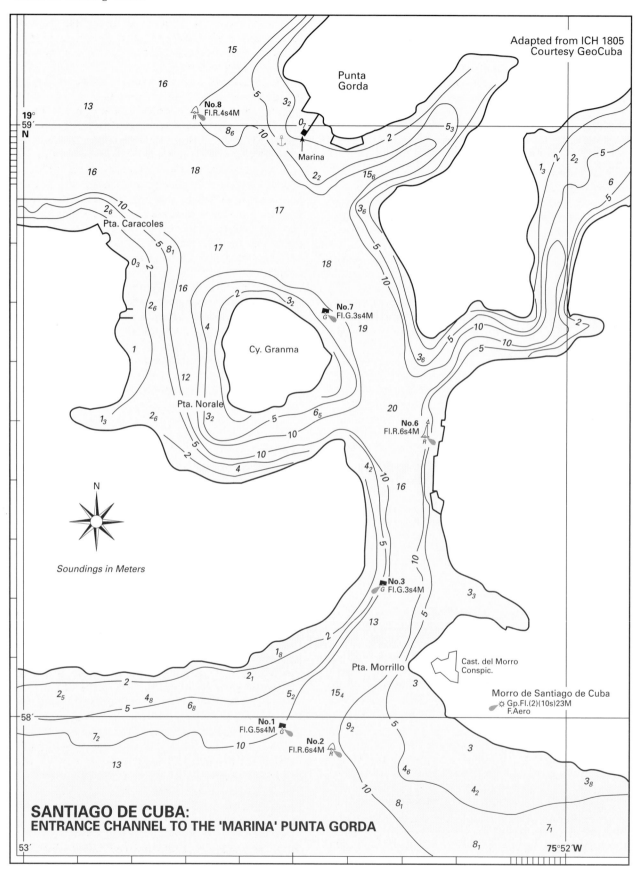

Adapted from ICH 1805
Courtesy GeoCuba

15

Punta
Gorda

16

13

No.8
Fl.R.4s4M

19°
59'
N

8_6

3_2

0_7

↓ Marina

5_3

2

16

18

2_2

15_6

17

2_6 10

Pta. Caracoles

3_6

8_1

1_3

2_2

5

5

6

17

18

5

0_3 2

16

2

3_2

No.7
Fl.G.3s4M

19

10

2_6

4

Cy. Granma

10

2

2_6

1

3_6

5

10

2

12

3_2

5

20

No.6
Fl.R.6s4M

1_3

2_6

3_2

5

6_5

10

Pta. Norale

10

16

5

4_2

2

4

N

Soundings in Meters

5

10

No.3
Fl.G.3s4M

3_3

13

2

1_8

Pta. Morrillo

3

Cast. del Morro
Conspic.

2_1

2_5

4_8

5_2

15_4

5

Morro de Santiago de Cuba
✷ Gp.Fl.(2)(10s)23M
F.Aero

5

6_8

No.1
Fl.G.5s4M

9_2

3

4_6

7_2

10

No.2
Fl.R.6s4M

4_2

3_8

13

10

8_1

8_1

7_1

SANTIAGO DE CUBA:
ENTRANCE CHANNEL TO THE 'MARINA' PUNTA GORDA

53'

75°52'W

more or less in a line running parallel to the shore from the tip of the jetty, so anchor to the west of this. Here the bottom drops off rapidly to 9m; if you anchor in 4 or 5m with about 20m of rode you will be about right. An anchor light will be needed at night since there is a certain amount of traffic.

Clearance procedures

Santiago is a port of entry for Cuba so you will most likely be greeted by the full range of officials, including (for the first time between here and the Marina Hemingway) someone from the Ministry of Transport to check the cruising permit for your boat, or issue one if you don't have one. There have been reports of some low-level soliciting of bribes.

Checking out Simply notify the marina officials ahead of time and they will get the various officials to the dock, and arrange the escort from the Guarda to the mouth of the bay.

Marina facilities

This is not much of a marina. In fact, it has little more than the one beat-up jetty. Nevertheless, water is available (you have to ask them to turn it on since the pipes leak too badly to leave it on all the time; it was also the worst-tasting water we got in Cuba), and electrical connections can be made (even more dubious than usual – see Chapter 1). Ashore there are scruffy showers and toilets, and a diesel pump ($0.45 per liter; the diesel will have to be hauled in cans since there is only a foot or two (0·3–0·6m) alongside the fuel dock).

The marina charges $0.45 per foot per day (high, considering the poor facilities; we recommend a vociferous complaint), and $0.30 per foot per day to anchor out (we recommend an outraged howl).

Santiago has two marine railways, both of which could handle the largest yacht.

Bahía de Guantánamo and Caimanera

The Bahía de Guantánamo is of course Guantánamo Bay, the American base, and a bone of contention between Cuba and the USA ever since Castro's accession to power. The base, however, does not occupy the entire bay – the northern half is still Cuban territory, and here will be found the small port of Boqueron, on the east side of the bay, and the town of Caimanera, on the west side of the bay.

Except for emergencies, the American base area is off-limits to all visiting boats, but there is no restriction on sailing through the base area (daylight hours only) into the Cuban zone. You simply have to call the Americans (VHF Ch 16 – call *Guantánamo Base*) when approaching the limits of their zone, requesting permission to pass through.

They will likely ask for a few details about the boat and crew, and then give you clearance to pass through (in our case, with the admonition: 'You will be entering communist territory: Be Careful!').

There is little reason to go to Caimanera beyond curiosity (actually, quite a compelling reason), and the fact that it makes a convenient break in the otherwise 65M passage between Santiago and Baitiquiri (or the 95M passage between Chivirico and Baitiquiri, if Santiago is given a miss as suggested above). The Bahía de Guantánamo at Caimanera provides excellent protection in most conditions, with some attractive vistas to the distant mountains, although in a strong northeaster there is enough of a fetch to allow an uncomfortable chop to build up. In this case, protection can be found 2M to the north of Caimanera in the lee of Punta Manatí.

A pleasant hotel has been built at Caimanera on a small hill overlooking the town. It is mostly used by Cuban tourists who come to ogle the American base from a small tower, with binoculars supplied by the management; they were quite envious when they discovered we had sailed right through the base! We preferred the view over the saltpans behind the town. The hotel welcomes sailors to its bar and restaurant.

Approaches

There are no off-lying hazards on the approaches to the Bahía de Guantánamo. Simply come to a position at approximately 19°53·0'N 75°11·3'W and sail in on a heading of 021°.

Passage to Caimanera

The channel through the base is wide, deep, and well marked (see plan). At the time of this writing, on the bluff on the east bank of the bay beneath a conspicuous radar dome and a field of antennas, could be seen the barbed-wire and watchtower-enclosed prison camps constructed to house thousands of Cuban refugees (emptied in 1996). Further in are likely to be a couple of American warships.

As you approach the northern limits of the American zone you can pass either side of Cayo del Medio, after which you will see a smart watchtower, flying the Stars and Stripes, with a fence stretching into the distance to the east and west of the channel. A little beyond this the Cubans have constructed a substantial concrete barrier across the channel, with a single passage through the center (large enough for a ship – no problem here).

Once in the Cuban zone you leave a green buoy to port (i.e. pass to the east of it) and then head for the docks visible in front of the town of Caimanera. One of these docks is clearly marked 'Pilot'. You can either moor to the end of the dock which is

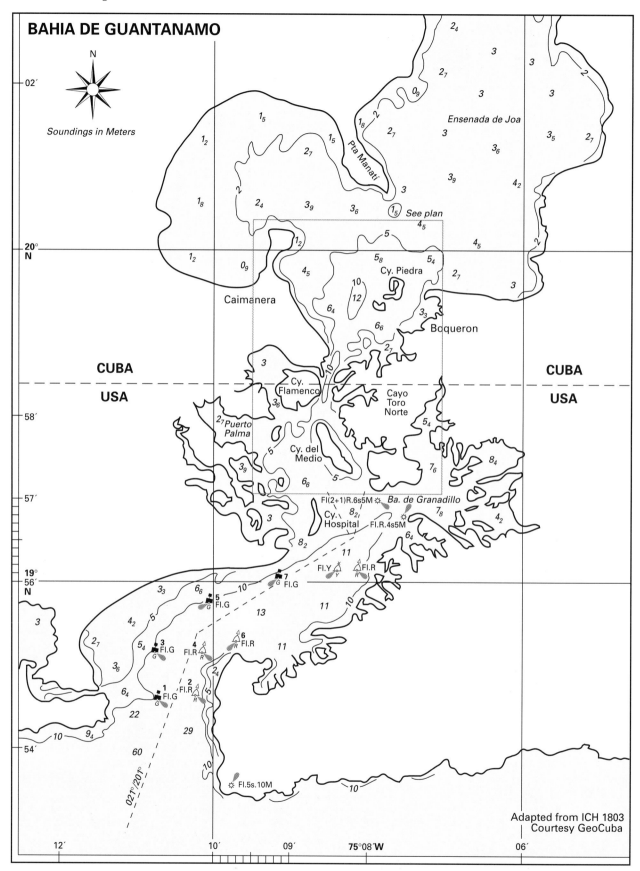

BAHIA DE GUANTANAMO

N

Soundings in Meters

Ensenada de Joa

Pta Manatí

See plan

Cy. Piedra

Caimanera

Boqueron

CUBA

USA

Cy. Flamenco

Cayo Toro Norte

Puerto Palma

Cy. del Medio

Fl(2+1)R.6s5M   Ba. de Granadillo

Cy. Hospital   Fl.R.4s5M

Fl.Y   Fl.R

7 Fl.G

5 Fl.G

3 Fl.G

4 Fl.R   6 Fl.R

1 Fl.G

2 Fl.R

021°/201°

Fl.5s.10M

Adapted from ICH 1803
Courtesy GeoCuba

75°08'W

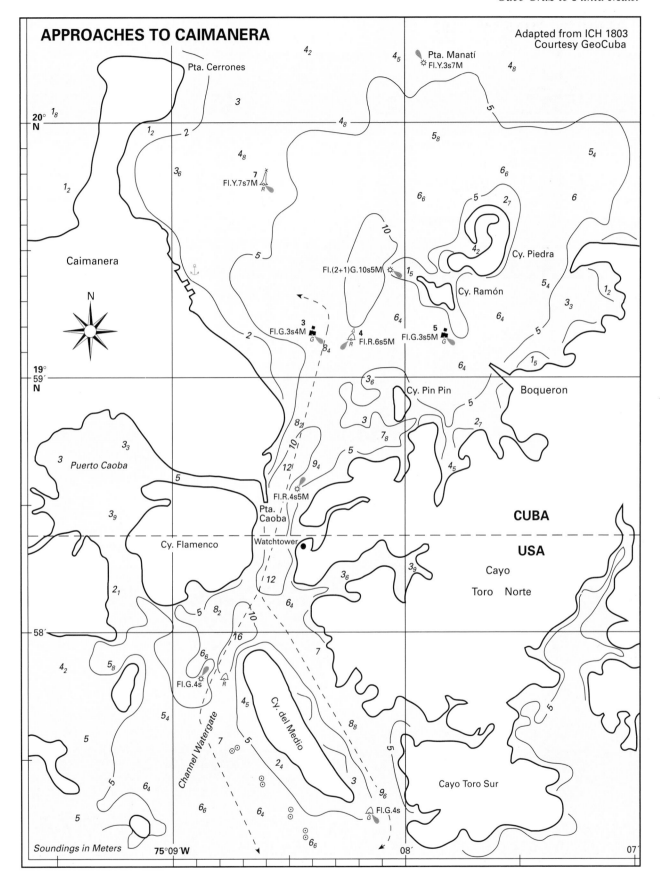

APPROACHES TO CAIMANERA

Adapted from ICH 1803
Courtesy GeoCuba

Pta. Cerrones

4_2

4_5

Pta. Manatí
Fl.Y.3s7M

4_8

3

4_8

20° N 1_8

1_2 2

5_8

5_4

4_8

3_6

7
Fl.Y.7s7M
R

6_6

5_4

6_6

5

6_6

2_7

6

1_2

Caimanera

5

10

Fl.(2+1)G.10s5M

1_5

4_2

Cy. Piedra

Cy. Ramón

5_4

N

6_4

6_4

3_3

3
Fl.G.3s4M
G

8_4

4
R Fl.R.6s5M

5 5
Fl.G.3s5M
G

5

1_5

6_4

1_5

19° 59′ N

3_6

Cy. Pin Pin

5

Boqueron

3

2_7

7_8

8_2

10

5

4_5

CUBA

12

9_4

Fl.R.4s5M

3 Puerto Caoba

3_3

Pta.
Caoba

USA

3_9

Cy. Flamenco

5

Watchtower

3_6

3_9

Cayo
Toro   Norte

58′

2_1

12

6_4

4_2

5_8

5

8_2

10

7

5_4

16

6_6

Fl.G.4s
R

5

4_5

8_8

6_4

Cy. del Medio

5

5

7

5

9_6

Cayo Toro Sur

6_4

2_4

3

6_6

6_4

9_6

Fl.G.4s
G

6_6

Soundings in Meters   **75°09′W**

08′

07′

immediately to the north of the pilot dock (1·6m depth), or else anchor out. For once there is not a Guarda post in sight, but rest assured, it is not far away (just up the street leading away from the head of the dock). If you wait a few minutes, the officials will show up and clear you in.

Note The bay is reported to be subject to violent squalls that arrive with little warning, so two anchors are recommended.

Bahía de Puerto Escondido

The Bahía de Puerto Escondido is a totally protected pocket bay 7M to the east of the Bahía de Guantánamo. It would make an excellent stop during a passage along the south coast. Unfortunately, it is currently off-limits to visiting boats. Nevertheless, we have included a plan (but without being able to check any of the details) in hopes that in the future this bay will be open to visiting sailors.

Reportedly, the entrance is hard to pick out from offshore, although just to the east is a reasonably conspicuous saddle-shaped hill. The channel narrows to 30m in places. A heading of 336° for the tip of a rocky peninsula visible inside the bay will carry you more or less up center channel.

Ensenada Baitiquiri

At Baitiquiri a narrow cleft in the hills opens out into a substantial, well protected lagoon. The entrance is extremely narrow (down to 15m), with

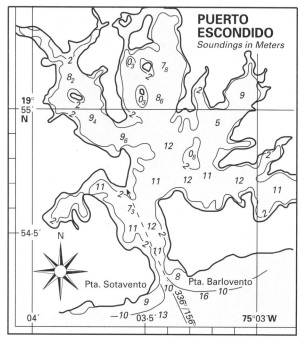

Adapted from an old DMA survey
Courtesy DMA

dangerous, drying coral on both sides. The channel runs in a generally NW direction, so that when the wind is strongly in the SE, which it was when we went in, 2–3m swells drive straight up the channel, producing some confused, breaking seas with the potential for broaching and no room to regain control of the boat if you should broach. In other words, in heavy seas this is not an entry for the fainthearted; it left me feeling a little weak in the knees.

Having said this, the entry is otherwise straightforward. Once the various marks have been located, and the boat placed in the right position to go in, there is no reason to be intimidated, even in rough conditions. Since Baitiquiri is the only well protected anchorage between Santiago de Cuba and Baracoa on the north coast, a distance of about 90M, it is generally a very welcome spot in which to layover for a while, and in any case is worth visiting in its own right – the small rural village ashore is attractive, while the surrounding countryside and hills are beautiful, with some lovely hiking.

Note After the downing of the two American planes in February 1996, the Guarda were not allowing cruisers to explore ashore. We don't know if this policy has been relaxed yet.

Approaches and entry

There are no off-lying hazards either to the west or the east of the bay. Simply come to a position at approximately 20°01·0'N 74°50·8'W, from where the small metal-frame lighthouse (Fl.6s) on the east side of the entrance will be clearly visible. Further up the channel you should be able to pick out a green and a red post (both lit, although only the green was working in 1995 – Fl.G.4s). Beyond the posts are some mangroves on the west side of the channel.

You should line up the outer edge of the mangroves midway between the two posts, on a bearing of 322°, and then come straight in between the posts. The reef will close in on both sides until at the posts, and beyond them, the channel is only 15m wide. The bottom comes up rapidly from great depths to 6m between the posts, and 3m just beyond them, but then deepens again to 4–5m. If heavy seas are running the most dangerous moments are in the final run up to the posts where there is the greatest likelihood of getting caught in a breaking sea with the least room to maneuver – it is important to keep the stern of your boat to the waves and keep moving fast enough to maintain steerageway. Once at the posts you will be out of the seas.

At the posts change course to a heading of 333°, directly for the dock and building (used for shipping salt) that will be visible on the inside of the bay. When in the bay curve to the west and anchor anywhere – the depths in the center are a fairly

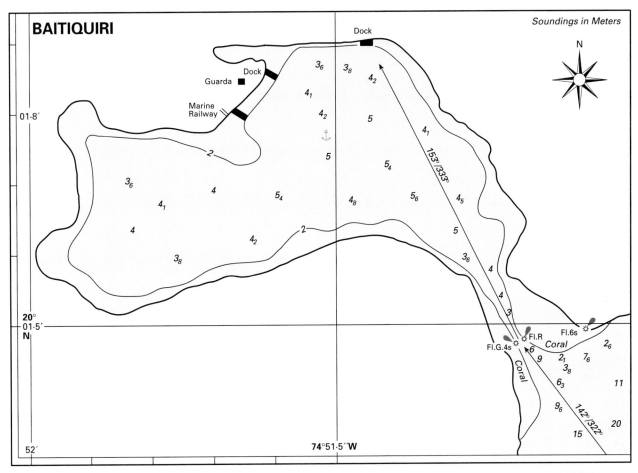

Adapted from an old DMA survey
Courtesy DMA

uniform 3–4m. The Guarda post is on the fish dock to the west of the salt dock – they will soon row out to check your papers.

South coast between Baitiquiri and Punta Maisí

There is no overnight protection to be found between Baitiquiri and Punta Maisí, and in fact none to be found between Punta Maisí and Baracoa (with the possible exception of the Ensenada Mata – see the next chapter). The mountains slowly decrease in height the further east you go toward Punta Maisí, so the katabatic effect is less pronounced. The trade winds reassert themselves both day and night, although the wind and seas tend to be calmer at night, and there is often still a wind shift toward the south in the daytime.

If going from Baitiquiri to Baracoa, the initial course is more or less due east for 35M as far as Punta Caleta, after which you bear off to the NE for another 12M before Punta Maisí is rounded. Thereafter, in prevailing conditions you will have the wind either on your beam or at your back which,

after more than 600M of windward work along the south coast, will come as a welcome change!

The best time to do the passage from Baitiquiri to Punta Maisí is generally at night (setting sail around 2200–2400 hours), since the conditions are easiest. But the authorities do not allow a departure from Baitiquiri between 1800 and 0600 hours, so it will have to be an 1800 start, at which time you may face lumpy and unpleasant seas for a while. Whatever the conditions, you should not hurry since it would be a great shame to arrive at Punta Maisí before dawn: the stretch of coastline between Punta Maisí and Baracoa (see next chapter) is arguably the most beautiful in Cuba and should not be missed.

If going from Baracoa to Baitiquiri, in prevailing conditions there will be no problems. However, this is a 75M run at the end of which you must make a daylight entry into Baitiquiri. This would seem to suggest an overnight passage. However, you should not miss the stretch of coastline from Baracoa to Punta Maisí, which is arguably the most beautiful in Cuba. So we would recommend an afternoon departure (1500–1600 hours), taking your time so as to arrive at Baitiquiri after 0700 hours.

175

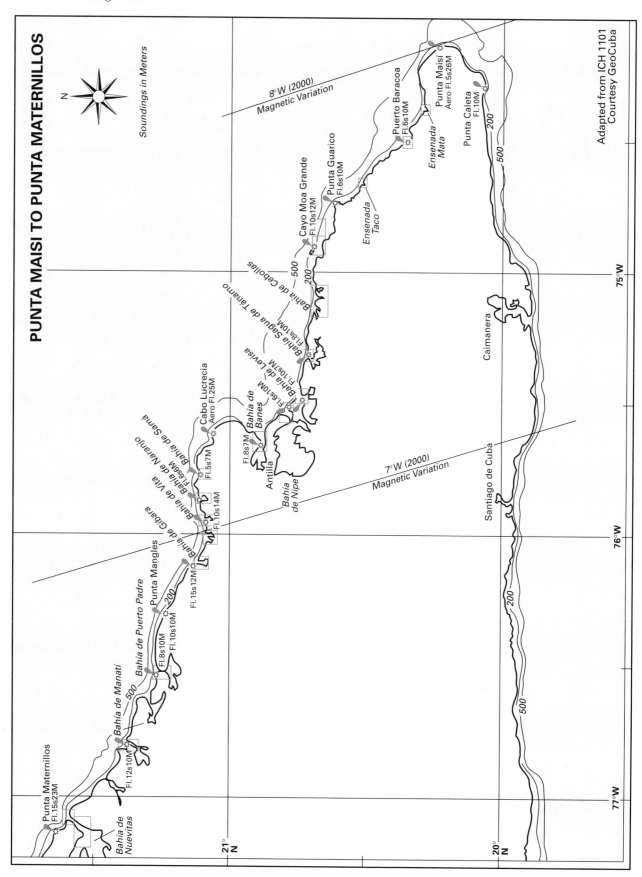

PUNTA MAISI TO PUNTA MATERNILLOS

N

Soundings in Meters

8°W (2000)
Magnetic Variation

Puerto Baracoa
Fl.6s10M

Punta Maisí
Aero Fl.5s26M

Ensenada
Mata

Punta Caleta
Fl.10M

200

500

Cayo Moa Grande
Fl.10s12M

Punta Guarico
Fl.6s10M

Ensenada
Taco

500

200

Bahía de Cebollas
Fl.8s10M

Bahía Sagua de Tánamo

75°W

Bahía de Leví sa
Fl.10s7M

Caimanera

Fl.6s10M

Cabo Lucrecia
Aero Fl.25M

Bahía de
Banes

Fl.5s10M

Fl.8s7M

7°W (2000)
Magnetic Variation

Bahía de Naranjo
Fl.6s6M

Bahía de Sama

Fl.5s7M

Antilla

Bahía
de Nipe

Santiago de Cuba

Bahía de Vita
Fl.10s14M

Bahía de Gibara

Fl.15s12M

Punta Mangles

200

Bahía de Puerto Padre

Fl.8s10M

Fl.10s10M

500

76°W

200

500

Bahía de Manatí

Punta Maternillos
Fl.15s23M

Fl.12s10M

500

77°W

Bahía de
Nuevitas

21°
N

20°
N

Adapted from ICH 1101
Courtesy GeoCuba

8. Punta Maisí to Punta Maternillos

The most notable features of this 200M stretch of the Cuban coastline are the 'pocket bays' – sizable bays and lagoons with narrow, deep-water channels connecting them to the sea. All of them offer superb protection in any conditions. Several of them are also exceedingly pretty, with the potential for much interesting gunkholing in protected waters. Unfortunately, some are currently off-limits to visiting sailors (*prohibido* – see the text), while freedom of movement is severely restricted inside most of the others; hopefully, this is a situation that will change in the future.

Aside from these pocket bays, the eastern half of this region is dominated by dramatic mountains which, although not as high as the Sierra Maestra in the south, are in many ways more beautiful, being covered with a lush, green carpet of vegetation and millions of coconut trees. In the western half of the region the mountains recede inland to be replaced by low hills, terminating in some low coral cliffs between which are many a lovely sandy beach; further west still are mile after mile of sandy beach. Some of the beaches have been developed as tourist resorts – there is a sprinkling of very substantial hotels with all the usual tourist facilities – but by and large the coastline is still virgin.

All-in-all this region has some lovely cruising, some great anchorages, and a wide range of things to do.

Winds

The year-round average wind is from the ENE at 10 knots. Seasonal variations are, once again, a more northerly tendency in the winter months, and a more southerly tendency in the summer months. Northers are less common than further west, but still relatively common in the wintertime, particularly in January and February. They tend to be somewhat muted by the time they reach this part of the coast, but nevertheless can pack quite a punch. In the summertime, quite strong winds, frequently also out of the north, are often associated with the passage of tropical depressions.

There is a marked daily wind pattern, with the winds being light at nighttime and then building throughout the day until they are often blowing at 20–25 knots by mid-afternoon, after which they once again die. We did not detect, and the Cuban pilot does not mention, any significant shifts in the change of direction during the course of a day.

Currents and tides

The predominant current offshore is the branch of the Antilles Current that flows up the Old Bahamas Channel toward the NW. This, however, is relatively weak (typically about 0·8 knots), but has been known to increase to as much as 3 knots. However, it is considerably influenced by the wind, and at times will reverse its direction altogether. Closer inshore, the currents tend to be wind driven, and are neither strong enough nor consistent enough to allow useful generalizations.

The tidal range throughout the region is about 0·5m (20in), with maximums as high as 0·9m (3ft) and minimums of 0·3m (1ft). In general, there are no significant tidal currents, although there may be strong currents in the narrow entrances to many of the pocket bays. Tides are semi-diurnal (i.e. occur twice daily).

Sailing strategies

Given the general orientation of this coastline on a NW/ SE axis, any time the wind is north of east it should be possible to ease the sheets regardless of the direction of travel. However, if the wind is at all south of east (primarily the summer months), any passage from west to east is likely to be a hard beat.

These general considerations need to be somewhat qualified in respect to the stretch of coastline from the Bahía de Nipe to Punta Lucrecia. Here the coastline is broadly on a north/south axis. When sailing from east to west, if the trade winds are blowing steadily out of the NE, in order to avoid a beat sailors should consider sailing direct from the Bahía de Cayo Moa around Punta Lucrecia to the Bahía de Naranjo.

At times, considerable swells drive up the Old Bahamas Channel. If the wind builds during the course of the day, as it so often does, these become larger and are worsened by an increasingly uncomfortable chop in the afternoon. On these days, early morning passages (in either direction) are recommended. Nighttime passages can be even smoother. Such passages are made simple by the fact that there are a series of major lighthouses along this coast, with at least one in sight almost all the time. However, it should be noted that several of these lights are set well inshore of reef areas, so the lights should never be approached closely without decent inshore charts and accurate fixes.

Charts and magnetic variation

ICH *1133, 1132, 1131* and *1130* cover this stretch at a scale of 1:150,000. In addition, there are detailed charts of Cayo Moa Grande and all the major pocket bays. Finally, there is the chart book (Region 5: Punta Maisí to Punta Maternillos) which covers this region.

Magnetic variation decreases from 8°00'W (January 2000) at Punta Maisí to 6°30'W at Punta ·Maternillos. In all areas, it is increasing annually at a rate of about 9'W.

Punta Maisí to Baracoa

This relatively short stretch of coastline is arguably the most beautiful in Cuba. Mountainsides covered in verdant tropical vegetation and thickets of coconut trees end in dramatic cliffs at the base of which are numerous small beaches. The most spectacular scenery is found where the Río Yumurí flows out to sea through a narrow, sheer-sided canyon.

You should make every attempt to sail between Punta Maisí and Baracoa in daylight, coming as close in to shore as you feel is prudent in the prevailing conditions. There appear to be no hazards more than 300m off the shoreline, and most of the time you can sail a good deal closer than this. However, I do have an 1825 Spanish chart that shows a reef up to ⅓M offshore at the west end of the bay to the west of Río Yumurí, so take care!

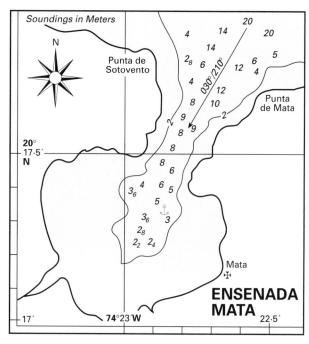

Adapted from an old DMA survey
Courtesy DMA

Ensenada Mata

The Ensenada Mata is a delightful bay, surrounded by steep hillsides covered in coconut trees. Unfortunately its entrance faces to the NE so that when the NE trades are running the swells drive straight up into the bay, making it a rolly and uncomfortable anchorage. At other times, however, the bay provides a good deal of protection. In any event, it is worth a visit, and if too uncomfortable you can beat a retreat to Baracoa, 8M to the NW.

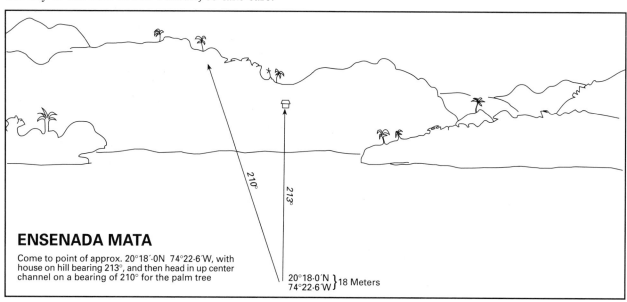

ENSENADA MATA

Come to point of approx. 20°18'·0N 74°22·6'W, with house on hill bearing 213°, and then head in up center channel on a bearing of 210° for the palm tree

20°18·0'N
74°22·6'W } 18 Meters

Approach and entry

Come to a position at approximately 20°18·0'N 74°22·6'W, which is more or less on the 20m line. Looking into the bay you will see a small house up on a hillside (bearing 213°), somewhat to the right (west) of mid-channel (see sketch). Come in up the center of the channel on a heading of 210° for the head of the bay. The channel is relatively wide, and quite straightforward. Once inside the two (inner) rocky headlands, anchor reasonably soon, more or less in the middle of the bay, since the bottom shoals on all sides (the best protection will be found by easing over toward the village on the east side of the bay, but you will not be able to get very close in).

When leaving, sail midway between the rocky headlands on a heading of 030°, and maintain this heading at least until over the 10m line in order to avoid coral on both sides of the entrance.

Baracoa

Baracoa may have been visited by Columbus (a matter for some argument). In any event, it is the site of one of the first seven towns in Cuba (founded by Diego de Velazquez, the first Governor of Cuba). In spite of this illustrious pedigree, there is not a great deal of surviving colonial architecture, and what there is is mostly run down. Nevertheless, the town is worth a visit, if only to enjoy its wonderful location with the dramatic flat-topped mountain of El Yunque in the background, and coconut-clad hillsides all around. The anchorage is reasonably well protected, but subject to uncomfortable swells when the NE trades are blowing (i.e. primarily in

the winter months). At such times, the entrance can be quite rough.

The city is technically a port of entry to Cuba, but the officials have little experience clearing in pleasure boats, so be prepared for the process to take some time. Also, make sure the immigration officers give you a visa – a *tarjeta del turistica*. We have had two reports from boat owners who were not issued visas, causing problems further down the line. Two hotels provide bars, restaurants, swimming pools, phone and fax services, and car rentals (a good place from which to rent a car for the day to explore the Río Yumuri and surrounding countryside). An airport has flights to Havana.

Approaches and entry

There are no off-lying dangers when approaching Baracoa from any direction. The harbor is at the NW corner of a large, open bay (the Bahía de la Miel). El Yunque, with its flat top and steep sides, is unmistakable from many miles out. You come in on a more or less westerly heading for the mountain. As you get closer, you will be able to pick out the harbor entrance just to the north of the Malecón (the sea wall) behind which are a number of white apartment buildings (one of which has a light, Fl.6s, on its roof), with a conspicuous ocher building on a hillside to the south. A position at approximately 20°21·4'N 74°29·7'W will put you right outside the harbor, which is then entered on a heading of 255°.

Once inside the harbor entrance you will see a large hulk, with a light on its stern (Fl.G.4s), beached immediately to the south. Simply hook around to the SSW of this wreck and anchor off the dock in 3–4m. The officials will soon be out (the full range; this is a port of entry). You will probably be asked to put out a stern anchor, since this is the custom here. When going ashore you can leave the dinghy somewhere on the main dock, or else dinghy over to the dock at the base of the hotel on the north side of the harbor.

When leaving, be sure the Guarda return your customs paperwork (which they will have collected on your arrival) as well as issuing you a new *despacho*; they have a tendency to keep the customs form (the *guia de recala*), which can cause problems further down the line.

Note Diesel is available on the dock (3m alongside, but watch out for a shoal that extends to the west and NW of the northern tip of the dock) at $0.35 per liter (1995) but with a $12.50 charge for using the dock.

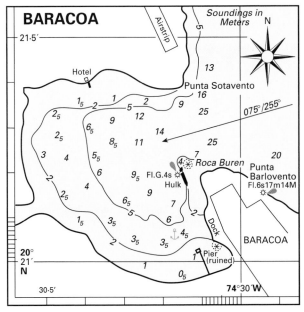

Adapted from DMA 26245
Courtesy DMA

Baracoa to Cayo Moa

This is a lovely stretch of coastline with verdant mountains inland, coconut-clad hills nearer the coast, and the occasional beach between rocky headlands. There are one or two interesting bays and river mouths, but with the exception of the Ensenada Taco all are exposed to the NE, and therefore subject to uncomfortable swells when the wind is from this direction. In addition, the mouths of several potential anchorages are obstructed by a power line that runs along the coast (a powerboat can get under this power line to explore the Ensenada Navas and the Ensenada Cayaguaneque, but a sailboat cannot. These are both straightforward entries up center channel, anchoring when the bottom comes up).

Ensenada Maravi

At the Ensenada Maravi the power line is high enough to clear most masts (I would guess the clearance is more than 20m; we had no trouble getting our 16m mast beneath it) giving access to a small bay into which the Río Maravi flows (obstructed by a sand bar and a bridge). This bay is surrounded by lovely hills clad in coconut trees and royal palms, making a beautiful lunch stop.

The inlet cuts into the coast to the SW and as such is wide open to NE swells, but when the wind is in the SE it is quite calm. The channel is clearly marked with two green buoys to port and two red buoys to starboard, leading to a couple of big-ship dolphins intended for loading lumber from the sawmill on the northern shore of the inlet.

Entry and anchorage

Come to a position at approximately 20°26·0'N 74°33·0'W and proceed on a bearing of 220° midway between the buoys. The water is initially exceedingly deep (more than 30m), shoaling to 24m between the inner set of buoys, and then abruptly shoaling to just over a meter a little beyond the ship-mooring dolphins. Anchor on the north side of the inlet just beyond the dolphin and beneath the palm-clad hillside.

Ensenada Taco

Here's a wonderful anchorage, a small 'pocket' bay entered through a narrow channel which provides access to a lovely, superbly protected lagoon, and with no power line across the mouth.

Entry and anchorage

The entrance is easy enough, but since it involves transiting a relatively narrow, unmarked channel it requires attention to detail. First come to a position at approximately 20°31·6'N 74°39·7'W, and then maneuver so that the midpoint of the NW side of the channel (this will be easy enough to pick out) bears 248° (see sketch). Come in for this midpoint, making whatever allowance may be necessary to compensate for any tidal set.

Once inside an imaginary line drawn between the two headlands at the mouth of the channel, come to a heading of 210°, straight up the center of the channel. The depths going in will steadily shoal to a minimum of 7m about midway through the entrance, and then increase again on the inside to 10m or more in the center of the bay, shoaling toward the edges (note that these shoals come up quite suddenly, so maneuver with caution).

The Guarda have a post just outside the bay (on

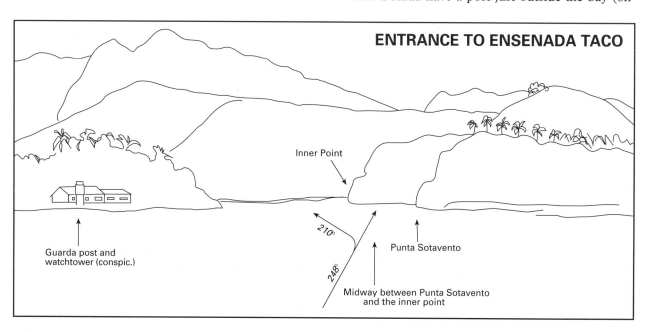

ENTRANCE TO ENSENADA TACO

Inner Point

Guarda post and watchtower (conspic.)

210°

248°

Punta Sotavento

Midway between Punta Sotavento and the inner point

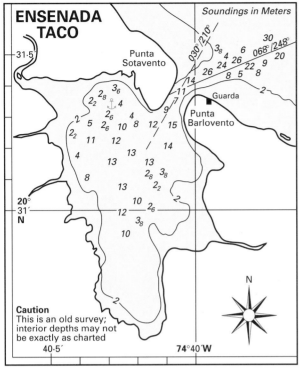

ENSENADA TACO

Soundings in Meters

Punta Sotavento

Guarda

Punta Barlovento

Caution
This is an old survey; interior depths may not be exactly as charted

Adapted from an old DMA survey
Courtesy DMA

the south side, with a conspicuous watch tower). They will soon arrive to check your papers.

Ensenada Yamaniguey

The Ensenada Yamaniguey is a more than 3M long inlet running on a north/south axis behind the reef and a small cay, Cayo del Medio. There are entry channels both to the south of Cayo del Medio (marked by a small red buoy) and to the north of the cay (unmarked, but clearly visible as a gap in the otherwise breaking reef). I have an old chart that shows deep water in both channels leading behind Caya Medio. Unfortunately the swells were running too strongly onto the reef for us to explore this one, but clearly if the chart is correct an exceedingly well protected anchorage will be found on the inside (particularly useful in a norther).

Bahía de Cayo Moa

The Bahía de Cayo Moa is a long bay fronted by an almost continuous barrier of reef and cays. A couple of exceedingly deep channels cut through this reef to give access to a well protected lagoon. The northernmost of these channels leads directly to the port of Moa, a major nickel exporting facility which is quite active at the present time, with ships both unloading and loading in the port, and also anchoring out in front of the port area and unloading or

loading via barges. Ashore there is one nickel refinery in operation (laying down a pall of smoke and dust across the surrounding countryside, and turning the water in the harbor bright red) and another huge facility under construction (although activity seems to be suspended at the present time). To the west is the ugly town of Moa where all the workers are housed.

There is no reason to visit either the port (where you will only be in the way), or the town. In fact, the only reason for coming here is to anchor overnight, taking advantage of the excellent protection afforded by the reef and cays. This can, in fact, be one of the more pleasant anchorages along this coast, since there is likely to be a good breeze to keep the bugs at bay.

Approaches

The reef at Moa extends further offshore than at any other point for miles in either direction, with strong onshore currents at times. Taken together, these two factors make the approach from the east (actually SE) or the west (NW) potentially hazardous, as can be seen from the considerable amount of wreckage atop the coral.

From the southeast, you must clear Punta Guarico, where the reef comes out about ¼M from the headland. This may not sound like much, but the two conspicuous wrecks attest to the fact that it is easy to misjudge! Beyond Punta Guarico a course of 295°, making any adjustments necessary to compensate for the tide, will parallel the reef, bringing you to the two entrances at Moa. Note that if proceeding to the northwestern entrance, it is essential to remain to seaward of the outer channel marker until you pick up the entry range (see below) – don't cut the corner.

From the west, in order to clear the reef, it is necessary to keep a good 2M off the mainland on the approach to Cayo Moa Grande, remaining well offshore until east of 74°57·0'W (the northernmost extension of the reef is at approximately 20°44·0'N 74°57·6'W). At this time Cayo Moa will be clearly visible to the ESE – you need to clear the cay by ¾M. Beyond the cay you will see the buoys marking the big ship channel into Moa. Stay well outside of a line drawn to the outer channel marker until you pick up the entry range (see below) – don't cut the corner.

Entry

There are two channels into the protected waters behind Cayo Moa and the reef. The northwestern channel, a big-ship channel, is wide, deep, and well marked; the southeastern channel is wide enough (300m) and deep (30–40m), but quite intricate and without a single marker, with the sides shoaling out dramatically to dangerous reef. This southeastern

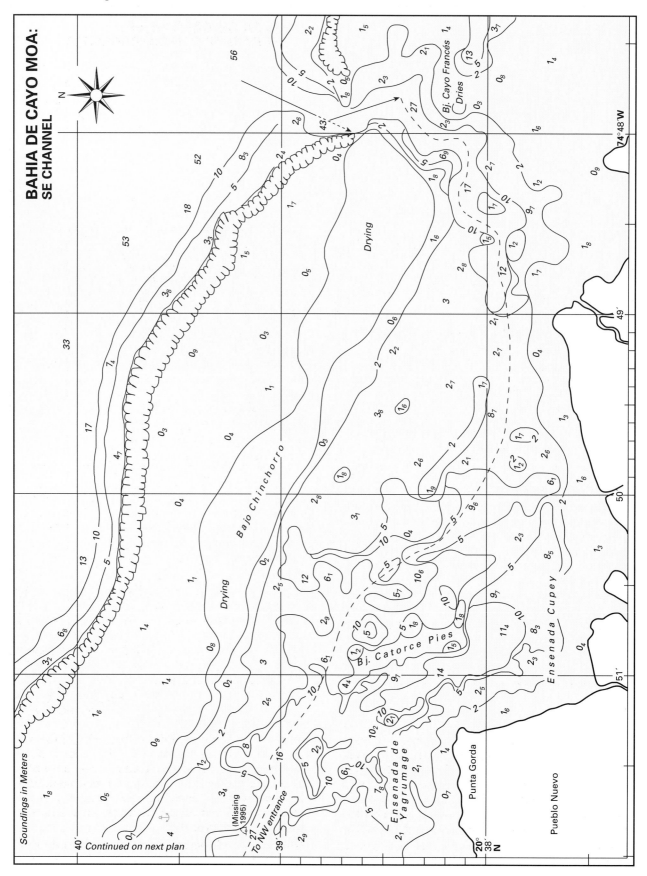

BAHIA DE CAYO MOA: SE CHANNEL

Soundings in Meters

Continued on next plan

Bajo Chinchorro

Drying

Drying

Drying

Bj. Catorce Pies

Ensenada de Yagrumage

Ensenada Cupey

Bj. Cayo Francés Dries

To NW entrance

(Missing 1995)

Punta Gorda

Pueblo Nuevo

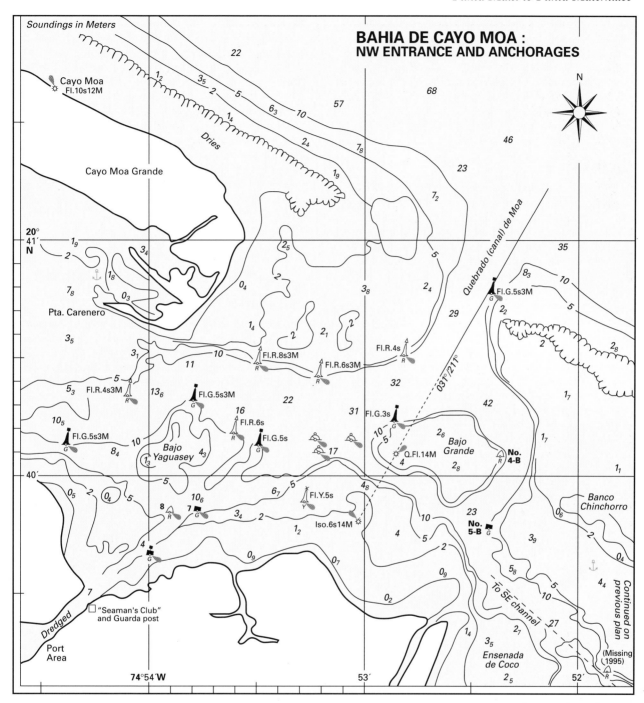

BAHIA DE CAYO MOA :
NW ENTRANCE AND ANCHORAGES

Soundings in Meters

Cayo Moa
Fl.10s12M

Cayo Moa Grande

Dries

20°41'N

Pta. Carenero

Quebrado (canal) de Moa

03°/211°

Fl.R.8s3M

Fl.R.6s3M

Fl.R.4s

Fl.G.5s3M

Fl.R.4s3M

Fl.G.5s3M

16
Fl.R.6s

Bajo
Yaguasey

Fl.G.5s

17

Fl.G.3s

Q.Fl.14M

Bajo
Grande

No.
4-B

Fl.G.5s3M

No.
5-B

Banco
Chinchorro

Fl.Y.5s

Iso.6s14M

To SE channel

"Seaman's Club"
and Guarda post

Continued on
previous plan

(Missing
1995)

Dredged
Port
Area

Ensenada
de Coco

74°54'W   53'   52'

Adapted from ICH 1786
Courtesy GeoCuba

channel should only be attempted in calm conditions and good light, and even then we would not want to transit it without a first-class chart, and electronic plotting equipment, particularly since once inside the reef quite a bit of relatively intricate navigation is still needed to proceed toward Moa, with many shoals and isolated rocks to be avoided.

Southeast channel Come to a position at approximately 20°39·2'N 74°47·8'W and proceed

on a SSW heading toward the inner edge of the reef on the west side of the channel. When abeam of the reef on the east side of the channel, curve to the SSE to avoid the shoal to the west, and then hook back in a generally SW direction, after which it gets too complicated for written instructions but at least you will be in calm waters!

Northwest channel Come to a position at approximately 20°41·2'N 74°52·2'W. The entrance to the channel is marked with a green buoy (*No. 1*) which is left to port (i.e. you pass to the west of it). The channel is entered on a heading of 211° for the range markers (clearly visible). Once inside, you curve either to the west (down the well marked channel), or the SE (leaving the red *No. 4-B* nun, conical, buoy to starboard – i.e. passing to the east of it), and then proceed to one of the anchorages (see below).

Anchorages

If all that is wanted is a quiet anchorage free of bugs, then in prevailing winds the preferred location is to the SE of the ship channel, behind the reef and its inner shoal (Bajo Chinchorro), but the Guarda may not be too happy about this choice. Instead they may direct you to an anchorage behind Cayo Moa. Both anchorages provide excellent protection in prevailing winds (NE to SE) but not in a norther.

Bajo Chinchorro Deep water runs up to the back of Bajo Chinchorro in several places (see plans). Any of these areas are suitable as an anchorage. From the SE channel you will just have to pick your way up toward the back of Bajo Chinchorro. From the NW channel, once inside the reef take the SE branch past red *No. 4-B* buoy, head toward green *No. 5-B* buoy, and then from this buoy come east into the lee of Bajo Chinchorro, anchoring in 3–4m.

Cayo Moa Grande Come down the main ship channel until south of the tip of Cayo Moa Grande, and then continue on a westerly heading out of the channel (the bottom will suddenly shoal to 2·5–3m) until south of Punta Carenero (the spit of land with a beach off its tip). Hook around 200m to the west of this spit, watching out for the shoal that extends south and west of it, and then anchor to the NW of it in 3–4m.

During a norther, better protection can be found in the early (NW) phase in the Ensenada de Coco (see plan) but as soon as the wind moves into the north the swells will come down the NW channel, at which time you will want to move to the Cayo Moa anchorage.

Bahía de Moa to the Bahía de Nipe

In this 40M stretch of coastline, which runs in a more or less east/west direction, the mountains that dominate the scenery in southeastern Cuba recede inland, to be replaced by the coastal lowlands and mangroves that predominate elsewhere. However, the mangroves are still broken up by patches of higher ground and low cliffs, with a beach here and there.

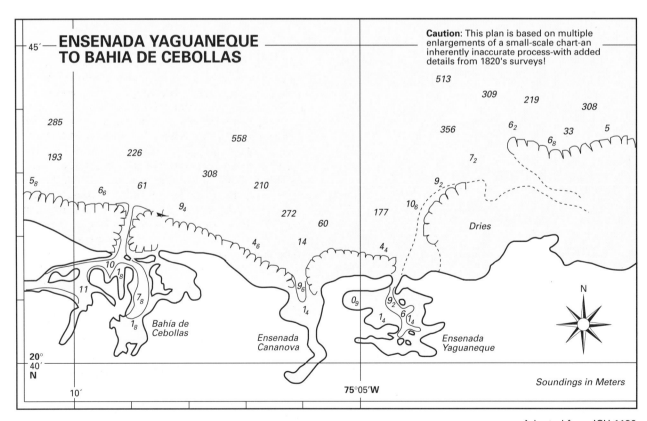

Adapted from ICH 1132
Courtesy GeoCuba

To the west of Cayo Moa there are three bays – the Ensenada Yaguaneque, the Ensenada Cananova, and the Bahía de Cebollas – with relatively deep (several meters up to 30m) entrances through the fringing reef, and with a fair amount of protection on the inside (Cananova is mostly shoal). Unfortunately, none of the entrances are marked, added to which the sides of the channels run abruptly into shallow coral heads. In addition, both the Ensenada Yaguaneque and the Báhía de Cebollas have very narrow entrances. In typical conditions considerable swells roll in from the NE, making these dangerous reef passages: *these are calm conditions, good-light entries only.* We came close to losing our boat trying to do a survey in 25–30 knot winds, and after that chickened out, so the only advice we can offer is: *Be careful!*

Bahía de Tánamo

Midway between the Bahía de Moa and the Bahía de Nipe lies the pocket bay of Tánamo with a narrow, deep-water (20m or more) channel opening out into a substantial bay containing numerous secluded and well protected anchorages. The bay was *prohibido* at the time of our visit and so we were unable to enter it. We understand that in 1997 it was opened to visiting boats. We have included a plan of the entrance, although we have not checked the details. The entrance can be rough when heavy swells are running, particularly when the tidal current of up to 3 knots (more in the rainy season) is ebbing against an onshore wind. Entry and exit should, if possible, be timed for slack water (40–45 minutes after the times of high water and low water on shore).

Approaches and entry

Because of its narrow, twisting entrance the mouth of the bay is difficult to pick out from offshore. To find it, come to a position at approximately 20°43·5'N 75°19·5'W from where the outer channel marker (a green *No. 1* buoy) is clearly visible. The channel is entered on a heading of 180° for a range light on the bank 1M ahead, leaving the *No. 1* buoy to port (i.e. passing to the west of it). As the range light is approached, the channel makes a sharp turn to the west, and then ⅓M later (at Punta Gitana) the bay itself begins to open out with Cayo Juanillo immediately to the south.

Anchorage

Between Cayo Juanillo and Punta Gitana there is a well protected bay (Ensenada Carenero) in which to anchor, while in the NE corner of this bay there is an even more protected inlet (Caleta El Conde) with 4–5m depths. The rest of the bay will have to wait for the future!

Bahías de Levisa and Cabonico

These are two more pocket bays sharing a common, deep-water entrance. As at Tánamo, both bays were *prohibido* during our visit, so the plan is provided in hopes of a relaxation of the regulations, or in case of emergency need. Once again, strong tidal currents are found in the channels, with rough water when the ebb tide is running against an onshore wind. Entry and exit should, if possible, be timed for slack water (40–45 minutes after the times of high water and low water on shore).

Entry

The entrance to the bays is at the SW corner of this section of the coastline and therefore relatively easy to locate. In any event, come to a position at approximately 20°45·0'N 75°28·3'W, from where the outer channel marker (a green *No. 1* buoy) will be clearly visible. This is left to port (i.e. pass to the west of it). Note that this buoy sits a little south of the northern extremity of the reef to the east of the bay, and so, if coming from the east, on no account cut the corner down to the buoy. The channel into the Bahía de Levisa is well marked from this outer buoy; that into the Bahía de Cabonico branches off to the SE without further buoyage (the Bahía de Cabonico contains numerous shoals and so is not considered important for navigation). We have no information on the interiors of the bays.

Bahía de Nipe

The Bahía de Nipe is Cuba's largest pocket bay. On the south side of its entry lies Cayo Saetía. This cay has been stocked with African game and developed as an African-style safari resort with a safari-style hotel, jeep tours of the game, and exotic hunting for those who want it. Perhaps of more interest to most cruisers is the fact that the cay has some of the most beautiful coastal scenery in Cuba, with lovely red and ocher cliffs enclosing small sandy beaches, backed by rolling verdant hillsides. Unfortunately, currently (1996) the Guarda prohibit the use of a dinghy to go ashore anywhere in the bay, so you will just have to drool, or be somewhat *illegado.*

The hotel has a dock on the south side of the peninsula at the inner end of the entry channel to the bay. Visiting sailors are expected to anchor in the vicinity of the dock, and to then use the hotel launch to go to and from their boat, and to use one of the hotel jeeps to travel from the dock to the hotel (quite a distance away – $2.00 per person per one-way trip in 1995). Similarly, to visit any of the gorgeous bays and beaches you are expected to use the hotel launch.

After waiting 2½ hours to check out of Moa the morning we sailed to the Bahía de Nipe, and then waiting 3½ hours to check into Nipe, we had had a

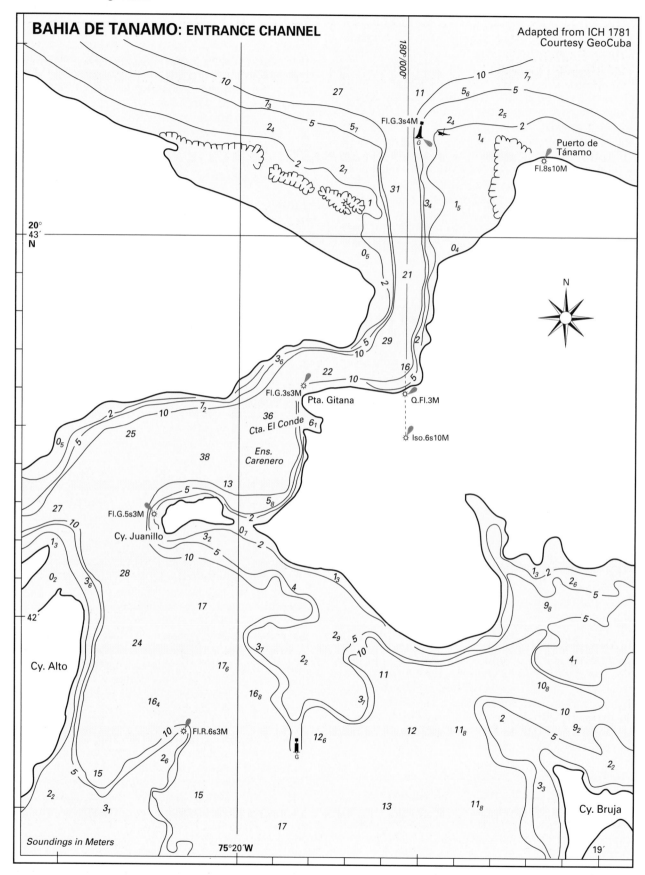

BAHIA DE TANAMO: ENTRANCE CHANNEL

Adapted from ICH 1781
Courtesy GeoCuba

180°/000°

10

27

11

10

7_7

7_3

5

5_7

5_6

5

2_4

FI.G.3s4M

2_4

2_5

2

G

1_4

Puerto de
Tánamo

2

2_7

1

31

3_4

1_5

FI.8s10M

**20°
43′
N**

0_5

0_4

2

21

5

0_5

5

29

2

10

16

3_6

22

10

5

FI.G.3s3M

Pta. Gitana

Q.FI.3M

2

10

7_2

36
Cta. El Conde

6_1

0_5

5

25

38

*Ens.
Carenero*

5_8

5

13

2

5_8

FI.G.5s3M

Cy. Juanillo

3_2

0_7

2

Iso.6s10M

27

10

5

1_3

10

1_3 2

2_6

0_2

3_6

28

10

1_3

5

9_8

5

42′

17

4

2_9

4_1

Cy. Alto

24

17_6

3_7

2_2

10

5

11

10_8

10

16_4

16_8

3_7

12

11_8

2

9_2

10

FI.R.6s3M

12_6

5

2_6

G

2_2

5

15

13

11_8

3_3

Cy. Bruja

2_2

3_1

15

Soundings in Meters

75°20′W

17

19′

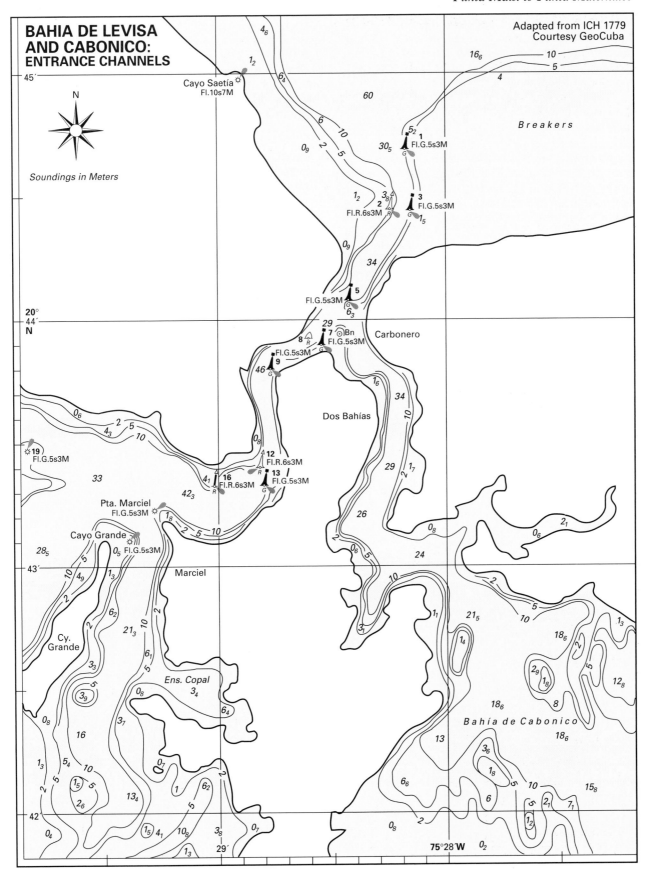

**BAHIA DE LEVISA
AND CABONICO:
ENTRANCE CHANNELS**

Adapted from ICH 1779
Courtesy GeoCuba

N

Soundings in Meters

Cayo Saetía
Fl.10s7M

Breakers

1 Fl.G.5s3M

2 Fl.R.6s3M

3 Fl.G.5s3M

5 Fl.G.5s3M

Carbonero

8

7 Bn
Fl.G.5s3M

9 Fl.G.5s3M

Dos Bahías

20°
44′
N

19 Fl.G.5s3M

12 Fl.R.6s3M

16 Fl.R.6s3M

13 Fl.G.5s3M

Pta. Marciel
Fl.G.5s3M

Cayo Grande
Fl.G.5s3M

Marciel

Cy.
Grande

Ens. Copal

Bahía de Cabonico

75°28′W

187

bellyful of officialdom for one day and argued forcefully against this bureaucratic control and supervision, but to no avail. We hope you have better luck – the Bahía de Nipe looks like it has some wonderful gunkholing.

Approaches

The Bahía de Nipe is exceptionally easy to enter in any conditions with a very deep, mile-wide entrance slowly tapering to a ½M wide channel which is well marked. There are no off-lying dangers to the north or the east beyond the narrow band of reef fringing the coastline in places. However, tidal currents of up to 3 knots are found in the channel; when the ebb is flowing against swells and seas from the NE this can make the entrance quite rough, so it is best to time entry and exit for slack water (40–45 minutes after the times of high water and low water on shore).

Entry

Come to a position at approximately 20°49·0'N 75°31·6'W, about 1M to the north of the metal-frame lighthouse (Fl.6s). From here a couple of (red) range lights can be seen on the hillside to the SSW, on a bearing of 202°. You head for the range until the channel opens out to the west. You continue down the channel until past the green *No. 3* buoy off the tip of Punta Carenero, from where the Guarda post (normally complete with gunboat) can be seen on the point. Hook around to the west of the buoy (don't cut inside it) and proceed slowly to the south past the Guarda post; if you are lucky you may get past to anchor off the hotel dock (see below), but then again you may be told to stop and anchor while the officials are rounded up (which may take an hour or two since they must come from the port of Antilla, well inside the bay). If you have to anchor you will need to come in almost to the beach, since the bottom drops off precipitously with depths of 20m or more.

Anchorage

The hotel dock is tucked around Punta Campeador, to the south of the Guarda post. A shoal extends to

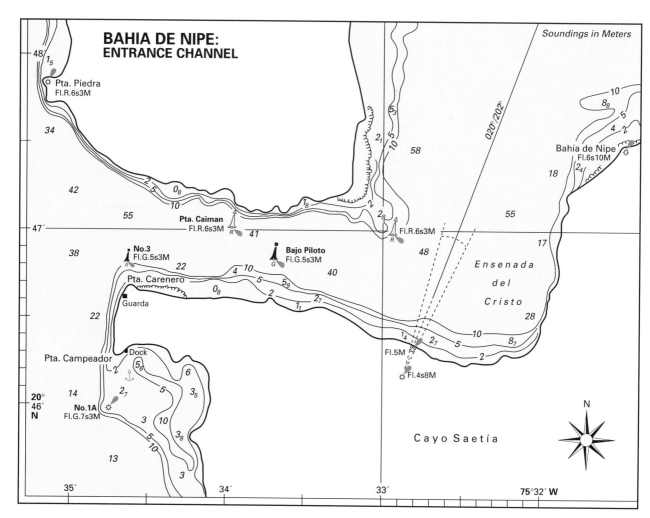

Adapted from ICH 1779
Courtesy GeoCuba

the south, and *slightly to the west*, of Punta Campeador, beyond which is a green buoy (*No. 1A*). From the Guarda post, sail south toward the buoy, staying to the west of a line drawn between Punta Campeador and the buoy until about half the distance between the two, and then turn to the east. The depths will rapidly shoal to 2·5m and then increase again to 4–5m. You can anchor anywhere in this area. The hotel dock is immediately to the north.

Bahía de Nipe to the Bahía Vita

There are no natural harbors in the first stretch of this coastline other than the totally protected pocket bay of Banes, but this is another that is currently *prohibido*! We have included a plan in case the prohibition should be lifted, or in case of emergency need. It should be noted that in prevailing NE to SE winds the entrance, which is hard to pick out from offshore, is more or less dead downwind with the coastline funneling the swells and waves toward the bay. The entrance itself is through a steep-sided canyon with several hairpin bends and tidal currents of up to 6 knots. *This can be a particularly rough entry, and a difficult exit!* It is best to time a passage for slack water (40–45 minutes after the times of high water and low water on shore).

North of the Bahía de Banes the fine old masonry lighthouse at Punta Lucrecia, with a grandiose colonial lighthouse keeper's house beneath it, is visible for many miles in either direction. There are no off-lying dangers anywhere along here, allowing you to cruise close inshore in 20–60m depths, enjoying the scenery. However, there are frequently substantial swells rolling in from the Atlantic, overlaid by an increasingly uncomfortable wind-driven chop as the day wears on, so morning passages are recommended.

Bahía de Samá

The Bahía de Samá is a pretty 1½M deep inlet on a north/south axis, with a conspicuous rocky outcrop on its western side (Punta Sotavento) and a couple of beaches on the inside backed by attractive hills. The bay is being developed as a sport-fishing base by Marlin, a Cuban tourist company, with tourists being bussed in from the nearby resort at Guada-lavaca. In 1995 a floating dock had just been installed, and other facilities were under construction.

The bay is wide open to the north making it dangerous to enter and untenable as an anchorage when the wind is from the NW to the NE (most of the wintertime) but it is quite calm, making a lovely overnight stop, when the wind is in the SE (the summer months). A walk up the hill from the Marlin dock provides some great views over the bay and the surrounding countryside.

Approaches
From the east, there are no off-lying dangers: simply stay ¼M or more offshore.

From the west (Bahía de Naranjo), note that the reef extends almost 1M offshore on the east side of the entrance to the Bahía de Naranjo, with reef and shoal water extending up to ½M offshore as far as Punta Cayuelo; thereafter there are no off-lying dangers.

Entry and anchorage
Come to a position at approximately 21°07·7'N 75°46·2'W, and maneuver so that the west bank of the bay at the head of the new dock is bearing 180°, and then come in for this point. Once off the light at Punta Sotavento, adjust your course to stay in mid-channel. The depths will steadily shoal to 6–9m off the light, down to 3m off the tip of the dock.

Anchor just beyond the dock over toward the small beach on the eastern shore in 3m.

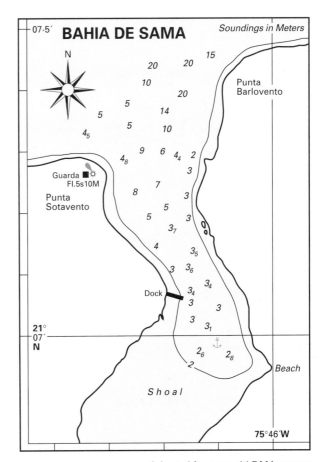

Adapted from an old DMA survey
Courtesy DMA

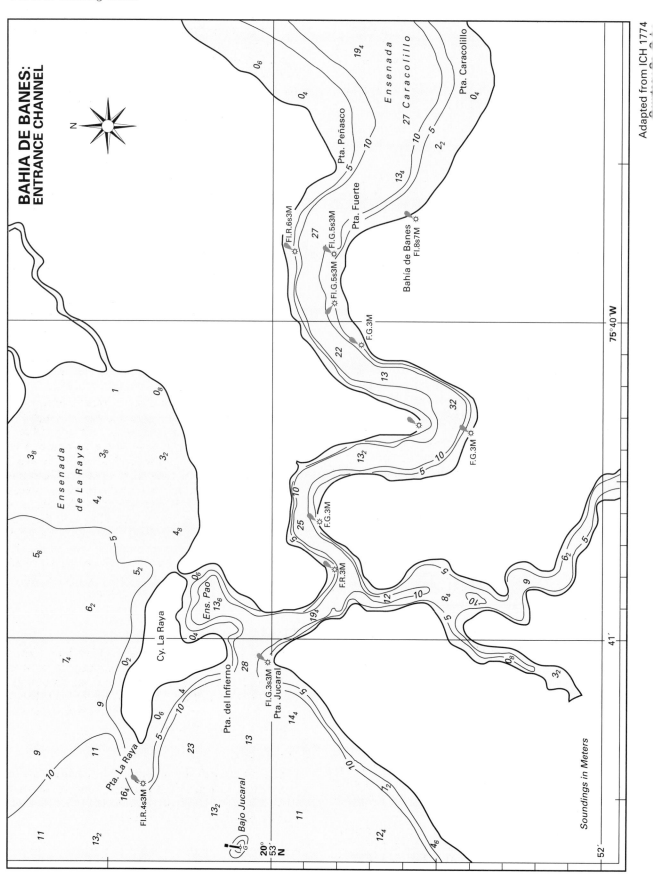

BAHIA DE BANES:
ENTRANCE CHANNEL

Adapted from ICH 1774

Soundings in Meters

Note that immediately to the south of the anchorage the entire bay has shoaled in to just over 1m; the British Admiralty and DMA charts showing 2 and 3 fathoms (4 and 5m) down the bay are based on old surveys and are now completely erroneous.

Note also that some Cuban charts show the light on the east headland, whereas it is now on the west headland.

Bahía de Naranjo

The Bahía de Naranjo is an attractive, relatively small, pocket bay with a narrow entrance opening out into an enclosed and well protected lagoon. The bay is in the process of being developed as a major base for 'nautical tourism', serving the collection of hotels that line the coast from the Bahía de Samá to the Bahía Naranjo (including the hotel complexes at Guadalavaca). To date (1995) a substantial aquarium has been constructed plus a small 'marina' (designed to meet the needs of local dive and sport-fishing boats rather than visiting sailors); the rest of the bay has been declared a national park.

The bay has a straightforward, deep, all-weather, entrance (although it can be rough when the wind is out of the north), inside which is an exceptionally well marked channel (minimum depth 5m) to the marina where the officials will clear you in (this is a port of entry to Cuba, making it an excellent point at which to check in if coming from the Bahamas). The marina has no dock space for visiting boats (you will have to anchor off) but diesel, gasoline and water are all available. The anchorage off the marina is well protected in all conditions. With a planing dinghy, the aquarium is an easy ride away, where you can swim with dolphins ($10 for adults; $5 for children), feed them ($2), or get kissed by a sea lion!

North of the aquarium, on the east side of the bay, there is a small dinghy dock and beach. From here a short trail leads to the Sol Río del Mares hotel – a very fine hotel with a full range of tourist facilities, including dive trips. The hotel can also be reached via a short taxi-ride from the marina. The hotel restaurant is open to visiting sailors with excellent buffet-style meals (breakfast $5; lunch and dinner $15); there are also two beach restaurants (á la carte). The hotel can arrange helicopter or bus rides or tours to Santiago, Holguin, Cayo Saetía and Baracoa, or else rent you a car or jeep.

Approaches

A substantial reef area extends almost 1M to the north of the hotel on the east side of the entrance into the bay. This needs to be given a wide berth. Otherwise there are no off-lying dangers.

From the east, between the Bahía de Samá and the Bahía de Naranjo you will pass a number of major hotels on lovely beaches tucked in behind a fringing barrier reef. Coming from the east, these are the first substantial tourist complexes on this coastline (there will be many more as you go further west). Nearing the Bahía de Naranjo you must progressively work further offshore until at the entrance to the bay you are at least 1M off. You must stay well off (north of 21°07·8'N) until the metal-frame lighthouse (Fl.6s) on the east side of the channel bears 185° *or less* – do not cut this corner.

From the west, you can simply parallel the coast a couple of hundred meters off until the final mile or so when the coastline recedes to the SE. You must continue east for another ½M, staying north of 21°07·1'N until the lighthouse (Fl.6s) bears 110° *or more*.

Entry and anchorage

Come to a position at approximately 21°07·3'N 75°53·3'W from where the entrance to the bay will be clearly visible with the lighthouse on the east side. Up inside the bay you will be able to see a conspicuous white building (part of the aquarium complex). Bring this building onto a bearing of 150° and then head straight for it, midway between the two buoys marking the channel mouth (red *No. 2* and green *No. 3*, both lit).

Once inside the outer channel buoys, follow the markers to the marina. After passing through the last pair of markers (two lit posts, red *No. 18* and green *No. 17*) anchor in front of the marina in 5 or 6m. The fuel dock is on the south shore of the small bay immediately to the east of the marina. To reach it, come past the north side of the marina, staying reasonably close to the marina where the depth is 3m or more; 2m can be carried alongside the fuel dock itself. In 1995 diesel was $0.75 a liter (expensive), and gasoline $0.90 a liter (normal). Water is available on the same dock but you will need to supply the hose and jury-rig a connection to their standpipe; the flow-rate is slow.

Bahía de Vita

The Bahía de Vita is a small pocket bay with a narrow, deep-water entrance leading to a well protected anchorage in attractive surroundings. Inside is the small port town of Puerto Vita, but it has little in the way of supplies. Nevertheless, this is a pleasant overnight stop.

Approaches

There are no off-lying hazards to either the east or the west – it is simply a matter of staying at least ¼M offshore. The lighthouse on Punta Barlovento can be seen from several miles out.

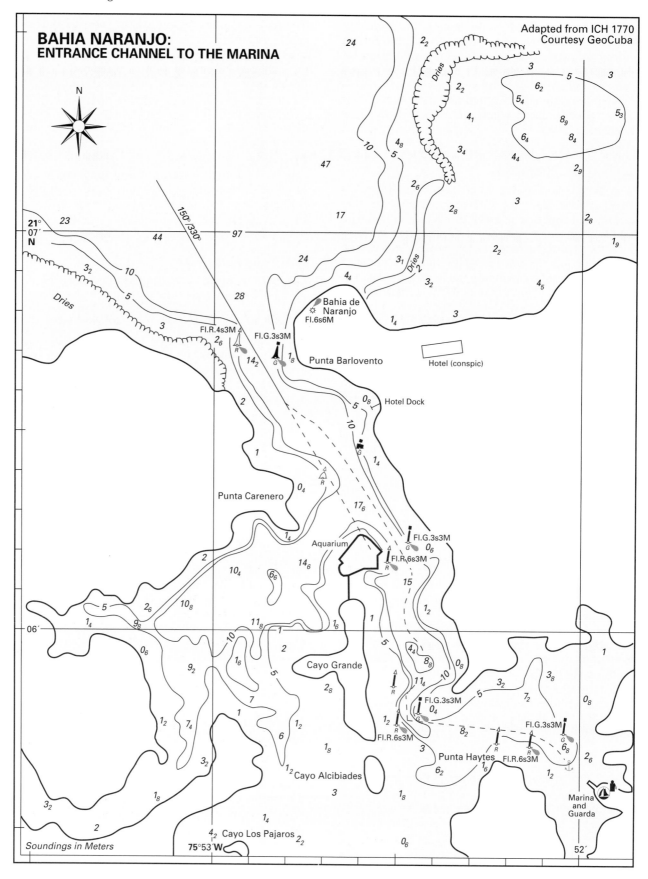

BAHIA NARANJO:
ENTRANCE CHANNEL TO THE MARINA

Adapted from ICH 1770
Courtesy GeoCuba

N

150°/330°

21°
07′
N

Dries

Dries

Dries

Fl.R.4s3M

Fl.G.3s3M

Bahia de
Naranjo
Fl.6s6M

Punta Barlovento

Hotel (conspic)

Hotel Dock

Punta Carenero

Aquarium

Fl.G.3s3M

Fl.R.6s3M

Cayo Grande

Fl.G.3s3M

Fl.R.6s3M

Punta Haytes

Fl.G.3s3M

Fl.R.6s3M

Marina
and
Guarda

Cayo Alcibiades

Soundings in Meters

75°53′W

Cayo Los Pajaros

06′

52′

Entry and anchorage

The channel is relatively narrow with a couple of doglegs. The first part is wide open to seas from the north and NW, in addition to which it is funnel-shaped which can lead to some rough and unpleasant cross seas. In such conditions it is important to get lined up on the channel well before entering, and to then enter with sufficient speed to maintain steerageway.

Come to a position at approximately 21°06·0'N 75°58·2'W, WNW of the lighthouse, from where you should be able to pick out a green buoy on a bearing of 134°. Set a course to leave this buoy (*No. 1*) close to port (i.e. come to the west of it), and then continue on this heading to pass midway between the next pair of buoys (red *No. 2* and green *No. 3*). By now you will be in calm waters and can follow the rest of the markers down the channel and around to the port area. Just north of the red *No. 4* buoy there is a Guarda post, but you can sail by and check in at the main post in the port area. To do this, either anchor off or else approach the commercial dock and wait for instructions.

There is plenty of water NE of the commercial dock in which to anchor out of the way of any port operations.

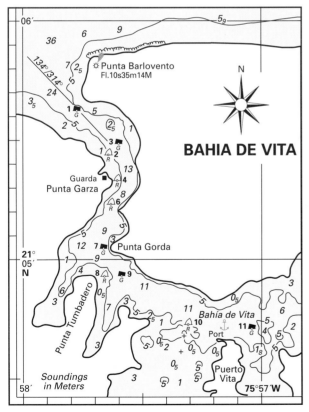

Adapted from DMA 26250
Courtesy DMA

Bahía de Vita to the Bahía de Puerto Padre

This 35M stretch of coastline includes a number of places of interest and several potential anchorages in settled easterly or southeasterly conditions, but no anchorage with good all-around protection.

Bahía de Bariay

The Bahía de Bariay, just 3M to the west of Puerto Vita has a pretty beach (Playa Blanca) but is chiefly interesting as (one of) the claimed sites at which Columbus first set foot on Cuban soil. For Columbus buffs there is a small monument ¼M to the south of Playa Blanca. On the attractive headland on the west side of the bay there are some intriguing ruins which we were unable to explore.

Entry and anchorage

There are no off-lying hazards either to the east or the west of the bay, but since it is wide open to the north, it is unsafe to enter in anything other than settled easterly or southeasterly conditions.

The bay is quite shoal throughout its southern half. The only reasonably protected anchorage which will accommodate a 2m draft is in the NE corner of the small bay which contains the village of Playa Blanca. Even here, swells tend to follow the curve of the coastline around from the east into the bay, making this somewhat rolly at times. The Columbus monument is down the road that leads out of the south side of town.

Bahía de Jururu

The Bahía de Jururu is a small pocket bay which has a shallow bar about a ½M in, obstructing the entry channel. To compound problems, the channel is narrow, with a relatively shoal (4m) bar across its mouth, and then another shoal almost completely across the channel just inside the mouth, necessitating a sharp dogleg. Finally, with any kind of seas or swells out of the north, there are likely to be breaking waves right across the entrance. In short, *in all but the calmest conditions this is a dangerous entry that should not be attempted*, which is a great shame, because the bay is quite enticing from the outside, displaying vistas of a calm anchorage and a small beach, with green fields running down to the shoreline and a picturesque mountain in the background.

It was not calm enough for us to enter when we were there. We have included a plan in case you should have better luck.

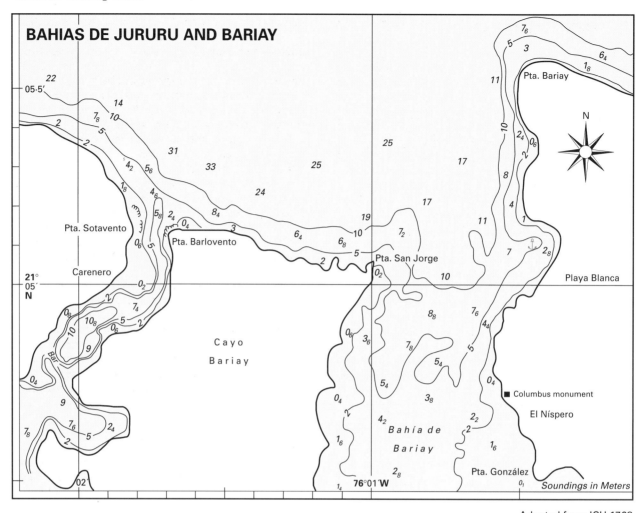

BAHIAS DE JURURU AND BARIAY

Adapted from ICH 1768
Courtesy GeoCuba

Puerto Gibara

Puerto Gibara is the site of one of the oldest cities in Cuba. It contains a number of fine colonial buildings, but many of them are crumbling.

Unfortunately, the bay is wide open to the north (completely untenable in a norther), with the swells sweeping in, even when the wind is in the SE. This is an exceptionally rolly and uncomfortable anchorage in which you always seem to be broadside to the swells! Sometimes better protection can be found in the SE corner of the bay, rather than off the town dock, but the Guarda are unlikely to allow you this far out of their sight, and it is a long dinghy ride to town. In short, Gibara is best by-passed in the boat, and visited by car from some other anchorage.

Approaches and entry

There are no off-lying dangers to either the east or the west. The red-and-white striped Punta Rasa lighthouse 2½M to the north of Gibara is conspicuous from several miles out. Once at the bay, simply sail up the center until east of the dock

in front of the city, and then head toward the dock and anchor. Note that the dock was formerly much longer, with another sizable dock to the south of it; there are reports of remnants of submerged pilings, so approach with care.

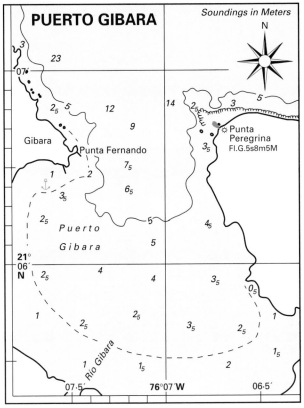

PUERTO GIBARA

Soundings in Meters

N

Gibara

Punta Fernando

Puerto Gibara

21° 06′ N

☼ Punta Peregrina Fl.G.5s8m5M

Río Gibara

07·5′   **76°07′W**   06·5′

Adapted from DMA 26250
Courtesy DMA

Bahías de Puerto Padre, Manatí and Nuevitas

The Bahías de Puerto Padre, Manatí and Nuevitas are three large pocket bays set into a low-lying coastline which is almost entirely one long, near virgin, sandy beach, broken up by a few low-lying rocky segments. Unfortunately, this coastline has no secure anchorages outside of these bays.

The three bays all deserve substantial comment. However, at the present time the Guarda require visiting boats to all three bays to dock at dirty commercial facilities within the bays, and do not allow gunkholing. For this reason, there is very little reason to enter these bays, except to seek shelter (which requires a fair amount of extra mileage to transit the entry channels to the various port facilities), or to clear in or out of Cuba (all three are ports of entry).

Rather than sail to the interior of these bays when seeking shelter, it would seem that all that is necessary is to anchor somewhere just inside the mouth of the entry channels, but this is not advisable. Even where the Guarda permit anchoring in the channel (Manatí and Nuevitas, but not Puerto Padre) you will find tidal currents of up to 3 knots with rocky bottoms swept clean by the

currents. It is very hard to set an anchor, and there is the constant worry that with a change of tide the anchor may come loose, allowing you to be swept ashore or into the ship channel. If you use an all-chain rode, all night long you will have to listen to it dragging across the bottom. In short, irrespective of the protection afforded by the channels, you are unlikely to get a good night's sleep.

Finally, given the strong currents in the entry channels, when the tide is ebbing against an onshore wind, the approaches to these channels can be extremely unpleasant with confused cross seas and severe tidal rips (the approaches to the Bahía de Nuevitas can be particularly uncomfortable). It is best to time an arrival or departure for slack water, which is some time after the time of high water or low water on shore (in the case of Nuevitas, as much as 2–2½ hours later).

Until the interiors of the bays are opened up to sailors, in our opinion you might as well keep sailing and by-pass them altogether. This results in a 120M or more passage between the Bahía de Naranjo (or the Bahía de Vita) and Cayo Confites (or one of the nearby reef anchorages – see below) – the longest sail in a circumnavigation of Cuba (although it can always be broken up, if necessary, by putting into one of the bays).

Bahía de Puerto Padre

The Bahía de Puerto Padre is home to the commercial port of Carúpano, situated on Cayo Juan Claro, to the SW of the entry channel. This cay is connected to the mainland by a causeway. The town of Puerto Padre is some distance off in the far SW corner of the bay.

The port authorities here are particularly restrictive in their attitude toward visiting boats. In general, they do not allow anchoring inside the entry channel, requiring boats either to leave or to proceed on to Carúpano. At Carúpano they like you to stay on a dirty commercial dock, which is in a good state of repair but has rather high fenders for cruising boats. From here it is a 5 mile taxi ride to the town (which is quite pretty).

Approaches

From the east, there are no off-lying hazards until a few miles short of the bay, at which time the reef begins to separate from the shoreline until it is almost ¾M offshore north of Punta Tomate (at the east side of the entrance to the bay; just prior to this, there is a reef anchorage which is entered by closing the coast at approximately 76°30′W longitude, and then hooking around to the east behind the reef). To stay clear of the reef, on your final approach to the Bahía de Puerto Padre keep the lighthouse on Punta Mastelero (Fl.8s) on a bearing of 225° *or less* until you pick up the channel markers.

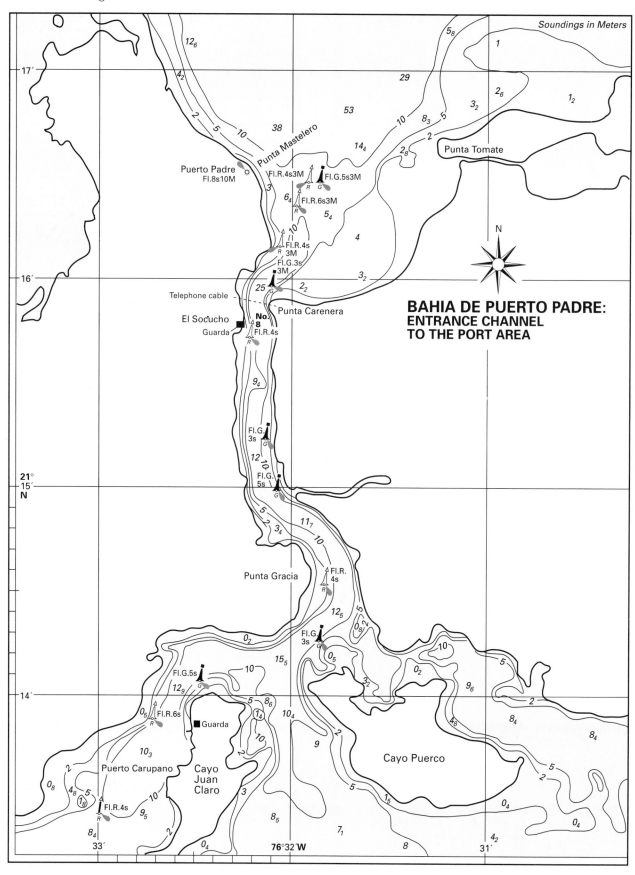

Soundings in Meters

12₆

5₈

1

17′

4₂

29

2₆

1₂

53

3₂

2

10

8₃

5

38

14₄

2₈

Punta Tomate

Punta Mastelero

Puerto Padre
Fl.8s10M

Fl.R.4s3M
R

Fl.G.5s3M
G

6₄

Fl.R.6s3M
R

5₄

N

4

Fl.R.4s
3M
R

10

BAHIA DE PUERTO PADRE:
ENTRANCE CHANNEL
TO THE PORT AREA

16′

25

Fl.G.3s
3M
G

2₂

3₂

Telephone cable

Punta Carenera

El Socucho

No
8

Guarda

Fl.R.4s
R

9₄

Fl.G.
3s
G

12

10

21°
15′
N

Fl.G.
5s
G

5

2

3₄

11₇

10

Punta Gracia

Fl.R.
4s
R

12₅

5

0₈

2

Fl.G.
3s
G

0₅

10

15₅

0₂

0₂

3₂

9₆

2

Fl.G.5s
G

10

8₄

14′

12₉

5

8₆

0₅

Fl.R.6s
R

14

10₄

2

8₄

8₄

Guarda

10

9

5

10₃

2

Cayo Puerco

2

Puerto Carupano

Cayo
Juan
Claro

3

5

0₄

0₈

4₈

5

10

0₄

1₈

Fl.R.4s
R

9₅

8₅

7₁

8

4₂

8₄

33′

0₄

76°32′W

31′

Adapted from ICH 1766

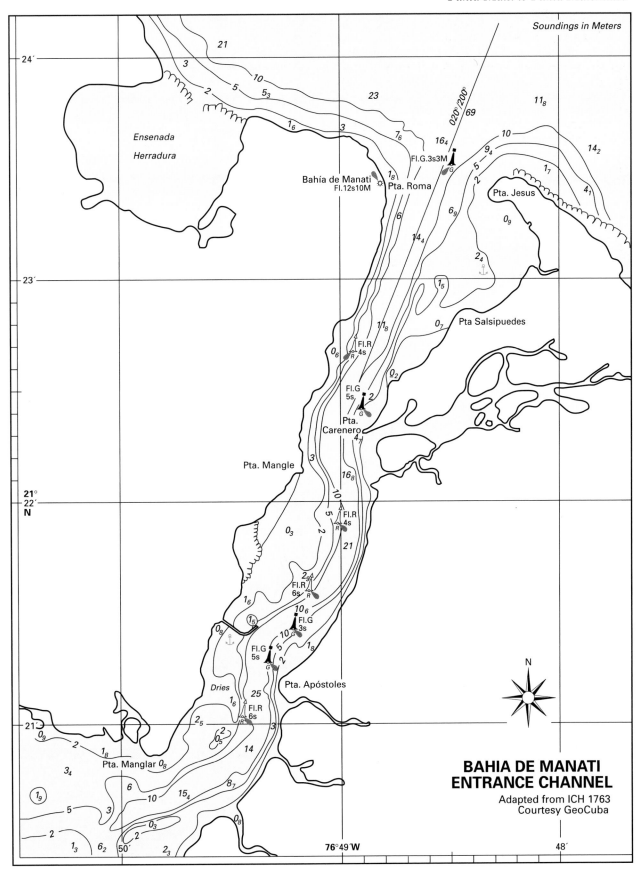

Soundings in Meters

Ensenada
Herradura

21

3

10

5

5₃

23

11₈

2

1₆

3

7₆

020°/200° 69

16₄

10

14₂

Fl.G.3s3M

9₄

5

Bahía de Manati
Fl.12s10M

1₈

Pta. Roma

6

6₉

2

1₇

Pta. Jesus

4₁

14₄

0₉

2₄

1₅

11₈

0₇ Pta Salsipuedes

0₆

Fl.R
4s
R

0₂

Fl.G
5s

2

Pta.
Carenero

G

4₇

Pta. Mangle

3

16₈

10

5

Fl.R
4s
R

2

21

0₃

2₉

Fl.R
6s
R

1₆

1₅

10₆
Fl.G
3s
G

10₃

5

1₈

0₈

Fl.G
5s
G

2

N

Dries

25

1₆

Fl.R
6s
R

2₅

2₀₅

3

Pta. Apóstoles

14

0₉

2

1₈

Pta. Manglar 0₈

8₇

3₄

6

10

15₄

1₉

5

3

0₃

0₈

2

2

**BAHIA DE MANATI
ENTRANCE CHANNEL**
Adapted from ICH 1763
Courtesy GeoCuba

1₃

6₂

50′

2₃

76°49′W

48′

197

From the west (Bahía de Manatí), note that the reef extends almost 1½M offshore at Punta Cobarrubia, and continues to run well offshore past the Cañon Punta de Piedra up to the northern tip of Cayo Guincho (north of the entrance to the Bahía de Puerto Padre). It is best to stay well out along this entire stretch, although there are a couple of small breaks in the reef just east and SE of Punta Cobarrubia that allow you to tuck in behind this reef.

Entry

Work south to a position at approximately 21°16·5'N 76°31·9'W which is just to seaward of the outer channel buoys (green *No. 1*, Fl.G.3s, and red *No. 2*, Fl.R.4s). From here a couple of lit red buoys (*No. 4* and *No. 6*, which are left to starboard – i.e. you pass to the east of them) lead toward the mouth of the channel on a bearing of 201°. At red *No. 6* buoy you change to a heading of 214°, aiming for a dock on the west side of the channel. At the mouth a green lit buoy (*No. 7*) is left to port (i.e. you pass to the west of it), and you come onto a southerly heading straight down the center of the channel.

There is a Guarda post at the dock on the west side of the entrance just past the green buoy. If you intend to proceed to Carúpano, you might try sailing by, but they will likely hail you; if you intend to try and anchor near the mouth of the channel you will have to check in regardless. The dock has 2·5m alongside. If the swells are running onto the dock, you can anchor on the margins of the channel just to the SW of the red *No. 8* buoy to the south of the Guarda dock (which is where you will be told to anchor if allowed to spend the night here; just in case you drag during the night, the Guarda will require you to post an anchor watch).

To go to Carúpano, follow the channel markers to the bay, where you will be faced with three channels. Take the western channel around to the north and west of Cayo Juan Claro, which brings you to the port area. The Guarda post is close to the northwestern tip of the cay.

Bahía de Manatí

The Bahía de Manatí is an almost entirely shoal pocket bay, but with a deep-water entrance leading to a substantial commercial dock about ⅔ of the way down the channel. This dock is pretty much disused, and the small town alongside it is now little more than a fishing village. The interior of the bay is almost entirely mangroves.

The entry is straightforward enough, and the Guarda here are more friendly and flexible than at either the Bahía de Puerto Padre or the Bahía de Nuevitas, but the protection afforded by the channel and the bay are not as good in a norther as at the

other two bays (at all other times the protection is good).

Approaches and entry

There are no off-lying dangers to either the east or the west of the bay. The entrance to the bay is not conspicuous, but the lighthouse on Punta Roma, the west headland, can be seen from several miles out.

To enter, come to a position at approximately 21°24·0'N 76°48·4'W and proceed on a bearing of 200°, leaving the green *No. 1* buoy (Fl.G.3s) to port (i.e. you pass to the west of it). In the course of the next 2M the well marked channel winds over to the east bank to avoid a large shoal on the west side, before curving back to the large, commercial dock. If it is calm, you should come alongside the outer edge of the dock (it is shoal on the inside), but be warned that the dock has large wooden fenders set well above deck height for most cruising boats making it next-to-impossible to moor with adequate protection for the boat or its rigging. The alternative is to anchor with the fishing boats to the south of the dock (but not too far south, since it gets exceedingly shoal). The bottom here is reportedly foul with rubble, so it is advisable to rig a tripping line.

Anchorages

Just inside the east headland at the entrance to the channel there is a small cove with a lovely sandy beach. Although the cove is mostly shoal, 2m can be carried well down into the SE corner, which is reasonably well protected in prevailing winds. After clearing in, the Guarda will let you anchor here.

If conditions make this an unsuitable anchorage, you can either anchor in the lee of the dock (which is only a partial lee in northers because the dock has an open construction), or else head down into the northern part of the bay, but this has a great deal of shoal water while the channels are unmarked.

Canón las Nuevas

A narrow, deep-water channel leads through the reef at the Canón las Nuevas. Reportedly, a 2m draft can be carried almost to the head of the narrow bay.

Bahía de Nuevitas

The Bahía de Nuevitas is one of Cuba's larger pocket bays. On the inside are a number of small cays, the port of Tarafa, and the town of Nuevitas. The bay itself is mostly mangroves and not particularly interesting, and the town does not have a lot to offer.

Because of the size of the bay, the relatively narrow entrance channel has particularly strong tidal currents of up to 4·5 knots, and even more on the ebb during the rainy season. When the ebb tide

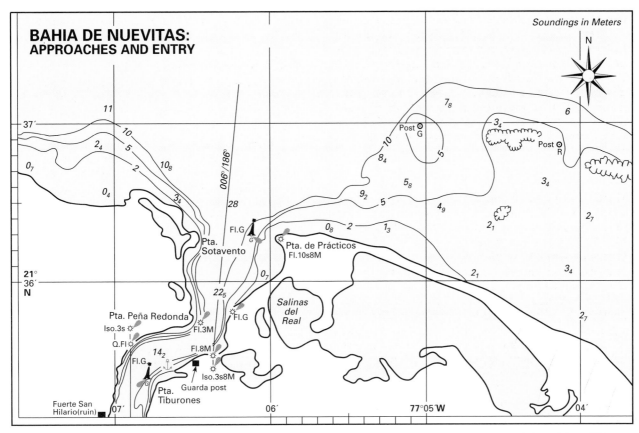

BAHIA DE NUEVITAS:
APPROACHES AND ENTRY

Soundings in Meters

Adapted from ICH 1411
and ICH 1760
Courtesy GeoCuba

meets an onshore wind, the approaches can be especially rough. Timing your arrival and departure for close to slack water is even more important here than at the other pocket bays. Note the previous comment that slack water is 2–2½ hours after the times of high water and low water on shore.

As at Puerto Padre, there is a Guarda post at the mouth of the channel as well as at the port of Tarafa. In settled conditions the Guarda permit anchoring on a rocky shelf near the mouth of the channel (the protection is good except in northers) but the holding is poor. If you feel comfortable leaving your boat under these circumstances, you can dinghy to the Guarda dock and have them call a taxi to take you to the hotel zone of Santa Lucía, a few miles down the coast to the east, or else arrange to be picked up from the ruined Fuerte San Hilario on the west side of the channel, from where a short drive will bring you to the magnificent lighthouse at Punta Maternillos (which can also be visited in settled conditions in a planing dinghy).

Approaches and entry

The lighthouse at Punta Maternillos (at approximately 21°39·8'N 77°08·5'W), 4M to the NW of the entrance, is conspicuous from many miles in either direction.

From the east, the reef gradually extends further offshore the closer you get to the bay. To the NE of Punta de Prácticos, the east headland for the channel, it is almost 1½M offshore.

The final section of reef has a break which is navigable with up to 2m. This break is marked with a red post. Further to the west the reef ends so that it is possible to hook around it and into its lee, with the depths shoaling from 4m down to less than 2m the further east you go once inside the reef. This western end of the reef is marked with a green post. In settled conditions a moderate amount of protection can be found off an attractive beach behind the reef, with the Santa Lucía hotel zone a longish dinghy ride to the east, but the holding is poor in a rocky bottom.

From the west, it is important to stay well offshore (up to 1½M) on the approaches to the Punta Maternillos lighthouse in order to avoid a long, near-drying reef (there are various breaks in this reef, with potential anchorages on the inside – see the next chapter). Once past the reef to the east of Punta Maternillos head directly for the light (which looks like a small rocket) on Punta de Prácticos.

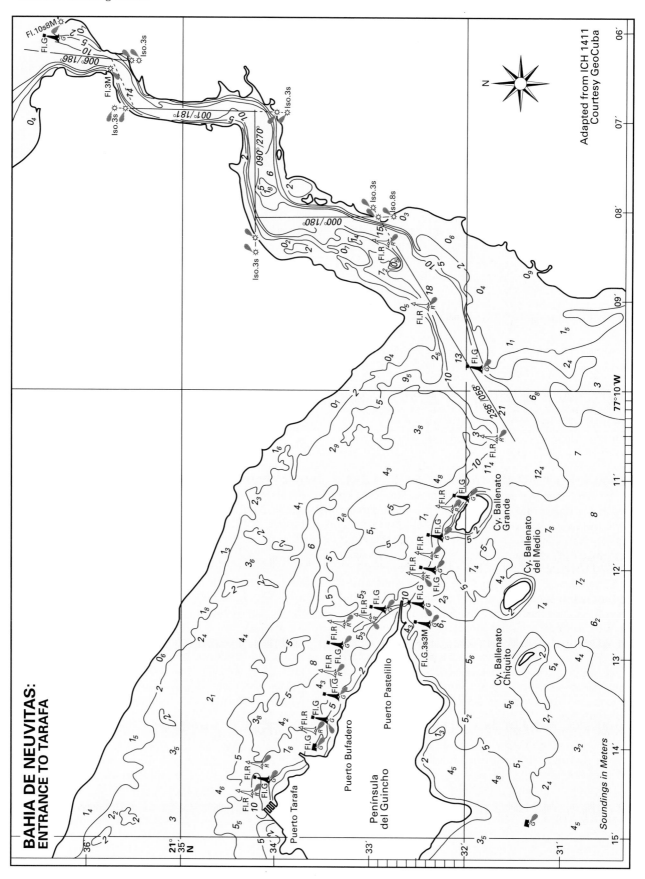

**BAHIA DE NEUVITAS:
ENTRANCE TO TARAFA**

Adapted from ICH 1411
Courtesy GeoCuba

Soundings in Meters

Puerto Tarafa

Puerto Bufadero

Puerto Pastelillo

Peninsula
del Guincho

Cy. Ballenato
Chiquito

Cy. Ballenato
del Medio

Cy. Ballenato
Grande

Entry

Come to a position at approximately 21°37·0'N 77°06·2'W and head in on a bearing of 186°, leaving the green buoy off Punta de Prácticos to port (i.e. you pass to the west of it). Ahead you will see a set of range lights. As you approach the range lights, the channel makes a sharp turn to the west. A Guarda post is on the east bank about midway through this turn.

If you are intending to go to Tarafa you can try sailing past the Guarda post and continuing down the channel, but you will probably be hailed. If you simply want to stop for the night at the entrance to the channel, you will need to check in. In any event, the Guarda will likely want you to come alongside their gunboat (if present – 3m on its outboard side) or the small dock in front of the Guarda building. If the conditions are too rough to do this (a norther) you can anchor in 3–4m on the margins of the east side of the channel, just beyond the Guarda dock (in 1995 there were a couple of charter boats anchored here).

Beyond the Guarda post the channel makes several sharp turns, but throughout its 5M length it is extremely well marked with buoys and ranges. Toward the south end it is particularly important to stay within the marked channel since outside it there are a number of shoal areas that come up with little warning. Once into the bay, the channel heads in a generally WNW direction for another 6M to the port of Tarafa, where you will have to come alongside one of the large, dirty commercial piers to clear in (if the swells make this unsafe, it may be better to anchor off to the west of the western pier). The Guarda have been known to try and insist that visiting boats stay on the dock and pay a commercial rate of $5.00 per meter for the privilege, but they should back down if you protest strongly enough.

The Bahía de Nuevitas is large enough to have unpleasant seas at times. Depending on the wind direction, good protection can be found on one side or the other of the Península del Guincho (on which the port of Tarafa and town of Nuevitas sit), or behind the cays to the SW of the peninsula (Cayos Ballenatos), but it may be difficult to persuade the Guarda to allow you to anchor in the location of your choice. In any event, if you move around to the west side of the port area, stay clear of the shoal that sticks out from the SW end of the docks, and continues around Punta de los Tanques to the west.

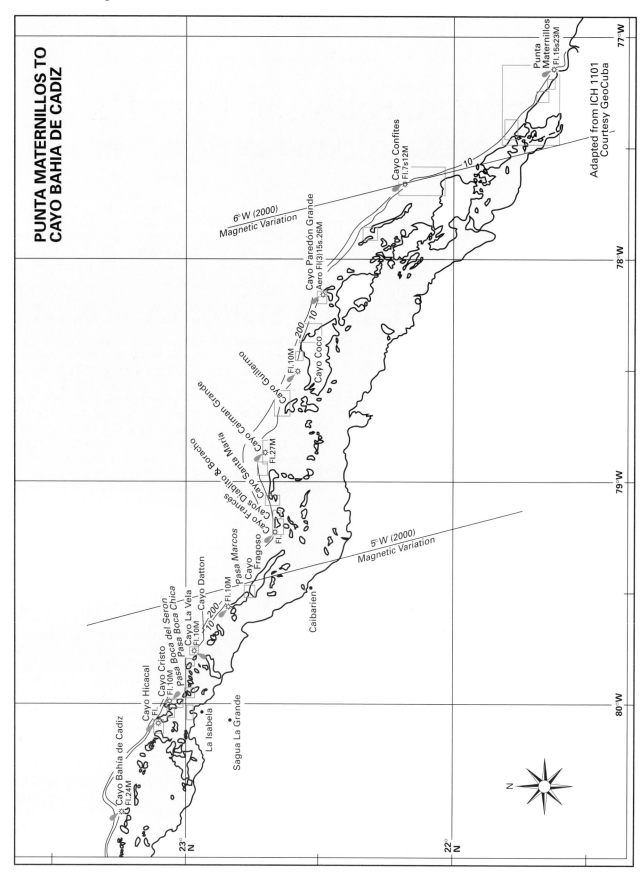

PUNTA MATERNILLOS TO CAYO BAHIA DE CADIZ

Punta Maternillos Fl.15s23M

Cayo Confites Fl.7s12M

6° W (2000) Magnetic Variation

Cayo Paredón Grande Aero Fl(3)15s.26M

Cayo Coco

Cayo Guillermo Fl.10M

Cayo Caiman Grande

Cayo Santa Maria Fl.27M

Cayos Diablito & Boracho

Cayo Francés Fl.

Cayo Fragoso

Pasa Marcos

Cayo Datton

Cayo La Vela Fl.10M

Pasa Boca Chica

pasa Boca

Cayo Cristo del Seron Fl.10M

Cayo Hicacal Fl.

Fl.10M

200

10

Caibarién

La Isabela

Sagua La Grande

5° W (2000) Magnetic Variation

Cayo Bahía de Cadiz Fl.24M

Adapted from ICH 1101 Courtesy GeoCuba

N

23° N

22° N

77° W

78° W

79° W

80° W

200 70

10

9. Punta Maternillos to Cayo Bahía de Cádiz

In this 210M stretch, a succession of cays (grouped in the Archipiélago de Camagüey, and the Archipiélago de Sabinal) line the coast of Cuba. Between the cays and the mainland are a number of large, mangrove-rimmed lagoons.

The lagoons are of little interest to us, especially since the depths are almost all shoal. By contrast, on the seaward side of the cays we find mile after mile of gorgeous unspoiled sandy beach fronted by an intermittent barrier reef sprinkled with small islets that invite exploration. Between the reef and the cays there is a great deal of relatively protected water with first-class sailing conditions. There are numerous potential anchorages, both on the larger cays and also behind a number of the smaller islets out on the reef. In addition, the reef itself is broken in many places, providing opportunities to enter and anchor in its lee.

Aside from a couple of small cities on the mainland, the occasional tourist development or isolated fishing station are the only signs of human habitation, although this may change in the future since the Cuban government is busy constructing causeways and roads, with the intention of developing several major tourist centers. All-in-all, this section of coastline, particularly that between Cayo Coco and Cayo Francés, is, in our opinion, one of the finest cruising grounds in Cuba.

Note, however, that the degree of protection provided by many of the anchorages is quite variable. In settled prevailing winds – NE to SE – just about any cay or section of reef to windward will break the moderate seas and swells, creating a reasonably comfortable anchorage, but in heavy seas, and particularly northers, most of the reef entries are dangerous, while a number of the anchorages are exceedingly uncomfortable at best, and untenable at worst (added to which the holding is often poor – thin sand over rock and coral rubble – so there is a good chance of dragging).

So if cruising this coast in the winter months it is essential to keep track of the weather, and to seek suitable shelter well before a norther strikes. By contrast, during the summer months, when the winds tend to be light and the swells quite small, it is possible to do a good deal more exploring in the waters behind the reef than we have done for this guide (but the mosquitoes will be fearsome from June to September). On balance, the best months to be cruising this coast are March to May, with the early winter months (November and December) as a less attractive option.

Winds

Average winds are from the ENE at about 10 knots. Seasonal variations include a succession of northers in the winter months (with the greatest incidence in January and February), and sometimes quite extended calms in the summer, broken by the strong winds associated with the passage of tropical depressions. According to the Cuban Pilot, May and November also have a relatively high incidence of strong winds, but the wind direction is not given.

The daily wind pattern typically consists of lighter winds at night, building steadily until mid-afternoon, and then easing.

Currents and tides

The Antilles Current is the major offshore current, but in spite of the narrowing of the Old Bahamas Channel (at this point called the Nicolás Channel) which takes place in the waters immediately off the coast, rather than sped up, the current is, if anything, weaker here than elsewhere (the average speed is about 0·5 knot). This current is heavily influenced by the winds, building to up to 2 knots with a SE wind, but reversing direction, and running at anything up to 3 knots to the SE, with a strong NW wind (associated with the passage of a cold front).

Closer inshore there are no predictable currents, with the exception of tidal currents in a number of the narrow passages and channels between the cays. In places these achieve speeds of up to 3 knots. The tides themselves average something less than ½m (18in), with maximums up to 0·8m (32in) and minimums of as little as 0·1m (4in). The tide is semi-diurnal (i.e. it occurs twice daily).

Sailing strategies

Given the generally SE to NW axis of this stretch of coastline, so long as the wind is north of east it should be possible to make a reasonable passage toward the east as well as to the west. However, the minute the wind moves toward the east, or south of east, any passage in this direction will be a hard slog, although a certain amount of it can be done in relatively protected waters behind the reef. In contrast, a westward passage will generally be a downwind run in which a powerboat may roll and fishtail, sometimes alarmingly, whereas a sailboat, with its sails checking its motion, will have a fast and comfortable ride.

Nighttime passages are complicated by the fact that although there are a number of substantial lighthouses to act as reference points, these are often well inside the line of the cays and reefs. Since the bottom comes up without warning along the edge of the reef, it is essential to keep well offshore for safety's sake, but this then puts you into the International Maritime Organization's (IMO) Traffic Separation Scheme, which covers all shipping in the Nicolás Channel (the scheme is necessary because of the narrowness of the channel). The shipping lanes are clearly marked on the charts – you need to either keep out of them, or make sure you are in the correct one!

Charts and magnetic variation

ICH *1130* (also mentioned in the previous chapter), *1129*, *1128* and *1127* cover this stretch at a scale of 1:150,000. In addition, there are detailed charts of the ports of Caibarien and La Isabela. Finally, there is the chart book (Region 6: Punta Maternillos to Bahía de Cádiz) which covers this region.

Magnetic variation (January 2000) decreases from 6°30'W at Punta Maternillos to 4°30'W at Cayo Bahía de Cádiz. In all areas it is increasing at an annual rate of approximately 9'W.

Punta Maternillos to Cayo Confites

From the magnificent lighthouse at Punta Maternillos the reef runs in an almost continuous line to the NW, but with many a break allowing passage to the inside. Behind the reef is one long stretch after another of virgin beach, with hardly a sign of human presence. We have by no means investigated all the breaks in the reef, but those covered below will be more than enough to get you started on an exploration of this region.

In the daytime, when sailing this stretch of coastline you need do little more than keep one eye on the reef and stay ¼M off (at which point you will frequently be off soundings).

At night a great deal more caution is required, since the bottom comes up with incredible speed (on one occasion our depth sounder went from no reading straight to 10m, at which point the reef was no more than 200m – 30 seconds sailing time – away). There are no lighthouses between those at Punta Maternillos and Cayo Confites, and few lights ashore, while there are sometimes onshore currents, making this a dangerous coast (as is evidenced by the amount of wreckage on the reef). It is essential to stay well offshore and to keep a close track of your position, but note that once you get beyond 3½M outside the reef you will be straying into the big-ship traffic separation scheme.

Punta Central

Punta Central is 3½M to the NW of Punta Maternillos. The reef is broken up immediately off the point, allowing passage to the inside where it is possible to anchor in 2–3m. However, the protection is not good and the holding is poor. The only reason for mentioning this spot is that in calm, settled conditions it affords an opportunity to visit the Punta Maternillos lighthouse by dinghy (a planing dinghy will be needed). There are no significant features on the coastline to serve as a guide when passing through the reef, so this is a good-light, calm-conditions entry only.

The reef entry is complicated by the fact that there are actually three breaks in the reef, increasing in width as you progress from the SE to the NW. The one to the SE (at approximately 21°41·2'N 77°11·3'W) is the most clearly defined since the coral protrudes on both sides, but it is also the narrowest. Those to the NW (at approximately 21°41·5'N 77°11·7'W and 21°41·8'N 77°12·9'W) are quite wide, but the ends of the reef are harder to pick out – it is important to keep pretty well to the center of the charted breaks until well inside the line of the reef, and only then to turn to the SE (toward the lighthouse), anchoring when the bottom shoals.

Estero la Palma and Punta Piedra

To the east of Estero la Palma the reef terminates about 1M offshore, beginning again onshore at Estero la Palma and extending to a little more than ½M offshore at Punta Piedra (3M to the NW), at which point it temporarily terminates once again.

At both places reasonable protection can be found in prevailing conditions by simply hooking around to the west of the open end of the reef, and then sailing to the SE into its lee. At Estero la Palma you come in at approximately 21°43·6'N 77°16·6'W. At Punta Piedra you come in at approximately

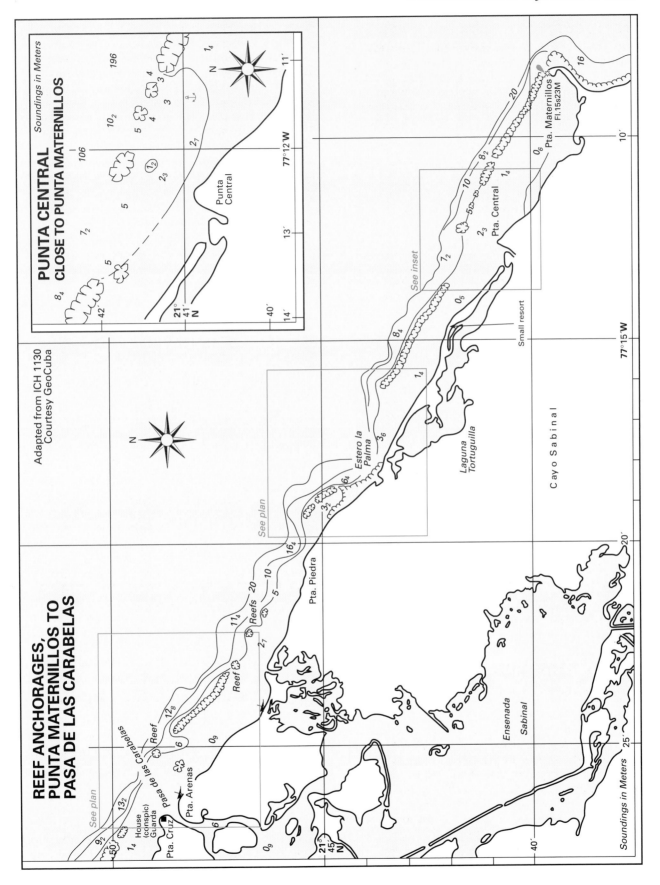

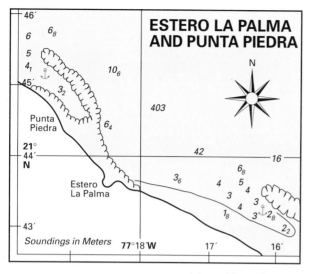

ESTERO LA PALMA AND PUNTA PIEDRA

Soundings in Meters

Adapted from ICH 1130
Courtesy GeoCuba

21°45·7'N 77°19·6'W (giving the breaking section of reef a wide berth since partially submerged reef extends some way beyond it). In both cases, once inside the line of the reef, sail to the SE into its lee until in a comfortable depth to anchor (the bottom shoals gently the further SE you go). The holding is generally poor in a rocky bottom.

Pasa de las Carabelas

The Pasa de las Carabelas, which can be identified by a conspicuous white Guarda post on the north side of its entry, is a mostly deep channel through the cays into the interior lagoon of the Bahía la Gloria. We had hoped to find a clear path into the pass, since this would then give access to a completely protected all-weather anchorage on the inside. Unfortunately, the mouth of the seaward side of the channel is obstructed by a shifting sandbar which had much less than 2m over it when

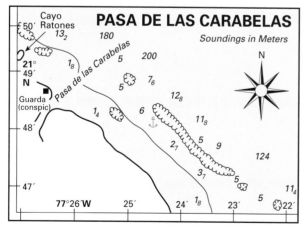

PASA DE LAS CARABELAS

Soundings in Meters

Adapted from ICH 1130
Courtesy GeoCuba

we were there.

In the process of poking around, we found that there is a minimum of 2·5m behind the reef that extends for a little more than 2M to the SE of the Pasa de las Carabelas. You can anchor at any point with quite reasonable protection in prevailing winds. However, it is important to note that on their charts the Cubans have missed an isolated patch of reef to the SE of this reef, and another ½M to the NW of the reef, so take care when entering.

At the south end, a position at approximately 21°46·8'N 77°22·6'W will bring you in about midway between the uncharted reef patch, and the next (charted) patch to the SE.

At the north end, a position at approximately 21°48·7'N 77°24·8'W will bring you in about midway between the charted end of the reef and the uncharted reef patch to the NW.

In both cases the reef should be entered on a southwesterly heading.

Quebrado Aguas del Inglés

The Quebrado Aguas del Inglés (which is not named on the charts) is found close to the southern end of Cayo Romano. It is an almost 2M wide break in the reef, creating an easy entry through which to duck in behind the reef to the south.

The south end of the break is at approximately 22°03·4'N 77°36·8'W. The north end is at approximately 22°04·6'N 77°37·6'W. You can enter at any point between these two positions, maintaining a generally westerly track until inside the line of the reef, and then hooking to the south. The bottom will shoal from about 7m as you pass through the reef, down to 3m tucked well behind the reef. The area appears to be free of substantial coral heads, but there are some smaller bits of coral and one or two shallower patches (we found nothing with less than 2·5m in this area). However, don't stray too close to Cayo Romano since there are some more substantial coral heads over toward the beach (good snorkeling).

Cayo Confites and Cayo Verde

Cayo Confites is a lovely little cay with a couple of anchorages that are well protected from all but the south and SW. Unfortunately, the cay, which is home to a detachment of the Guarda, and also the Cuban control station for the Old Bahamas Channel traffic separation scheme, is considered a military zone and as such is off-limits to civilians. However, the Guarda will generally make an exception regarding the beach at the southern tip of the cay, allowing visiting sailors ashore at this point but no other.

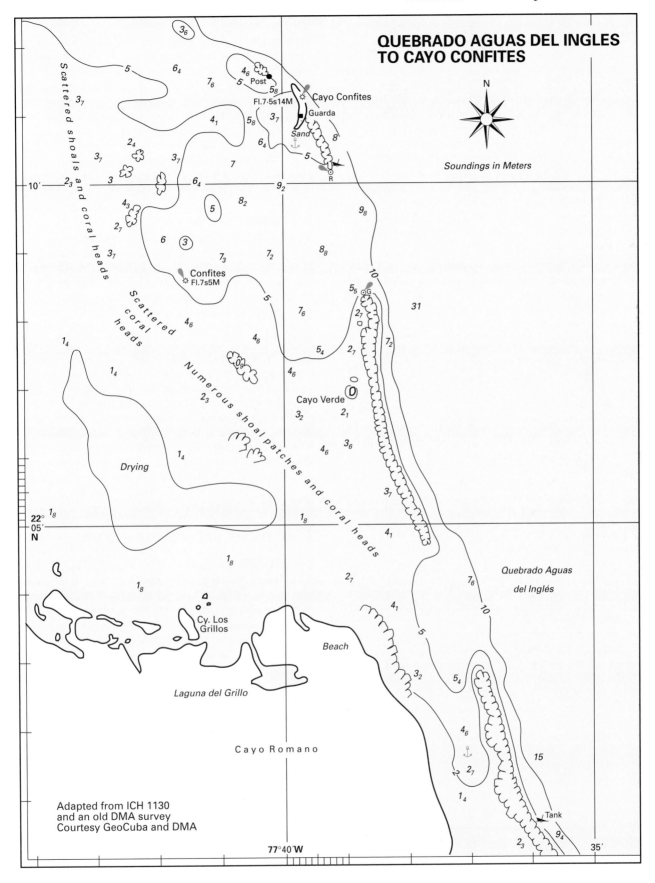

QUEBRADO AGUAS DEL INGLES
TO CAYO CONFITES

N

Soundings in Meters

3₆

Scattered shoals

5   6₄   7₆   4₆   Post

3₇   5   5₈   Cayo Confites
Fl.7·5s14M   Guarda
4₁   5₈   3₇
2₄   6₄   Sand   8
3₇   3₇   7   5
2₃   3   6₄   9₂   R
and coral heads   8₂   9₈
4₃   5
2₇
6   ③   7₃   7₂   8₈
3₇   10
Confites   5₅   G
Fl.7s5M   2₇
Scattered   7₆   31
coral   5   2₇   7₂
heads   4₆   5₄   2₇
1₄   4₆
Numerous   4₆
1₄   0₉
2₃   Cayo Verde   Ⓓ
1₄   3₂   2₁
Drying   shoal   4₆   3₆
1₄   patches   3₇
1₈   1₈   4₁
22°   1₈   and   7₆   Quebrado Aguas
05′   2₇   coral   10   del Inglés
N   1₈   heads   4₁
1₈   5
2₇   4₁
ᙅ   Cy. Los   3₂   5₄
Grillos   Beach
Laguna del Grillo   4₆   15
Cayo Romano   2₇
1₄   Tank
Adapted from ICH 1130   2₃   9₄
and an old DMA survey   35′
Courtesy GeoCuba and DMA
77°40′W

Cayo Verde is another small cay some 4M to the south of Cayo Confites. It too has good protection from all but the south. There are no restrictions on going ashore here, but the cay is not as pretty as Cayo Confites, consisting of mostly low rock covered with scrubby vegetation. However, there is some reasonable snorkeling on small coral patches nearby, with a fine selection of fishes (and some large lobster!).

The anchorage at Cayo Confites provides reasonable protection in a norther, as well as in prevailing winds.

Note The light shown on Cayo Verde on some Cuban charts no longer exists; the only light is a grey, metalwork tower (Fl.7·5s) on Cayo Confites.

Approaches

From the southeast, it is reportedly possible to sail from the anchorage at the Quebrado Aguas del Inglés up the inside of the reef to Cayo Verde and Cayo Confites, but the southern end of this passage has numerous isolated coral heads so good light is needed. Nearing Cayo Verde the channel is clear, with the exception of a clearly visible shoal area extending a short distance to the SW of Cayo Verde. From here it is a clear run into the lee of Cayo Confites.

The more usual approach is through the marked reef entry to the SSE of Cayo Confites (see below). If this entry is used, just be sure to stay well outside the line of the reef until the green beacon bears 270° *or less* (as you approach the beacon the reef curves out to the east, while the beacon is set well inside the reef – if you cut the corner you will hit the reef).

From the northwest (Cayo Paredón Grande), the stretch of coastline between Cayo Paredón Grande and the northern end of Cayo Cruz is particularly dangerous since the reef is intermittent, with isolated patches occurring up to 2M outside the main line of the reef, very close to the deep water offshore. Unless gunkholing in calm conditions (see below) you should stay well out until past the Bajo Tributarios de Minerva, an isolated shoal to the north of Cayo Cruz at approximately 22°21·0'N 77°51·7'W. From here you can head directly for Cayo Confites (on a heading of 132° *or more*, depending on how wide a clearance you give the shoal).

In calm conditions, as you near Cayo Confites you can head directly down to its west (leeward) side, taking care to avoid an area of shallow, breaking reef just to the NW of the northern tip of the cay. This reef has a post marking its southern end, where there is a relatively narrow channel between the northern tip of the cay and the post. Once in the lee of Cayo Confites, it is a clear run down to Cayo Verde.

In rough conditions it is better to stay offshore until south of Cayo Confites and to then come in through the marked reef entry (see below).

Reef entry

SSE of Cayo Confites there is 1½M wide break in the reef, with lit beacons on either side of the channel (the red one at the north end; the green one at the south end). To enter, come to a position at approximately 22°09·3'N 77°38·1'W and then head in in a westerly direction. Once inside the line of the reef, hook to the south for Cayo Verde, or to the north for Cayo Confites.

Anchorages

Cayo Verde Depending on the winds and seas, you can anchor either to the NW or the SW of the cay, taking care to avoid the coral patch due north of the cay, and the shoal extending from its SW tip. The depths shoal gently from about 3m as you approach the cay. Holding is none too good in a rocky bottom covered in thin sand – a Danforth-type anchor works best.

Cayo Confites Depending on the winds and the seas, you can either anchor behind the reef to the south of the sand spit at the southern tip of the cay, or come up into the lee of the cay just to the north of the Guarda dock. The depths shoal gently from about 3m as you approach the reef or cay. Holding is none too good in a rocky bottom covered with thin sand – a Danforth-type anchor works best.

Cayo Confites to Cayo Paredòn Grande, Cayo Coco and Cayo Guillermo

It is approximately a 35M sail between Cayo Confites and Cayo Paredón Grande with no secure anchorages and a good deal of potentially dangerous coral. The reef becomes highly intermittent to the NW of Cayo Confites, with the main line further inshore but isolated patches up to 2M to seaward of the main line.

Some of these patches are very close to the deep water of the Old Bahamas Channel. On the wrong heading, there are just a few seconds between being off soundings and being on the reef. The dangers are sometimes compounded by relatively strong onshore currents. *For those coming from the SE, who have grown accustomed to navigating simply by keeping one eye on the reef a couple of hundred meters to port, it is essential to either head well offshore, or to start maintaining a very accurate plot of the boat's position.*

Regardless of the direction of your travels, if the conditions are at all rough the only prudent course of action is to keep well offshore. But in calm conditions, with an early start from either Cayo

Confites or Cayo Paredón Grande, there is time to do some exploring, and there is much to see. The cays have mile after mile of gorgeous pristine beach, with excellent snorkeling on much of the coral. A couple of spots we would recommend are tucked into the lee of the northern tip of Cayo Cruz (see below), and off the beach on the western side of Cayo Paredón Grande, but in truth with the Cuban charts, a GPS, and the right light you could work into a dozen lovely beaches, and anchor alongside a hundred gorgeous coral heads. However, be careful, keep a close eye on the weather, and *head offshore at the first sign of the wind or seas kicking up, and in plenty of time to reach a safe anchorage before nightfall.*

West of Cayo Paredón Grande lie the tourist cays of Cayo Coco and Cayo Guillermo, with numerous beautiful beaches and a fair sprinkling of reasonably well protected anchorages.

Note The Cubans have recently built a road to Cayo Cruz, continuing all the way to the lighthouse at Cayo Paredón Grande, so you had better cruise this region before it becomes another Cancun!

North tip of Cayo Cruz

Between Cayo Cruz and Cayo Mégano Grande (to the NW of Cayo Cruz) there is a mile-wide break. Shoal water and coral extends about ¼M to the north of Cayo Cruz, and well out to the east of much of Cayo Mégano Grande, with a mass of drying sandy flats blocking all passage south between the two cays. However, in settled easterlies a pleasant lunch-time stop will be found

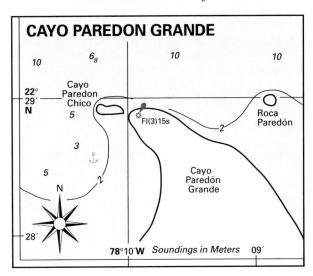

CAYO PAREDON GRANDE

Adapted from ICH 1129
Courtesy GeoCuba

immediately to the west of the northern tip of Cayo Cruz (but no further south). Just be careful when approaching or leaving to avoid the Bajo Tributarios de Minerva, and the two isolated coral patches 1M to the north, and 1½M to the NNW, of Cayo Cruz.

Cayo Paredón Grande

What a lovely cay this is! On the east side is an enticing, unspoiled beach. Offshore there is a good deal of lovely coral. And towering above everything is the magnificent yellow-and-black checkerboard lighthouse, Fl(3)15s. The view from the top of the lighthouse over the surrounding cays and reef is spectacular. The anchorage is wide open to the north and west (no good in a norther), but the protection is quite good in prevailing easterlies.

Approaches

From the southeast, there are scattered patches of dangerous coral almost out to the deep water of the Old Bahamas Channel (see above). These terminate due east of the northern tip of Cayo Paredón Grande, so any approach that has the lighthouse on a bearing of 265° *or less* will (just) clear these hazards (the last one being a large drying rock called Roca Paredón). Once past Roca Paredón, if conditions allow it you can sail within a couple of hundred meters of the shoreline to get a photograph of the lighthouse, after which you round the little cay (Cayo Paredón Chico) to the west and anchor soon after in the lee of the cay (see below).

From the northwest, intermittent reef extends from the northern half of Cayo Paredón Grande to the northern tip of Cayo Coco. A heading of 112° *or more* on the lighthouse will keep you outside the reef (just outside toward Cayo Coco; well outside as you near Cayo Paredón Grande).

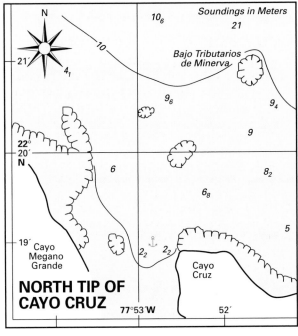

NORTH TIP OF CAYO CRUZ

Adapted from ICH 1129
Courtesy GeoCuba

Anchorage

The bottom shoals well out from the west side of Cayo Paredón Grande. Once past the western tip of Cayo Paredón Chico you should proceed slowly into the lee of the cay and then anchor in 2–3m, finding a patch of sand (of which there are many) in which to drop your anchor. As good a spot as any is immediately due south of the western tip of Cayo Paredón Chico, with the lighthouse bearing approximately 040°. In the rainy season, when the mosquitoes are fierce, it might be advisable to anchor further offshore.

Cayo Coco

Cayo Coco has miles of beautiful beaches which are aggressively being developed for tourism, but even so the island is large enough for the impact to be confined to relatively small stretches of the coastline.

Much of the island is inaccessible to visiting sailors, but there is a 'marina' development (PuertoSol) on the SE coast which offers quite good shelter in most conditions (including a norther), and from where a taxi can be hired to reach the hotel district, while at the NW tip of the island there is a reef anchorage off Punta Coco close to miles of lovely, pristine beach, untouched by the tourist industry.

Approaches

From the east (Paredón Grande), care must be taken in approaching the east coast of Cayo Coco since there are a fair number of scattered reef areas and shoal patches, between which there is a great deal of deep water. The easiest way to get to both the marina and the Punta Coco anchorage is to come outside all the reef, keeping the lighthouse on Paredón Grande on a backbearing of 112° *or more* (i.e. a heading of 292° or more).

For the marina, when west of 78°18·5'W follow the directions below.

For Punta Coco simply continue on the 292° heading until off the north coast of Cayo Coco, and then curve to the west paralleling the shoreline, remaining ¼M or more offshore (in rough weather it is advisable to stay further offshore since the relatively shoal water to the north of Cayo Coco can result in some unpleasantly steep seas). Once past Punta Coco, see the directions below.

From the west, there is a line of scattered coral patches between the Cayos Guillermitos and Punta Coco. The safest course of action is to stay outside of this area, keeping the northern tip of Cayo Coco on a bearing of 105° *or more*, although it is quite possible to navigate well inside this line but in this case you will need the Cuban charts and will need to maintain a precise plot of your position.

For Punta Coco, see below.

For the marina, continue around the northern coast of Cayo Coco at least ¼M offshore (in rough weather further offshore, since the relatively shoal water to the north of Cayo Coco can result in unpleasantly steep seas), until you can see the lighthouse on Cayo Paredón Grande. Remain far enough offshore to keep the lighthouse on a bearing of 112° *or more*. When east of 78°19·6'W, see the directions below.

Marina entry and anchorage

There is no channel as such to the marina, although by the end of 1995 there are plans to have a properly marked, dredged (3·5m) channel, so what follows may be redundant before it is published.

From outside the line of the reef you need to come through a large break, whose eastern edge is at approximately 22°31·7'N 78°18·4'W (note that the reef here extends to the west of its charted position on the Cuban charts), and whose western edge is at approximately 22°32·2'N 78°19·8'W – a median position of approximately 22°32·0'N 78°19·2'W will keep you well clear of both reef areas.

Head in a southerly direction to a position at approximately 22°31·2'N 78°19·2'W, which is a little to the west of an isolated coral patch. The depths are highly variable, mostly over 4m but with isolated patches of not much over 2m at low water, so this is not a recommended entry in a deeper draft vessel in rough conditions.

At the position above, you will be able to see Cayo Queche, an isolated cay to the east of Cayo Coco, on the horizon. Maneuver to place its eastern edge on a bearing of 140°, then head directly for this eastern tip, maintaining this bearing (i.e. making any corrections necessary to compensate for a tidal set). The depths will steadily shoal until off the tip of the conspicuous sandy shoal that comes out from Cayo Coco there is (barely) 1·8m at low tide (this is the controlling depth for the channel; the tip of the shoal is currently marked with a small, hard-to-see stake).

When the tip of the long rubble dock is more or less due south, head straight for it, coming into the lee of its northern side (by the time this is published, there should be a considerable breakwater from the tip of the dock, hooking back into the land, with provision for a number of boats to moor Mediterranean-style on the inside in minimum depths of 2m). The 'marina' currently has no water, dock-side electrical hookups, or fuel. They do monitor VHF Ch 16 and if requested will assist in guiding boats to the dock.

The Guarda have a post at the head of the dock; they will soon be out to check your papers.

When leaving, head more or less due north from the tip of the dock until the eastern tip of Cayo

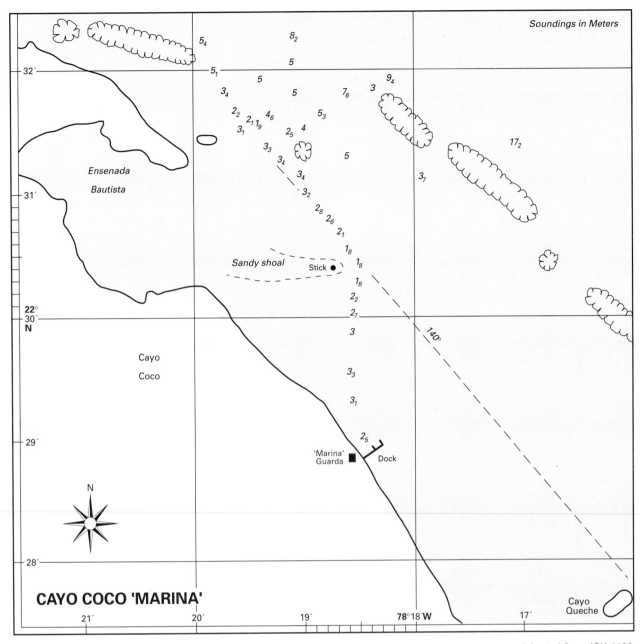

Soundings in Meters

CAYO COCO 'MARINA'

Adapted from ICH 1129
Courtesy GeoCuba

Queche is on a back-bearing of 140°, and then continue on a heading of 320°, making whatever course adjustments are necessary to keep Cayo Queche on the back-bearing of 140°. When east of the isolated cay to the east of Cayo Coco, head due north into deep water.

Note There are plans to dredge and mark another channel to the marina from a break in the reef, which is to the NE of the dock, down to the tip of the dock, passing through a charted sand patch. Longer-term plans include the construction of a 400-berth marina in the Ensenada Bautista, an exceedingly well protected location on the eastern side of Cayo Coco.

Punta Coco entry and anchorage

To the west of Punta Coco there are a couple of substantial reef patches. Between the two patches is a reef entry that leads into the lee of the sickle-shaped eastern reef patch. The reef breaks almost all swells creating a reasonably comfortable anchorage in all but northers and strong northeasters. There is plenty of attractive coral while Punta Coco, 1M to the east, and the beach to its south, are lovely and well worth visiting in the dinghy.

To enter the anchorage come to a position at approximately 22°33·8'N 78°27·2'W and head in a

211

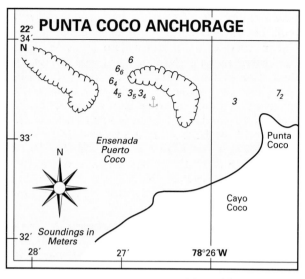

PUNTA COCO ANCHORAGE

Adapted from ICH 1129
Courtesy GeoCuba

Cayo Guillermo

Cayo Guillermo has some great beaches and lovely coral which are the basis for a major tourist development. Numerous small *cabañas* are grouped around a central pool/bar/restaurant complex. The hotel (Villa Cojimar) welcomes visiting sailors. The restaurant serves buffet-style meals at $15 per person. There is an international phone (☎ 30 10 11) and fax (33 55 54), car rentals, and diving ($27 per dive; dive instruction available). You can even rent a room for two people, with all meals included, for $72 per night.

A rickety wooden dock at the SE tip of the cay is used to get the guests on and off the dive boats, charter boats, and so on. A 2m draft can be carried alongside the tip of the dock, and there is ample room to anchor off its head in 3m, but the access channel has a controlling depth of 1·6m at low tide, although 2m can be got through at high tide. This anchorage can be used in a norther, although it is likely to be uncomfortable (it is wide open to the north, but there is enough shoal water to break up the worst of the seas).

North of Cayo Guillermo are two lovely, grass-clad rocky cays, the Cayos Guillermitos, both of which have well protected anchorages in prevailing winds. The only inhabitants are numerous birds (mostly terns – please stay off the islands during nesting season, from March to the end of June).

southerly direction between the two reef areas, with the depths shoaling to about 4m. When at latitude 22°33·5'N head due east into the arc of the reef, anchoring when the bottom shoals to about 3m. The entry and path into the back of the reef appear to be free of coral heads until close in to the reef, but nevertheless this should be treated as a good-light, calm-conditions entry only.

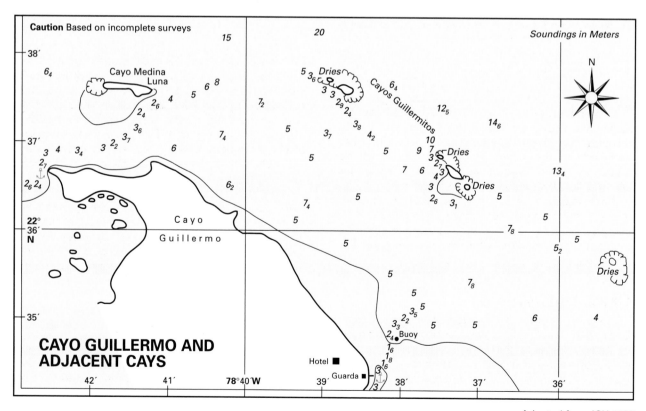

CAYO GUILLERMO AND ADJACENT CAYS

Adapted from ICH 1129
Courtesy GeoCuba

Behind the NW tip of Cayo Guillermo there is a particularly well sheltered anchorage in prevailing winds (but wide open to a norther), but with not much to see ashore (mostly mangroves).

Approaches to the hotel dock

The 5m line makes a broad arc around the bay between Cayo Guillermo and Cayo Coco, with intermittent patches of reef well to seaward more or less on a straight line between the northern tip of Cayo Coco and the Cayos Guillermitos. You can pass between these reef patches in numerous places, making for a position on the 5m line at 22°35·3'N 78°37·8'W from where you will be able to see a white buoy more or less to the south, with the dock beyond.

Come past the buoy leaving it 10m or so to port (i.e. you pass to the west of it) and then aim for a point a little to the east of the tip of the dock, on a heading of approximately 210°. On the approach to the buoy the depths will shoal fairly rapidly from 6 or 7m to 2·5m, and then beyond the buoy, in a conspicuous sandy area, reduce to as little as 1·6m at low water, before increasing again to over 3m off the dock.

The north side of the dock is shoal. On the south side, the inner edge of the channel leads away to the SW more or less in line with the tip of the dock, with the water shoaling very abruptly to well under 2m on the landward side of this line. A narrow slot has been dredged into this shoal to allow a 1·8m draft to be brought alongside the south side of the dock, but there is very little room to maneuver. Rather than try and come alongside, it might be better to simply anchor off just to the SE of the dock. The bottom is surprisingly hard; we had trouble setting a plough, whereas the Danforth-type took an immediate hold.

This anchorage is exposed to the east and can be somewhat rolly, especially since there is a tide through the channel which often sets the boat broadside to the waves. Better protection will be found by proceeding a little further down the channel toward the highly visible causeway.

When taking a dinghy in to the hotel dock, note that the cross boards have been nailed down with excessively long nails which protrude on the underside, so take care when bringing an inflatable alongside!

Cayos Guillermitos

The Cayos Guillermitos consist of two small cays. Both cays have attractive anchorages on their western sides with good protection in prevailing winds, but exposed in northers. Both are outside the line of the reef, and can be approached from any direction.

Eastern cay The eastern cay has a rocky caylet to both its SE and its NW (neither shown on the Cuban charts). Shoal water with some scattered coral extends a short distance to the east and west of these two caylets. Another shoal lines the south coast, extending to the SW of the center part of the cay in a series of conspicuous sandy patches. To the north of this sandy shoal there is a small cove on the western side of the cay with deep water (3m) almost onto the beach and up to the south side of the small caylet to the NW. To anchor, come into this cove from any point between the NW and SW and then drop the hook when the bottom shoals out close inshore.

Western cay The western cay has a rocky drying caylet to its NW (not shown on the Cuban charts), with a shoal area containing scattered coral that extends further to the west than the reef area shown on the Cuban charts, so if approaching from the NW stay well clear of this side of the cay. Shoal water also extends to the south of the eastern half of the island. But on the western side, where there is a small cove, deep water (3m) runs in close to the shoreline. To anchor, come into this cove from any point between the WNW and SW and then drop the hook when the bottom shoals out close inshore.

Anchorage off NW tip of Cayo Guillermo

The NW tip of Cayo Guillermo is a rocky headland. Immediately to the south, on the western side of the cay, there is a bay which affords complete protection from easterly winds but is wide open to northers. To reach this bay you can either work along the north coast of Cayo Guillermo, or come down from the north, leaving Cayo Media Luna ¼M or more to port (i.e. passing to the west of it) and heading directly for the headland. If coming along the coast of Cayo Guillermo, you need to stay over toward Cayo Guillermo (¼M or so off the coast) since it is quite shoal up toward Cayo Media Luna.

Once at the headland, it can be rounded fairly close inshore (but watch out for fishing nets just south of it), after which you are in the lee of the cay. The bay to the south and SE is shoal, so you should come in slowly toward the beach close to the headland and anchor when the depths reduce to about 2m.

Cayos Santa María

The Cayos Santa María are a pretty group of cays with an impressive red-and-white striped lighthouse on the central one (Cayo Caimán Grande). The cays contain several anchorages that are well protected in prevailing winds, and one way or

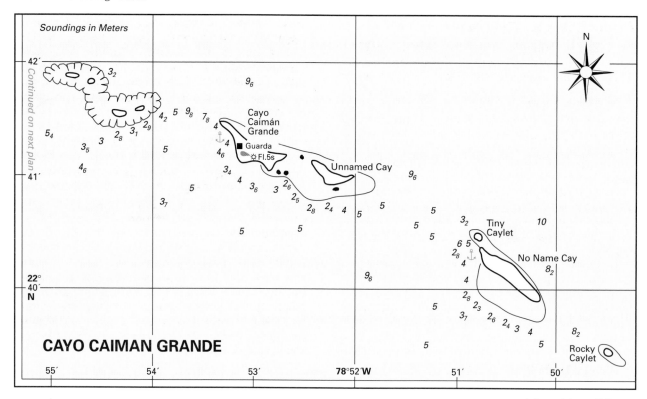

Soundings in Meters

CAYO CAIMAN GRANDE

Adapted from ICH 1128
Courtesy GeoCuba

another a fair amount of protection can also be found in a norther.

Approaches

From the east, the area between Cayo Media Luna (the cay to the north of Cayo Guillermo) and the Cayos Santa María is relatively free of coral, but this just makes the few patches that do exist all the more dangerous. All can be avoided by staying to seaward of an imaginary line drawn between the Cayos Guillermitos and the light on Cayo Caimán Grande (a bearing of 285° *or less* on the light).

This approach will bring you north of a small rocky caylet, and then just north of a larger cay with a tiny caylet off its western end. There is then a mile-wide break between this cay and the next cay (an unnamed cay to the east of Caimán Grande). If offshore, you can come south through the center of this break (at approximately 22°40·8'N 78°51·5'W.) to anchor in the lee of the cay to the east (see below), or else proceed to the anchorage at Cayo Caimán Grande (see below).

Instead of sailing outside the reef areas, a smoother run will be had by working through the relatively shoal water on the inside, but to do this you will need the Cuban charts and a GPS, and will need to keep close track of your position.

From the west, a heading of 090° *or less* on the light stays clear of all dangers. If you stray north of this line (which corresponds to 22°41·2'N latitude)

you will end up in some quite shoal areas south of Cayo Caimán (to the west of Cayo Caimán Grande) and also south of the unnamed cays between Cayo Caimán and Cayo Caimán Grande (these unnamed cays are foul with shoals and rocks and should be given a wide clearance).

Eastern cay (no name)

At the eastern end of the Cayos Santa María there is a small rocky caylet, and then a substantial cay with no name. An extensive area of relatively shoal water extends up to 1M to the south of the no name cay, but apart from some coral heads south of the SE tip of the island there appears to be at least 2·5m over the entire shoal, with considerably more in most places, and no coral heads.

At the western tip of the cay there is a little cove with a sandy beach. To the NW is a tiny rocky caylet. Between the two is a very shallow shoal. Relatively deep water (3m) runs almost onto the beach and then around to the caylet to the north. In prevailing winds a beautiful, protected, little anchorage will be found by coming in from the west until almost on the beach, and then dropping the hook in the edge of the sand extending to seaward from the beach. The holding in the sand is good; off the sand it is not too good. A refreshing breeze comes in through the slot between the cay and the caylet.

Cayo Caimán Grande

An anchorage suitable for vessels of any draft will be found on the western side of Cayo Caimán Grande. There are no problems entering here. The water along the south coast of Cayo Caimán Grande is relatively deep and free of hazards, as is that to the west and in the break to the north between Cayo Caimán Grande and the small cays to the west. If entering from the north, come to a position at approximately 22°41·6'N 78°53·7'W and head south.

To anchor, simply come into the lee of the cay and anchor when close inshore, under the watchful eye of the rather splendid Guarda post. Protection is excellent in prevailing winds, but not good in a norther (but in this case, you can just hang off the south shore of the cay). You can dinghy around to a beat-up steel dock on the south shore, where a path leads to the Guarda post and from there to the lighthouse, and ascend the lighthouse to get a wonderful view over the surrounding cays.

Cayo Caimán

Cayo Caimán is a pretty, grass-covered rocky cay with a single palm tree and a single conspicuous pine tree, which can be seen from miles away, on its summit. To the south of the cay is a floating fishing station.

Approaches

From the east, shoal water extends to the SE and south of the cay. To avoid it you should stay south of latitude 22°41·4'N until the conspicuous tree is to the north of you, and then curve around toward the cay, staying to the west of the fishing station (which is on the edge of the shoal).

Note For those coming from offshore, there is a 1½M wide gap between Cayo Caimán and the rocky caylets to its east, with a relatively deep-water passage through it. However, there is a dangerous rock awash about midway across this gap (the channel runs to the west of it) while coral extends some way out from the east side of Cayo Caimán into the channel: this passage should be treated as a good-light, calm-conditions, entry. If in doubt, come to the west of Cayo Caimán (see below).

From the west, the approaches are clear, with the exception of a reef that extends ½M to the west of the western tip of the cay. This reef terminates in a dangerous drying rock. Beyond this, there are no off-lying hazards.

Anchorage

The water is relatively deep on the south shore close into the western tip of the island, but then gradually shoals the further east you go, with the edge of the shoal water curving to the SSE past the fishing station. You can anchor anywhere in the lee of the SW side of the island.

Cayo Santa María to Cayo Francés

Another lovely area! The north shore of Cayo Santa María is one long beach, currently undeveloped, but a causeway has been built out from the mainland so it will not be long before the hotels and condominiums appear. To the west of Cayo Santa María a substantial bay contains numerous drying rocks and small cays, with a fair sprinkling of gorgeous little beaches between rocky headlands. On the south side of this bay are yet more,

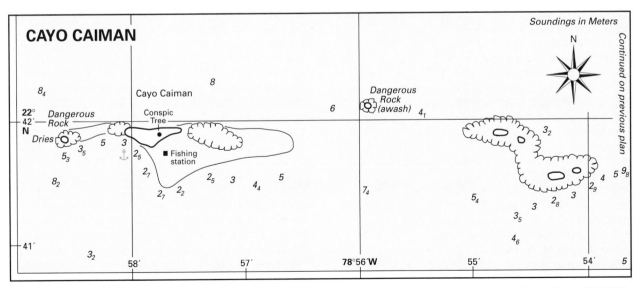

Adapted from ICH 1128
Courtesy GeoCuba

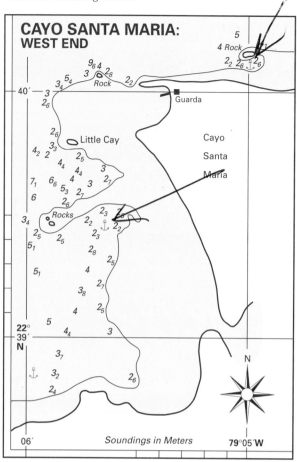

CAYO SANTA MARIA:
WEST END

Guarda

Little Cay

Cayo
Santa
Maria

Rock

Rocks

22°
39′
N

06′   *Soundings in Meters*   79°05′W

Adapted from ICH 1128
Courtesy GeoCuba

number of good anchorages. One way or another, you should plan on spending some time here.

Cayo Santa María

In calm conditions it is possible to anchor off the beach on the north shore (relatively deep water runs almost to the shoreline, especially at the western end) but there is no protection. At the western tip of the island there is a small, rocky caylet more or less on the 2m line. By hooking around its western end it is possible to carry 2m between it and the beach for a beautiful lunch stop.

The western tip of Cayo Santa María ends in a rocky point, with an off-lying rock to the west. South of this rock is a tiny caylet. Shoal water, with scattered coral extends from the tip of Cayo Santa María to the rock, and then arcs to the west on its way down to the caylet. The edge of the shoal then runs to the SE toward the coastline, before coming back out to the SW in a narrow, shallow spit that terminates in two or three substantial drying rocks. South of this spit there is a good deal of reasonably deep water (2·5–5m) all the way down to the beaches in the south.

In prevailing winds you can anchor anywhere off this western coast with excellent protection. In a norther, good protection can be found by tucking in to the south of the shoal spit.

Cayo Diablito and Cayo Borracho

These are two rocky cays with attractive little patches of sand. Good protection can be found in any conditions in the sound that is bordered by the two cays to the north, and Cayo Cobos to the south.

completely undeveloped, spectacular beaches (but there is now a road). Scattered around the bay are some great coral patches. Here and there are a

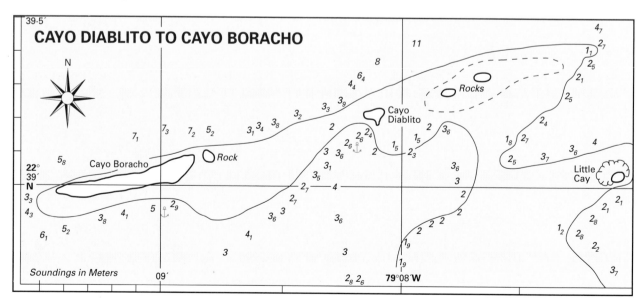

CAYO DIABLITO TO CAYO BORACHO

N

Cayo Boracho

Rock

Cayo
Diablito

Rocks

Little
Cay

22°
39′
N

Soundings in Meters   09′   79°08′W

Adapted from ICH 1128
Courtesy GeoCuba

Approaches and anchorages

From the east, all approaches to the sound from south of the cays are blocked by various shoals, so to enter the anchorages you have to keep to the north of the reef and cays as far as a break between Cayo Borracho and Cayo Francés. On the way to this break, note that a shoal runs between Cayo Diablito and Cayo Borracho more or less on a line between the north coasts of the two cays, but with a slight extension northward at the east end of Cayo Borracho. To the north of this there is deep water with no hazards. Come west in this deeper water to a position at approximately 22°39·0'N 79°09·8'W, and then head south past the western tip of Cayo Borracho.

Note that shoal water, with scattered coral, extends a little more than 200m to the west of Cayo Borracho, so don't cut the corner. Once south of Cayo Borracho you can head east fairly close inshore and anchor at any point. If continuing to Cayo Diablito, at the eastern end of Cayo Borracho you must come approximately 300m south in order to avoid a shoal with scattered coral that extends over toward Cayo Diablito. At Cayo Diablito, anchor a couple of hundred meters off the south shore.

From the west, you can come around the north shore of Cayo Francés, where there are no off-lying

hazards, to the position at approximately 22°39·0'N 79°09·8'W, and then proceed as above.

Alternatively, come through the channel (the Canal de las Piraguas) to the south of Cayo Francés (see below).

Cayo Francés

Cayo Francés is not particularly interesting, being mostly mangroves, but it does have a couple of good, all-weather, anchorages.

The cay is wedge-shaped, with deep-water all along the north shore, and the 2m line close inshore along the southern shore. At the northwestern tip of the island a shoal extends south. Inside of this shoal there is a well protected anchorage. To the south of Cayo Francés are numerous small mangrove cays surrounded by extensive shoals. Between them and Cayo Francés is a channel, the Canal de las Piraguas, which also is extremely well protected.

Approaches

From the east, you can either stay offshore and hook around the western tip of Cayo Francés, or pass through the break between Cayo Francés and Cayo Borracho (see above) and head down to the Canal de las Piraguas (see below).

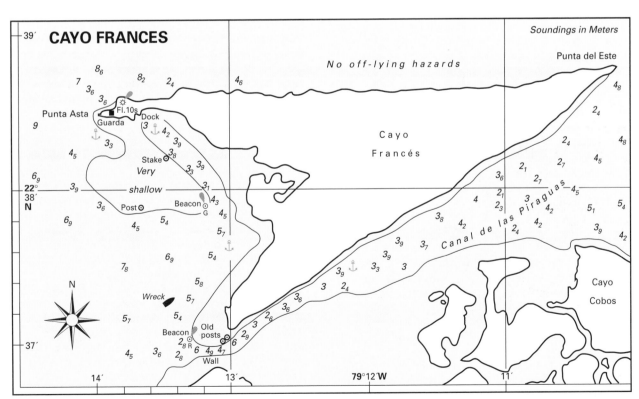

Adapted from ICH 1408 and
an old DMA survey
Courtesy GeoCuba and DMA

From the west, stay well off Cayo Fragosa when approaching Cayo Francés, since shoal water extends almost 2M out in places. A heading of 122° *or more* on the Cayo Francés light (a white concrete tower, Fl.10s), or the Guarda post at the tip of the island, stays (just) to seaward of these hazards.

Anchorages

Canal de las Piraguas The canal is shaped like a funnel, with the open end to the east. Water is deep (3m or more) from the eastern tip of Cayo Francés down to the rocky headland to the south (on Cayo Cobos). Proceeding westward along the canal, the water is relatively deep into the mangroves on the south side of Cayo Francés, but an extensive shoal extends to the west of Cayo Cobos, gradually narrowing the canal until it is only about 100m wide at the southwestern tip of Cayo Francés. Here the canal has a dogleg, marked on its north side by the remains of an old beacon (a couple of posts protruding just above water level) and a concrete beacon (red). The canal is up to 6m deep at this point, with a very abrupt wall on the south side which is visible in most light conditions.

The best place to anchor is about midway along the south shore of Cayo Francés, but watch for the relatively shoal patch in mid-channel at around longitude 79°11'W (it has just over 2m over it at its shallowest point).

West coast The anchorage inside the shoal is well marked. Coming from the Canal de las Piraguas, as soon as you round the southwestern tip of Cayo Francés you will see a large ferro-cement wreck – you can pass either side of this on the way to a green beacon a mile to the north.

You leave the green beacon close to port (i.e. you pass to the east of it), and then proceed NW on a heading just a little to the east of the lighthouse, anchoring off the dock (good holding).

Coming from the west, you must pass south of the post that marks the SW corner of the shoal, and then head east to the green beacon, after which you proceed as above.

Caibarien

Caibarien was once a prosperous sugar-exporting town. However, it has no deep-water access so the sugar was loaded onto barges to be transported out to ships anchored off Cayo Francés. Nowadays, of course, sugar is exported in bulk, so Caibarien has been put out of business, although it is still a port of entry to Cuba.

The city has quite a bit of colonial architecture and an abundance of lovely turn-of-the-century buildings with impressive facades, most of which are crumbling but some of which have been tastefully restored. Although it is quite a detour (15 miles

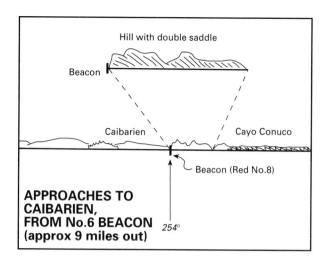

APPROACHES TO CAIBARIEN, FROM No.6 BEACON (approx 9 miles out) 254°

from Cayo Francés, with nowhere to go afterward except back to Cayo Francés – see below) if you have the time we think the town is worth a visit.

The charts show minimum depths of 2·7m in the approach channel, but in reality the controlling depth is closer to 2m. Once at the port area it is possible to carry 1·8m to the old city docks, which are a short walk from the town center, but the controlling depth is in fact closer to 1·6m. Boats with a 2m draft will have to anchor well off.

Approaches and entry

The only approach is down a marked channel from Cayo Francés. There would appear to be a channel from the east through the Bahía Buenavista, but this is now closed off by a causeway (fishing boats can get under the bridge, but a sailboat cannot). There would also appear to be a channel from the west through the Bahía de San Juan de los Remedios, but this is closed off by shoal water (1·4m) at the NW end of the bay.

The channel from Cayo Francés leads past the sea buoy (at approximately 22°38·4'N 79°15·1'W) on a heading of approximately 214° to a red lit beacon (*No. 4*) about 3½M away. The sea buoy can be passed on either side; the beacon is left to starboard (i.e. you pass to the east of it). Approaching the beacon there is a shoal patch (just under 2m) less then ¼M to the east, so you should hold over toward the beacon, passing it 50–100m off. At the beacon the depths are about 2·5m.

The next beacon (red *No. 6*) is 1½M to the SW, with very variable depths, which reduce to 1·8m close to the beacon (there are a number of keel stripes in the bottom to prove it). A little over 2m will be found by giving the beacon 100m clearance; more if you pass it a little more than ¼M to the east. This beacon, too, is left to starboard.

From the *No. 6* beacon the next beacon, which is 4M away on a bearing of 254°, is barely visible, but if you put the boat on the correct heading you will see on the horizon a low hill with a couple of saddles

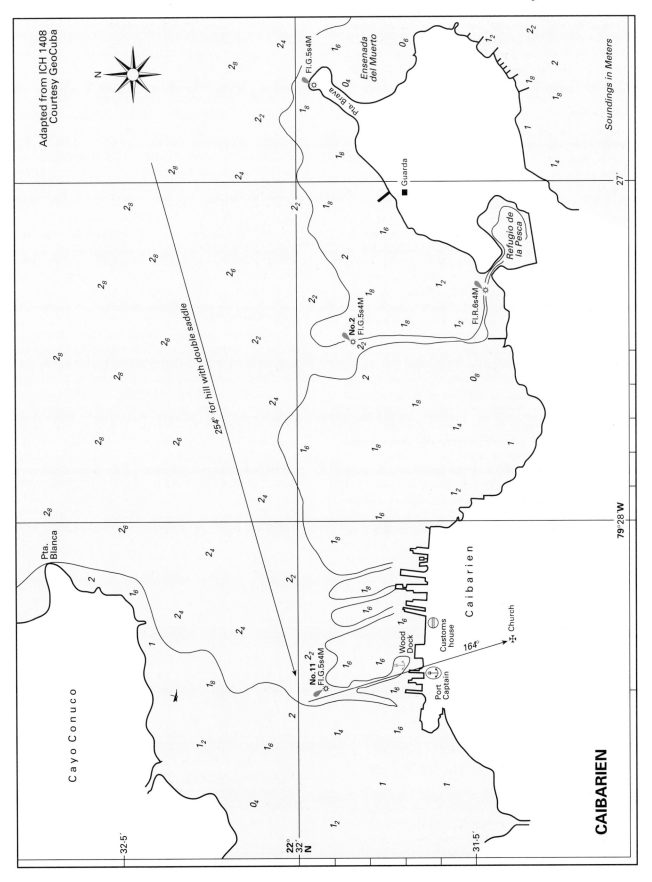

Adapted from ICH 1408
Courtesy GeoCuba

Soundings in Meters

Ensenada
del Muerto

Pta. Brava

Fl.G.5s4M

Guarda

Refugio de
la Pesca

Fl.R.6s4M

No.2
Fl.G.5s4M

254° for hill with double saddle

Cayo Conuco

Pta.
Blanca

No.11
Fl.G.5s4M

Wood
Dock

Customs
house

Port
Captain

Caibarien

164°

Church

CAIBARIEN

79°28' W

27'

32·5'

31·5'

22°
32'
N

and a steep edge to the east (see sketch); the beacon will be more or less lined up with this steep edge. In any event, just aim for the hill until the beacon is visible, and then leave it to starboard once again, continuing on toward the hill for another 4M. As you approach Caibarien you will be able to see the steel-frame light on Punta Brava.

Anchorages

The port area – for vessels drawing less than 1·8m. Keep heading for the hill, leaving Punta Brava almost ½M to port (i.e. passing to the NW of it). Once you are south of Cayo Conuco you will be able to see a red beacon (*No. 11*) to the SW. You make a broad arc around to the south, passing just to the west of the beacon (15m), and then heading towards the church spire (approximately 164°). The controlling depth of 1·6m at low tide occurs as you round the beacon (we carried 1·8m with some bumping).

Close to shore you will see a well restored building (the customs house) on the waterfront to the left with a substantial wooden dock out front. To the right of this is another substantial wooden dock, while ahead of you will be various pilings. Anchor just off the pilings in a small 2m pool, using a Bahamian moor to prevent your boat from swinging into the pilings or onto the nearby shallows. The Port Captain's office, where you check in, is straight ahead.

Off the Guarda dock – for vessels drawing over 1·8m. You come past Punta Brava a couple of hundred meters off, from where you will see a green (*No. 2*) beacon ahead. Anchor off the Guarda dock, which will be to port (i.e. to the south), outside of an imaginary line drawn between Punta Brava and the green beacon. You will have to dinghy in to the Guarda dock to clear in, and get a ride to town from here (the Guarda will try to get you to go to the port anchorage, insisting that 2m can be carried all the way, and telling you that their man will show you the way, but don't believe a word of it; their man got our 1·8m draft stuck, and it wasn't even low tide!).

Leaving Caibarien

Once off Punta Brava, keep the hill with the double saddle on a back-bearing of 254° until you pick up the channel markers.

Cayo Francés to la Isabela

To the NW of Cayo Francés is Cayo Fragosa, a 22M long cay without a single decent anchorage. Off the coast of Cayo Fragosa are one or two shoals and reef areas up to 2M offshore, close to where the bottom drops away into very deep water.

Between the northern end of Cayo Fragosa and the channels into La Isabela there are numerous small, mangrove cays, which at times are set several miles inside the 10m line. On the shelf between these cays and the 10m line are numerous shoals (some of them uncharted) and a number of rocks (one or two uncharted). In particular, there is an uncharted, low-lying, and particularly dangerous caylet right on the 10m line at approximately 22°59·0'N 79°48·4'W.

To navigate inshore in this area it is necessary to have the Cuban charts and a GPS, to keep a close and constant plot of your position, to maintain a bow watch, and to only sail in calm conditions and good light. It is much better to simply stay outside the 20m line, heading into deeper water anytime the bottom starts to come up.

The following are potential reef entries and anchorages.

Pasa Marcos

To the NW of Cayo Fragosa are the Cayos Pajonal. There is a substantial break between Cayo Fragosa and the Cayos Pajonal, with Cayo del Medio in the center, the Pasa Marcos to the north of Cayo del Medio, and what appears (on the Cuban chart) to be plenty of water to enter the sheltered sound inside the Cayos Pajonal. However, this entire area

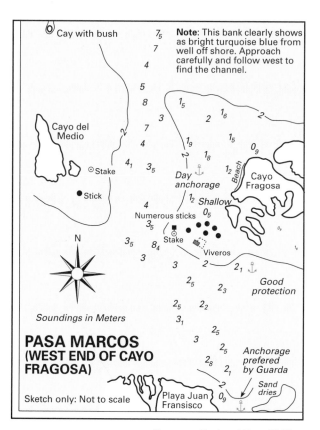

Courtesy Ned and Kate Phillips

has substantial shifting shoals, while the channel through the Pasa Marcos is completely unmarked. At times, significant tidal currents flow across the entrance. Further, if any seas are running they tend to drive up whatever channels exist.

It may be possible to carry 1·8m through the Pasa Marcos (we have been told it is), but the conditions were not suitable for us to confirm this. Even if it is possible, this is very much a calm-conditions, goodlight entry.

Note Ned and Kate Phillips have written to say that the channel runs between an extensive shoal to the NW of Cayo Fragosa, and another shoal to the east of Cayo del Medio (see their plan). There is an attractive lunchtime anchorage off the beach at the western tip of Cayo Fragosa. To the south is a shoal area with numerous stakes and *viveros* (fish farms). If a course is shaped around this shoal and the stakes and platforms, they report that a sheltered anchorage will be found off the south coast of Cayo Fragosa. However, the Guarda would not allow them to stay here, and instead moved them to a more exposed anchorage at Playa Juan Francisco, on the mainland.

Canal de las Barzas

This is another channel in an area with numerous shoals, significant cross-currents, and onshore seas in prevailing winds. The only beacon is well inside the pass; the channel is not at all clear. Reportedly, 2m can be carried inside, but we declined to try.

Cayo Datton

Cayo Datton is a mere speck of a cay to seaward of the Cayos Pajonal (at approximately 22°53·4'N 79°40·6'W). It is, however, set on a north/south axis,

with shallow reef extending to the north and NW, so that in prevailing easterly conditions it makes a pleasant sheltered anchorage (but it is not good in a norther).

Approaches

From the east, it is possible to come south of the isolated rock ½M to the east of Cayo Datton, aiming for the southern tip of the cay and simply rounding this into its lee, but the cay is hard to pick out against the cays behind it. It is easier to stay outside the 10m line until past the rock, and to then come south between the rock and Cayo Datton (at about longitude 79°40·5'W), hooking around the southern end of Cayo Datton into its lee.

From the west, stay outside the 10m line until 1M or so off, and then head SW to come into the lee of the island.

Anchorage

The water shoals well out from the western shoreline. Come in slowly from the west for the center of the cay and anchor in turtle grass when the bottom shoals to about 2·5m (it comes up quickly soon after this).

Note To the SW of Cayo Datton are numerous sticks. These have no navigational significance (they were once used for setting fishing nets).

Cayo la Vela

This is a speck of a cay, identifiable by its metal-frame lighthouse, at approximately 22°56·6'N 79°45·4'W. The cay is set on a substantial shoal. It provides a fair measure of protection in prevailing conditions. Since shoal water extends from the cay

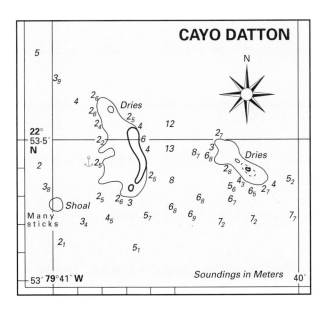

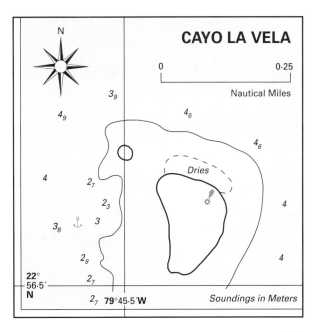

southward, the only approach is from the west. Boats coming from the east must come north of the cay until past the isolated rock just to its west, and then curve south into its lee. The bottom shoals a couple of hundred meters out from the shoreline, so you will have to anchor well off.

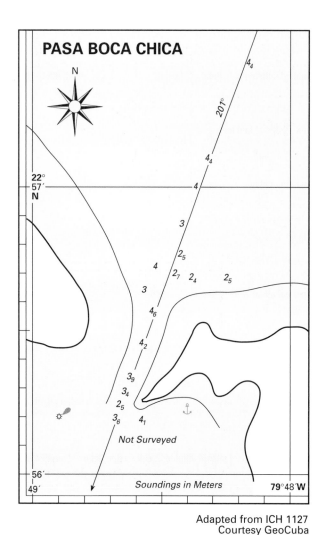

Adapted from ICH 1127
Courtesy GeoCuba

Pasa Boca Chica

The Pasa Boca Chica is a relatively deep (minimum 2·5m) channel between the cays which leads to a bay that is exceptionally well protected from the north and east (excellent refuge in a norther). The entry is straightforward. However, if coming from the west, beware of the dangerous, uncharted caylet mentioned above (at approximately 22°59·0'N 79°48·4'W).

Entry and anchorage

Come to a position at approximately 22°57·4'N 79°48·2'W, and then proceed on a heading of 201°. You will see the two headlands framing the entrance to the channel, with a distant headland more or less in the center of the channel. To the left, beyond the furthest mangroves, you will see a couple of faint hills. Go straight for these, holding to the bearing of 201°, and making any allowance necessary to compensate for tidal set.

Minimum depths approaching the channel will be a little more than 2·5m. At the entrance to the channel there are shoals on both sides – just stay more or less in the middle in 3–4m. As you go through you will be coming across to the eastern side of the channel until at the inner edge you simply round the sandy spit to the east about 100m off, arriving in a well protected bay where you anchor.

Pasa Boca del Seron

The Pasa Boca del Seron is a somewhat winding, but mostly deep and wide, channel that leads into the Puerto Sagua la Grande, the bay in which La Isabela is situated. Entry and passage are uncomplicated, although there are strong tidal currents (up to 3 knots); when the ebb is flowing against an onshore (north) wind it can be quite rough at the mouth. Once inside, there are numerous protected spots in which to anchor, although the boat will lie to the current rather than the wind.

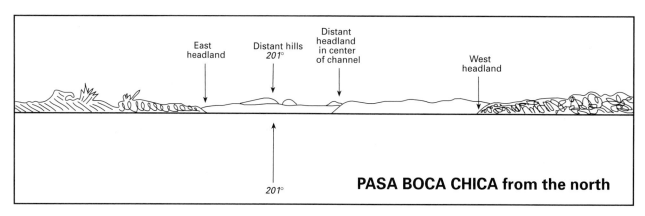

PASA BOCA CHICA from the north

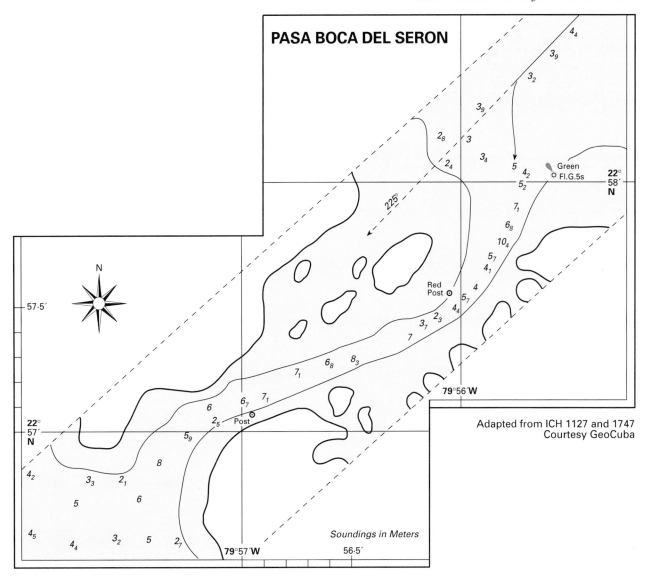

PASA BOCA DEL SERON

Green ☼ Fl.G.5s

22°
58'
N

Red
Post ⊙

79°56'W

Post ⊙

22°
57'
N

79°57'W

56·5'

Soundings in Meters

Adapted from ICH 1127 and 1747
Courtesy GeoCuba

Approaches

The entrance to the Pasa Boca del Seron is marked with a sea buoy (at approximately 23°00·7'N 79°53·5'W).

From the east, the buoy should be approached on a heading of 288° *or less* to stay outside of several dangerous shoals, and also the uncharted, rocky caylet mentioned above.

From the west, the buoy should be approached on a heading of 113° *or more* to avoid various off-lying hazards.

Entry and passage from the north

Once at the sea buoy you will be able to see a break in the mangroves (the only break in the mangroves) on a bearing of 225°. Head directly for this break until you can pick out a green beacon to port (i.e. to the east) then adjust your course to leave this beacon 100m or more to port (i.e. pass to the west of it).

Minimum depths on the approach to the beacon should be about 3m. Once past it the channel deepens to up to 10m, making a broad arc around to the SW, leaving a red post to starboard in the process, and then arcing back rather more to the south, leaving a green post to port.

The channel is relatively wide and deep, but with steep edges at times. It is more or less midway between the various cays. If the water begins to shoal out, make a couple of experimental zigzags to see where the deeper water lies. You will, at any rate, be able to pick out the deep water when the tide is running at full flood or ebb, since the current attains speeds of up to 3 knots, creating considerable turbulence in the channel.

At the southern end of the pass, don't cut the corner if heading to La Isabela since a shoal extends a couple of hundred meters off the west headland. For La Isabela, see below.

Entry and passage from the south

From the SW (La Isabela) the channel is hard to pick out against the mass of mangroves. To the west of it is another channel (Pasa Boca de Canete) with several channel markers at its south entry. This should not be confused with the Pasa Boca del Seron whose entrance is 1M further to the SE.

To find the channel, come to a position at approximately 22°56·5'N 79°57·7'W, from where the entrance will be clear enough. Proceed up the center of the channel, toward the NE. At the green post curve to the east, leaving the post to starboard. From here you should be able to see the red post, which is left to port, curving around toward the north to exit with the green beacon 100m or so to starboard (i.e. you pass to the west of it). Once past the green beacon take up a heading of 031° until you see the sea buoy, and then head for it.

La Isabela and the Puerto Sagua la Grande

La Isabela is reported to be a nice town with regular train service (5 times a day) to the larger town of Sagua la Grande inland, where there is an *agromercado* and dollar store. Unfortunately, we never even set foot ashore! The Guarda insisted that we go on their dock, and we refused since the approach channel is relatively shoal (reportedly less than 1·8m at low water) and at the time it was on a lee shore with a moderate breeze and waves. Having argued ourselves to a stalemate, we ended up simply leaving. We hope you have better luck.

The town is at the southeastern corner of a substantial bay, the Puerto Sagua la Grande. The northern rim of this bay is formed by a series of cays, between which are several navigable channels. Here and there are a number of well protected anchorages (but mostly surrounded by mangroves and not very interesting). The channels and anchorages are covered below, working from SE to NW across the bay.

Approaches and entry to La Isabela

This was once an active port, but is now more or less dead. Nevertheless, it still has an exceedingly well marked ship channel (the Canal Boca de Maravillas) beginning at the sea buoys (at approximately 23°02·0'N 79°58·0'W). The channel is subject to strong tidal currents (up to 3 knots) and when the ebb tide is running out against a northerly wind it can be exceedingly rough – it is best to time an entrance or exit for slack water. Alternative channels (which also have strong currents and can be rough) are the Boca del Seron (for boats coming from the east – see above) and the Boca de Sagua la Grande,

Pasa Cristo, or Pasa Boca Ciega (for boats coming from the west – see below).

The town of La Isabela is on a peninsula. The ship channel leads directly to the main port area, which is on the leeward (western) side of the peninsula and therefore well protected in prevailing winds, whereas the Guarda dock, where you are supposed to clear in and where they like you to moor, is on the windward side of the peninsula. To come to the Guarda dock, give the tip of the peninsula a wide clearance (½M), and then follow the markers into the mouth of the Río Sagua la Grande up to the Guarda dock. According to the very detailed Cuban harbor chart, the controlling depth is 1·5m. The Guarda claim otherwise, but we have heard this before . . .

Note Mike Stanfield of *Janetta Emily* has provided the following directions: 'Approach from the NE down the ship channel. At buoy *19* head 160° towards the wreck marked by the Boca del Río Sagua light, avoiding the two shoal patches shown on the chart approximately 300m north of the light. When about 10m west of the wreck come onto a heading of 235° towards the hammerhead wharf and Guarda post at approximately 22°56·5'N 80°00·5'W.' Mike reports minimum depths of 3m. No wonder the Guarda were so annoyed when I refused to believe them!

Ensenada del Jorobado

The Ensenada del Jorobado is a 2–3m deep bay 3M to the north of La Isabela. This bay is well protected in both northers and prevailing winds. To enter it, follow the ship channel (Canal Boca de Maravillas) to the red *No. 16* buoy, and then head to the NW from just north of the buoy (not south of it, since there are a couple of very shoal patches). Once into the Ensenada del Jorobado, come up the center of the bay and anchor when it begins to shoal to about 2·5m.

Pasa Boca Ciega

The Pasa Boca Ciega is a deep-water pass through the cays to the west of the Canal Boca de Maravillas. The pass is relatively narrow, not straight, unmarked, subject to strong currents, and has a very shallow shoal at its south end which is passed to the east or north. All-in-all, unless the light is right, and the seas on the outside calm, this is not a pass to use.

Pasa Cristo

The Pasa Cristo is a wide, relatively shoal, pass between Cayo Iguana and Cayo Esquivel del Sur. It has variable depths, with a considerable number of unmarked shoals. A minimum 2·5m draft (perhaps more) can pass through, more or less in center

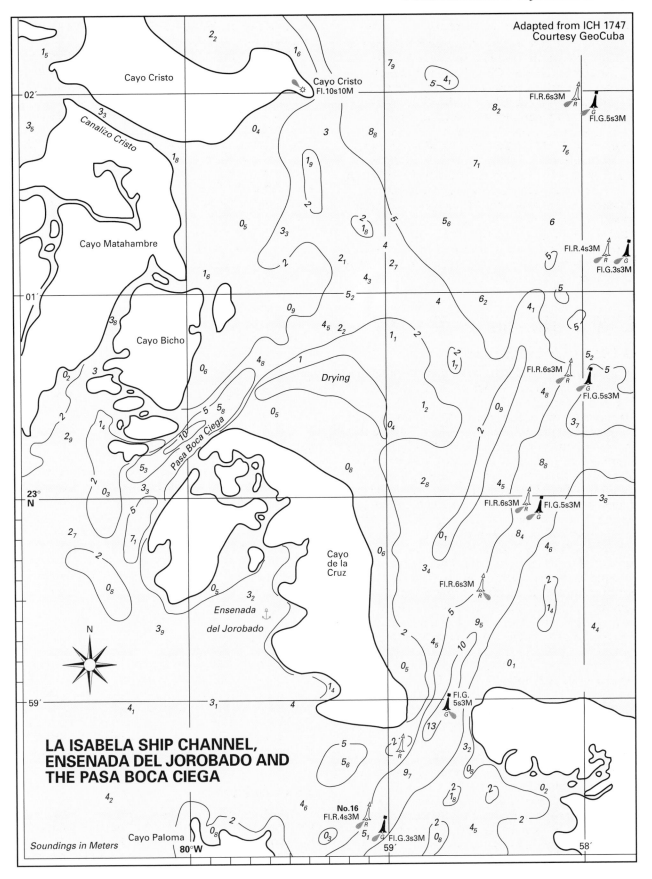

Adapted from ICH 1747
Courtesy GeoCuba

LA ISABELA SHIP CHANNEL, ENSENADA DEL JOROBADO AND THE PASA BOCA CIEGA

Soundings in Meters

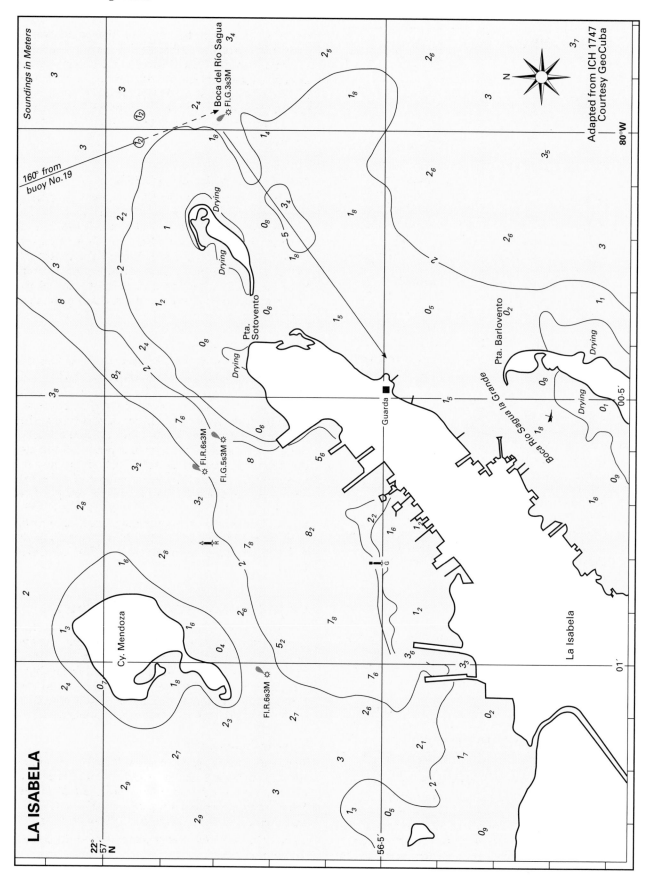

LA ISABELA

Soundings in Meters

Adapted from ICH 1747
Courtesy GeoCuba

N

80°W

Boca del Río Sagua
Fl.G.3s3M

160° from
buoy No.19

Drying

Drying

Pta.
Sotovento

Drying

Fl.R.6s3M
Fl.G.5s3M

R

G

Guarda

Pta. Barlovento

Drying

Boca Río Sagua la Grande

Drying

La Isabela

Cy. Mendoza

Fl.R.6s3M

22°
57'
N

00.5'

01'

56.5'

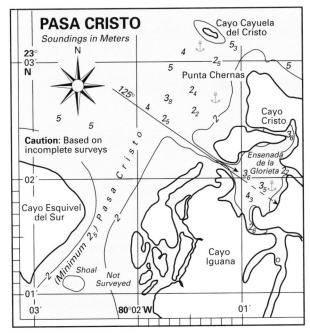

PASA CRISTO
Soundings in Meters

Caution: Based on incomplete surveys

Adapted from ICH 1747 and 1127
Courtesy GeoCuba

channel, but passing to the east or west of a substantial shoal at the south end. However, since there are no channel markers this is a good-light, calm-conditions passage.

At the seaward end of the pass there is a small cay, Cayuela del Cristo. West of this cay there is plenty of deep water; east of it there is a 3–4m deep channel between the cay and the reef that extends about ¼M to the NW of Punta Chernas (the headland at the NE entry to the pass). In prevailing winds a sheltered anchorage can be found in the lee of Cayo Cayuela del Cristo or the reef off Punta Chernas.

Ensenada de la Glorieta

A mile to the south of Punta Chernas there is a large lagoon, the Ensenada de la Glorieta, which forms a completely protected anchorage in any conditions (good for northers), but with nothing to look at but mangroves.

The entrance to the lagoon is between a couple of shoal areas. To enter it, come through the Pasa Cristo until you can look into the furthest part of the lagoon, on a bearing of 125° down the center of the entry channel. Proceed on this heading, making whatever allowance is necessary to compensate for any tidal set (which might be quite strong). Once inside the line of the mangroves at the entrance to the lagoon head to the north side of the channel to avoid a shoal in the center, and then continue straight into the lagoon. Inside there seem to be fairly uniform depths of 3–4m.

When leaving, stay over to the north side of the

channel, following the edge of the shoal water (which is especially visible as you pass out of the entrance into the Pasa Cristo). Once outside, head directly for the northern tip of land on the west side of the Pasa Cristo (311°), making whatever adjustments are needed to compensate for any tidal set. Continue on this heading until at least ¼M outside the lagoon.

Boca de Sagua la Grande

The Boca de Sagua la Grande is the west entrance into the Puerto Sagua la Grande. It is wide, relatively deep, reasonably well marked, and free of hazards. For boats coming from the west, it makes sense to enter here and sail through the protected waters of the bay to La Isabela; for boats coming from the east it makes sense to sail from La Isabela to this pass, rather than using the main ship channel to go back out to sea.

Approaches and entry

The mouth of the channel is marked by a red, lit sea buoy, which is at approximately 23°05·5'N 80°06·3'W. This buoy can be left on either side, although it is intended to be passed to the east. From here, so far as we could see, any course to the south will find at least 3m, but for the more cautious there are a series of beacons and posts delineating the deeper water (5m or so). To find the first of these (a red beacon, which is a couple of miles in) head approximately 206° from the sea buoy, after which you follow a course of approximately 125° past a couple of posts, continuing until La Isabela bears about 152°; you can then head straight for La Isabela, passing ½M or so to the SW of Cayo Levisa.

Cayo Hicacal (Esquivel del Sur)

Cayo Hicacal is a small cay which forms the northwestern tip of Cayo Esquivel del Sur. At the northwestern tip of Cayo Hicacal there is a small promontory on which there is a steel-frame light structure. In prevailing winds the area just to the south of the light structure makes a well protected anchorage, although it is wide open to northers.

Approach and entry

From the inside, you can cut well to the east of the marked Boca de Sagua la Grande channel, heading directly for the light structure from the SW. If the bottom begins to shoal, simply jog a little to the west and then come back toward the light once again.

From the outside, simply come around the point, 100m or so off.

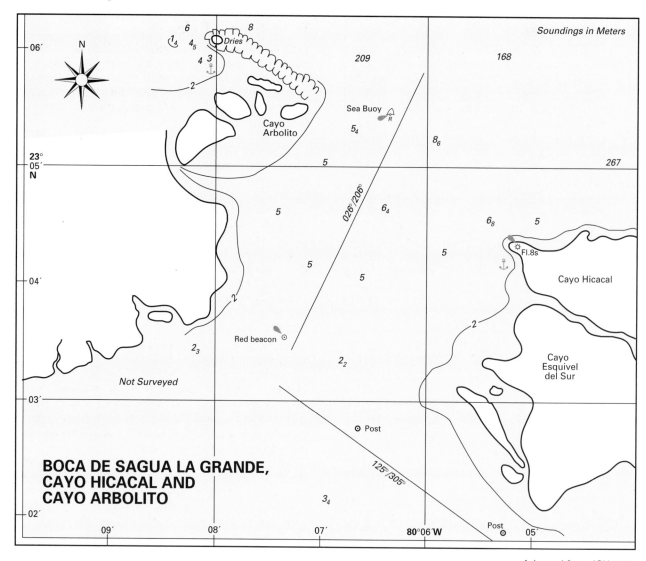

Soundings in Meters

**BOCA DE SAGUA LA GRANDE,
CAYO HICACAL AND
CAYO ARBOLITO**

Adapted from ICH 1127
Courtesy GeoCuba

Anchorage

2–3m can be carried quite close to the small beach to the south of the light, but then the bottom comes up quite fast, so it is best to anchor in about 2·5–3m.

Cayo Hicacal to Cayo Bahía de Cádiz

This is a potentially dangerous stretch of coastline with numerous sections of drying, and near-drying reef strung out on a SE to NW axis along the 10m line. The reef extends northward to the Arrecife de Nicolao (at approximately 23°14·4'N 80°21·8'W), at which point it is fully 5M north of the nearest cays. Inside the line of the reef the cays are almost entirely mangroves and as such uninteresting. There is simply no reason to go inside the line of the reef except to enter the anchorages listed below; the rest of the time you should stay outside the 20m line.

Cayo Arbolito

A solid section of reef closes the coastline at Cayo Arbolito, and then steadily diverges toward the NW. The reef ends after a mile or so, making it possible to hook around it to the west, coming into its lee. In prevailing winds this makes a pleasant reef anchorage (more attractive than the anchorage across the Boca Sagua la Grande at Cayo Hicacal), but it is wide open to northers.

Approaches and entry

Come to a position at approximately 23°06·4'N 80°08·2'W from where you will be able to see a small patch of always-dry reef (with a tiny bit of vegetation on it). This more or less marks the western extremity of the reef. Head south and then east into the lee of the reef, with the bottom shoaling from 6m down to 3 or 4, and then creep into whatever depth you feel is comfortable further in behind the reef.

Cayo Mégano de Nicolao

There is no cay at Cayo Mégano de Nicolao; simply one tiny hump of sand with a few scraps of vegetation. However, there is a substantial near-drying reef which breaks just about all seas from the NE to the SE, making this a lovely reef anchorage right out in the middle of nowhere.

Approaches

The waters surrounding Cayo Mégano de Nicolao contain a fair number of hazards, so great care must be exercised on the approaches. Fortunately, there is a buoy immediately to the south of the reef (at approximately 23°13·0'N 80°19·4'W) which can be used to get yourself oriented.

From the east, stay outside the 20m line until the buoy is on a bearing of 290° or less and then head straight for it.

From the west (Cayo Bahía de Cádiz), once around the shoals and reef immediately to the north of Cayo Bahía de Cádiz head due east (090°) until you pick up the buoy, and then maneuver to place the buoy on a bearing of 090°. Now head straight for the buoy, making whatever course corrections are needed to keep it on a constant 090° bearing. On this course you will cross a relatively shoal area (down to 3·5m) and then pass midway between a reef to the south, and an obstruction to the north, both of which will be about ¼M off.

Anchorage

Once in the vicinity of the sea buoy, simply hook around into the lee of the reef to the north and anchor in 3–4m somewhere in the area west of the tiny sand cay.

Pasa (Boca) Falcones

The Pasa Falcones is a substantial break between the Cayos Falcones (just south of the Cayo Bahía de Cádiz) and Cayo Blanquizal. The pass has fairly uniform depths of 3–4m, shoaling gently the further you go into the Bahía de Santa Clara, the large bay to the south.

On the southern side of the Cayos Falcones is a conspicuous fishing camp built on piles a couple of hundred meters out into the bay. The piles are driven into an extensive shoal, much of which dries at low tide. This shoal hooks out from the cays a little to the north of the fishing station, and then curves SW, following the coast, ending at the southern tip of the fishing station. If you come to the south of the southern end of the fishing station, and then hook north inside it, you come into a wonderfully protected anchorage which almost always has a breeze and so is free of bugs.

Approaches

The entrance to Boca Falcones is completely straightforward from either the north (Cayo Bahía de Cádiz) or the east (north of Cayo Blanquizal). However, there are reef and shoal areas off both Cayo Bahía de Cádiz and Cayo Blanquizal, so these cays should be given a good clearance; there is also, of course, the reef area around Cayo Mégano de Nicolao (see above).

Once clear of the various shoals and reef patches in the approaches, head for a position at approximately 23°09·7'N 80°28·4'W and then head for the fishing station which will be clearly visible. (For a plan see next chapter).

Anchorage

The entry is straightforward. You simply come around the fishing station, which has almost 3m at its southern end, and then come north midway between the buildings and various piles on one side, and the mangroves ashore on the other side. The further you sail toward the small point to the NE, the better the protection. Just off the mangroves are several abandoned metal frameworks which delineate the edge of the shoal water (the southern frame is submerged at high water, the northern one submerged at all times). The water is deep to within 20 or 30m of the mangroves to the NE, but when it does shoal, it does so quite suddenly. The holding is good.

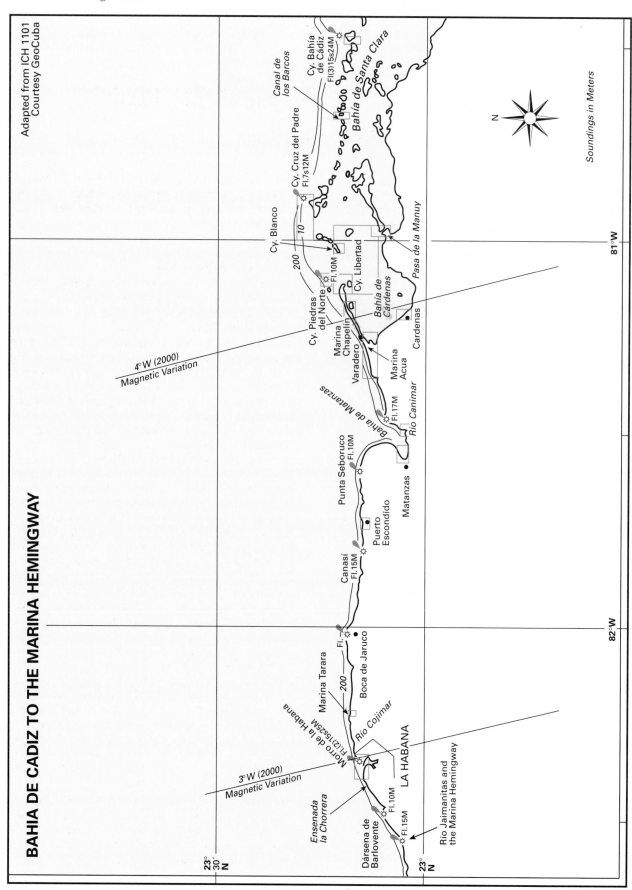

BAHIA DE CADIZ TO THE MARINA HEMINGWAY

Adapted from ICH 1101
Courtesy GeoCuba

Soundings in Meters

N

4° W (2000)
Magnetic Variation

3° W (2000)
Magnetic Variation

81° W

82° W

23° 30' N

23° N

Canal de
los Barcos

Cy. Bahía
de Cádiz
Fl(3)15s24M

Bahía de Santa Clara

Cy. Cruz del Padre
Fl.7s12M

Cy. Blanco

Bahía de
Cárdenas

Cy. Libertad

Pasa de la Manuy

Cy. Piedras
del Norte
Fl.10M

Marina
Chapelín

Varadero

Marina
Acua

Cardenas

Bahía de Matanzas

Fl.17M

Río Canimar

Punta Seboruco
Fl.10M

Matanzas

Puerto
Escondido

Canasí
Fl.15M

Fl.
Fl.200

Boca de Jaruco

Marina Tarara

Río Cojimar

Morro de la Habana
Fl.(2)15s25M

LA HABANA

Ensenada
la Chorrera

Fl.10M

Dársena de
Barlovente

Fl.15M

Río Jaimanitas and
the Marina Hemingway

230

10. Cayo Bahía de Cádiz to the Marina Hemingway

Between the Bahía de Cádiz and the Península de Hicacos, some 40M to the west, a series of primarily mangrove cays line the coast of Cuba. Behind the cays are two large bays, the Bahía de Santa Clara, and the Bahía de Cárdenas, both of which are broadly navigable by vessels up to 2m in draft, creating the possibility of an 'inside' passage along this part of the coast. Although the interior areas of the bays are dominated by mangroves, and as such are not particularly interesting (except for the bird life, notably large numbers of flamingos), we enjoyed picking our way through the various canals, and were exceedingly happy to be on the 'inside' as one cold front after another swept across the region during our explorations (in February).

To seaward of the cays there is an intermittent reef which, apart from a section to the west of Cayo Cruz del Padre, provides few opportunities to anchor in protected waters and therefore constitutes little more than a navigational hazard. The reef ends on the eastern side of the entrance to the Bahía de Cárdenas, and does not re-occur until well west of Havana. The western side of the entrance to the Bahía de Cárdenas is formed by the Península de Hicacos which is, on its seaward side, one long beach. Here we find Varadero, Cuba's leading tourist development, while immediately offshore lies the lovely little island of Cayo Piedras del Norte.

To the west of Varadero the coastline is mostly inhospitable with almost no opportunities to anchor or find shelter until the Marina Hemingway, 70M away. The eastern section of this coastline has some dramatic cliffs. Further west the cliffs give way to miles of beaches which terminate in the dramatic fortress of El Morro at the entrance to the Bahía de Havana. From here to the Marina Hemingway the shoreline is mostly built up. The one or two well protected inlets that do exist are all currently off-limits to visiting boats.

Winds

As elsewhere on the northern coast, average winds are from the ENE at about 10 knots. Seasonal variations include a succession of strong northers in the winter months (with the greatest incidence in January and February) and periods of calm in the summer months, broken up by the effects of tropical depressions, including northerly winds of 40–50 knots. Winds tend to be light at night, and build throughout the day.

Currents and tides

Offshore, the Antilles Current flows to the NW up the San Nicolás channel to converge with the Gulf Stream which sweeps in from the west and then hooks to the NE off Havana. The Antilles Current is typically weak (½ knot or so) and much affected by the wind (increasing to up to 2 knots with an ESE wind; reversing and flowing at up to 3 knots to the SE with a strong NW wind). The Gulf Stream is far more predictable, but is far enough offshore not to have much influence on coastal sailing (with the exception of that stretch of coastline from Havana to the Marina Hemingway, which has a fairly consistent NE current of about 1 knot).

Inshore, currents are generally weak and unpredictable, with the exception of tidal currents in some of the channels between the cays. These can attain speeds of up to 4 knots. The tides themselves are semi-diurnal (twice daily), though the pattern is increasingly irregular the further west you go. The average tidal range decreases from about 0·5m (20in) at the Bahía de Cádiz down to not much more than 0·25m (10in) at the Marina Hemingway. Within the Bahía de Santa Clara and the Bahía de Cárdenas, the tides are less than this.

Sailing strategies

Boats with a draft of less than 2m can sail through the interior areas of the Bahía de Santa Clara and the Bahía de Cárdenas in protected waters, making passages to both the west and the east relatively comfortable and easy in this stretch. But from the Bahía de Cárdenas to the Marina Hemingway it is a 70–80M passage in open water with little or no potential shelter along the way.

From east to west, so long as northers are avoided the wind should be at your back, making this an easy run. The last stretch should be made as close inshore as possible to avoid the current that runs to the NE along the coast.

From west to east, it can be a hard beat to windward. The best time to make this passage is at night when the wind and seas tend to be a little calmer. The coastline is well lit, with a string of major lighthouses, and no off-lying dangers until the eastern tip of the Península de Hicacos is reached (at which point you can head into the protected waters of the Bahía de Cárdenas). If the boat is well found, and the crew do not mind heavy-weather sailing, a favorable wind will be found during the early stages of a norther, but the winds are likely to blow at 25–30 knots, and maybe more.

Charts and magnetic variation

ICH *1126* and *1125* cover the coastline from the Bahía de Cádiz to just east of the Marina Hemingway at a scale of 1:150,000. In addition there are detailed charts of the Bahía de Cárdenas and the Bahía de Matanzas, and exceedingly detailed charts of the approaches to the port of Cárdenas, the Marina Acua, and, of course, Havana harbor. Finally, there is the chart book (Region 7: Bahía de Cádiz to Marina Hemingway) which covers this region.

Magnetic variation decreases (January 2000) from about 4°30'W at the Bahía de Cádiz to 3°00'W at the Marina Hemingway. In all areas it is increasing annually at a rate of about 8'W.

Bahía de Cádiz and Canal de Rancheria

The Bahía de Cádiz is dominated by the exceedingly tall black and white lighthouse (Fl(3)15s) on Cayo Bahía de Cádiz. In settled easterlies a reasonably well protected anchorage will be found to the SW of the light, but the more the wind is toward the NE, the greater the chance of an uncomfortable cross swell working its way into the anchorage.

A completely protected anchorage can be found for the night in a canal that cuts through the center of the Cayos Falcones from the Bahía de Cádiz to the Boca Falcones (Canal de Rancheria – see below), but the entrances are quite shoal (the controlling depth at both ends is 1·5m at low water; something over 1·8m at high water). A second excellent anchorage with an easy entry and minimum depths of 3m will be found on the south side of the Cayos Falcones by rounding Cayo Bahía de Cádiz to the north and then proceeding down the eastern side of the cay, and of the Cayos Falcones, for approximately 3M (see the end of the previous chapter for written directions).

The lighthouse on Cayo Bahía de Cádiz is a marvel and is well worth a visit. To get there you take the dinghy through the mangrove canal that separates the cay from Cayos Falcones. Midway through this canal, there is a fork to the north which winds through the mangroves for some distance before coming out at a dock beside the light.

The lighthouse was constructed in 1862 out of massive steel panels (25mm thick at the base) which were bolted together, entirely by hand. It has a spiral staircase with 199 steps, and then another 20 or 30 steps up to the observation platform and the light, with a magnificent view over the surrounding cays. As with many other Cuban lighthouses, the mechanism that turns the light is the original clockwork mechanism. This must be wound up twice a night. In addition to the trips to the top needed to wind this up, the lighthouse keepers go up each morning to put sunscreens over the windows (to protect the impressive fresnel lens from the sun) and then go up at nightfall to remove the screens.

Approaches to the Bahía de Cádiz

From the east, the safest course of action is to stay outside the 20m line until past the Arrecife de Nicolao (at approximately 23°14·4'N 80°21·8'W), after which you can aim directly for the lighthouse (visible from many miles away). When nearing the cay, stay ½M off the NE tip, and ¼M off the NW tip.

From the west, there are various reef patches close to the 10m line on the approaches to the cay, so the safest course of action is to stay outside the 20m line until past a position at approximately 23°15·0'N 80°37·0'W after which you can head directly for the light (110° *or more*), curving down toward the west side of the cay once past the Arrecife Lavanderas (at approximately 23°13·3'N 80°32·5'W).

Anchorage

Proceed slowly toward the area SW of the lighthouse, anchoring when the bottom shoals to 2–3m. The holding is none too good, but there are a number of small patches of sand – if you drop the hook in one of these it should get a pretty good bite.

Cayos Falcones canal (Canal de Rancheria)

This canal cuts through the Cayos Falcones from the Bahía de Cádiz to the eastern end of the Bahía de Santa Clara. It is relatively shoal at both ends (1·5m at low tide), and the south end in particular is not always easy to follow. Once inside the north end of the canal, there is plenty of room to anchor (on a muddy bottom), providing good protection in all conditions.

From the north The canal entrance is hard to detect. You should head for the south end of the Bahía de Cádiz to a point near 23°11·3'N

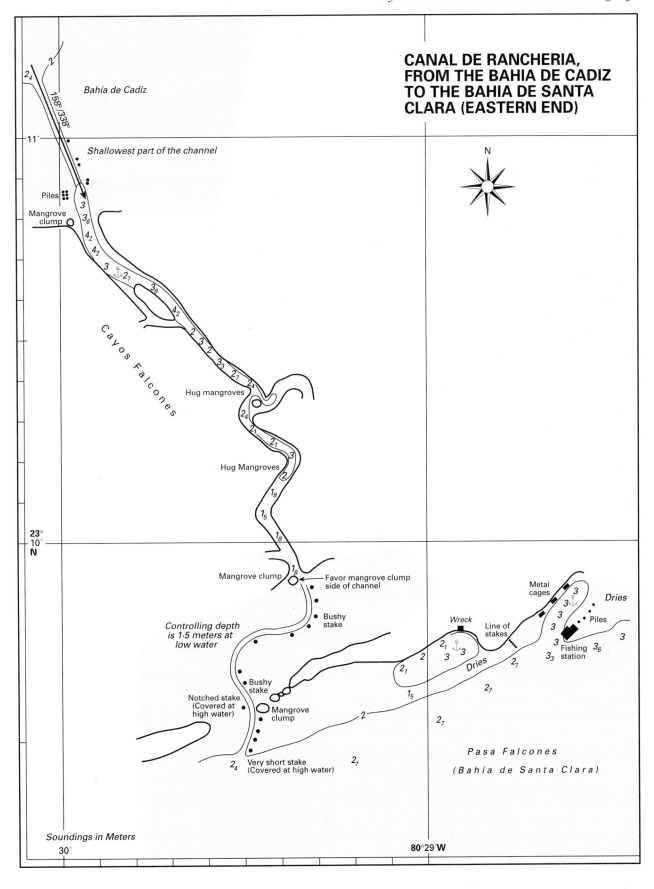

CANAL DE RANCHERIA, FROM THE BAHIA DE CADIZ TO THE BAHIA DE SANTA CLARA (EASTERN END)

N

Bahía de Cadiz

158°/338°

Shallowest part of the channel

Piles

Mangrove clump

Cayos Falcones

Hug mangroves

Hug Mangroves

Mangrove clump

Favor mangrove clump side of channel

Bushy stake

Controlling depth is 1·5 meters at low water

Bushy stake

Notched stake (Covered at high water)

Mangrove clump

Very short stake (Covered at high water)

Metal cages

Dries

Wreck

Line of stakes

Piles

Fishing station

Dries

Pasa Falcones (Bahía de Santa Clara)

Soundings in Meters

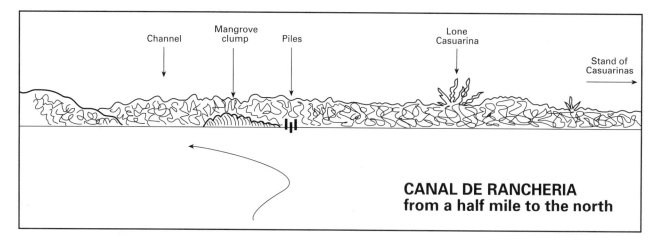

Channel   Mangrove   Piles   Lone   Stand of
           clump   Casuarina   Casuarinas

**CANAL DE RANCHERIA
from a half mile to the north**

80°30·1'W. To the west of the canal entrance (well to the west) is a very conspicuous stand of casuarinas, and then a little to the east of this is a single casuarina that is quite conspicuous. As you approach from the north, it will look something like the sketch. The bay will slowly shoal to about 2·4m. A little to the east of the lone casuarina you should, with binoculars, be able to pick out a group of pilings, and just to the east of the pilings an isolated clump of mangroves. These mangroves mark the west side of the channel.

Come in slowly for the group of pilings until you can pick out the line of stakes which mark the east side of the channel. You need to get lined up to come in on a heading of about 158°, leaving these stakes just 5–10m to port (no more than 10m) as you come in, making whatever allowance is necessary to compensate for the sometimes strong tidal set.

Approaching the first stake the depth will decrease to 1·8m, and then there is one shoal spot of about 1·5m between the first and second stake. After the third stake you must curve to the east to keep the next two stakes just 5–10m to port, and then curve back to the west and head for the center of the channel. The depths will steadily increase to 3m.

Once inside you should favor the west bank about midway toward the island, and then curve back to take the east channel past the island. The area to the north of the island makes a well protected anchorage with enough of a breeze most of the time to keep the bugs under control. Proceeding down the channel, at the next small island you must stay tight to the mangroves on the western bank, and then again after the next major bend. The channel now shoals – you will need someone on the bow to guide you.

Toward the south end it looks like there is no channel at all – just mangroves ahead, at which point the channel appears to take a sharp turn to the west. However, ignore the turn and keep on for the mangroves. A narrow channel will open up between the mangrove clump in center channel and the eastern shore. You should favor the mangrove clump

going out, and then follow the line of stakes, leaving these to port.

This last section of the channel is both narrow (10–15m in places) and shallow (as little as 1·5m at low tide). You should once again leave the stakes just 5–10m to port (certainly no more than 10) and should have someone on the bow to give additional guidance. The channel will come back to a southerly heading, hugging the west bank of a mangrove clump as you come out into the Boca Falcones. At this time, a number of stakes will be visible to the west – these should be ignored. Once past the mangrove clump there are three more stakes, but the last is almost submerged at high water. In any event, you will see a distinct cay on the horizon bearing 190°. If the last stick is not visible, aim just to the east of this cay after passing the second to last stick, heading south for 100m, and then head directly for the cay until into deeper water (2·4m), hoping you don't run aground in this final stretch (the channel is not at all well defined during this last stage)!

From the south Come to a position at approximately 23°09·3'N 80°29·6'W. Looking more or less north, things will resemble the sketch. You need to head west sufficiently to be able to pick out the Bahía de Cádiz lighthouse above the distant mangroves, bearing 012/3°, at which time it will be lined up on the western side of a distinct clump of mangroves, while more or less directly astern will be a distinct cay on the horizon bearing 190°.

Come in slowly for the west edge of the mangrove clump until you can pick out the channel stakes. The first one may be submerged at high tide. If it is not visible, line up the next two and then aim a little west of them (20m or so) on the run in, finally coming toward the stakes to leave them 5–10m off the starboard side. This first stretch is quite shoal (1·5m at low tide) and without a clearly defined channel until the second stake is reached – if you get this far without running aground, you are doing OK! Come past the west side of the mangrove clump and then follow the line of stakes as shown on the plan. If a forked stake is just visible (it is submerged at

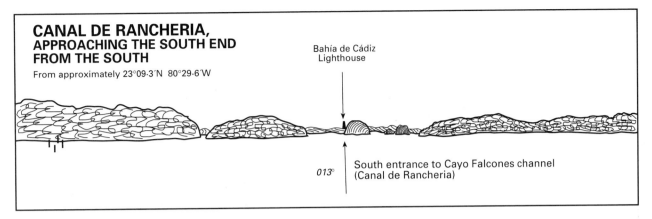

**CANAL DE RANCHERIA,
APPROACHING THE SOUTH END
FROM THE SOUTH**

From approximately 23°09·3'N 80°29·6'W

Bahía de Cádiz
Lighthouse

013°

South entrance to Cayo Falcones channel
(Canal de Rancheria)

high tide) leave this to port, and ignore the stakes further to the west of it.

The channel makes an inverted 'S' to bring you into the mangroves through a narrow gap between a mangrove clump and the cay itself. You should favor the mangrove clump side of the channel. Once inside, ignore the branch to the west, continuing north. At the small island, keep tight over to the mangroves on the western shore, and then at the larger island stay in the eastern channel.

Coming out at the north end, stay 5–10m off the stakes (no more), leaving them all to starboard, going more or less north to begin with and then curving to the NNW after the first two stakes. The shallowest part of the channel (1·5m at low water) is alongside the last two stakes, after which the depths slowly increase as you head NNW up the center of the bay.

Bahía de Cádiz to the Península de Hicacos (on the outside)

This is not a particularly hospitable or attractive stretch of coastline, being mostly mangroves ashore with intermittent patches of reef offshore. The reef is frequently well offshore and very close to the 10m line, which makes it potentially quite dangerous. As a result, many cruisers will likely choose the inside passage through the Bahías de Santa Clara and Cárdenas (see below), but for those who choose to stay on the outside, in settled or calm conditions, and in good light, there are a couple of areas worth exploring.

Cayo Cruz del Padre and its associated reef

Cayo Cruz del Padre (at approximately 23°16·8'N 80°53·9'W), has an odd-looking lighthouse that can be seen from several miles off. A considerable area of breaking reef extends to the WNW, with shoal water behind the reef. Further west the reef curves to the WSW, with a relatively deep channel between it and the cays behind. This reef has several navigable breaks allowing access to the protected water in the sound behind the reef. There are numerous opportunities to anchor here in settled and reasonably calm conditions, and to explore the coral.

Approaches and entry

From the east, after rounding the northern edge of the reef to the NW of Cayo Cruz del Padre, follow the line of the reef around until you come to a position at approximately 23°17·0'N 80°59·3'W (the depths will reduce to 6–8m). Sail in on a heading of 145° through a ½M wide break in the reef, maintaining a bow watch (there are some little bits of scattered coral, but we saw nothing of any size). The depths gradually reduce to a minimum of 2·5m well inside, and therefore out of the wave action, and then increase again.

Maintain the 145° heading until near latitude 23°16·0'N, at which time you can sail either east or west in the lee of the reef. If sailing east, head for the Cayo Cruz del Padre lighthouse (approximately 080°) until the bottom begins to shoal a couple of miles short of the light. If sailing west, head for the Cayo Piedras del Norte lighthouse (approximately 260°); on this heading you will sail out from behind the reef after a couple of miles, and can continue to Cayo Piedras del Norte or some other destination.

From the west, come to a position at approximately 23°15·5'N 81°02·0'W with the Cayo Piedras del Norte lighthouse on a back-bearing of 260°, and the Cayo Cruz del Padre lighthouse on a bearing of 080°, and sail toward the Cayo Cruz del Padre light. Depths will diminish to about 3m before increasing to mostly 5m or more for 3–4M, after which they shoal out. Anchor anywhere in a protected spot behind the reef.

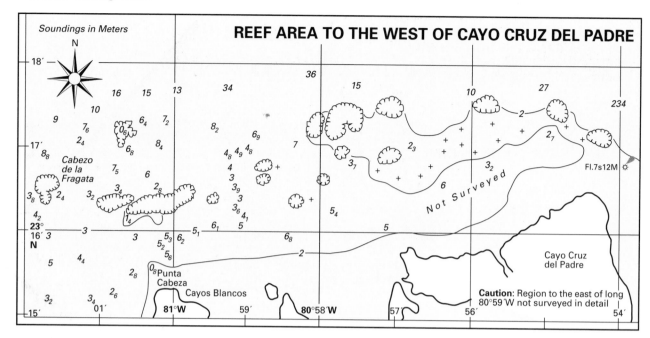

Adapted from ICH 1126
Courtesy GeoCuba

Cayo Piedras del Norte

Cayo Piedras del Norte is a beautiful, photogenic little island to the north of the entrance to the Bahía de Cárdenas. It has a great mixture of coral and beach, including shells, fossils, small caves (on the eastern and northeastern shore), blow holes, and a panoramic view from the top of the lovely stone lighthouse (in spite of the fact that this is a military observation post, the guards are happy to take you up and show you around). There is an extensive field of coral heads extending 200–300m offshore from the north and NE coast, in depths of 1·5–3m. If it is not too rough, there is some interesting snorkeling out here. Closer to the beach, there are colorful fishes flitting around the ruins of an old jetty.

The island makes an excellent day stop in settled weather, using either the Cayo Libertad or Cayo Blanco anchorages overnight (see below), but is not recommended as an overnight anchorage because of poor holding and uncertain protection if the weather changes. In heavy weather it is not possible to anchor off the island because of swells sweeping around it. Cayo Piedras del Norte is a popular stop for charter boats operating out of the Marina Chapelín and the Marina Gaviota, so to secure a good spot in an anchorage, head out early.

Approaches and anchorages

The approaches to the cay are free of dangers, with the exception of Cayo Monito and Cabeza del Coral, which are clearly marked. Closer inshore, beware the extensive area of coral that extends 200–300m or more to the NE, with some depths of a little over 1m well offshore. Aside from this area,

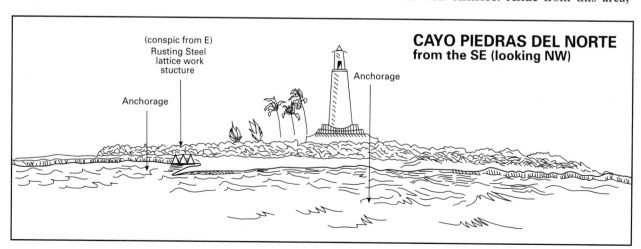

CAYO PIEDRAS DEL NORTE

Soundings in Meters

N

15′

5

4₈ 3₆ 3 3 3 3 Isolated coral heads 3

2₄ Rock 2 Coral 1₅ 3₆

4₈ 4₂ Coral Beach Blow Hole

6 4₂ Ruined Jetty

3 3 3₉ 2₇ Beach 3

Sand Steel Beach 2₇

23° 14.5′ N 5₄ 2₇ 2₇ Sand

3₆ Stakes 2₇

6 2₇ 4₈ 330°

07·5′ 81°07′W

most of the island can be approached quite closely.

There are three anchorages on the island, one of which should provide reasonable protection in settled conditions. These are:

1. To the SE of the light. Approach the light on a heading of 330° and anchor in 2·5–3m in a sand bottom when 100–150m off the beach. Holding is poor (thin sand over rock). A Danforth-type anchor will set the best. Note that shoal water extends further offshore to the west of this anchorage, while the bottom is rocky to the NE.

2. In the bay to the west of the light. Approach from the SE, and then curve in toward the small beach. You can come almost onto the beach, but note the small shoal extending off the south end of the beach area, and the submerged jetty extending 50m or more off the shoreline to the north (the end of the jetty has just 1·5m over it). Holding is once again poor (thin sand over rock).

3. In the bay to the NW of the light, between the two off-lying islets. Approach from the NW toward the eastern islet, and anchor over toward this islet in 3–4m just inside a line drawn between the northern extremities of the two islets. Holding is poor in a rocky bottom. There is an extensive area of rocks and coral in the western and southern parts of the bay, so don't try to get too far inshore. There is no beach; to go ashore it will be necessary to take the dinghy around to one of the beaches.

second is to enjoy the bird life. The bay, which is almost uninhabited, is home to herons, egrets, ibis and numerous other species, and above all flamingos, which we have found in several different places on the shallow flats, particularly in the large bay on the south side of Cayo Genoves. (But please note that the flamingos are extremely shy and easily disturbed; they should be observed with binoculars from a distance. Unless you have at least a 300mm lens, and preferably a 600mm lens, you will not be able to get worthwhile photographs so it would be better not to try).

The eastern end of the bay is accessible from seaward via the Boca (Pasa) Falcones (see the previous chapter) and the Canal Sierra Morena, but must be exited via the same channels. At this eastern end the center of the bay has depths of 2·0–2·7m, shoaling on all sides toward the edges of the bay. There are several small towns on the south shore which are probably accessible with a draft of 1·8m or less, but we have not confirmed this.

The center section of the bay is impassable to boats with a draft of more than a meter. With less than a meter, passage can be made via the Canalizo Nicolas (Sanchez) and the Pasa Balizas.

The western end of the bay has fairly uniform depths of 2–3m, gradually shoaling toward the edges (sometimes 1M or more out from the mangroves). Its perimeter is featureless, with the exception of a large white building on the southern shore (the La Tela salt works) which is conspicuous from miles away.

Canal de los Barcos

The Canal de los Barcos is a 3M long channel winding through the mangroves, leading to the northern side of the Bahía de Santa Clara. The controlling depth in the canal is 1·8m, which is found at the extreme southern end (in protected

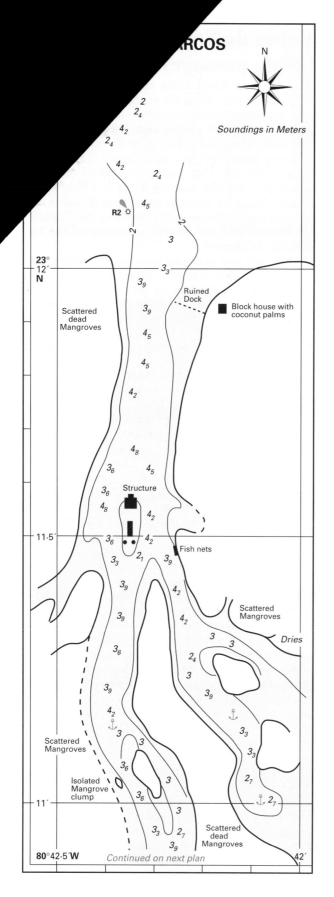

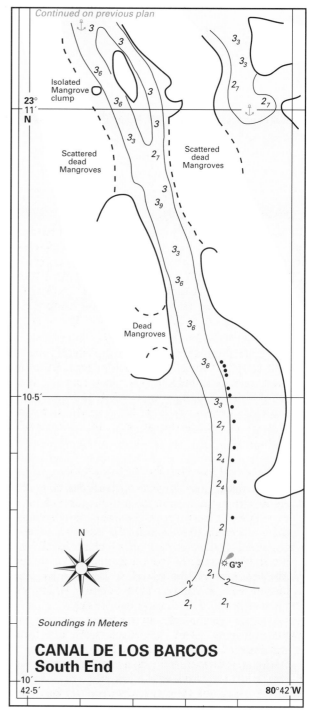

CANAL DE LOS BARCOS
South End

Soundings in Meters

waters). The approaches to the canal from the north lead from the 5m line across a wide shoal area, with fairly uniform depths of 2–3m up to 1M offshore.

The canal in places is plenty wide enough to anchor. In addition, there is a branch leading off into the mangroves which contains several secluded and protected spots suitable for anchoring.

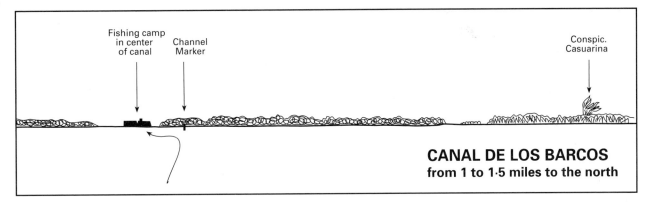

CANAL DE LOS BARCOS
from 1 to 1·5 miles to the north

Labels on sketch: Fishing camp in center of canal — Channel Marker — Conspic. Casuarina

Approaches from offshore

From the east There is a dangerous reef extending almost 2M offshore to the east of the canal. To clear its northernmost extension you must stay north of 23°15·0'N (this will put you within a couple of hundred meters of the reef at one point) until as far west as 80°40·0'W, at which point you should head WSW to close the coastline approximately 1M north of the canal (23°13·0'N 80°42·3'W).

From the west There is a dangerous patch of coral almost 2M out to the NW of the channel (Arrecife Lavanderas). To avoid it you must stay north of 23°14·3'N until as far east as 80°44·0'W at which point you should head ESE to close the coastline approximately 1M north of the canal (23°13·0'N 80°42·3'W).

Entrance and passage from the north

A very extensive shoal, with depths down to 2m close to shore, must be crossed before the channel can be entered. This is no place to be if any seas are running, although the shoals do seem to have a calming effect on the waves as you close the shore.

From offshore the channel is not easy to pick out. However, there are a couple of isolated conspicuous casuarina trees to the west of the channel which will get you oriented. The channel itself is approximately ½M to the east of the easternmost of the two casuarinas. From 1M to 1½M north of the channel it looks something like the sketch.

Inside the channel is a fishing station (which sits on piles in the center of the channel). This is far easier to pick out than the channel marker. Any heading for this fishing station from the north seems to be free of danger. As you close the shore you will pick up the channel marker (a red beacon, *No. 2*) at which time you should take up a position that brings you in from the north 20–30m to the east of the beacon (i.e. you leave it to starboard). Note that there are shoals extending north of the beacon on both sides of the channel, so you should be in position for the final approach a couple of hundred meters out, making whatever adjustments are necessary to compensate for the tide which can set strongly across here.

Once past the beacon, continue in mid-channel toward the fishing station. At this time several channels will begin to appear, with no indication of which one to take. The correct one is due south of the fishing station (one or two others have deep water, but all are eventually closed off by shoals).

The fishing station is on a shoal which can be taken on either side. The western channel is the deeper, but be sure to favor the stakes on the fishing station shoal, rather than the mangroves on the western shore, as you come round the south end of the shoal, since shoal water extends well out from the mangroves at this point.

½M south of the fishing station there is an island in mid-stream which can be taken on either side. In any event, be aware of the extensive shoal in mid-channel extending northward from the tip of the island. The western channel is once again the deeper, but its western side is not clearly delineated since this is a fairly open area of primarily water with scattered (mostly dead) mangroves. However, to the east of the general run of the mangroves is one isolated clump of living mangroves. The channel runs midway between this clump of mangroves and the island.

South of the island there is a long shoal in center channel, with shoal water extending well out from the western shore – you must maintain a course to clear the two. Thereafter, you should stay pretty much in mid-channel until you pick out the line of stakes, and the channel marker (another beacon), delineating the southern end of the channel. The stakes and beacon are left 10–20m to port (i.e. you pass to the west of them). The channel is quite narrow opposite the first stake, and narrower still as you approach the beacon. It shoals steadily to just 2m, with the depth only slowly increasing after you have cleared the channel and entered the Bahía de Santa Clara.

Entrance and passage from the south

Head for a position at approximately 23°10·0'N 80°42·2'W. The channel marker (a green beacon, *No. 3*) should be approached from a southerly direction, and should be left to starboard (i.e. you pass to the west of it). As you close the beacon, the water will shoal to about 2m. You will be able to pick out a series of stakes leading in a northerly direction. These delineate the east side of the channel.

Come into the channel leaving the beacon and all the stakes 10–20m, but no more, to starboard. The channel is very narrow to begin with, with the shallowest depth (2m) immediately north of the beacon, after which the depths steadily increase until by the end of the stakes there are 3m or more. Note that there is another narrow section immediately after the last stake, so be sure to maintain the 10–20m distance off the stakes at this point.

Beyond the stakes the course is broadly north up the center of the channel between the mangroves, but paying attention to fairly extensive shoals that push out from both banks from time to time. Almost a mile in, the channel splits around an island. This can be taken on either side, but note the extensive shoal to the south of the island, and the shoal jutting out from the western bank – both have a number of keel marks in them! The western channel is slightly wider and has the deeper water.

North of the island come back into mid-channel, but not too soon, since there is another extensive shoal from the north tip of the island up the center of the channel. Another ½M further on there is a large shoal in mid-channel with a substantial building set on piles on top of it (a fishing station). This too can be taken on either side, with the deeper water once again being on the western side.

There is then a clear run up mid-channel to the northern marker (a red beacon, *No. 2*), which is left 20–30m to port. North of the beacon, there is shoal water with as little as 2m in places, and gradually deepening to 5m at 1M out – this is no place to be if any seas are running. We have not found any deep-water channels across this shoal. We maintained a heading of pretty much due north until clear of the coast (note that there is often a strong tide across here and a considerable adjustment may be needed to the heading). In any event, whether heading east or west, note that there are dangerous reefs well offshore in both directions; these should be given a good clearance.

Anchorage

The canal is wide enough to anchor in many places, and in fact we spent a comfortable night just to the north of the island in mid-stream. But a more secluded anchorage will be found by taking the southeastern fork at the fishing station. You can anchor anywhere down here, with none but the birds on the nearby mudflats to keep you company. We rode out a norther here in tranquil comfort. Wherever an anchor is dropped, the bottom is very

soft and the holding not too good. A Danforth-type anchor will set better than a plough or Bruce. Tidal currents are quite strong, so the boat is likely to lie to the current rather than the wind, reversing every six hours.

Passages through the west end of the Bahía de Santa Clara

From the east Once through the Canal de los Barcos, a course of 225° is held, aiming for a point about 1M west of the La Tela saltworks. When about 2M NE of the saltworks, the course is altered to 260° until the channel marker for the Pasa de la Manuy is picked up.

From the west Once clear of the Pasa de la Manuy, a heading of 080° is maintained down the center of the bay for a point approximately 2M NE of the La Tela saltworks, at which point the course is altered to 045° until the channel marker for the Canal de los Barcos is picked up.

Pasa de la Manuy

The Pasa de la Manuy connects the Bahía de Santa Clara with the Bahía de Cárdenas. The controlling depth of 1·8m is found at the south end, while there are just 2m at the NW end of the channel.

Approaches and passage

From the south (Bahía de Santa Clara) There are no distinguishing features at this end of the Bahía de Santa Clara. You will simply have to keep on heading west until you pick up the channel

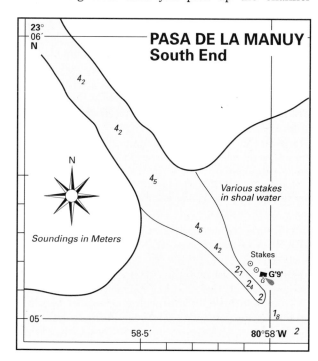

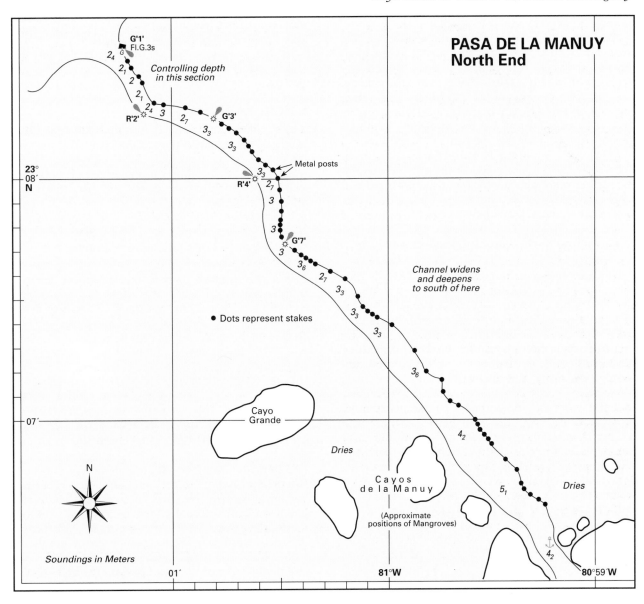

PASA DE LA MANUY
North End

G'1'
Fl.G.3s
2_4
2_1
2
2_1
2_4 3
R'2' 3
2_7
3_3 G'3'
3_3

23°
08'
N

3_3
R'4'
2_7 Metal posts
2_7
3
3
G'7'
3
3_6
2_7
3_3
3_3
3_3

Controlling depth
in this section

Channel widens
and deepens
to south of here

● Dots represent stakes

Cayo
Grande

Dries

3_6

C a y o s
d e l a   M a n u y

(Approximate
positions of Mangroves)

4_2

5_1

Dries

4_2

N

07'

01'

Soundings in Meters

81°W

80°59'W

---

through the mangroves (it is wide and straight, and visible from some distance). A position at approximately 23°05·0'N 80°57·8'W will put you ¼M off the entrance buoy (green, *No. 9*) in about 1·8m at low tide. Approach the channel on a heading of about 320°, with the buoy lined up with the eastern side of the entry. This heading puts you toward the eastern side of the channel. Leave the buoy some 10–20m to starboard (i.e. you pass to the west of it – although this is a green buoy, the channel is considered to be running in the opposite direction, and so the green buoys are left to starboard and the red to port), maintaining the 320° heading until the water deepens, at which point you simply come into center channel.

Off the buoy the depth is a little over 2m, and then once past the buoy it increases fairly rapidly to more than 4m. Thereafter the passage is pretty straightforward (see the notes below for the north end of the channel).

From the north (Bahía de Cárdenas) Come to a position at approximately 23°08·8'N 81°01·5'W, at which point the entrance buoy (green *No. 1*) will be clearly visible. The channel is entered, leaving the buoy 10–20m to port (i.e. you pass to the west of it), and then continuing leaving all the stakes a similar distance to port. The depth in this first stretch is a little over 2m at low tide. After the first ½M the depth increases first to 3m, and then gradually to 4m or more. The channel is relatively narrow in one or two places in the first mile (particularly around the red *No. 4* beacon) but then opens out somewhat as it deepens, becoming easy to follow. However, you may need to make a considerable adjustment to your heading to compensate for tidal currents, which can be quite strong.

There is deep water (4–6m) in the section with the mangroves on either side, and plenty of room to anchor anywhere (the channel is more than 200m wide). But south of the mangroves the channel steadily narrows until off the green buoy (*No. 9*) it is narrow and not clearly discernible. Then it peters out altogether into an area with depths of about 1·8m, which gradually deepen to fairly uniform depths of 2–2·5m in the Bahía de Santa Clara itself. The stakes at this south end of the channel tend to be further onto the shoals than at the northern end and so should be given a little more clearance. When exiting the channel it is best to hold a heading of about 140°, to leave the buoy some 10–20m to port (i.e. you pass to the west of it), and to simply keep pressing on until the deeper water of the bay is encountered.

Anchorage

The drying mudflats lining both sides of the channel to the north of the section that runs through the mangroves are home to numerous birds, including flamingos, several varieties of egrets, herons and sandpipers, terns, and ibis. This is a bird-watcher's dream. An excellent anchorage, in 3–4m with good holding, can be found on either side of the channel anywhere around the northern end of the mangroves, with protection from all but the NW (during a norther this might be quite uncomfortable, particularly if the wind is blowing against the tide).

Bahía de Cárdenas

The Bahía de Cárdenas is a substantial, relatively shallow bay ringed by mangroves. There are few spots of great interest, but the bay does contain a number of good anchorages which provide useful stopovers when traversing the coast of Cuba, one or two of which make excellent refuges in the event of a norther. The northern perimeter of the bay (the Península de Hicacos) is also home to no less than three marinas – Acua, Chapelín, and Gaviota – which are useful for supplies of fuel and water, and for checking in and out with the various authorities.

The bay can be entered from the east (via the Pasa de la Manuy, which links the Bahía de Cárdenas with the Bahía de Santa Clara), from the north (via the Canal de Buba or by sailing past Cayo Blanco), and at its west end through the Marina Acua (but at the present time this channel is limited to vessels with less than 2m draft, and less than 5m in height – see the section below on the Marina Acua).

The northern part of the bay, from the Pasa de la Manuy to the region between Cayo Buba and Cayo Blanco, contains several shoals with less than 2m over them, many of which come up very suddenly – the bow may be aground before the depth sounder

gives a warning; you need to maintain a bow watch when maneuvering close to the shoals.

At the southern end of the bay is the city of Cárdenas.

Canal de Buba

The Canal de Buba is the main ship channel into the Bahía de Cárdenas. Although the channel is narrow in places, it is extremely well buoyed (red to starboard when heading in), including a number of buoys not shown on the existing Cuban charts, so entry and exit are straightforward. However, there are sometimes tidal currents of up to 4 knots in the channel; when the tide is ebbing against a north wind, it can be quite rough. So in general it is best to time an entry or exit for slack water.

From the outside, it is best to make for the sea buoy, which is at approximately 23°13·6'N 81°05·3'W. This keeps you clear of various shoal patches to the north of the eastern tip of the Península de Hicacos. Once at the sea buoy the first pair of channel buoys should be visible, more or less due south, a little more than 1M off.

In the vicinity of Cayo Buba extremely shoal water is found immediately to the west of the canal, whereas there is at least 2·8m to the east, so it is best to stay on the east side of the channel (keep an eye on the buoys, and adjust your course for any tidal set).

If going to Cayo Libertad, or the marinas Gaviota, Chapelín or Acua (see below for all these) once past red buoy *No. 14*, head west out of the channel. If going to Cárdenas, continue toward the SW. For the Pasa de la Manuy, the simplest course is to stay in the canal until past the long shoal at the southern end of Cayo Diana (its southern tip is at 23°08·5'N) and then head east until you pick up the green buoy at the northern entry into the pass (see above).

From the inside, the canal can be picked up at numerous spots. If coming from the Pasa de la Manuy, there are several shoals on the direct path (to the NW), so it is best to either head NNW (between Cayo Romero and Cayo Surgidero), or east (until past the long shoal that extends south of Cayo Diana).

If coming from the south side of the Península de Hicacos (Marinas Acua, Chapelín and Gaviota, or Cayo Libertad), it is necessary to stay about ½M south of Cayo Buba, picking up the canal at red buoy *No. 14*.

Cárdenas

Cárdenas is one of Cuba's larger ports. From a distance it can be picked out by a tall chimney belching black smoke. This spreads a greasy fallout for miles. The water in and around Cárdenas is

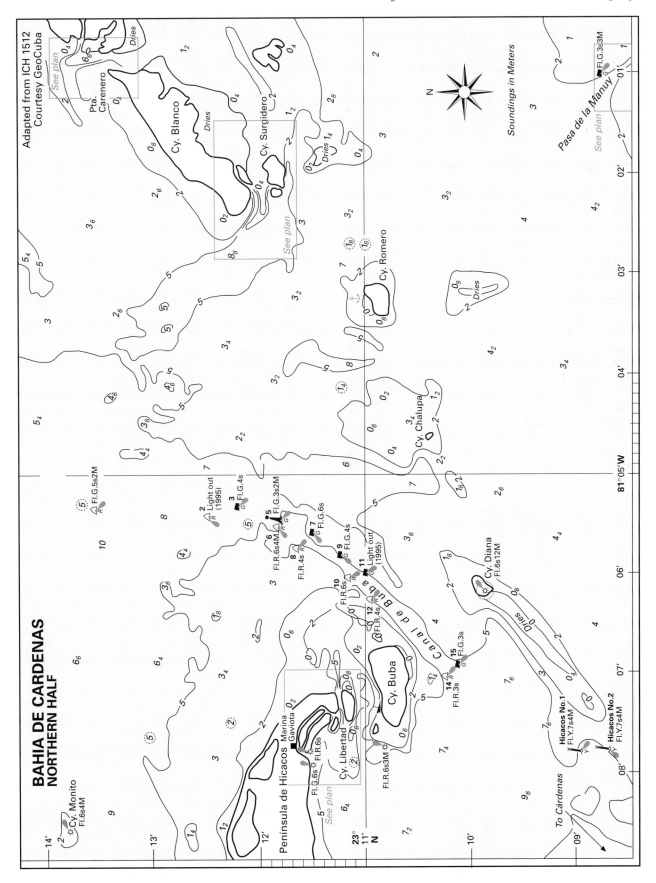

BAHIA DE CARDENAS
NORTHERN HALF

Adapted from ICH 1512
Courtesy GeoCuba

Soundings in Meters

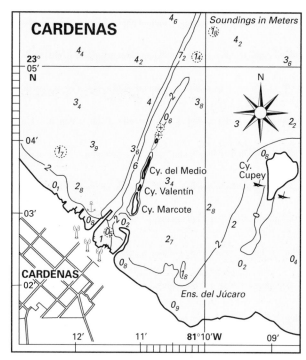

CARDENAS

Soundings in Meters

23° 05' N

CARDENAS

Cy. del Medio
Cy. Valentín
Cy. Marcote

Cy. Cupey

Ens. del Júcaro

81°10'W

Adapted from ICH 1512
Courtesy GeoCuba

filthy, and the air smells of sulfur. The port has no facilities for visiting yachts.

Depending on the wind conditions, it is possible to anchor out in the bay immediately north of the town, or else find protection behind one of the old spoil heaps that line the ship channel into the harbor, but even so there is no place to land a dinghy (the one tiny beach is filthy and strewn with boulders; the smaller docks nearby are all state-owned commercial wharves). In addition, the arrival of a foreign yacht is likely to cause something of a sensation with the security forces. We anchored off and dinghied ashore, only to be met by a Lada (Soviet-built Fiat) which screeched to a halt in front of us as we stepped out of our dinghy, with the uniformed officers leaping out to intercept us. It took a while before we received permission to go to town for a couple of hours.

Cárdenas itself is another crumbling city, although it does have a scattering of nice colonial buildings and a certain decaying charm. Transportation is currently almost all by horse-drawn buggy. We got a ride to the farmers' market (*mercado libre*), where our 'cab' waited for us, and then back to our dinghy, for ten pesos ($0.20), while we bought a considerable supply of fresh vegetables for another 100–200 pesos ($3-$4), but when we got back to the dinghy we were charged $5 for leaving it on the dock for two hours!

Cárdenas is worth visiting primarily to go to the market, which should be done in the morning. However, rather than sail there, the best way to do a shop would be to anchor your boat behind Cayo

Siguapa (see below) and to catch a bus to Cárdenas from Varadero.

Cayos Blanco and Surgidero

Cayos Blanco and Surgidero are both mostly mangroves, and as such at first sight are not particularly interesting. However, Cayo Blanco has some lovely unspoiled sand beaches, whilst in the shallow lagoon to the east of the two cays are numerous mudflats which are home to many herons and other birds – this is a peaceful, uninhabited area which has some great dinghy exploration for nature lovers. Best of all, there are a number of well protected anchorages with good holding.

Approaches and anchorages

Southern Cayo Blanco anchorages There are several excellent anchorages in the vicinity of the south coast of Cayo Blanco. All are entered via a channel that curves around the southwestern tip of the island. Due to extensive shoals to the north, south and east, the approach must be made from the west, heading for the center of the conspicuous white sand beach at the tip of Cayo Blanco. As the cay is neared, a clear white sand shoal to the west of the island is easy to pick out. The deepest water (6m or more) is found just off this sand. The course curves gently around the shoal to close the southern tip of the island, coming past the beach no more than 5–10m off.

Just beyond the beach is a dock which can also be passed close to (2·4m alongside), but immediately past the dock you must swing out a few meters to the south to stay in the channel, which then continues 20m or so off the mangroves. It is possible to anchor anywhere in this area in 4–5m, with good protection from all but the west (this would be an uncomfortable anchorage in the early stages of a norther). The holding is good in a silty/sandy bottom.

A small channel runs to the north from this main channel, and then a second, wider channel leads north into the mangroves. This second channel is navigable with a draft of 2m or more, but only with a certain amount of weaving around shoal areas. It is entered by keeping tight to the mangroves on the western side of the entrance (there is a substantial shoal jutting out from the eastern shore). After 100m or so the channel widens sufficiently to permit anchoring, but two anchors will be needed (fore and aft) to prevent the boat swinging into the mangroves when the tide turns. The bottom is very soft soupy mud that does not have particularly good holding, but this is unlikely to matter since the anchorage is completely protected from all directions. The biggest problem is the bugs, which will swarm aboard at dusk if there is no breeze.

Should you continue further east up the main

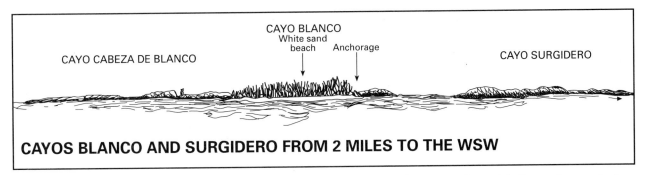

CAYOS BLANCO AND SURGIDERO FROM 2 MILES TO THE WSW

channel, you will find it splits, with one channel curving south to Cayo Surgidero, hugging the northern shore of Surgidero and then curving back to the white sand beach at the tip of Cayo Blanco, while the other channel continues east and then curves toward the south. There are numerous places in which you could anchor in these channels, with excellent protection from all directions.

Cayo Surgidero anchorage Cayo Surgidero is divided by a relatively deep (3m or more) channel, with the deep water running almost into the mangroves on both sides. This is an exceedingly well protected spot (particularly in a norther), but with enough of an air flow to keep the worst of the bugs at bay in most circumstances. The channel can be entered either by coming in on an ESE heading for the northwestern tip of the main part of the cay, or else from the south.

The southern entry is straightforward enough, but crosses a shoal area with depths of 1·8m, and even shallower shoal water close by on both sides. The procedure is as follows. Come in from the west 200m or so south of the cay (but no more than 300m south or you will run foul of another shoal). As you pass the small western cay, you will see the slot between the two halves of the cay open up. Next, you will see a series of mangrove clumps in the widening slot, and then clear water to the west of these clumps.

There is one mangrove bush at the west end of these clumps, and then a larger clump, and then a break between this clump and the next one to the east. This break should be lined up on the western tip of the main part of Cayo Surgidero, at which point a low spot in the mangroves on the horizon will also be lined up with the break and the tip of

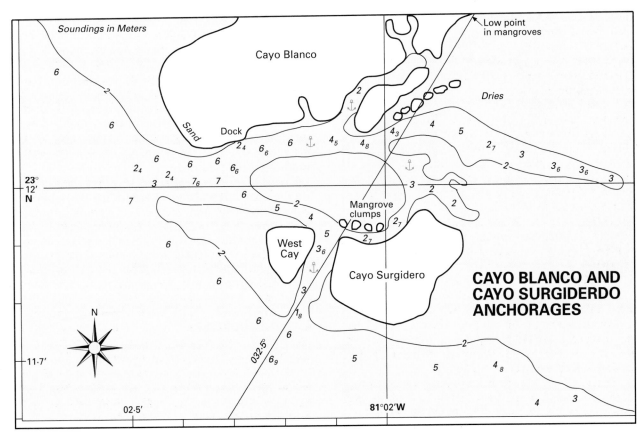

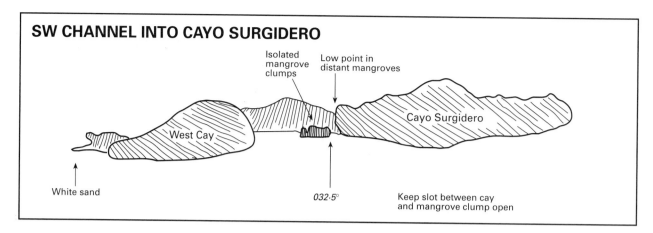

SW CHANNEL INTO CAYO SURGIDERO

Isolated mangrove clumps

Low point in distant mangroves

Cayo Surgidero

West Cay

White sand

032·5°

Keep slot between cay and mangrove clump open

Cayo Surgidero, and the whole lot will be bearing 032/3°. Now head straight in, making whatever course adjustments are necessary to compensate for the tide, which can run quite strongly across here.

To come out, simply head for the isolated clump of mangroves on the horizon bearing 213/4°.

Northern Cayo Blanco anchorage Another well protected anchorage can be entered by rounding the northern tip of Cayo Blanco (Punta Carenero) and heading down a channel directly to the south (Canal de Carenero). You can anchor anywhere in the channel. This channel cuts between extensive drying mudflats which you will share with the birds and no one else.

The hard part is the initial entry, since the north

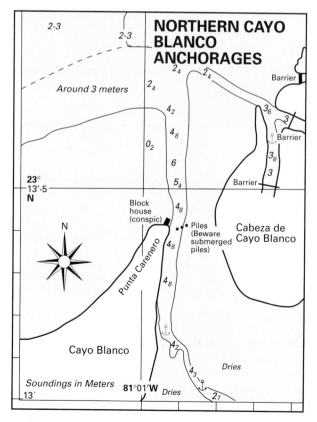

NORTHERN CAYO BLANCO ANCHORAGES

2-3

2-3

2_4

2_4

2_4

Barrier

Around 3 meters

2_4

4_2

3_6

3

4_8

0_2

Barrier

6

3_6

23°
13'·5
N

5_4

3

Barrier

Block house (conspic)

4_8

N

Piles (Beware submerged piles)

Cabeza de Cayo Blanco

Punta Carenero

4_8

4_8

4_2

Cayo Blanco

Dries

4_3

Soundings in Meters **81°01'W** *Dries*

2_7

13'

shore of Cayo Blanco is fronted by extensive shoals with varying depths. The initial approach must be made from the west a ¼M north of Cayo Blanco in 2–3m. There is no clearly defined channel at this point – the water simply shoals slowly to both the north and the south. The deeper water is found by maintaining a heading of about 070° until north of Punta Carenero, which can be distinguished by an old concrete block house. Once north of the blockhouse, you curve to the south. The channel rapidly deepens and becomes more clearly defined, with the deeper water over toward the western side. By the time you approach the block house the western side will have a shear natural wall 3m deep, undercut at its base in places, with just centimeters of water on the flats to the west (so you won't want to run out of the channel!).

Immediately past the block house, there are a series of piles (the remains of a defensive barrier) coming out from the eastern shore. Depending on the state of the tide, the last 2 to 6 piles may be just submerged, extending well into the channel, so be sure to keep over to the western shore. Beyond this you can anchor at any point. The channel appears to go a long way into the mudflats, but we have only followed it for ½M or so.

There is another deep-water channel which forks off the main entry channel north of the block house, continuing ESE and then curving south into the mangroves. Once again, protected anchorages can be found in the mangroves, but it is not possible to go very far because all channels are closed off by the remains of defensive barriers (which are just submerged at high tide, so take care!).

Cayo Libertad

Cayo Libertad is just south of the eastern tip of the Península de Hicacos. To the NW of the cay there is an anchorage with good holding in 4m. It has protection from all but the south and west. Ashore, between the mangroves, are a number of small sandy beaches and fishermen's homes. In the

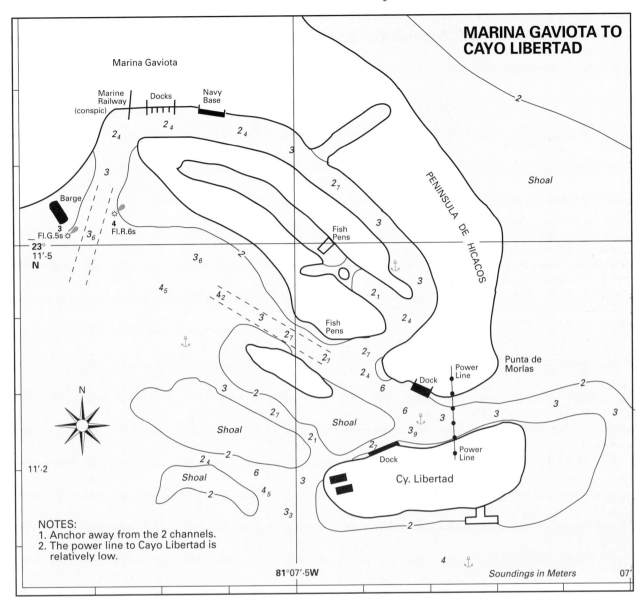

MARINA GAVIOTA TO CAYO LIBERTAD

NOTES:
1. Anchor away from the 2 channels.
2. The power line to Cayo Libertad is relatively low.

81°07'·5W   Soundings in Meters   07'

mangroves to the north is a Cuban naval base, complete with gunboats, next to which is the Marina Gaviota. Three miles to the west is the Marina Chapelín.

Approaches

From the Pasa de la Manuy There are several shoal areas between the Pasa de la Manuy and Cayo Libertad, which are frequently difficult to see in the somewhat muddy water. The safest approach to the cay is to head due west once clear of the Pasa de la Manuy, passing a little more than 1½M south of Cayo Diana to intersect the ship channel at the *Hicacos No. 2* marker. From here you can go due north to pass to the west of the Cayo Buba beacon (on the west side of Cayo Buba).

From the outside The approach is via the Canal de Buba, the main ship channel to Cárdenas (see above).

In order to clear a shoal south of Cayo Buba, it is necessary to come down the Canal de Buba as far as red buoy *No. 14*, ½M south of the cay (there are passages across the shoal closer to the cay, but it is better to simply give it a good clearance). Once at buoy *No. 14*, head due west until due south of the Cayo Buba beacon which is located about ⅓M west of Cayo Buba, and then come due north to leave the beacon to starboard.

From the Cayo Buba beacon Continue due north toward some conspicuous buildings until 200–300m west of the small, unnamed cay to the NW of Cayo Libertad, and then anchor in 4m (don't cut in toward Cayo Libertad since it's west end is beset with shoals, some of them barely covered at low water).

From the west From Cayo Siguapa or the Marina Chapelín (see below) come east into the last substantial cove on the west side of the Península de Hicacos and then anchor.

Anchorage

Anchor in the southern half of the bay in order to keep clear of the main exit channels from the Cuban naval base and the Marina Gaviota. An anchor light is highly recommended since the gunboats sometimes come out at night.

Alternative anchorages

1. A deep-water channel runs east to west between Cayo Buba and Cayo Libertad, extending 1M to the ENE of Cayo Buba, but then closed off by shoal water at its east end. The shoals provide reasonable protection, although some swells do find their way into this anchorage from time to time (particularly when the wind is blowing either from the east or the west against the tide). There is, however, almost always a good breeze. We found the holding to be poor (a rocky bottom) in the middle of the channel, but better over toward Cayo Buba (just to the NE of the wreck).

   From this anchorage, a narrow channel with 3m depths curves around the east end of Cayo Libertad, but is obstructed on the north side of the cay by a relatively low-lying power line (my guess would be 5–6m clearance) which runs from the Península de Hicacos to Cayo Libertad.

2. A deep-water channel (minimum depth of 2·7m) runs close inshore up the western side of Cayo Libertad (identified by the conspicuous white buildings), and then hugs the north shore of the cay (it is necessary to stay within 3–5m of the shore until up to the dock, since there is a shoal just to the north). Once past the east end of the dock (which has 2m alongside) you can curve north toward the dock on the other shore (which also has 2m alongside).

   There is plenty of room to anchor between the two docks, west of the power line, in 3–4m. The channel continues to the north close to the southern shore of the Península de Hicacos, and then branches with the NE arm going up to the naval base and marina, and the NW arm cutting through to the anchorage in the bay.

3. 200m up the channel from Cayo Libertad to the naval base and marina, the channel widens to create a small basin which forms a totally protected anchorage. 3m can be carried almost into the mangroves on both sides. However, there is a good deal of boat traffic through here, so you should keep off to one side and be sure to set an anchor light. Alternatively, you could tuck into the south end of the dead-end channel between the bay and the marina channel: here you will not

be disturbed by any traffic. Once again, there is deep water into the mangroves on both sides. In both channels your boat may lie to the tidal current rather than the wind, so two anchors may be needed to keep the boat from swinging into the mangroves when the tide changes.

4. During a norther, good protection will be found by simply anchoring in the lee of the Península de Hicacos. You can tuck fairly close into shore about ¼M west of the Marina Gaviota, off a small sand beach (immediately to the west of which is a small inlet in which it is possible to carry 1·8m).

Marina Gaviota

The Marina Gaviota is tucked up in the mangroves to the north of Cayo Libertad. It can be entered via the marked channel immediately to its south (presently made conspicuous by a beached barge on the west side of the channel), or by curving around through the mangroves in the channel that is found just north of Cayo Libertad (see above). In either direction, there is a minimum of 2·4m.

The marina is fully occupied by charter boats catering to the tourists in the Varadero strip, so you are unlikely to find a berth, but it does have water and a fuel dock with both diesel and gasoline. In addition, it would be possible to clear in and out here, but I imagine it might take some time since I doubt that it is done very often and the officials may be unsure of the procedures. The marina also has a marine railway which is clearly capable of handling substantial vessels with a draft of up to a little under 2m, but it might be difficult to arrange a haul out or to get work done (although there are a number of reasonably well equipped workshops on the site). In any event, the marina is worth a visit by dinghy just to look at the lobsters and turtles in pens on the dock, and to see the gunboats parked next door.

The marina monitors VHF Ch 06.

Marina Chapelín

The Marina Chapelín is found about midway along a more than 2-mile canal that runs through the mangroves on the south side of the Península de Hicacos. The marina is primarily a base for tour boats catering to the tourists in Varadero. There are a number of sailboats and sport fishing boats available for day charters and the occasional diving trip. When there is space available, the marina will take in private boats. The charge is $0.45 per foot per day, which includes water and electricity. There are no showers or toilets. Diesel is available ($0.50 a liter in 1995). There is talk of adding new docks specifically to cater to visiting boats. The marina monitors VHF Ch 72.

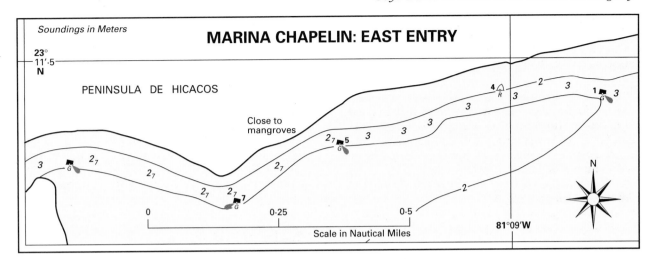

MARINA CHAPELIN: EAST ENTRY

Soundings in Meters

PENÍNSULA DE HICACOS

Close to mangroves

Scale in Nautical Miles

81°09'W

Address Marina Chapelín, Carretera Punta Hicacos, 1½ Km de Sol Palmeras, Varadero, Cuba. ☎ 66 7093 and 66 7550.

Approaches

From the east The entrance channel runs between extensive shoals for more than 1M. The channel is not quite straight, but is reasonably well buoyed. However, in places it is quite narrow, so care will have to be taken to adjust the course for any tide set.

Heading in, the entrance is marked by a lighted green buoy (*No. 1*) which is left immediately to port. ¼M in is an unlit red buoy (*No. 4*) which is left to starboard. There is then almost ½M before the next green buoy (*No. 5*). After *No. 5* (left to port) the channel comes quite close to the mangroves before curving a little to the south to the green *No. 7* buoy (also left to port). From *No. 7* it is a straight shot to the unnumbered green buoy at the entrance to the canal (left to port). There is a minimum of 2·7m in the channel, and 4m or better once inside the canal.

From the west The marina canal can be entered from the west, but the channel runs between shallow banks without the benefit of channel markers. However, it is a fairly straightforward entry, maintaining a heading of almost due north

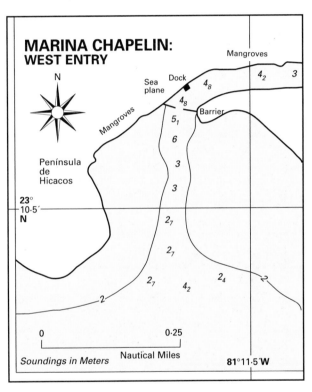

MARINA CHAPELIN: WEST ENTRY

Mangroves

Sea plane   Dock

Barrier

Península de Hicacos

Soundings in Meters   Nautical Miles

81°11·5'W

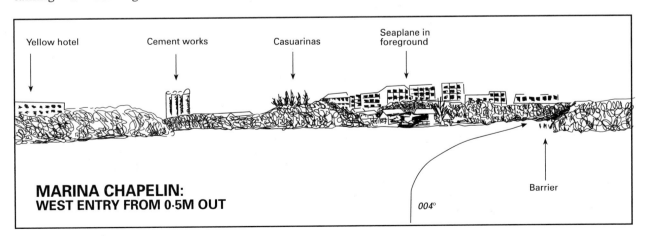

Yellow hotel   Cement works   Casuarinas   Seaplane in foreground

Barrier

004°

MARINA CHAPELIN:
WEST ENTRY FROM 0·5M OUT

(approximately 004°) for a small dock at the entrance to the canal (you may need to adjust your course to counteract tidal influences). The dock itself is not conspicuous, but behind it is a fair amount of new construction (major hotels), while alongside (to the west) you can often see a seaplane parked on the canal bank (see sketch). As you come in the water shoals to 2·7m, and then deepens again. Closer in you will see piles running across the channel, with a cable strung between them. In the center of this barrier is a gap leading into the canal, which then has consistent depths of 4m or more all the way to the marina.

Marina Acua

The Marina Acua is a port of entry into Cuba. It is a similar development to the Marina Hemingway, also dating from the 1950s. A substantial lagoon has been dredged and bordered with cement walls, which are all in surprisingly good condition. At the east end of the lagoon a channel runs under a couple of drawbridges into the Bahía de Cárdenas; at the west end of the lagoon a canal (Canal de Paso Malo) cuts through the isthmus of the Península de Hicacos to give entry to the lagoon.

Originally the minimum dredged depths for the development were 3–4m, but substantial silting has occurred in the western channel, reducing its depth to less than 2m at low water (we found out the hard way!); the eastern channel will carry 4m, but one of the drawbridges is no longer operative so entry at this end is restricted to boats no taller than 5m. However, the canal should be dredged, and the bridge fixed, by the end of 1995.

The marina monitors VHF Ch 68. If contacted on your approach, when you arrive the staff will have the various officials standing by to take care of your paperwork.

The marina is an excellent place in which to check in or out of Cuba, to pick up or drop off crew, or to leave a boat for a while, with a new airport just 10 miles out of town (direct flights to Canada and the Bahamas, as well as to Havana, Santiago de Cuba and Cayo Largo).

The one drawback is that whenever the wind is at all in the south, it carries the fumes of the local oil fields and refineries over the marina, producing a sulfurous stink and depositing a fine, greasy layer on the boat.

Approaches

From the east Come just to the south of the red *No. 14* buoy in the Canal de Buba and then head a little south of east (263°) for 8M to a position at approximately 23°08·4'N 81°15·5'W (staying at least ¼M south of Cayo Gordo en route). This will

bring you to the channel to the north of Cayo Siguapa. The channel curves around the cay, and then makes a sharp turn to the WNW, passing under the drawbridges into the marina lagoon (sailboats should make sure that the bridge is operative before coming this way).

The channel around Cayo Siguapa has several lighted channel markers although the first one shown on the chart (green *No. 31*) no longer exists, while the second (green *No. 29*) is no longer lit, and the light on the third (green *No. 27*) was not working in 1995. The lights on the rest were operative. Note that the green markers are left to starboard, and the red to port, since the channel is considered to be running from the marina to the bay. The channel has tidal currents up to 3 knots, especially at the bridge. Once inside the lagoon, it is necessary to keep over toward the southern shore (keep south of the principal channel markers but north of the two stakes) between Isla del Este and the marina docks.

If the bridge is not operative, boats with masts taller than 5m can pass along the north shore of the Península de Hicacos to enter the marina through the Canal de Paso Malo (see below). The only off-lying dangers on the north shore of the Península de Hicacos are a small bank (Los Colorados – minimum depth 1·4m – ½M to the north of Punta Hicacos), and Cayo Monito, Cayo Piedras del Norte, and Cayo Mono, which are stretched out on a line to the NE, with Cayo Monito the closest inshore (1½M due north of Punta Hicacos).

When going west it is better to stay ½M or more off the coastline, since this will generally put you in a favorable current of up to 1 knot. The shoreline, which is one long strip of white sand punctuated with a few low-lying headlands in the eastern half of the peninsula, is heavily built up with vacation homes and moderately high-rise hotels. The marina entry is described below.

From the west The coastline west of the marina entry channel is deep until close inshore with no off-lying dangers. Any approach that stays ½M offshore will be in deep water. The marina can be entered via the Canal de Paso Malo (see below) or by rounding the eastern tip of the Península de Hicacos and doubling back in the peninsula's lee.

If heading east to round Punta Hicacos, you can stay just 200–300m off the beach in 3–5m of water right up to Punta Hicacos. This has the advantage of keeping you out of an unfavorable current which is often found a little further out. ½M north of Punta Hicacos is a shoal (Los Colorados) with a minimum depth of 1·4m. 2m can be carried between the beach and this shoal, but there is then an extensive bank with isolated shoal patches below 2m stretching almost 3M to the ESE so it might be just as well to go north of the Los Colorados shoal, and then east 3M into the deep water of the Canal du Buba.

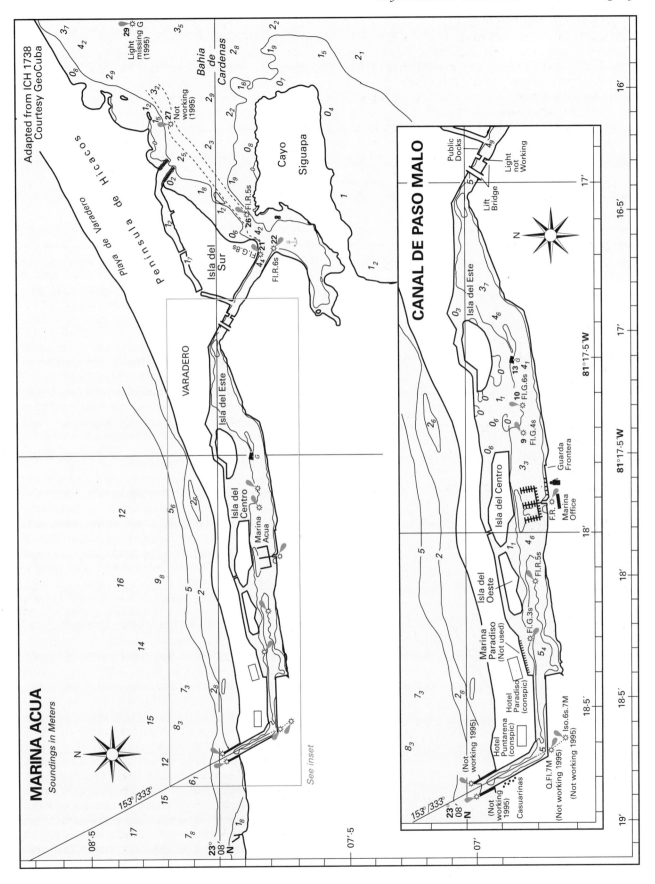

MARINA ACUA
Soundings in Meters

Adapted from ICH 1738
Courtesy GeoCuba

N

153°/333°

VARADERO

See inset

Peninsula de Hicacos

Playa de Varadero

Isla del Sur

Isla del Este

Isla del Centro

Marina Acua

Bahía de Cárdenas

Cayo Siguapa

Light **29** missing G (1995)

27 Not working (1995)

26 Fl.R.5s

21 Fl.G.8s

22

8

Fl.R.6s

CANAL DE PASO MALO

N

Public Docks

Light not Working

Lift Bridge

Isla del Este

13 Fl.G.6s

10

9 Fl.G.4s

Guarda Frontera

F.R.

Marina Office

Isla del Centro

Isla del Oeste

Fl.R.5s

Marina Paradiso (Not used)

Hotel Paradiso (conspic)

Fl.G.3s

Hotel Puntarena (conspic)

Q.Fl.7M (Not working 1995)

Iso.6s.7M (Not working 1995)

(Not working 1995)

Casuarinas

(Not working 1995)

81°17·5'W

153°/333°

N

23° 08'

23° 08'

251

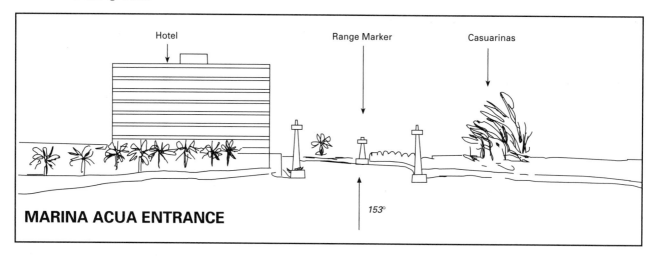

MARINA ACUA ENTRANCE

153°

Canal de Paso Malo

The entrance to the Canal de Paso Malo (at approximately 23°08·0'N 81°18·7'W) is not at all clear until close inshore. However, immediately to the east are two substantial hotels (currently, the westernmost hotels in the Varadero strip), which can be picked out from miles offshore. The channel runs alongside the western edge of the western hotel. The entry is distinguished by two low-lying walls (breakwaters) projecting into the Florida Straits. Both walls are capped by lighted masonry towers (neither light was working in 1995).

The entrance is approached on a heading of 153°. As you close the coast, beyond the channel markers will be seen a white masonry range post (with a height of 7m); as you get even closer you will see a smaller range marker (height 3m) directly in front of the taller one (neither range light was working in 1995). From time to time there may be various lattice work towers visible from offshore which look like they may be aids to navigation, but these should be ignored since they are the derricks of oil-rigs in an oilfield less than a mile inland.

Approaching the entrance you come on soundings quite close inshore, and then the bottom rapidly shoals to 4m between the tips of the breakwaters. A little further in silting has reduced the depth to 1·8m in center channel at low tide. However, deeper water (a little over 2m) can be found by moving over to the eastern side of the channel (immediately after passing through the entrance to the breakwaters) but staying at least 3m away from the wall, since a rocky ledge projects into the channel from its base. As you draw parallel to the sand dunes to the west of the channel, make your way over diagonally toward the western side of the channel, aiming for the center of the group of casuarinas immediately beyond the sand dune. Now come down the western side of the channel (once again, at least 3m away from the wall) until past the hotel, at which point you should return to mid-channel, with the depth

increasing to 5m (note that by the time this is published the channel should have been dredged to 5m, making these maneuvers unnecessary).

Just as at the Marina Hemingway, during the early (NW) phase of a norther, heavy seas drive up into the channel, burying the breakwaters in foam, while the combination of the rapidly shoaling channel, a tidal flow of up to 3 knots, and deflected seas off the walls creates a tumultuous situation in the mouth of the channel, particularly when the tide is ebbing (you should try to time an entry or exit for slack water). Entry under these conditions is not advised, and if attempted must be done at sufficient speed to maintain steerageway (otherwise the boat may broach and get driven onto one of the walls). Until the canal is dredged, with a 2m draft, at low tide you can still expect to bang the bottom fairly hard in the wave troughs. If the boat should stick before it is past the worst of the waves, it may get slewed around, thrown onto its beam ends, and pounded sideways over the sand or into the wall (this canal is called 'Paso Malo' – 'Bad Pass' – for good reason!).

Once past the hotel, the channel makes a sharp turn to the east. It is clearly marked all the way to the docks at the Marina Acua (passing the docks of the disused Marina Paradiso en route). The lights on the various channel markers within the lagoon were working in 1995. When approaching the Marina Acua, someone will be on hand to direct you to a slip, at which point you will be boarded by various officials who will take care of the paperwork.

Clearance procedures

If checking into Cuba for the first time, the normal protracted procedures are to be expected, but if just clearing in from another Cuban port the clearance procedure is generally quite brief, with a perfunctory search of the boat. When leaving the marina to go cruising, simply notify the marina office of your intentions, itinerary and departure time. They will pass this information onto the immigration officers and the Guarda who will come to the boat with the necessary paperwork when you depart.

Charges and facilities

The docks of the marina are solidly constructed and in good condition, with electricity and water for every slip (although the electricity has to be jury-rigged as usual, with potentially dangerous consequences – see Chapter 1). The marina charges are $0.35 per foot per day. There are no public showers or toilets, but fuel (both diesel and gasoline) and ice are available on a fuel dock located next to the Guarda post (in 1995, diesel was $0.45 a liter; gasoline $0.90 a liter). The fuel dock has 3m alongside.

The marina is home to KP Winter, a sailboat charter company with a fleet of Beneteaus from 40–50ft (12–15m). These are available for day charters, skippered charters of a week or more, or bareboat charters (but the skipper must have an official captain's license). The charter company much prefers to put a captain aboard. Prices range from $2,500 per week, for a 40ft boat in low season, to $5,500 per week for a 50ft boat in high season (December to March, and August). These prices do not include provisions, the captain, or any other charges. The ☎ and fax is 33 5462.

The marina also has various sport-fishing boats available for charter.

It is possible, in an emergency, to haul boats on the hard next to the Guarda post, but to do this a crane and spreader bars must be brought in.

Anchoring out

When clearing in with the authorities, you may wish to immediately seek a permit to cruise the Bahía de Cárdenas. As soon as this is issued, you can save yourself the marina charges by leaving and anchoring out in any one of a half dozen good anchorages in this region (see the previous notes). The closest to the marina and Varadero is in the lee of Cayo Siguapa. Here a well protected bay (in all conditions) has fairly uniform depths of 3–4m, but with a rather soft bottom – you will need to check that the anchor has a good bite. The shoreline is uninteresting (mangroves) but Varadero is no more of a dinghy ride from the anchorage than it is from the Marina Acua.

Provisions/things to do

To get into Varadero, take the dinghy across to the north shore of the lagoon and tie it up on the waterfront either to the west or the east of the bridge. It would be wise to lock it securely.

The central feature of Varadero is its gorgeous sand beach. This first attracted Cubans, who began to build substantial beachfront homes after the turn of the century. It then caught the attention of the government, which has turned the Península de Hicacos into one long tourist trap with all the amenities you would expect, including western-style restaurants, bars, discos and nightclubs. This is not, however, the place to experience Cuba, or meet Cubans (who, apart from the necessary workers, and the prostitutes and their pimps, are kept away from the tourists).

The town is laid out with the Avenida 1 and Autopista del Sur running west to east from the bridge, intersected by short north/south Calles, starting with number 1 a little to the west of the bridge and going up to number 69 to the east, after which come the most exclusive hotels. There is a modern hospital (expensive) and pharmacy at the east end (Calle 64), with a post office and telephone office close by. Another post office is located more centrally (between Calles 39 and 40), with a bank (Banco Financiero International) on Calle 32 (this is one of the few places in Cuba at which you can obtain cash with a credit card). Just about all the hotels have a tourist desk with tourist information. Cars can be rented from Havanautos (between Calles 7 and 8, and on Calle 56). The bus station is on Calle 36.

Food stores are hard to find. The Varazul Hotel (Calle 15) has some supplies including fresh bread, butter and fruit.

Marina Acua to the Marina Hemingway

The coastline along this entire stretch is generally inhospitable, with no secure anchorages (except in the Río Canimar – see below) for vessels with a draft of more than 1m. In any event, anchorage is prohited between Matanzas and Havana except for the locations mentioned below. Deep water is found close to shore (at some points a boat is off soundings within 100m of the shoreline) so a depth sounder will often not give adequate warning of the approaching coastline – if sailing close inshore, it is essential to maintain a good watch. Only at one spot, off Guanabo, does shoal water extend more than 1M off the coast, and here it is particularly dangerous since there is an isolated reef patch with just 2m over it 1M out (at approximately 23°11·2'N 82°08·5'W).

To the west of the Marina Acua the beaches of Varadero give way to cliffs, some of which attain a considerable height, and then a substantial stretch of low cliffs behind which is a narrow coastal shelf which has been developed as an oilfield. When the wind is from the south a sulfurous stench carries for miles offshore. Finally, there are once again long stretches of sandy beaches nearing Havana.

There is normally little current close to the coast.

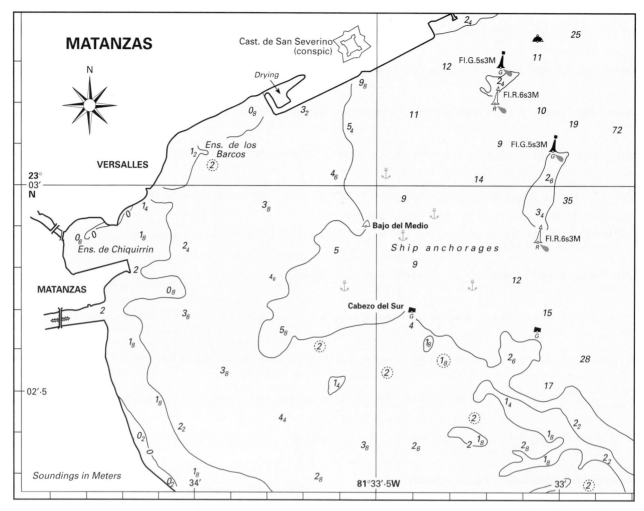

MATANZAS

Cast. de San Severino (conspic)

Drying

VERSALLES

Ens. de los Barcos

23° 03' N

Ens. de Chiquirrin

MATANZAS

Bajo del Medio

Ship anchorages

Cabezo del Sur

02'·5

Soundings in Meters

34'

81°33'·5W

Adapted from ICH 1735
Courtesy GeoCuba

A mile or two out there is often a west-setting current of up to 1 knot. As you progress further out, you come into the east-setting Gulf Stream which strengthens the further offshore you go.

Matanzas

Matanzas is a commercial port at the SW extremity of the Bahía de Matanzas – an extremely deep, wide-open bay cutting into the north coast of Cuba.

Matanzas is one of those places that should be bypassed. The entire bay is open to swells from the north, and therefore offers little protection. If you enter you may have a pilot put aboard who will attempt to levy pilotage fees. The pilot will want to escort you to a commercial dock charging commercial dock fees. If you insist on anchoring out, the Guarda will try to get you to use an expensive water taxi to go ashore, rather than your dinghy, and so on. Although Matanzas has some attractive features, it is not worth the likely hassles trying to see them.

Río Canimar

The Río Canimar empties into the SE corner of the Bahía de Matanzas. We have not sailed up it, but it reportedly has an exceedingly secure mooring alongside a new dock belonging to the Hotel Canimao, which is about 1½M up the river. The following information comes from the Cuban chart and reports from other cruisers.

The mouth of the river can be picked out from well offshore. From a position at approximately 23°03·3'N 81°30·3'W you sail in on a heading of 155°, which puts the east bank of the river in transit with the center of the bridge. Once abeam of the conspicuous Castillo del Morillo you come south to favor the west bank of the river (there is an extensive shoal coming out from the east bank), and then ease back toward mid-channel to pass under the bridge (reportedly, 25m clearance), remaining in center channel beyond the bridge (but note the mid-channel shoal shown on the chart ¾M beyond the bridge). Minimum depths are reported as 2·4m.

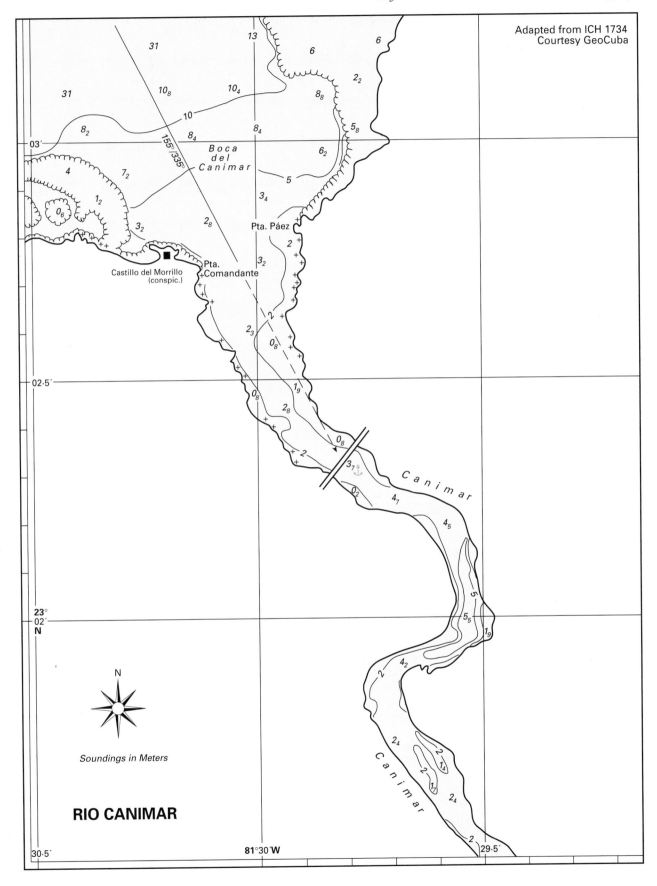

Adapted from ICH 1734
Courtesy GeoCuba

31

31

31

13

6

10₈

10₄

6

2₂

8₈

8₄

10

5₈

8₂

8₄

03′

B o c a
d e l
C a n i m a r

4

7₂

155°/335°

6₂

5

3₄

1₂

0₆

3₂

2₈

Pta. Páez

2

Castillo del Morrillo
(conspic.)

3₂

3₂

Pta.
Comandante

2₃

2

0₈

02·5′

1₉

0₈

2₈

C a n i m a r

0₈

2

3₇

0₂

4₇

4₅

5

23°
02′
N

5₅

1₉

4₂

N

2

2₄

2₄

Soundings in Meters

2₄

1₄

2

1₇

C a n i m a r

2₄

RIO CANIMAR

2

30·5′

81°30′W

29·5′

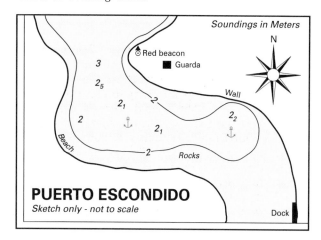

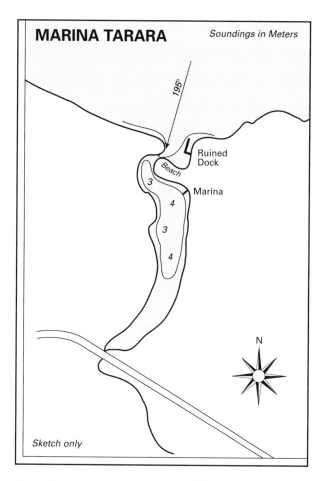

Puerto Escondido

Puerto Escondido (at approximately 23°08·8'N 81°43·6'W) is recognizable from offshore by its dramatic cliffs, although the entrance to the Río Escondido, in which there is a small harbor, is hard to pick out since the river comes in from the east behind a low-lying rocky promontory. The entry channel is close to the cliffs in the SW corner of the bay, midway between two rocky headlands.

On the east headland at the river mouth there is a red triangular mark (which is left to *port* going in – i.e. you pass to the west of it) and a conspicuous building that looks like a small hotel but is in fact a Guarda post. Between the headlands you will find 3m which rapidly shoals to a little over 2m with rocks dead ahead and to port, and a small beach at low tide off to starboard. The channel makes a sharp turn to the east and narrows, with some nasty rocks on the south side. It soon shoals to less than 1·8m.

If the wind is south of east, this is a neat place in which to stopover, although there is room for at most two boats, and two anchors will be needed to prevent your boat swinging onto various shoals and rocks (shoal-draft boats can anchor further in with a little more room). If the wind is at all north of east, this is a potentially dangerous entry which should not be attempted, especially if any sizable seas are running.

Marina Tárara

To the west of Puerto Escondido the coastline continues to be rugged and we get into the oilfield. A limestone ridge over 100m high in places runs along the shoreline. This ridge is cut by a number of rivers, forming interesting gorges which look like tempting exploration, but all are reportedly obstructed by shoal water. The Río Canasi (at approximately 23°08·6'N 81°46·9'N) looks particularly inviting. Its mouth can reportedly be entered by vessels with a draft of up to 2m, but the

river shoals to less than 1m within two tenths of a mile.

8M east of Havana (at approximately 23°10·8'N 82°12·8'W) is the Marina Tárara, in a sheltered lagoon from which the Río Tárara flows into the sea. The lagoon is 3–4m deep, but currently the entrance has little more than 1m over the sandbar at low water. Dredging to 3m is underway but it remains to be seen whether this will be completed, and if it is, how rapidly the channel will silt up once again – check the entry depth with a reliable source before trying to go in.

The bay into which the Río Tárara flows has rocky headlands to both the east and the west. (Note that there is a similar bay a couple of miles to the west, so make sure you have the right one!) The entrance to the river is not easy to spot from offshore since it comes into the bay from behind a low-lying rocky spit. However, there is a substantial (ruined) concrete jetty on the east headland of the bay, and a conspicuous sandy beach on the south side, both of which can be picked out. The entrance to the river is immediately to the west of the sandy beach.

The bay is entered on a heading of approximately 195° on a course that comes close to the west headland. The west shore is then hugged (15–20m off) all the way into the river (at which point you want to be just 5m off the west bank) and around the first sharp bend (to the west) after which you can ease into center channel as you curve around to the east into the lagoon. The lagoon currently shoals toward its edges so it is not possible to carry much more than 1m alongside the docks – a Mediterranean-style mooring is required (bow or stern to the dock).

In 1996 the marina was charging $0.35 per foot per day, which included water and electricity (the usual dubious hookup – see Chapter 1). There is a bar and restaurant, a disco under construction, a swimming pool, and of course the lovely beach. This is both a cheaper and more restful place to dock than the Marina Hemingway, but without showers or laundry facilities, and not as well placed for exploring Havana.

To contact the Marina Tárara, ☎ (537) 33 5501/ 5510; fax (537) 33 5499.

Río Cojimar

East of Cojimar is an enormous, east-European style housing estate, visible for miles and incredibly ugly!

At Cojimar (approximately 23°10·2'N 82°17·6'W) a colonial fort guards the entry to the Río Cojimar. The river is entered between the fort (on the western shore) and the rocky cay in the center of the bay. Past the fort, the river makes a sharp turn to the east. Although it is reportedly possible to carry 2m as far as the dock by the fort, thereafter the bottom shoals to less than 1m. There is little protection to be had here (although this is where Ernest Hemingway used to keep his boat, so maybe we missed something).

Havana Harbor

Havana Harbor is closed to visiting cruising boats, although if conditions are too dangerous to enter the Marina Hemingway (a strong norther) the port authorities will allow you to dock, and to clear in or out, in Havana. The entry is deep and

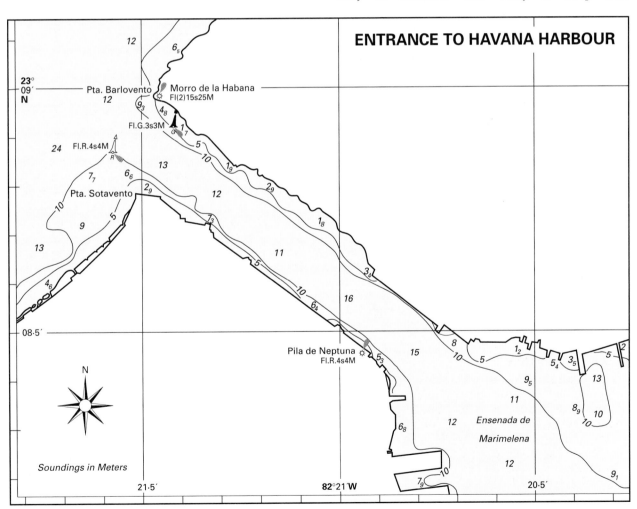

ENTRANCE TO HAVANA HARBOUR

Adapted from ICH 1730
Courtesy GeoCuba

straightforward; once inside you will be told where to go. This is a busy commercial harbor, one of the filthiest we have ever seen (right up there with Santiago de Cuba), with a heavy coating of oil on the water, a perpetual stench of oil and sewage, and no facilities for small boats. We would have to be pretty desperate before we took our boat inside. However, it is well worth making a pass across the entrance to the harbor just to photograph the formidable fortifications of El Morro, on the eastern side.

To the west of the harbor entrance there is a continuous sea wall (the Malecón) for several miles, after which the coastline consists of low-lying rocks.

Ensenada la Chorrera

Just west of Havana (at approximately 23°08·0'N 82°24·6'W) lies the Ensenada la Chorrera, into which flows the Río Almendares. The east side of the channel (actually the south side, since the river hooks to the west) is marked by an attractive colonial fort which has been restored and converted to a restaurant. The river is navigable in its lower stretches by vessels with a draft of up to 2m, and would make an excellent spot in which to moor a boat while exploring Old Havana. However, it is currently closed to visiting boats (and in fact if you sail close to shore at this point the Guarda are likely to send out a gunboat and tell you to stay further off).

Between the Ensenada la Chorrera and the Río Jaimanitas (at the Marina Hemingway) is a dredged (2m deep) 30m wide channel into the Ensenada Cubanacan, but this too is closed to visiting boats.

Río Jaimanitas

Immediately east of the Marina Hemingway is the Río Jaimanitas, which reportedly has a deep-water entry between the west shore (a substantial sea wall in front of the Old Man and the Sea hotel) and the small, low-lying rocky cay in the mouth of the river. However, this river is used solely by local craft.

Appendix

Key terms (with their abbreviations) used on the ICH charts

Acopio (Ac)	Storage facility	*Estación de prácticos (Est. Prac)*	Pilot station
Aduana (Adu)	Customs		
Advertencia (Adv)	Warning	*Este (E)*	East
Algas (Alg)	Seaweed	*Estero (Esto)*	Creek
Arena (A)	Sand	*Estrecho (Estr)*	Narrows
Arrecife (Arrf)	Reef		
Astillero (Ast)	Shipyard	*Fango (F)*	Mud
		Faro (F.)	Lighthouse
Bahía (Ba)	Bay	*Fondeadero (Fond)*	Anchorage
Bajo (Bj)	Shoal	*Fuerte (Frte)*	Strong
Bajamar (B.M.)	Low tide		
Baliza (Bz)	Beacon	*Isla (I.)*	Island
Banco (Ban)	Bank		
Barlovento	Windward	*Lago (La)*	Lake
Boca	Entrance	*Laguna (Lag)*	Lagoon
Boya	Buoy		
Buque (Buq)	Ship	*Malo (Mal)*	Bad
		Malecón (Mcon)	Sea wall (with road)
Cabezo (Cbzo)	Coral head	*Manglés (Mang)*	Mangroves
Cabo (Cab)	Cape	*Muelle (Mu)*	Dock
Caleta (Cta)	Cove, inlet		
Canal (Can)	Channel	*Navegable (Nav)*	Navigable
Canalizo (Clzo)	Small (shoal) channel	*Nivel (Niv)*	(Sea) level
CAP (Casa A Pilote)	Fish station on piles	*Norte (N)*	North
Capitanía	Port captain's office		
Castillo (Cast)	Fortress	*Obstáculo (Obst)*	Obstruction
Cayo (Cy)	Cay	*Oeste (W)*	West
Cayuelo (Cylo)	Little cay		
Centro (Ctro)	Center	*Pasaje (Pas)*	Passage
Chico	Small	*Pedraplén*	Causeway
Chimenea (Chim)	Chimney (conspic.)	*Peligroso*	Dangerous
Conspícuo (Consp)	Conspicuous	*Península (Pen)*	Peninsula
Construcción (Const)	Construction	*Pequeño (Peq)*	Small
Coral (Cor)	Coral	*Pesca (Pes)*	Fish
Corriente	Current	*Piedra (P)*	Stone
Costa (Cst)	Coastline	*Pilote*	Piling
		Playa (Py)	Beach
Dársena (Dar)	Dock	*Pleamar (PM)*	High tide
Destruído (Des)	Destroyed	*Práctico (Prac)*	Pilotage
Dique flotante (Dique Fl)	Floating dock	*Profundidad (Prof)*	Depth
Dragado (Drg)	Dredged	*Puente (Pte)*	Bridge
		Puerto (Pto)	Port
Ensenada (Ens)	Bay	*Punta (Pta)*	Point
Entrada (Ent)	Entrance		
Espigón (Espg)	Jetty, pier	*Quebrada (Qba)*	Break (in a reef – fem.)
Esponja (Esp)	Sponge	*Quebrado (Qbo, qbo)*	Break (in a reef – masc.)

259

Restinga (Rest)	Ledge; low-lying cay
Refugio (Rfg)	Refuge
Río (R.)	River
Roca (R)	Rock
Rompeolas (Rolas)	Breakwater
Rompientes (Rpte)	Breakers
Salina (Sa)	Saltpan
Sierra (Srr)	Mountain range
Sotavento	Leeward
Submergido (Sgdo)	Submerged
Sucio (suc)	Foul
Sur, sud (S)	South
Surgidero (Surg)	Open roadstead
Torre (To)	Tower

Index